Visit us at

www.syngress.com

Syngress is committed to publishing high-quality books for IT Professionals and delivering those books in media and formats that fit the demands of our customers. We are also committed to extending the utility of the book you purchase via additional materials available from our Web site.

SOLUTIONS WEB SITE

To register your book, visit www.syngress.com/solutions. Once registered, you can access our solutions@syngress.com Web pages. There you may find an assortment of valueadded features such as free e-books related to the topic of this book, URLs of related Web sites, FAQs from the book, corrections, and any updates from the author(s).

ULTIMATE CDs

Our Ultimate CD product line offers our readers budget-conscious compilations of some of our best-selling backlist titles in Adobe PDF form. These CDs are the perfect way to extend your reference library on key topics pertaining to your area of expertise, including Cisco Engineering, Microsoft Windows System Administration, CyberCrime Investigation, Open Source Security, and Firewall Configuration, to name a few.

DOWNLOADABLE E-BOOKS

For readers who can't wait for hard copy, we offer most of our titles in downloadable Adobe PDF form. These e-books are often available weeks before hard copies, and are priced affordably.

SYNGRESS OUTLET

Our outlet store at syngress.com features overstocked, out-of-print, or slightly hurt books at significant savings.

SITE LICENSING

Syngress has a well-established program for site licensing our e-books onto servers in corporations, educational institutions, and large organizations. Contact us at sales@syngress.com for more information.

CUSTOM PUBLISHING

Many organizations welcome the ability to combine parts of multiple Syngress books, as well as their own content, into a single volume for their own internal use. Contact us at sales@syngress.com for more information.

SYNGRESS®

How to Cheat at Administering Office Communications Server 2007

Anthony Piltzecker Technical Editor

Rand Morimoto
former Cyber-Security Adviser to the White House

Ron Barrett
Rabon Bussey
Adam Gent
Dustin Hannifin

Mohan Krishnamurthy
Matt McGillen
Paul Summitt

KEY	SERIAL NUMBER
001	HJIRTCV764
002	PO9873D5FG
003	829KM8NJH2
004	BPOQ48722D
005	CVPLQ6WQ23
006	VBP965T5T5
007	HJJJ863WD3E
008	2987GVTWMK
009	629MP5SDJT
010	IMWQ295T6T

PUBLISHED BY
Syngress Publishing, Inc.
Elsevier, Inc.
30 Corporate Drive
Burlington, MA 01803

How to Cheat at Administering Office Communications Server 2007

Printed and bound in the United Kingdom

Transferred to Digital Print 2011

ISBN 13: 978-1-59749-212-6

Publisher: Amorette Pedersen
Acquisitions Editor: Andrew Williams
Technical Editor: Anthony Piltzecker
Project Manager: Gary Byrne

Page Layout and Art: SPI
Copy Editor: Audrey Doyle
Indexer: SPI
Cover Designer: Michael Kavish

For information on rights, translations, and bulk sales, contact Matt Pedersen, Commercial Sales Director and Rights, at Syngress Publishing; email m.pedersen@elsevier.com.

Technical Editor and Lead Author

Anthony Piltzecker (CISSP, MCSE, CCNA, CCVP, Check Point CCSA, Citrix CCA), author and technical editor of Syngress Publishing's *MCSE Exam 70-296 Study Guide and DVD Training System,* is a Consulting Engineer for Networked Information Systems in Woburn, MA. He also contributed to *How to Cheat at Managing Microsoft Operations Manager 2005* (Syngress, ISBN: 1597492515).

Tony's specialties include network security design, Microsoft operating system and applications architecture, as well as Cisco IP Telephony implementations. Tony's background includes positions as IT Manager for SynQor Inc.; Network Architect for Planning Systems, Inc.; and Senior Networking Consultant with Integrated Information Systems. Along with his various certifications, Tony holds a bachelor's degree in Business Administration. Tony currently resides in Leominster, MA, with his wife, Melanie, and his daughters, Kaitlyn and Noelle.

Contributing Authors

Ron Barrett (MCP, CCNA, Citrix CCA) is a technology professional/author specializing in network infrastructure and emerging technologies. For the past nine years he has worked in various capacities for several major financial firms and dot-coms. Ron has also worked as a technical author the last seven years while holding the post of IT director for a financial services firm in Manhattan, NY. He also has been a member of CPAmerica for the past four years, holding the posts of vice-chairman and chairman of the Technology Executive Committee. Now turning his attention full-time to writing and technical education, he is currently developing training clips for ClipTraning.com. Ron is the coauthor of the newly released *Administrator's Guide to Microsoft Office Servers 2007* (Sams, 2007).

"I would like to thank my wife, Alicia, and my children, Ronald and Emma, for all their support and patience."

Rabon Bussey (MCSE, CCNA, Citrix CCA) is a practice leader for NWN, a Microsoft Gold and a Microsoft Voice Partner headquartered in Waltham, MA. NWN Corporation provides clients with a complete range of networking services and solutions. NWN brings its clients the premier products in the industry, tailored to their specific needs and situations. Rabon is a key contributor to the business and practice development. Rabon has more than 20 years' experience in the industry, and his focus is currently on unified communication.

Rabon currently offers strategic consulting to NWN clients based in the Carolinas. He resides in Greensboro, NC, with his wife, Caryn, and three girls.

Adam Gent (MCSE: Messaging & Security, MCTS: LCS, Security+) is a technical consultant with Datapulse Ltd. Datapulse is a Nortel Developer Partner specializing in attendant consoles, call billing applications, and value-add applications for Office Communications Server (OCS). Adam works with the company's Product Group to architect and manage products that relate to OCS. He also works with customers consulting on the deployment of OCS within enterprises.

Adam holds a bachelor's degree in computer science from Cardiff University and is a member of the British Computer Society.

Dustin Hannifin (Microsoft MVP – Office SharePoint Server) is a systems administrator with Crowe Chizek and Company LLC. Crowe (www.crowechizek.com) is one of the nation's leading public accounting and consulting firms. Under its core purpose of "Building Value with Values®," Crowe assists both public and private companies in reaching their goals through services ranging from assurance and financial advisory to performance, risk, and tax consulting. Dustin currently works in Crowe's Information Services delivery unit, where he plays a key role in maintaining and supporting Crowe's internal information technology (IT) infrastructure. His expertise resides in various Microsoft products, including Office SharePoint Server, System Center Operations Manager, Active Directory, IIS, and Office Communications Server. Dustin holds a bachelor's degree from Tennessee Technological University and is a founding member of the Michiana IT Professionals Users Group. He regularly contributes to various blogs and newsgroups. Dustin, a Tennessee native, currently resides in South Bend, IN.

Mohan Krishnamurthy Madwachar (MCSE, MCNE) is the GM – Network Security, Almoayed Group, Bahrain. Mohan is a key contributor to Almoayed Group's Projects Division and plays an important role in the organization's Network Security initiatives. Mohan comes from a strong networking, security, and training background. His tenure with companies such as Schlumberger Omnes and Secure Network Solutions India adds to his experience and expertise in implementing large and complex network and security projects.

Mohan holds leading IT industry standard and vendor certifications in systems, networking, and security. He is a member of the IEEE and PMI.

Mohan would like to dedicate his contributions to this book to his projects team colleagues: Nogen, Chamikar, Saurabh, Ramkumar, and Sachin.

Mohan has coauthored three books: *Designing & Building Enterprise DMZs* (ISBN: 1597491004), *Configuring Juniper Networks NetScreen & SSG Firewalls* (ISBN: 1597491187), and *How to Cheat at Securing Linux* (ISBN: 1597492078) published by Syngress. He also writes in newspaper columns on various subjects and has contributed to leading content companies as a technical writer and a subject matter expert.

Matt McGillen (MCSE, MCP+I) is a solution architect with PointBridge. He has more than 10 years of IT consulting experience in government, legal, financial, and healthcare sectors. He is currently focused on designing and developing unified messaging and unified communications solutions for complex business environments. Past projects have included extensive work with Cisco IP Telephony, Cisco Contact Centers, and the entire Microsoft Unified Communications stack.

Matt holds a bachelor's degree from the University of Illinois and resides in Oak Park, IL, with his wife and three children. He blogs about unified communications at https://blogs.pointbridge.com/Blogs/mcgillen_matt/default.aspx.

Rand Morimoto (Ph.D., MCSE, Microsoft MVP) has been in the computer industry for more than 30 years and is an internationally known expert in Windows networking, Microsoft Exchange messaging, Office Communications Server unified communications, and SharePoint collaboration. Dr. Morimoto speaks at more than 50 conferences and conventions around the world and writes several best-selling books each year on Microsoft networking technologies. Rand is currently the president of Convergent Computing, an IT consulting firm in the San Francisco Bay Area that he founded more than 20 years ago that has 60+ consultants designing, implementing, and supporting Microsoft technologies for some of the largest organizations in the world. Dr. Morimoto is the former Cyber-Security adviser to the White House and is currently a Regent for St. Mary's College. He also is a board member for the Chabot Space and Science Center and the Institute of International Education.

Paul Summitt (MCSE, CCNA, MCP+I, MCP) holds a master's degree in mass communication. Paul has served as a network, an Exchange, and a database administrator, as well as a Web and application developer. Paul has written on virtual reality and Web development and has served as technical editor for several books on Microsoft technologies. Paul lives in Columbia, MO, with his life and writing partner, Mary.

Contents

Chapter 1

Unified Communications

Solutions in this chapter:

- **History of Communication**

- **IP Communication: How It Works and Why It's Revolutionizing Communication**

- **Understanding Presence**

- **Microsoft and Unified Communications**

☑ **Summary**

☑ **Solutions Fast Track**

☑ **Frequently Asked Questions**

Introduction

Unified communications are like relationships. We all want 'em, we all have 'em … what do we do with 'em? (with respect to Jimmy Buffet for that one). In all seriousness, you should ask yourself some important questions regarding unified communications:

- What is my (or my company's) view of unified communications?

- What kind of real ROI can I find from unifying my independent systems?

- Realistically, how can I integrate my systems while not destroying my budget?

- Which components or products make the most sense for my business?

In this chapter, we will explore these very questions, and help you come up with the answers. Because this book focuses on Microsoft technologies, we will also look at many of the Microsoft products that have brought us to the present-day solution that we will be focusing most of our attention on in this book: Office Communications Server (OCS) 2007.

Before we look forward, it's a good idea to step back and look at how we got to "today." To begin, we will review the progress and history of communication over the past 150 years, and how it has impacted where overall information delivery and communication are going.

History of Communication

You can breathe a sigh of relief. We're not going to take you all the way back to the caveman and discuss cave drawings. Likewise, Egypt and those amazing hieroglyphics are out. We're going to jump in right around the time of Mr. Alexander Graham Bell. Way back in 1876, Mr. Bell (not Antonio Meucci, as some conspiracy theorists believe) invented the first telephone (Figure 1.1), which was based on the same principles of the telegraph, which is essentially the transmission of wire signals over copper wiring. Bell spent numerous hours attempting to transmit sound over this medium, first in the form of a clock spring's twang, and then, on March 10, 1876, finally speaking those now-famous words, *"Mr. Watson—come here—I want to see you."*

Figure 1.1 A Replica of Bell's First Telephone

Over the next 100 years, Bell's invention would grow in popularity, ultimately ending the reign of the telegraph and eventually placing a phone in nearly every home within the developed world. Over the years, the shape, style, and price of the Plain Old Telephone System (or POTS) would change many, many times. It is important to understand that the result of this invention was the intercontinental mesh of telephone wires. These old "POTS lines" are the basis for why we have digital communication today.

If Bell's invention provided for the foundation of modern-day communication, the invention of the Private Branch Exchange (PBX; Figure 1.2) is the ground floor. Although the acronym "PBX" has been around since the days of the operator-assisted telephone call, it is generally used when referring to corporate telephone systems. The first readily available PBX solution was released in the early 1970s and comprised four core components:

- Switching matrix
- Control
- User stations
- Trunks

Figure 1.2 A Legacy PBX System

Basically, when a call was placed from a user station (keep in mind that a station can be a phone, an analog device such as a modem, a fax, and so on), the PBX is responsible for completing the call to either another internal station or the outside world via the Public Switched Telephone Network (PSTN)—"Ma Bell" in the early days, and the "Baby Bells" in the 1980s and 1990s. We are oversimplifying the call process, as a number of factors play into it, including Class of Service, or COS (does the caller have the right to place this call); Least Cost Routing, or LCR (which phone line is the least expensive to make this call); and many other pieces of the calling puzzle, all determined in milliseconds. The problem with the PBX was that it was massive in size and ran hot enough to keep an entire Alaskan community warm on a subzero day.

TIP

If you want to learn more about the history of the PBX, there is a fantastic Web site to visit: http://leegoeller.com. This is the home page of Lee Goeller, who has been an independent telecommunications consultant working with business customers as well as designers of telecom equipment for more than three decades.

Although arguments could be made for satellite communication and cell phones, the next great revolution in Internet Protocol (IP) communication was the invention of the IP-PBX. A company called Sphere is generally recognized as the inventor of the IP-PBX; however, it decided to go with Asynchronous Transfer Mode (ATM) communication as opposed to IP.

As such, the real revolution in IP-based communication came in late 1998–early 1999, when it was determined that "network convergence" could be provided over existing Ethernet implementations. The first IP-PBXs were incredibly crude, using IP-ready phones that plugged into any Ethernet port, without any focus on the quality of the call or the effect of data transmission on it. We will spend a lot more time discussing IP communication in the next section.

So far, we have spent this chapter discussing voice communication. However, we also need to spend some time discussing software-driven communication.

Software Communication

Although voice communication had a pretty big head start on software communication, any fool can see that software (or data-based) communication has made a fast and permanent impact on our society. We could spend time discussing many avenues, including services such as CompuServe (Figure 1.3) or community-owned Bulletin Board Systems (BBS), or go down the road of the "early" Internet, but the real boom in terms of software communication for both the business world and personal communication was the "Dot Com" boom of the late twentieth century.

Figure 1.3 A Screenshot of the Early CompuServe Service

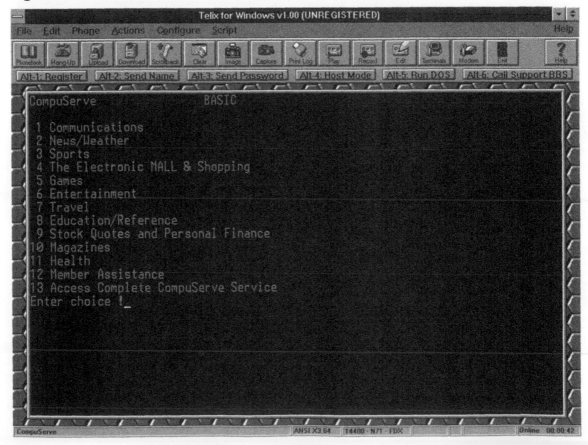

While many larger enterprise-type companies had already implemented internal-only mail solutions, the rest of the business world was pretty much left out in the cold regarding data communication. As dial-up Internet began to grow in popularity the "chosen few" were allowed modems (or, if you were really high-tech, you may have had a server with a modem bank) to go out and get e-mail on behalf of their company.

Likewise, instant messaging (IM) had just begun to pop up as a "cool" new way to communicate with friends and family. Although purists would claim that the UNIX operating system really offered the first IM communication (as many BBSs did), companies such as Tribal Voice (Pow Wow; Figure 1.4), AOL (AOL Instant Messenger/AIM), and ICQ began to pop up all over the place. Again, at first IM was really nothing more than a "gadget" that was used in home environments, and it was generally looked down upon in the corporate world.

Figure 1.4 PowWow Instant Messaging Screenshot (from Wikipedia)

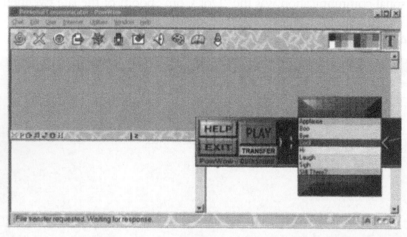

By the latter half of the 1990s, high-speed Internet as well as corporate Internet-capable e-mail was being implemented at a rapid rate within corporations around the globe. The Dot Com boom (it feels funny to say that, doesn't it?) was really beginning to pick up steam. Venture capitalists everywhere were throwing their money down the drain by the bucket load, funding startups that had absolutely no idea what to do with all their newfound cash! Religious battles between different mail solutions such as Microsoft Exchange, Lotus Notes, Novell GroupWise, and various open source mail solutions were beginning.

At the turn of the millennium, something pretty astounding happened: Investors recognized the fact that they weren't getting much (any?) ROI and started to pull back funding to these startups. However, a very interesting side effect to this Internet "boom" took place: the birth of true Voice over IP (VoIP) communication.

IP Communication: How It Works and Why It's Revolutionizing Communication

Anyone familiar with early VoIP can tell you fireside stories about the lack of quality, due to many reasons including packet delays, lost packets, and packets that arrived out of order. However, as companies (both vendors and end-users) really began to think about the potential cost savings of integrating systems, more innovation regarding IP communication began to occur. Although many traditional PBX providers, such as Lucent/Avaya and Nortel, initially laughed off the idea of integrated solutions, "data" companies such as 3Com, Cisco, and Alcatel took off as the "leaders" in this space. Thanks to some very wise acquisitions and a lot of research and development funds—plus the added bonus of owning most of the network infrastructure worldwide—Cisco really took off as the market leader in VoIP. To understand how VoIP works, we have to take a slightly deeper dive into the core components of a VoIP solution. The first thing to discuss is something we've already talked about: the switching mechanism.

Switching in the Voice World

If you think about how you make a phone call today from your home, some basic steps need to occur:

1. You have to pick up the phone, regardless of how you do it; lifting the handset, pressing Speakerphone, and so on. The first thing you will hear is a dial tone. This means the central office (CO) recognizes the fact that you want to do … something.

2. You dial a number, which the CO interprets and routes to the proper CO for the target, and ultimately rings at your intended recipient.

3. Once the other person answers the call (assuming someone or something is on the other end to do so), the circuit between you and the called party is "opened."

4. When you (or the other person) hang up, the circuit is closed, and all lines associated with the circuit are freed up. Figure 1.5 shows a diagram of a phone call between Bob and Lisa.

Figure 1.5 A Traditional Phone Call

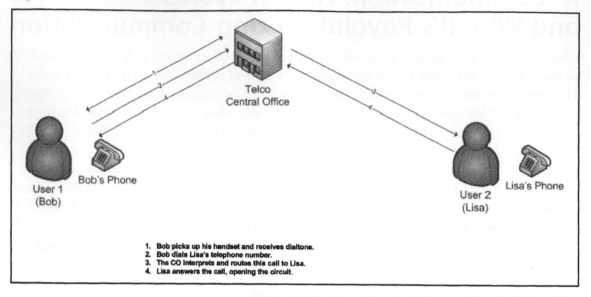

Telco
Central Office

Bob's Phone

User 1
(Bob)

Lisa's Phone

User 2
(Lisa)

1. Bob picks up his handset and receives dialtone.
2. Bob dials Lisa's telephone number.
3. The CO interprets and routes this call to Lisa.
4. Lisa answers the call, opening the circuit.

It is important to understand that while this conversation is occurring—be it 30 seconds, 30 minutes, or 30 hours long—it's always going to occur over the same circuit. In this scenario, we are always going to be passing some sort of *traffic*. It may be you speaking, the other person speaking, or simply background noise. This type of communication is known as *circuit switching*.

With data networks, we do not use circuit switching. Instead, we use *packet switching*. With packet switching, there is no need to pass traffic over the same circuit for a potentially endless period of time, much of which may be wasted time while no data is being passed. With packet switching, we can break up a larger piece of data into smaller "chunks" and distribute those chunks over an infinite number of paths. At a high level, here is how packet switching (Figure 1.6) works:

1. The first device—say, your laptop—is attempting to send a file to a file server. It breaks up that file into smaller packets (known as the *payload*) and tacks on the target system's address information.

2. Your laptop then sends that packet off to its gateway (which may be a switch, a router, etc.), and assumes that the gateway knows how to deliver the packet. In turn, the gateway may deliver the packet directly to the server (assuming it's on the same network segment), or it will pass it off to the proper next "hop."

3. When the server receives the packet, it begins to restructure the file, much like a jigsaw puzzle—but with a specific set of instructions on assembly.

Figure 1.6 Packet Switching

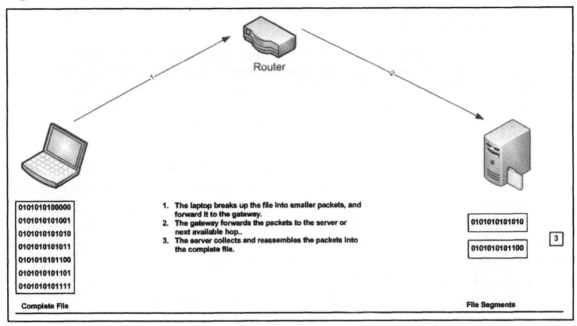

So, what did this mean for voice communication? Well, basically, it meant we could do more with less. By that, I mean that by leveraging this method of distributing our transmission, we no longer had to ensure that we had a 1:1 ratio of potential phone calls to phone lines. On the internal cabling front (from the wiring closet to the desk), it also meant that we no longer had to have cable runs for both data and voice. However, adding voice onto our existing data infrastructure was not quite that simple. We needed to address a number of items, possibly the most important of which is the quality of the call being transmitted.

Quality of Service

Taking what we've said regarding packet switching, logic would tell us that conversations would be broken up into various chunks, arriving out of order. So, if Alexander Graham Bell were alive today, a conversation over VoIP would have come across something like *"to see Mr. Wat—son here—I you. come want"* instead of *"Mr. Watson—come here—I want to see you."* Right? Wrong.

Early on, the early developers of VoIP were quick to grasp the idea that this wouldn't work. Likewise, they were quick on the ball to determine that if a voice call over IP didn't sound almost exactly the same as an analog call, it would never work. Therefore, they made a variety of "tweaks," including adding "comfort noise" to the call, and other things to reduce unwanted problems such as "jitter." One item was still outstanding in terms of voice transmission and the effect of the data network. This issue was related to the fact that nothing was stopping someone from transmitting a large file, streaming audio, and—oh yes—trying to make a phone call across the same 100 MB port. To address this, Quality of Service was born.

Whatis.com defines QoS as follows:

> "the idea that transmission rates, error rates, and other characteristics can be measured, improved, and, to some extent, guaranteed in advance. QoS is of particular concern for the continuous transmission of high-band-width video and multimedia information. Transmitting this kind of content dependably is difficult in public networks using ordinary 'best effort' protocols."

Basically, it comes down to the fundamental design of IP transmission—the fact that messages are sent using a best effort, and retries are often necessary to complete a transmission. As multiple data streams are passed over the same 100 MB pipe, each packet is, by default, given the same priority in terms of delivery. The obvious problem here is that in a voice conversation, a listener isn't going to understand the conversation if a packet is repeated at the end of the message. QoS was particularly important for voice so that voice packets could be "tagged" and given priority in the data stream. Traditionally, QoS has been managed almost exclusively on hardware devices such as routers and switches. With the introduction of OCS 2007, Microsoft has taken this to the next level, taking call quality out of the hardware and developing Quality of Experience (QoE). We will discuss this later in the book.

NOTE

There are many ways to handle QoS, and various protocols are involved, which can often be further complicated depending on the hardware vendor involved. Unfortunately, an in-depth explanation of QoS is far beyond the scope of this book. However, if you are interested in learning more about QoS, consider picking up *Administering QoS in Cisco IP Networks* by Michael Flannagan (Syngress).

Understanding Presence

For many people, the concept of presence can be a little hard to grasp at first. Microsoft defines presence as "the ability of a person or device to communicate with others and to display levels of availability." Quite often, when speaking with customers about presence, Microsoft assumes that IM is "presence." However, this just isn't true. IM is simply another way to *represent* presence. Many things make up presence, but any one item alone is not presence. Before we discuss what presence is, what it represents, and what it means in terms of business productivity, here is a list of some of the items that are a *piece* of the presence "pie" but cannot represent presence on their own:

- IM
- E-mail
- Cell phone
- Desk phone
- Physical locale

In a face-to-face conversation, this is usually the point where people begin to look at me as though I've gone completely insane and should be rushed to the nearest medical facility. In particular, physical locale is usually the final nail in that coffin. At this point, I'm intentionally trying to confuse people. First, it can be quite a lot of fun if you do it right. Second, and more important, it gets them thinking and asking questions in their heads, if not directing them toward me. Anyway, why am I saying these key components of communication alone cannot represent someone's presence? Because the fundamental concept of presence is communicating with a *person*. Take a moment to think about that.

If you were in your car on your drive to the office, and you needed to talk to one of your coworkers, you would not really be interested in determining whether your coworker was at his desk, on the road, at home, in a hotel, and so on. All you'd really want to do is speak to that person. How much time have you spent calling someone's cell phone, desk phone, (maybe) home phone, and so on trying to reach him, and in the end leaving possibly three or more voice messages without ever reaching him? What's even worse is when you leave those voice messages, simply to tell him that he needs to read an e-mail that you sent him! Talk about loss of productivity! In the end, it really should not be up to the caller to determine the best means to communicate with the called party. In some cases, communications problems can be easy to solve: Forward your desk phone to your cell phone or home number, right? Well, that can work in some cases, but what if you need to change the number you are forwarding to "on the fly"? For example, my cell phone doesn't get great reception at my house, but I will often work out of my home office. At other times, I'm on the road and need that call to go to my cell phone, but I don't want to have to go into the office to make that change.

By using a *presence engine*, we can control this call flow in a number of ways. First, we can implement and control basic call forwarding from a GUI console. In the case of Microsoft Office Communicator (MOC), this can be done on a PC or a Windows Smartphone, further extending your control of your presence—but we'll get to that a little later. A *true* presence engine must be able to take this a step further, or we're simply duplicating call control from a PBX. A presence engine has to be able to determine what to do with a call without you manually adjusting the call flow. For example, most of us keep our cell phones somewhere on our person, correct? Well, let's say you've put in a few hours of hard work in front of your PC, and you decide to take a walk to the lunch room for a cup of coffee; the president of your company is also in there and decides to spark up a conversation that goes for 20 minutes. You know you have an important call coming into your desk phone shortly, but you don't want to be rude. How great would it be if your PC could recognize the fact that you're away from your desk, intercept the call to your desk phone, and forward it to your cell phone?

This concept loops back around to the fundamental concept of presence. In this scenario, the person who is calling you doesn't want to have to worry about calling your desk, leaving a message, and then calling your cell phone. She wants one number to call. Why? Because she wants the most productive way to get in touch with you.

IM and Presence

We've talked a lot about voice communication, but what about IM and presence? IM has taken a much larger role in corporate communication, with a lot of that growth having to do with the generation of working professionals coming into the workforce over the past decade. Without realizing it, this generation has revolutionized the way we do business. Because many of these workers grew up with IM, text messaging, blogs, and so on, they have come to expect this type of "instant" and "freeform" communication in the workplace. In many cases, they actually consider e-mail to be a very slow form of communication! So, how does this need for instant gratification help the workforce? Let me give you an example.

In a previous position, I was in constant communication with the CTO of my company. He was a very nice person, but he was also very busy, and he often traveled between our five large regional offices, so communication with him was often difficult. I often had to play the "phone call" game, calling his desk line, cell number, desk line in other offices, and so on, to try to hunt him down. In the end, if I could not reach him, I would simply shoot him an e-mail and wait for a response. When I did get him on the phone, we both felt obligated to have a "polite" conversation first ("How's the weather in Boston? How are the kids? Did you catch the Sox last night?"), although we were both usually very busy. So, for a question that really required only 30–60 seconds of our time, we spent about five minutes on the phone!

Now, I'm not saying that we should all be cold and business-like all the time, but there is a time and a place for friendly conversations. Likewise, when I need someone to make a key tactical decision, I really want that person to make that decision right there and then. So, to address this issue, we installed Microsoft Live Communication Server (LCS) 2005. After installing LCS, I was able to do multiple things:

- I could tell when the CTO was online and in front of his PC.

- I could tell whether he was online but away from his PC, on the phone, or in a meeting and should not be disturbed.

- Most important, I could initiate that quick 15–30-second conversation for that tactical answer that I was looking for—and have a record of his response!

The LCS installation really started out as a "pet project," but once the other departments in the company caught wind of it, everybody wanted to get involved. For the sales team, it became a crucial piece of their sales process. The fact that they could be on a phone call with their customer, and at the same time IM their inside sales team for pricing information for that customer in "real time," was a huge advantage when trying to close a sale. Later, when we were able to extend this capability to our customers and partners, our communication network grew, and the gap between information requests and fulfillment shrunk.

Presence in Other Applications

Presence in a single application (such as MOC) is fantastic, but you won't be spending most of your time in front of the presence application. For everyone else, you will spend your time in various applications, such as Microsoft Outlook, or perhaps a CRM application or SharePoint portal site. Because we often have multiple applications running, it's important to be able to extend presence into these "presence-aware" applications. In some cases, we can even add presence into applications that are otherwise not presence-aware. The benefits to this can be pretty astounding. I mentioned Microsoft Outlook earlier—if you were to survey 100 service-oriented employees, you would probably find that the majority of them would agree they spend most of their time in front of e-mail. For many of us, it's also the first thing we check when we wake up in the morning and the last thing we check when we go to bed. With presence integration, we can gather a lot more information about the sender and recipients of the message (Figure 1.7). How beneficial would it be, at 11:00 P.M., to find out that Bob, who just sent you a critical e-mail, is online and available to chat? We will explore this a little later in this book.

Figure 1.7 Presence Representation in Outlook 2007

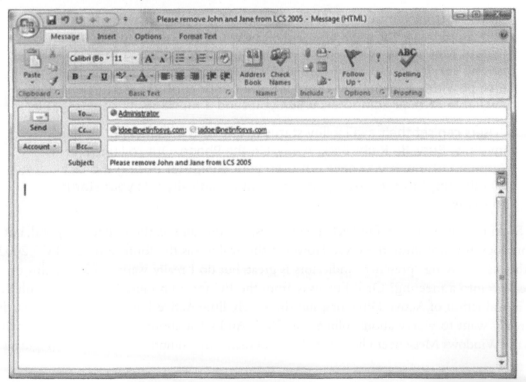

We're almost through with our unified communication primer. The last stop before we dive into OCS 2007 is to take a 50,000-foot view of Microsoft's history of unified communications, starting with Exchange 2000.

Microsoft and Unified Communications

It would be great to be able to say that Microsoft had always planned to be a player in the presence and unified communications spaces. However, that would be revising history just a bit. In truth, to an outsider, it appears as though Microsoft made several failed attempts at getting this type of technology off the ground. Sure, it had MSN Messenger out there for a long time, but on the corporate side, Mr. Gates was not too successful. In fact, there have been rumors that during its lifetime, the entire Communications Server product line had been scrapped, left for dead, but later revived. Although we could discuss earlier Microsoft products, such as NetMeeting, the first real push into the world of IM and presence came with Exchange 2000 Enterprise Edition, which included a feature known as the Instant Messaging Service.

Exchange 2000 and IM

The following paragraphs come directly from the official Exchange 2000 manual:

> "Microsoft Exchange 2000 Server Instant Messaging Service offers a fast and simple way for users on a TCP/IP network to communicate instantly. Instant Messaging complements e-mail in a way similar to the way telephone service complements postal mail; however, Instant Messaging also provides information about whether your contacts are present and available at their computers when you send a message.

> "Users can set their availability status to any of the following: Online, Invisible, Busy, Be Right Back, Away, On the Phone, Out to Lunch, or Appear Offline. If you have not used your computer during the last 20 minutes, Instant Messaging Service automatically sets your status to Away."

Sound familiar? If not, flip back a few pages. As you can see, the intent was good, but the technology was not quite there yet. However, this really was the foundation for LCS 2003. At this stage, having "presence" indicators is great, but do I really want to change this every time I go into a meeting? Or if I'm away from the PC for 20 minutes? And what with Y2K, the introduction of Active Directory, and those ugly little Active Directory Connectors, did we really want to worry about rolling out "IM"? And what about the fact that the IM client was the Windows Messenger client, which was outdated the minute it was released (Figure 1.8)?

Figure 1.8 Windows Messenger

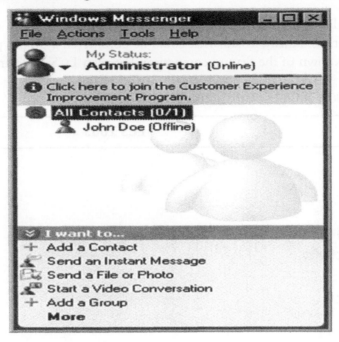

In any case, Microsoft made another run at this three years later. This time, however, it decided it was a better move to separate the product from the Exchange bundle.

LCS 2003

We're not going to spend much more than a couple of lines describing LCS 2003, simply because there isn't much to say. We were still forced to use the Windows Messenger client, and communications functionality was greatly limited to inside the corporate network in most cases. The only good things to say about LCS 2003 are:

- Microsoft began to offer presence services to other applications, such as Outlook 2003.

- Microsoft was wise enough to keep the product going, and improve it with LCS 2005.

SOME INDEPENDENT ADVICE

If you are a user of Exchange 2000 IM services, you probably already know that you can't get to LCS 2005 or OCS 2007 directly. The only way to get to these more recent presence technologies is to first migrate your 2000 IM services to LCS 2003. For more information, visit www.microsoft.com/downloads/details. aspx?FamilyId=94676200-EC51- 4B5F -B261-8B72FC996833&displaylang=en.

LCS 2005

LCS 2005 was truly a breakthrough for Microsoft regarding its unified communications and presence initiatives. Finally, it had what could be considered a proper presence solution. Table 1.1 is a breakdown of the feature comparison between LCS 2003 and LCS 2005.

Table 1.1 LCS 2003/2005 Feature Comparison

Feature	LCS 2003	LCS 2005
Secure IM		X
Federation (communication between two LCS installations)		X
Public IM connectivity		X
PBX integration		X
Up to 150 contacts		X
Exchange integration for Busy/Out of Office		X
Application sharing		X
Capacity planning toolkit		X
Microsoft Operations Manager 2005 support		
Archiving		X
Clustering (Enterprise Edition)		X
File transfer	X	X
Desktop sharing	X	X
Presence status	X	X
Live Meeting integration	X	X
"Do Not Disturb" setting	X	X
Integration with Microsoft applications	X	X

As you scrolled down Table 1.1, you probably noticed that a significant number of features really made LCS 2005 a "prime-time" application. With the exception of call control, everything that we have discussed up to this point as being a key piece of the "unified communications" world was being wrapped into this package. Let's talk about some of the more important features of the LCS 2005 product. Figure 1.9 shows LCS 2005 as seen via MOC 2005.

Figure 1.9 LCS 2005 (As Seen via MOC 2005)

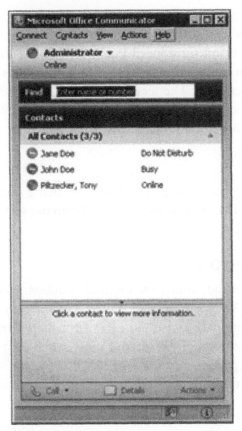

Secure IM

Microsoft was wise enough to recognize that communications going across IM needed the same encryption capability that e-mail solutions were already using. We had to be able to secure these IMs so that they were not passing in clear text, internally, to federated (outside third-party LCS implementation) partners, and to remote users working from home. To ensure that these IMs were secure, Microsoft provided for the use of the Transport Layer Security (TLS) protocol. TLS works in a client/server handshake arrangement, whereby the client initiates the communication to the server, and the server selects the strongest cipher and hash function and notifies the client. The client can then check the server's certificate for authenticity, and then begin communication. This was a major step in solidifying the place of presence in the corporate world. We could guarantee that communication would be secure, protecting confidential company information and also meeting regulatory requirements.

Public IM Connectivity

Honestly, without the ability to talk to the outside world, having an internal IM solution is incomplete. Imagine if your corporate e-mail was only able to send mail internally in today's world. To address this, Microsoft introduced Public IM Connectivity (PIC). PIC made it possible—for a fee—to communicate with MSN Messenger users, Yahoo! Messenger users, and AOL Instant Messenger users. The fee is fairly low (about $3/user/month, varying on the number of users), but it opens LCS to a whole new world. With the introduction of PIC, we needed a way to monitor and track IMs being sent both internally and externally.

Archiving

As mentioned, we needed a way to track IMs that were being transmitted to internal users, federated users, and public IM users. With the LCS Archiving service, we are able to record and recover IMs as needed.

Exchange Integration

With LCS 2003, we were already inside the Outlook mailbox. However, communication was only one-way. With LCS 2005, we were now able to automatically update our presence status by allowing the MOC client access into our calendar, which would automatically change our status to "In a Meeting" as appropriate, and show our next availability. Likewise, when we set our "Out of Office" message in Outlook, MOC was able to present this message to other MOC contacts when they would look at our status in a Microsoft application or the MOC client itself.

PBX Integration

Here's the big one. LCS 2005 was now able to tie into *certain* PBX systems, almost always with the use of a third-party gateway product. Typical functionality included the following:

- **Remote call control** The ability to answer and place calls to a desk phone (or software-based telephone)
- **Click-to-dial** Simply clicking on user properties in MOC, Outlook, or other presence-aware applications to make a phone call

- **Location-based forwarding** As described earlier, the ability to forward a call based on physical location and/or current status

- **"In a Call" presence** Ties directly to remote call control; shows your presence as "In a Call" when the desk phone is off the hook

Although this was all very exciting stuff in terms of PBX integration, there were two glaring holes in the solution. The first was internal call control (as opposed to relying on a third-party PBX), and the second was the complete lack of any voice mail solution. The latter was solved with the release of Exchange Server 2007.

SOME INDEPENDENT ADVICE

Several third-party gateway products are on the market today for integrating LCS 2005 with a PBX system. Some are exclusive to the manufacturer, such as Cisco's Unified Presence Server (CUPS), which ties LCS to Cisco Unified Call Manager. Some are more PBX-agnostic, such as the popular Genesys Labs product known as GETS. For more information on GETS, visit www.genesyslab.com/ products/enterprise_collaboration.asp.

Exchange 2007

Although there are many features to rave about in Exchange 2007, our focus here is on the Unified Messaging (UM) role of Exchange 2007. If you're not familiar with the UM role, Microsoft has provided (assuming you own the correct Client Access Licenses) the ability to use Exchange as a single-inbox solution. By single inbox, I am referring to the ability to store voice mail and e-mail within the same mailbox, and retrieve those messages via a PC or telephone.

With Exchange 2007, we are now able to redirect voice mail from a PBX to Exchange (again, this may require a third-party hardware gateway depending on your PBX) so that it can be picked up in Outlook, Outlook Web Access, or Outlook Voice Access (OVA). OVA is a new feature of 2007 that allows users to dial into a direct inbound dial (DID) number, or extension, and access their mailbox. E-mails and voice mails can be read back to the user, and all mailbox functions can be voice-controlled. Another exciting feature of OVA is the ability to manipulate your calendar—review your calendar, accept meeting invitations, clear your calendar, send "I'll be late" notices, and much more.

Exchange 2007 was the first major release of the official "Microsoft Unified Communications" strategy. We will discuss how Exchange 2007 integrates with OCS later in this book.

NOTE

As with QoS, trying to squeeze all of the exciting details about Exchange 2007 into this book, let alone this chapter, would be unreasonable. We recommend picking up *How to Cheat at Configuring Exchange Server 2007* by Henrik Walther (Syngress, 2007).

Summary

The times, they are a-changing. If you were to draw the evolution of communication in a timeline, you would see that the past decade has experienced the most rapid change in well more than 100 years. As our calendars get packed with more and more requests, and we need to do a better job of not only managing our time, but also indirectly impacting the time of others, we need better ways to streamline communication. The technology is now in place for us to move forward and take up this initiative, but it's up to us as the end-users to put the technology into action.

With many companies coming in and out of the unified communications world early in the process, Microsoft has slowly been building its arsenal of tools and suites before making its big splash into this world. We, the authors of this book—along with Microsoft—believe that OCS 2007 is now the foundation of this unified communications strategy. In the coming chapters, we will take a very in-depth look at this amazing new product from the folks in Redmond. Enjoy.

Solutions Fast Track

History of Communication

☑ The first readily available PBX solution was released in the early 1970s and comprised four core components: switching matrix, control, user stations, and trunks.

☑ Services such as CompuServe were early innovators of software-based communication.

☑ Early IM technologies were crude, and many did not survive the Internet bust.

IP Communication: How It Works and Why It's Revolutionizing Communication

☑ With *circuit* switching, communication always occurs over the same physical line (or set of lines).

☑ With packet switching, communication can occur via multiple data paths before reaching the target.

☑ The *payload* consists of smaller data segments that make up a larger file.

☑ QoS is defined as the idea that transmission rates, error rates, and other characteristics can be measured, improved, and, to some extent, guaranteed in advance.

Understanding Presence

- ☑ IM is simply just another way to *represent* presence.

- ☑ IM, e-mail, cell phones, desk phones, and physical locale are pieces of the presence "pie."

- ☑ The fundamental concept of presence is that communication is person-to-person, not person-to-device.

Microsoft and Unified Communications

- ☑ The Exchange 2000 IM series was Microsoft's first real attempt at a corporate presence solution.

- ☑ LCS 2003 built on the basics of Exchange 2000 IM, but still was not a fully functional presence engine, as it was still essentially a stand-alone solution.

- ☑ LCS 2005 introduced new features such as public IM connectivity, secure IM, federation, and PBX integration.

Frequently Asked Questions

Q: Why spend an entire chapter on the history of communication?

A: There are several reasons, but most important, it is essential to understand that many of these technologies have been around for a number of years, but have all functioned as independent "islands."

Q: Where can I learn more about VoIP in general?

A: A number of VoIP books are on the market. We recommend that you look at the selection available from Syngress Press. For a complete list, visit www.syngress.com/bookseries/?series=VoIP.

Q: Does Exchange 2007 UM work with any legacy PBX?

A: It's hard to guarantee that it will work with *any* PBX; however, the general rule of thumb is that if you can forward your voice mail to an extension, and have that extension exist off-Net, then yes, Exchange 2007 UM will work with any legacy PBX.

Q: Where can I learn more about Exchange 2007 UM gateways?

A: Visit www.microsoft.com/technet/prodtechnol/exchange/telephony-advisor.mspx.

Chapter 2

Microsoft Office Communications Server 2007

Solutions in this chapter:

- What's New in OCS 2007?
- Comparing the Editions
- OCS 2007 Server Roles
- Planning an OCS 2007 Installation

☑ Summary

☑ Solutions Fast Track

☑ Frequently Asked Questions

Introduction

Microsoft Office Communications Server (OCS) 2007 is Microsoft's latest version of Live Communications Server 2005. The product provides management for all synchronous communications that take place in real time. This includes instant messaging (IM), voice over IP (VoIP), and audio conferencing and videoconferencing. It will work with your company's existing telecommunications systems without major hardware upgrades. This means your business can deploy advanced VoIP and conferencing without tearing out its preexisting legacy telephone network.

OCS 2007 also provides improved presence control, a key benefit of the Microsoft unified communications package, which unites all the contact information stored in Active Directory with the various technologies that people communicate with today. Presence provides you with instant information regarding whether someone is available and allows you to contact people with a click of the mouse via IM, a phone call, or videoconferencing.

What's New in OCS 2007?

OCS 2007 is actually the first public version of this product. It builds on the underlying promises and capabilities of Live Communications Server 2005, but OSC 2007 is really much, much more.

New Features

OCS 2007 builds on the foundations that Live Communications Server 2005 and Microsoft Office Communicator (MOC) 2005 delivered—namely, presence and IM, federated communications, and remote call control. Newly available key features in OCS 2007 include a number of improvements to the IM and presence capabilities. Some of these improvements include integration with Microsoft Exchange Server distribution lists, as well as the addition of software-powered VoIP that allows users to make, receive, and manage voice (phone) calls using MOC 2007 running on their computers (as well as Universal Serial Bus [USB] telephone devices), and multiparty on-premises audio/video and Web conferencing. OCS 2007 also supports the Interactive Connectivity Establishment (ICE) framework of protocols. This allows your users to take advantage of the aforementioned new communications capabilities from wherever they are located—such as a hotel or a coffeehouse—without needing to establish a virtual private network (VPN) connection. Let's look at some of these new features a little more closely.

On-Premises Web Conferencing

OCS 2007 now provides enterprise users, both inside and outside the firewall, the ability to create and join real-time Web conferences that are hosted on your organization's internal servers. Meetings such as these are also referred to as *on-premises conferences* and can be scheduled or unscheduled. In other words, both scheduled (preplanned) meetings and unscheduled (on-demand) meetings can be hosted on your internal servers. These meetings can also include IM, audio, video, application sharing, slide presentations, and other forms of data collaboration, just like outside, hosted services.

We all know that for years now, Microsoft has offered hosted Live Meeting services via the Web. With the introduction of OCS 2007, Microsoft now allows you to bring that same functionality in-house. You or any other enterprise user can also invite external users to join in. An *external user* is anyone who doesn't have an Active Directory Domain Services account. People who are employees of your business's partners, with secure and authenticated identities in your partners' domain, can also join your conferences and, if invited to do so, can even act as presenters. Thus, many of those meetings you've previously outsourced to Microsoft or other companies (e.g., WebEx) can now be maintained inside your network. In addition, an Outlook plug-in, as seen in Figure 2.1, lets you use Outlook's familiar scheduling interface to set up conferences.

Figure 2.1 Outlook 2007 with Live Meeting Toolbar Plug-in (area enclosed in the rectangle in the upper left section)

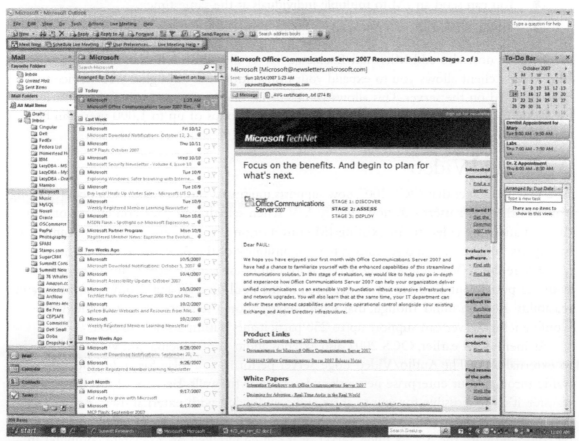

By using your own in-house server-based conferencing solution, you can provide your users with a more secure, controlled, and cost-effective collaboration experience. Adding RoundTable, another Microsoft product that we'll be discussing at length shortly, creates a totally immersive environment by providing a 360-degree view of the location including wideband audio and video by which the participants of your meeting communicate in real time. It's the closest thing to face-to-face interaction that you can experience.

Group IM

The first question that comes to mind when I hear the words *group IM* is "What the heck is it?" Microsoft's documentation says that group IM refers to an IM conversation that takes place among three or more people. Anyone who has ever used Microsoft, AOL, or Yahoo! Instant Messenger knows that you can create a group IM session in one of three different ways:

- You can start a conversation with one person and then invite additional parties to that initial two-person IM conversation.

- You can send an IM to multiple individuals at the same time.

- Within a domain, you can send an IM to a Microsoft Exchange Server distribution list.

You can now also add Microsoft Exchange Server distribution lists as contacts. The MOC 2007 client allows you to expand your distribution lists through a Web service that's been exposed on the server. This allows you to invite one or more members of a distribution list group to your IM session. Now your distribution groups of up to 1,000 users can be expanded, and your IM session can include as many as 100 different people.

Audio and Video

Also new is the fact that OCS 2007 now supports multiparty audio/video (A/V) conferencing. You and the other users can now specify A/V when scheduling your conference or you can add audio or video to an existing IM conversation or conference call. Management of multiparty audio and video sessions is the responsibility of the A/V Conferencing Server.

Where the A/V Conferencing Server is located doesn't really matter. It can be colocated with the pool Front-End Server or deployed in the pool on a separate computer for greater scalability. Keep in mind, though, that when deployed on a separate computer, the A/V Conferencing Server can support up to 250 participants within a single session.

As mentioned earlier, OCS 2007 also extends audio conferencing and videoconferencing to external users. The Audio/Video Edge Server performs as a relay for audio and video traffic through your enterprise network and corporate firewalls. Because of this information transfer, it's now possible for you to share audio and video with external users. As with the A/V Conferencing Server, where the A/V Edge Server is located doesn't really matter. It can be colocated with the Access Edge Server or it can be installed on a separate computer in the perimeter network. The MOC 2007 client supports peer-to-peer A/V communication for users both inside and outside the organization's firewall.

The question arises as to when you might use A/V conferencing as opposed to Live Meeting. Most IMs and the included A/V conferencing arise out of spur-of-the-moment communications (at least for me they do). Generally, my group has used it for small, last-minute, unplanned discussions, but I prefer using Live Meeting for meetings with planned agendas and larger groups of participants. A/V conferencing is limited to 250 participants when deployed on a single server. Also, if you are allowing external users access to the meeting and you don't have an A/V Edge Server, you will need to go with Live Meeting.

Enterprise Voice

Another of these new features is provided through the MOC 2007 client. This new feature is called Enterprise Voice, Microsoft's software-powered VoIP solution. MOC 2007 now offers Enterprise Voice, the IP telephony component of Microsoft's Unified Communications solution. Enterprise Voice combines software and telephony to give you what Microsoft calls a full-featured "softphone." With Enterprise Voice, MOC 2007 can become your main telephone in that it allows you to use your computer as your primary business phone.

Although MOC 2007 is the recommended application for use here, it is not the only one. The Tanjay phone is a stand-alone device that can be used, although the underlying code is based on the MOC 2007 application. We'll discuss client applications more fully shortly.

The combination of IM, conferencing, audio/video features, full integration with Outlook and Exchange Unified Messaging (UM), and Enterprise Voice allows you to choose the most appropriate way to communicate with your colleagues throughout your business. From your PC, you can place a call by simply clicking on an Outlook or Communicator contact. You can receive calls simultaneously on all your registered user endpoints; how you choose to answer your calls is up to you. You can also receive calls on your mobile phone or other mobile devices using this feature.

Enterprise Voice offers a large number of options that allow you to manage your everyday communications. Think about how Communicator's call control features, such as call holding, call resume, and call transfer, enable you to manage multiple phone calls at the same time. Each call is handled through a separate Conversation window, so you can efficiently manage your calls.

Enterprise Voice also provides robust call-forwarding and Do Not Disturb features integrated with the rich presence model available in Communicator. These features give you greater control of your time and your workday. For instance, you can manually set your presence state to Do Not Disturb and Communicator will then automatically forward to your voice mail all calls that originate from people other than your team members. Call-forwarding options allow you to forward all your calls to another phone, contact, or voice mail, or even simultaneously ring another number. To top it all off, using Enterprise Voice, you can add context to a call by adding a Subject line and an Importance indicator.

Here are some of the features available to you with Enterprise Voice. First, with Enterprise Voice any calls made to your work phone numbers are automatically converted to VoIP calls. You get VoIP calling features, but you still use the same familiar methods of placing calls to other work numbers.

Second, using Enterprise Voice you can manage multiple calls. Think about it. When you answer an incoming call, all other active calls are automatically put on hold. When you're finished with the one call, you can then easily resume any call on hold by simply selecting the Resume button in the Conversation window that represents that particular call.

Next, when you set your presence state to Do Not Disturb, you can control how many times you get interrupted during a given period. Keep in mind too that MOC 2007, by default, automatically redirects to voice mail incoming calls other than those from the specific team members you've chosen.

Imagine clicking a link within an e-mail and being able to call someone—with Enterprise Voice that's possible too. Also, just right-click the Presence button in an Outlook item and a context menu object will be displayed. That object will allow you to call a specified contact or contacts involved in the e-mail discussion.

As far as call forwarding and redirect to voice mail are concerned, there are new settings for both of these features that you can control. You can set call forwarding to automatically forward all your calls to voice mail if that's what you want. You can also control the time interval that an incoming call will ring before it is forwarded to voice mail. Another new feature allows you to redirect your incoming calls to voice mail from Communicator's actionable call alerts.

The MOC 2007 client also offers call-forwarding rules that are easy to configure. For instance, you can set call-forwarding settings to:

- **Forward call to** All of your incoming calls can be forwarded to another number. That number could be your mobile phone, a new phone number that you specified, or another contact number or voice mail.

- **Simultaneously ring this additional number** You can also set the call-forwarding settings to ring an additional number at the same time your default phone number rings if you're mobile or away from your desk. This feature also helps you to ensure that you receive your phone calls on your mobile phone, even if you're not logged into the MOC 2007 client on your computer.

- **Redirect unanswered calls** With MOC 2007 you now can configure call-forwarding settings to specify that if a call is not accepted within a specified time interval, the call is redirected to another number, contact, or voice mail.

- **Apply call-forwarding rules only during working hours** If you're running Outlook 2007 and Exchange 2007, you can configure your working hours in the

Outlook Work Calendar by selecting **Tools | Options | Calendar Options in Outlook**. Then you can use the **Call-Forwarding Settings dialog box** in MOC to apply the call-forwarding settings only during the work hours you set in the Outlook Work Calendar.

■ **Add Subject and Importance to a call** As mentioned previously, you can also add a conversation subject and an importance flag to a call, enabling the call recipient to quickly determine the reason for and urgency of the call.

Using Enterprise Voice, you can participate in IP voice sessions that cross through network address translators (NATs) and firewalls. This means that when you are working at home or on the road you can still call the enterprise from anywhere an Internet connection is available, without incurring long-distance charges or resorting to a VPN. You will be able to receive call notifications on your computer, configure call forwarding in MOC, and access voice mail either from your computer or by calling an access number. And best of all, you can enjoy these features without having to change your existing phone number and with minimal client configuration.

For business customers, Enterprise Voice also provides the following benefits beyond the productivity enhancements users can use. Keep in mind that only minimal hardware additions, and no extensive alterations to existing OCS 2007 and telephony infrastructures, are required. You don't have to lose the familiarity of your PBX system to enjoy the advantages of Enterprise Voice, as it can be partly or fully integrated with existing PBX systems. You can back out of it on user machines easily as your situation may require. Smart, least-cost routing algorithms are used for calls to the PSTN. VoIP infrastructure management is fully integrated with existing OCS 2007 administrative tools. And finally, bottlenecks and single points of failure in traditional communication networks are eliminated via a distributed architecture.

Microsoft RoundTable Communications and Archival System

OCS 2007 supports the Microsoft RoundTable communications and archival system, Microsoft's new 360-degree surround A/V conference room device that turns an online meeting into a true face-to-face experience. Attending a video conference by using RoundTable is much the same as attending a meeting in person. When you use RoundTable in conjunction with Microsoft OCS 2007 or Live Meeting 2007, a 360-degree view of the conference room, wideband audio, and video are provided to the participants, while the system tracks the flow of conversation among multiple speakers. The audio and video of your entire conference room are delivered to a remote meeting location for your co-workers to interact with in real time.

RoundTable offers the following features:

- **It's immersive and participatory** Everyone involved, no matter where they are, converses and shares information as though they are physically in the same room.

- **It's collaborative and affordable** Plug-and-play functionality makes RoundTable extremely easy to set up. No need for techies in most cases.

- **It makes your meetings valuable** Have you ever tried to remember what was said at a certain place in your notes where the coffee stain has all but wiped them out? No problem now. Simply record those meetings for later use both by yourself for note-taking purposes and by those who weren't able to make it to the meeting. These viewers will have the same meeting experience that those who attended had, plus they'll be able to fast-forward and rewind.

Enhanced Presence

MOC 2007 now provides new presence state levels to more accurately reflect your willingness and ability to communicate with others. It also now gives you more control over access to your presence information by assigning specific contacts to specified access levels. Let's take a closer look at some of these new features.

MOC 2007 introduces new presence states and icons. You now have many more options when it comes to presence states, including Inactive and Busy (Inactive) states. The actual presence state in now more accurately represented with the introduction of new presence buttons. Also, presence states now transition from Available, to Inactive, to Away. Intermediate Inactive states are determined by an idle-time setting you set. This setting monitors user activity on the computer to determine the transitions.

According to Microsoft Office Online (http://office.microsoft.com/en-us/help/HA102064651033.aspx), improved presence management allows various levels of access to be assigned to your contacts. This enables you to control who can see your contact information and how much of this information is visible. In other words, you can set up some of your people with certain access to your presence information. This determines what they can and can't see. You could, for example, set up John and Mary to let them see your mobile phone number and to let them interrupt you with an IM or phone call when you're in the Do Not Disturb mode. Meanwhile, you can give everybody else company-level access. That way, they see your work phone number, but not your mobile phone. Also, they can't interrupt you when you're in Do Not Disturb mode.

Remember that you can assign a Team access level to other contacts. This allows you to set a level of interruption management. This is simply a list of people who can contact you when your Presence status is set to Do Not Disturb. You're now also able to manually set your Presence status to Do Not Disturb. You can also do this for any incoming IM, Call, or

Conference alerts. Remember, though, that when you have set your Presence state to Do Not Disturb, you'll only be able to see urgent alerts from team members.

Location status is now available from the Presence menu in MOC 2007. You can select either the **Home** or the **Office** location, or you can enter a custom location. When you set the **Location** option, your location information becomes available on your Contact Card. Anyone to whom you've granted **Personal** or **Team** access levels can now see it.

To explain further, OCS 2007 provides the underlying structure on which client applications, such as MOC 2007, publish and subscribe to the various levels of presence information. This underlying structure includes categories and containers. We can define *categories* as pieces of information, such as status, location, or calendar state, pertaining to presence. In a similar way, *containers* are the logical carrier where client applications publish pieces of presence information. When that presence changes, client applications can publish just the individual category instead of the entire presence document.

Nine levels of presence are now available for use with the client applications. Those levels are:

- Available
- Inactive
- Away
- Busy (Inactive)
- Busy
- Do Not Disturb
- Offline
- Unknown
- Blocked

Also remember that six different categories of presence information are now available:

- Name/e-mail (your name and e-mail address)
- Basic contact information (your title and company)
- Detailed contact information (your work phone, work address, office number, SharePoint site, free/busy schedule, notes [out of office], and notes [personal])
- Additional numbers (mobile phone, home phone, and other phone)
- Location (current location, time away, and working hours)
- Meeting details

In MOC 2007, you can assign your contacts to one of the several presence levels mentioned earlier. Which level you choose depends on how much information about yourself you want each contact to see. Keep in mind that each presence level in this structure corresponds to one of the containers we discussed previously. Also remember that each container is associated with a particular amount of information about a user. You may want to assign some people to one level where they may be able to see only your name, job title, company, and e-mail address. At the same time, you might want other people to be assigned to another level where they might, for example, be able to see only your home and mobile phone numbers.

OCS 2007 keeps all of its clients notified of all presence-level changes, depending on the containers for which each client has permission. For example, as you move from one part of town to another as you travel, your supervisor and your spouse can be notified of your movements, whereas everyone else without those necessary permissions for that container are not notified. OCS 2007 supports this capability through the use of access control lists (ACLs) that are based on these containers and categories we've discussed.

There are five basic ACLs, listed here from most restrictive to least restrictive:

- **Blocked** Here, only the name and e-mail information can be seen by those you've given access.

- **Public** With this ACL, only the name/e-mail and basic contact information can be seen.

- **Company** Here, the name/e-mail, basic contact information, and detailed contact information are available to those who have access.

- **Personal** In this case, the name/e-mail, basic contact information, detailed contact information, additional numbers, and location can be seen by those you have given access.

- **Team** Finally, in this least restrictive ACL, the name/e-mail, basic contact information, detailed contact information, additional numbers, location, and meeting details can be seen. Also, these contacts are allowed to interrupt you should they need to talk to you.

Federation Enhancements

OCS 2007 supports all the federation and remote user scenarios that were previously enabled in Live Communications Server 2005. In addition, OCS 2007 introduces the following enhancements to existing federation support:

- Federated conferencing
- Support for partners with multiple domain names
- Improved monitoring and throttling capabilities for federated connections

Let's take a closer look at these three enhancements. Your company works closely with other companies on certain projects. At those companies, you have people who don't belong to your domain but still need to be allowed to access your conferences. Those users in those federated domains are considered to be authenticated as far as joining one of your on-premises conference is concerned. There is a difference, though. That difference is that those federated users can't join a meeting as presenters. They can still be presenters, but they must first join the conference as a participant; once they've joined, you can promote them to presenter status during the meeting. Keep in mind, though, that these users can't organize conferences hosted in your domain.

But what do you do if you have multiple domains in your enterprise? Simple: Enhanced federation now also uses subject alternate names (SANs) in certificates. If you want to make your domain capable of enhanced federation, all you have to do is install a certificate that supports SANs on your Live Communications Server 2005 SP1 Access Proxy or your OCS 2007 Access Edge Server.

Finally, with OCS 2007, you can actively monitor all connections made to your federated domains. This means you can limit traffic from any federated domain that's not on your Allow list. Additionally, OCS 2007 limits the number of internal users with which these federated domains can communicate. Monitoring of this activity takes place on your Access Edge Server using the **Open Federation** tab on the **Status** pane in the OCS 2007 Computer Management snap-in. If you find that a federated domain has a legitimate, but higher than average, volume of communications with your organization, you can add the domain to your Allow list. If you suspect malicious activity, you can block the domain.

Client Applications

Client applications are the tools that your users access, and they use the IM, presence, and conferencing features that are made possible by OCS 2007. Keep in mind that OSC 2007 and these client applications are symbiotic. Without the clients, the features exist as mere potential. Without the server, the clients can do nothing. Let's talk more about the OCS 2007 client applications.

As I mentioned earlier, MOC 2007 is not the only client available for use with OCS 2007. With that said, according to Microsoft, it is the recommended Unified Communications client for it. MOC 2007 exposes to the end-user the presence, IM, and multimodal conferencing features that OCS 2007 supports. That includes the expanded presence information and the ability to control who sees it, group IM based on Exchange Distribution Lists, and the addition of audio and video to IM conversations. But what other clients are out there that we could choose instead?

If you are more comfortable making calls using a phone than from the MOC 2007 software client, Microsoft has developed the MOC Phone Edition telephone. For the most part, this is a physical version of MOC 2007, with a similar user interface and similar functionality. Like MOC 2007, with the MOC Phone Edition you can place a call either by using the numeric touchpad or by simply clicking one of your contacts. The MOC Phone Edition also supports enhanced presence, Session Initiation Protocol (SIP) signaling, and a user experience similar to that of MOC 2007, all in a desktop telephone. You can also use the MOC Phone Edition to connect either from home or from the office.

Another client you could choose is the Live Meeting 2007 client. This client is the data collaboration and A/V client for both OCS 2007 and the Hosted Live Meeting service. This is important. Think about it—one client that provides a unified collaboration experience across both server-based and service-based conferencing products. That cuts down on software clutter on the client machine.

Finally, the Microsoft Outlook Add-in we talked about earlier is the conference scheduling client for OCS 2007. It's compatible with Microsoft Office Outlook 2000, 2002, 2003, and 2007.

Simplified Deployment and Management

To make deployment and administrative tasks much simpler, quicker, and easier, Microsoft has overhauled OCS 2007's setup and management tools, procedures, and capabilities. We'll discuss several of these improvements in this section.

Deployment Planning Improvements

OCS 2007 features improved scalability via a new, expanded Enterprise pool configuration that supports a single Front-End Server without a load balancer. Expanded load-balancer support now includes offerings from F5, Cisco, Foundry, and WebMux. New server roles can be deployed and managed for conferencing, media, VoIP, and external-user support. Users also now are able to delegate permissions setup, server management, user management, and other administrative tasks where read–only access is adequate. Other improvements include support for disjointed domain name system (DNS) namespaces and for Universal Groups.

Installation Improvements

Installation improvements to OCS 2007 include integrated setup and management of multiple server roles on a single computer. A new Deployment Wizard clarifies deployment by specifying prerequisites and providing guidance at every step. Scenario-based deployment options guide you from absolute zero to a functional system without having to leave the Deployment Wizard, and new wizards simplify configuration and reduce configuration mistakes. A new Streamlined Certificate Wizard provides step-by-step guidance through the certification process. A single computer running OCS now requires only a single certificate regardless of the number of colocated components, resulting in greatly streamlined certificate management. Deployment has been simplified by eliminating the need for Domain Add. Adding a server to a pool is much simpler, and a domain controller is no longer required to be available in the root domain of the forest.

Management Improvements

Management improvements include new conferencing and VoIP policies for specifying and managing usage entitlements; enhanced in-band provisioning for soft clients and devices; and a redesigned Status pane in the OCS 2007 administrative snap-in that makes configuration settings readily available without having to access individual property pages. New database queries and event logs are available through the Status pane of the snap-in.

Administration Improvements

Administration improvements to OCS 2007 include enhanced intelligent IM filter client version checking, for the purpose of allowing or blocking certain client versions and devices; improved archiving controls that enable global administrators to delegate per-user archiving; new call detail records (CDRs) that provide a way to collect IM, VoIP, and meeting usage statistics; new resource kit tools for CDR querying and reporting; and new resource kit tools for OCS 2007 environment discovery.

Monitoring and Troubleshooting Improvements

Monitoring and troubleshooting improvements include an enhanced MOM pack, which includes support for new server roles. A new tracing and logging tool, OCSLogger, for troubleshooting and debugging is available with the OCS 2007 administrative snap-in. You can use this tool to enable logging, collect and analyze logs, and package logs for sending to Microsoft Customer Support Services. This tool replaces the Flat File logging functionality in Live Communications Server 2005 SP1. A new log analysis tool, Snooper, is available from the resource kit tools for advanced analysis of protocol traffic (SIP, CCCP), troubleshooting voice call signaling, and viewing user and conference state information. A runtime diagnostics module monitors problems (such as server connection and DNS failures, certificate validation failures, client authentication failures, and domain validation issues) and raises MOM-enabled alerts. More detailed error information is conveyed by the server and client. Each error is associated with a unique ID, reason, and detailed parameters. RouteHelper is a resource kit tool that offers an alternative to the administrative snap-in for viewing, modifying, and testing Enterprise Voice number normalization rules, location profiles, voice policy, and routes.

New Deployment Tool

The new OCS 2007 deployment tool provides you with an end-to-end deployment solution that makes your life much simpler. This new tool provides step-by-step guidance not only through your installations, but also through the configuration and activation of all your server roles, as well as validation of the installed deployments.

The deployment tool will guide you through the end-to-end deployment process by means of a variety of new wizards that take most of the guesswork out of your normal, common deployment tasks. Those new wizards include the Setup Delegation Wizard,

Certificates Wizard, Create Enterprise Pool Wizard, Deploy Server Wizard, Add Server to Pool Wizard, Server Configuration Wizard, Activation Wizard, and Validation Wizard.

The Setup Delegation Wizard allows you permissions on the various Active Directory objects to delegate the various setup tasks, even when you aren't authorized.

The Certificates Wizard helps you to configure a certificate for your local server based on the selected server role and any earlier deployment configurations you may have set. Using this wizard, you can create a new certificate request, import a certificate, export a certificate, or assign an existing certificate. You can then either create the certificate request online and transmit it when completed or create and save the certificate request offline for submission at a later time. You are in control.

The Create Enterprise Pool Wizard allows you to create various Active Directory objects and the pool's backend databases.

The Deploy Server Wizard helps you to install and activate the Front-End Server and all conferencing server components on a single Standard Edition server.

The Add Server to Pool Wizard provides assistance with the installation and activation of the Front-End Server and all conferencing server components on a single Enterprise Edition: Consolidated Configuration server.

The Server Configuration Wizard provides step-by-step procedures for configuring each server role and pool.

The Activation Wizard requests the user input that is necessary to activate local servers.

And finally, the Validation Wizard provides easy-to-follow, step-by-step testing procedures allowing you to know for sure that a deployment has been installed, configured, and activated correctly. It also then checks for you to make sure that the deployment is working properly.

Management Console Improvements

You can manage your installation much more easily now that the OCS 2007 snap-in for the Microsoft Management Console (MMC) has been redesigned. Some of these changes include eliminating clutter, making descriptive text more specific, improving discoverability, and reducing the number of exposed settings to only those that administrators require for normal operations. The Status pane of this snap-in allows you to configure your forest, domains, pools, servers, and users with ease. You no longer have to navigate through the MMC to find the specific settings you're looking for. The Status pane also features a new Database tab. This tab allows you to query a pool's backend user and conferences databases. Each query is then displayed as an expandable item in a list.

Universal Group Support

An important fact to remember is that OCS 2007 supports the native mode Universal Groups available in the Microsoft Windows Server 2003 and Windows 2000 Server operating systems.

This means that as a member of any of these Universal Groups you can include other groups and accounts from any domain in the domain tree or forest. You'll also be able to be assign permissions in any domain in the domain tree or forest. Universal Group support, combined with administrator delegation, greatly simplifies management of your OCS 2007 deployment.

Enhanced In-Band Provisioning

You're also now able to customize your clients to meet the needs of your installation. Your control over enabling or disabling features you want is centralized and can be chosen according to your security policy and network infrastructure. This happens through in-band provisioning. This also provides a way to configure all your roaming clients, those outside the reach of your Group Policy. In-band provisioning is also now extensible. More settings are now provided by the server too.

The big question in my mind after reading all about this in Microsoft's preliminary literature was "What's it used for?" The answer is simple. OCS 2007 uses in-band provisioning to pass user identity and server configuration information to the client. The information conveyed in the user identity category is used to display the username and e-mail address in the client. The server configuration category contains such information as Address Book Server download URLs, group expansion Web service URLs, console installation URLs, and conference troubleshooting URLs.

Integrated Address Book Server

I know you've been sitting there with this question burning in the back of your mind and you wanted to ask but were afraid. The question? How do MOC 2007 clients get their Global user information? The answer is that it's provided via the Address Book Server. "But," you say, "in Live Communications Server 2005 SP1, Address Book Server was optional." You're correct. If you remember, it also had to be installed separately from the server. In OCS 2007, Address Book Server is required and is a fully integrated Front-End Server component. It's installed by default automatically as part of both Standard Edition and Enterprise Edition setups, so you can rest easier now.

Meeting Policies

Come to think of it, your job just got a whole lot easier with OCS 2007. As an administrator, you can now easily define a global meeting policy using the OCS 2007 administrative snap-in. An OCS 2007 meeting policy determines the maximum allowed meeting size, color definition for application sharing, types of supported media, and whether and how programs and desktops can be shared with federated and/or anonymous users. You can choose from one of five freely available predefined policies or you can define a custom policy.

CDRs

Are you one of those people who need to know how your network communications are being used? Although some people gather this type of information simply to justify their own existence (and in this time of paper-pushing bureaucrats who have no idea what IT means, it is sometimes necessary), being prepared for surges in network use and allotting the correct amount of resources to the heaviest uses are justifiable reasons for gathering this type of data. CDRs capture data about your users' activities, such as participating in IM conversations and starting and joining conferences. CDRs make it easy to collect both IM and meeting data and to then generate reports on their use. This data can then be used to determine network bandwidth load, employee usage patterns, and return on investment.

Now it comes down to choosing what data to capture. You, as the network administrator, can choose and specify which IM and conferencing usage data you want. IM data includes call details, file transfers, audio and video calls, and remote assistance calls. Meeting data includes the number of meetings, number of participants joining a meeting, number of data and A/V instances joining a meeting, and details about peer-to-peer IM sessions and group IM sessions.

CDRs also allow you to monitor the amount of IM and conferencing activity you want for the purpose of developing data and metrics about how productive your employees are and how they are using the network. Then you, as I said earlier, can use this data to justify your technology investments. You can also use it to determine the return on investment to show your bosses how good you are.

SOME INDEPENDENT ADVICE

An important thing to keep in mind when planning your installation is that if there is an outage, disruption, or other degradation of the power, network, or telephone services at your location, the voice, IM, presence, and other features of OCS 2007 and any device connected to OCS 2007 may not work properly. Voice communications via OCS 2007 depend on the availability of the server software and the proper functioning of the voice clients or the hardware phone devices connecting to the server software. Anywhere you install a voice client (e.g., a PC running MOC 2007 or a MOC Phone Edition device), you should make sure you maintain a backup option for users to call emergency services (911, 999, etc.) in case of a power failure, network connectivity degradation, telephone service outage, or other problem that may inhibit operation of OCS 2007, MOC 2007, or the Phone Edition devices. Such alternative options could include a telephone connected to a standard PSTN line or a cell phone.

Another thing you need to be aware of in your planning is that the use of a multiline telephone system (MLTS) may be subject to U.S. (state and/or federal) and foreign MLTS laws that require the MLTS to provide a caller's telephone number, extension, and/or physical location to applicable emergency services when a caller makes a call to emergency services (e.g., when dialing an emergency access number such as 911 or 999). Keep in mind that OCS 2007, MOC 2007, and MOC Phone Edition devices do not provide the caller's physical location to emergency services when a caller dials those emergency services. Compliance with such MLTS laws is the sole responsibility of the purchaser of OCS 2007, MOC 2007, and MOC Phone Edition devices.

Improved Features

Both OCS 2007 and MOC 2007 are filled with new and improved features that enhance your enterprise communications. For MOC 2007, new sign-in improvements include:

- Manual configuration of server name
- Sign-in user interface integration into a single screen
- Event logging

Let's look at these improvements more closely. Now you can manually configure both internal and external server names for how you will connect to OCS 2007 from both inside and outside the firewall. The sign-in user interface for the client is centralized now so that the sign-in address, username, and password are handled on one screen. It now also provides event logging of sign-in errors, complete with the how and why and even suggested steps you should take to make troubleshooting much easier.

At the same time, there are improvements to tabs in MOC 2007. Those improvements include:

- Improved user interface for tabs
- Contextual information

When you look at these two areas of improvement more closely, the tabs in the MOC 2007 client window are now more tightly wrapped into the Communicator user interface. Now the client user interface displays in the upper portion of the application's main window and tabbed content displays in the lower portion. This allows you to expand and collapse the content area for tabs as necessary (this is available with both the Remote Call Control [RCC] and Unified Communications [UC] configurations).

Also, developers can now send contextual information to a tabbed page in the client. This is possible by invoking a script in the tab page rather than using the traditional *GET/POST* method. This method enables a faster page refresh, but it also means that passing contacts by HTTP *GET/POST* is no longer supported. Support is available to pass contacts, groups, and distribution groups, or any combination thereof. Anyone using or wanting to use this feature must implement this script (this is also available with both the RCC and UC configurations).

The following improvements for audio and video devices are also available in the client:

- Support for audio USB devices
- A USB handset display
- A speakerphone button in the Conversation window
- Automatic audio and video setup

Let's look at these improvements a little more closely. MOC 2007 now supports telephony-class USB audio devices, including handsets and headsets. We talked about one of them earlier in the chapter. The client also now supports USB handsets with displays that show call alerts, call subject, and caller information and timer. Sounds are now integrated with USB handset displays to enhance your calling experience. A speakerphone button has been added to the client Conversation window. This means you can toggle your call audio between speakers and a USB handset or headset. Finally, the audio and video setup experience is significantly improved. Some of those new improvements include:

- **Automatic detection and selection of devices** This improved feature automatically detects and selects audio and video devices. That includes USB handsets and headsets, speakers and microphones, and Web cameras. As with other plug-and-play applications, if one of the devices is detached/reattached or a new device is attached, Set Up Audio and Video automatically reconfigures the devices for you.

- **Option to use high-fidelity speakers for call audio instead of speaker-phones** If you have USB handsets and headsets, Set Up Audio and Video provides you the option of selecting an alternative device (other than the USB handset or headset) for playing audio from calls. This allows you to play the audio from that call from your boss, for example, on high-fidelity speakers to make him sound better.

- **Option to select the device to play program sounds** Finally, you can also now use Set Up Audio and Video to select a device (other than the default audio device) to play program sounds such as a ring for an incoming call or an IM. This allows you to put it on those speakers and really annoy the person in the next cubicle.

One of the things you are going to get with MOC 2007 is improved manageability. You now have at your disposal new server configuration settings and policies allowing you far superior administrative control than you've had before. Telephony modes, location profile (for outbound call routing), the Uniform Resource Identifier (URI) for the A/V Authentication Service, the voice mail URI, and the Exchange UM URI can all now be configured and managed using the server Windows Management Instrumentation (WMI) settings.

Status and notification alerts are now combined into a single setting. Also, the busy mode alert has been discontinued and you don't have to worry about that anymore. Your alerts can also now be configured so that you receive conversation alerts, but not notification alerts.

You also have new logging options available now. You can choose to enable logging and to document how the MOC 2007 client performs. The client now provides a Turn on Logging in Communicator option. This goes hand in hand with the EnableTracing Group Policy. There is also a Turn on Windows Event Logging for Communicator option. This corresponds with the EnableEventLogging Group Policy. When turned on, errors are written to the system event log. You can then view them in the Windows Event Viewer.

The auto-archiving (DisableAutoArchive) policy is now separated into two policies: the IMAutoArchiving policy and the CallLogAutoArchiving policy. This provides you even more control over your archiving decisions.

Allowing access for users from outside your domain is now easier too. Settings to enable IPAudio, IPVideo, and AVConferencing, previously available only as Group Policy objects, can now be set up and provisioned in-band.

With MOC 2007, the connectivity between the client and the server is strengthened. When you first log on, your SIP URI is auto-populated. Connectivity between the client and the server for various DNS configurations is also strengthened. This is accomplished by retrying all servers returned by DNS.

The way error messages are handled has also been significantly improved. Error Message Reporting for both Enterprise Voice and Conferencing is now available. You can now just click a link in the error message and open a Web page for additional details and how you might be able to fix the error.

Improved Client

Client applications are the tools with which end-users access and use the IM, presence, and conferencing features that are made possible by OCS 2007. Without the clients, the features exist as mere potential. Without the server, the clients have nothing to do.

OCS 2007 supports the following client applications:

- MOC 2007 is the recommended Unified Communications client for OCS 2007. The MOC 2007 client exposes to the end-user the presence, IM, and multimodal conferencing features that OCS 2007 supports. This includes expanded presence information and user control over who sees it, group IM based on Exchange Distribution Lists, and the addition of audio and video to IM conversations. The MOC 2007 client is the application for synchronous communication. *Synchronous* means the communication takes place in real time. Examples of this include phone conversations as well as face-to-face conversations. MCO 2007 is therefore the primary tool for obtaining presence and directory information, IM, telephone calls, and A/V conferencing.

- MOC 2007 is an all-in-one client solution that helps you get more done by allowing you to communicate easily with clients and co-workers in different places and time zones using a variety of communication options, including IM, voice, and video. Integration with programs across the 2007 Microsoft Office system—including Word, Excel, PowerPoint, OneNote, Groove, and SharePoint Server—gives you many different ways to communicate with other information workers via a consistent and simple user experience.

- MOC 2007's innate and natural design makes it easy for you to use. Features including click-to-call and the ability to shift conversations from IMs to phone or videoconferences on the fly make it very easy to use. The client also helps you control incoming communications with alerts, automatic call forwarding, and the ability to manually set your status light. For example, you can set your status to Busy when you need to focus on something specific, and MOC 2007 will route all your incoming calls to voice mail.

  MOC 2007 also integrates the entire communications experience into the Microsoft Office system. Presence information appears wherever a contact's name appears: in a document workspace, on a Microsoft Office SharePoint Server site, or in an e-mail string. Also, with MOC Mobile 2007, you can have tools such as presence and click-to-call on your Windows Mobile-powered devices.

  So, while MOC 2007 is Microsoft's preferred UC client for OCS 2007, as I said earlier, it is not the only one. Here are some others.

- **MOC Phone Edition** As mentioned earlier, Microsoft has developed the MOC Phone Edition telephone for organizations or users who are more comfortable making calls from a phone-like device than from the MOC software client. Again, for most purposes, the MOC Phone Edition phone is a physical version of MOC 2007, with a similar user interface and comparable functionality. Like MOC 2007, the MOC Phone Edition allows you to place a call either by using a numeric touchpad or by clicking one of your contacts. Just like the software client, the MOC Phone Edition also supports enhanced presence, SIP signaling, and a user experience similar to that of MOC, all in a desktop telephone. Again, you can use the MOC Phone Edition to connect from home or in the office.

- **Microsoft Office Live Meeting 2007 client** The Live Meeting 2007 client is the data collaboration and A/V client for both OCS 2007 and the Hosted Live Meeting service. It provides a unified collaboration experience across both server-based and service-based conferencing products.

- **Microsoft Outlook Add-in** The Microsoft Outlook Add-in is the conference scheduling client for OCS 2007. It is compatible with Microsoft Office Outlook 2000, 2002, 2003, and 2007.

Comparing the Editions

Like its predecessor, Live Communications Server 2005, OCS 2007 is available in two editions: Standard Edition and Enterprise Edition. Both support the full suite of IM, presence, conferencing, and VoIP features. Let's look at each one now.

Standard Edition

The Standard Edition server hosts all the necessary server components and services, as well as the database for storing the user and conference information, on a single Front-End Server. Because it requires a minimal hardware investment and minimal management overhead, the Standard Edition configuration is ideal for small and medium-size businesses as well as for branch offices. It is intended for deployments with fewer than 5,000 users either in total or at a particular location where high availability is not a requirement. The Standard Edition provides full functionality for small organizations.

Enterprise Edition

The Enterprise Edition of OCS 2007 separates the server functionality from data storage to achieve higher capacity and availability. An Enterprise Edition pool typically consists of two or more Front-End Servers, each fronted by a hardware load balancer and connected to a backend database. (If needed, it is also possible to deploy a single Front-End Server without a load balancer.) Optionally, certain conferencing components can be deployed on separate computers for higher capacity and availability. The Enterprise Edition is appropriate for medium, large, and very large organizations.

Enterprise Edition: Consolidated Configuration is a pool configuration in which all the server components are colocated on the pool's Front-End Servers (the only exception is the placement of the backend database that must reside on a separate dedicated computer). Consolidated Configuration provides scalability and high availability while still being relatively easy to plan, deploy, and manage.

Enterprise Edition: Expanded Configuration, on the other hand, offers maximum capacity, performance, and availability for large organizations. Expanded Configuration enables your organization to scale up specific A/V or Web conferencing requirements independently from other Enterprise Edition server components. For example, if your A/V traffic increases more rapidly than other traffic, you can meet this increase by deploying only additional A/V Conferencing Servers rather than entire Front-End Servers.

OCS 2007 Server Roles

OCS 2007 conferences provide rich multimedia experiences that include data collaboration, group IM, audio and video, and multiparty audio conferencing. For each media type there is a corresponding conferencing server, or multipoint control unit (MCU), that manages and coordinates the use of that media type during the course of a meeting. OCS 2007 ships with four conferencing servers:

- **IM Conferencing Server** Provides server-managed group IM
- **Web Conferencing Server** Enables multiparty data collaboration
- **A/V Conferencing Server** Enables audio conferencing and videoconferencing
- **Telephony Conferencing Server** Enables audio conference integration with audio conferencing providers (ACPs)

Front-End Server

The IM Conferencing Server and Telephony Conferencing Server always run as separate processes on the Standard Edition server or Enterprise Edition Front-End Server. The Web Conferencing Server and A/V Conferencing Server can optionally be deployed on separate computers within an Enterprise pool.

With both the OCS 2007 Standard and Enterprise editions, the Front-End Server is responsible for the following tasks:

- Handling signaling among servers and between servers and clients
- Authenticating users and maintaining user data, including all user endpoints
- Routing VoIP calls within the enterprise and to the PSTN
- Initiating on-premises conferences and managing conference state
- Providing enhanced presence information to clients
- Routing IM and conferencing traffic
- Managing conferencing media
- Hosting applications
- Filtering *SPIM* (unsolicited commercial IM traffic)

Edge Server

An edge server is an OCS that resides in the perimeter network and provides connectivity for external users and public IM connections. Each edge server has one or more of the following roles: Access Edge Server, Web Conferencing Edge Server, or A/V Edge Server.

Edge servers enable your internal and external users to communicate using the MOC 2007 or Live Meeting 2007 client. Depending on your needs, you install edge servers in one or more of the following roles:

- **Access Edge Server** This used to be known as the Access Proxy. The main thing to know here is that this server handles all SIP traffic across your corporate firewalls. This SIP traffic is required to set up and validate connections. It doesn't handle data transfer and it doesn't authenticate users. Active Directory access is required to perform authentication. Authentication of inbound traffic is performed by the Director or the Front-End Server. A Director is an OCS 2007 Standard Edition server or Enterprise pool that doesn't host users and that resides inside an organization's firewall. Having a Director is not mandatory, but it is strongly recommended. Keep in mind that the Director role is used to route traffic to the proper pool or server. It also acts as a middleman between the Access Proxy role and other front-end servers. If a hacker manages to get in and compromises an Access Proxy server, he can't bring down Active Directory or any of the front-end servers. That's because the Director role takes the main force of any potential denial-of-service (DoS) attack. If a Director isn't deployed, this authentication is performed by the Front-End Server on the pool or on a Standard Edition server that you've designated to do so. Edge servers don't have Active Directory access because they're deployed in the perimeter network outside Active Directory. If you're using conferencing, remote user access, federation, or public IM connectivity in your enterprise, you must have an Access Edge Server.

- **Web Conferencing Edge Server** In relatively simple terms, the Web Conferencing Edge Server enables data collaboration with external users. It proxies Persistent Shared Object Model (PSOM) traffic between the Web Conferencing Server and the external clients. The Web Conferencing Edge Server has to approve any traffic from outside the domain before it ever sees it. The Web Conferencing Edge Server requires users outside the domain to use TLS connections and to obtain a conference session key.

- **A/V Edge Server** This server provides a single trusted connection point where both inbound and outbound media traffic can securely cross NATs and firewalls. Basically, it enables audio conferencing and videoconferencing and A/V peer-to-peer communications with external users who are equipped with the MOC 2007 client. Peer-to-peer communications travel between the clients and don't go through the A/V Conferencing Server. ICE is the industry-standard solution for multimedia traversal of firewalls. ICE is based on the Simple Traversal Underneath NAT (STUN) and Traversal Using Relay NAT (TURN) protocols. The A/V Edge Server is a STUN server. All users are authenticated to secure both access to the enterprise and use of the firewall traversal service that the A/V Edge Server provides. To send media inside the enterprise, an external user must be authenticated and must have an authenticated internal user agree to communicate with him or her through the A/V Edge Server. The media streams are exchanged by using the Secure Real-time Transport Protocol (SRTP), which is an industry standard for real-time media transmission and reception over IP.

Keep in mind that you can install these edge servers on a single computer or on separate computers. For reasons of economy and simplicity, the recommended deployment for most organizations is to colocate the Web Conferencing Edge Server with the Access Edge Server but to install the A/V Edge Server, which requires greater bandwidth, on a separate computer. Group IM and data collaboration with external users also require deploying an HTTP reverse proxy in the perimeter network.

Mediation Server

The OCS 2007 Mediation Server provides signaling and media translation between the VoIP infrastructure and a basic media gateway. A Mediation Server also links OCS 2007 with a PBX in both the departmental deployment and PBX integration topologies.

The Mediation Server is deployed as a stand-alone application inside the firewall. On the OCS side, the Mediation Server listens on a single mutual TLS transport address. On the gateway side, the Mediation Server listens on a single Transmission Control Protocol/ Internet Protocol (TCP/IP) transport address.

The main functions of the Mediation Server are as follows:

■ Translating SIP over TCP (on the gateway side) to SIP over mutual TLS (on the Enterprise Voice side)

■ Encrypting and decrypting SRTP on the OCS side

■ Translating media streams between OCS and the media gateway

■ Connecting clients that are outside the network to internal ICE components, which enable media traversal of NAT and firewalls

■ Acting as an intermediary for call flows that a gateway does not support, such as calls from remote workers on an Enterprise Voice client

From the perspective of the Enterprise Voice infrastructure, the combination of the basic media gateway and Mediation Server appears as a single entity. Together, they are the logical and functional equivalent of an advanced media gateway. When advanced media gateways become available, enterprises that deploy them no longer need a dedicated Mediation Server. Meanwhile, the basic-hybrid media gateway provides an interim solution for organizations that prefer to avoid deploying and managing a gateway and Mediation Server separately. A typical organization supports multiple gateway–Mediation Server combinations, depending on the number of office locations, the number and distribution of Enterprise Voice users, network traffic, and performance requirements.

Archiving and CDR Server

The Archiving and CDR Server provides the following capabilities:

- Archiving of all IM conversations for all users or for individual users that you specify
- Archiving of CDRs for all users

Messages from the OCS Front-End Server are sent through the Windows Server Message Queuing service to the Archiving and CDR Server, which uses a Microsoft SQL Server database to store archived information. An Archiving and CDR Agent is installed as part of every OCS Standard Edition server or Enterprise Edition server.

Although the Archiving and CDR Agent is automatically installed, to archive IM traffic and call data you must configure the Archiving and CDR Agent and the Archiving and CDR Server to which the Archiving and CDR Agent connects.

The Archiving and CDR Server receives the IMs and call data from the Archiving and CDR Agent and stores the information in a SQL database. The Archiving and CDR Server consists of three components:

- Destination queue, which is managed by Microsoft Message Queuing
- Archiving and CDR Service component
- Archiving backend database

The Archiving and CDR Server component reads messages from the Archiving and CDR Agent in the destination queue and writes the messages to the archiving backend database.

Communicator Web Access

What about Web access? What about a messaging client you can use that doesn't require anything more than a Web browser? Enter the 2007 version of MOC Web Access. By combining the power of Microsoft Exchange Server 2007 and Microsoft OCS 2007, this software provides access, presence, and IM anywhere to anyone with Web access. The application looks and feels like the desktop version of MOC 2007. Keep in mind too that the 2007 version of Communicator Web Access builds on the foundations laid by Live Communications Server 2005 with SP1 and the 2005 version of Communicator Web Access.

Using Communicator Web Access is as easy as typing a URL into your browser. That means you can access it from just about anywhere you have access to the Internet; from home, from the road, or even from a public Web kiosk. Keep in mind that there's no need for additional software or hardware.

Other than being able to access it from the Web, what other features does this application offer? Some of the features include:

- **Zero installation** As I said earlier, there's no additional software or hardware to be installed. You simply log in using a supported browser. Wonders never cease; you don't even have to install any ActiveX controls.

- **Multiple browser and operating system support** Remember, you will need a supported browser to use Communicator Web Access. Table 2.1, from the "Getting Started with MOC Web Access (2007 release)" document, discusses the supported operating systems, browsers, and authentication mechanisms. Notice that although Linux isn't supported, Communicator Web Access does work.

Table 2.1 Supported Operating Systems and Browsers

Operating System	Browser	Authentication Mechanism
Windows 2000 SP4	Microsoft Internet Explorer 6 SP1	NTLM Kerberos Forms-based Custom
Windows XP SP2	Internet Explorer 6 SP2 Windows Internet Explorer 7	NTLM Kerberos Forms-based Custom
	Mozilla Firefox 2.0 and later	Forms-based Custom
Windows Vista, Enterprise Edition	Internet Explorer 7	NTLM Kerberos Forms-based Custom
	Mozilla Firefox 2.0.0.3 and later	Forms-based Custom
Mac OS x 10.4.9	Apple Safari 2.0.4 Firefox 2.0 and later	Forms-based Custom

- **Digital certificate security (MTLS/SSL)** Remember that all communications between Communicator Web Access and OCS 2007 can be, and perhaps should be, secured with Secure Sockets Layer (SSL).

And those are only a few of the features available to you. But what can you do with all these features? Some of the tasks you can perform include:

- Manage contacts
- Set your presence
- View presence for others
- Write a personal note
- Send and receive IMs
- Forward incoming calls
- Redirect incoming audio calls

BEST PRACTICES ACCORDING TO MICROSOFT

Let's step back for a minute and look at the hardware requirements that exist for installation of OSC 2007 Server. The first thing we need to remember is that the requirements will vary depending on how you plan to set up your system configuration and the features you plan to install.

Your system hardware requirements are going to depend on the server role, configuration, and storage requirements you choose. Let's look at the requirements for the server configurations available to you. For a minimum configuration, you'll need the following components: a 3.2 GHz or equivalent dual-processor CPU; 2 GB of memory; a 2x 18 GB hard disk plus 2x 36 GB for colocated SE Server; 15 K rpm SCSI; a 1 MB cache; and a GBIT network interface card (NIC).

The aforementioned components should be the minimum configuration you might consider for either of these two configurations:

Standard Edition server configured as:

- Front-End Server, Web Conferencing Server, and A/V Conferencing Server
- Director
- Archiving and CDR Server
- Edge Server (one or more of the supported edge server roles)

Enterprise Edition server configured as:

- Consolidated Enterprise Edition server (Front-End Server, Web Conferencing Server, A/V Conferencing Server, and Internet Information Server [IIS] colocated on the server)

- Front-End Server in the expanded configuration (conferencing servers and IIS installed on separate computers)
- Web Conferencing Server in the expanded configuration
- IIS in the expanded configuration
- Archiving and CDR Server
- Small or medium-sized backend database server. For information on other configurations, go to http://www.microsoft.com/technet/prodtechnol/office/communicationsserver/evaluate/sysreqs/ocs-ee.mspx#ELB

Other requirements you should consider include the operating system. At a minimum, Microsoft recommends using Windows Server 2003 SP1R, but you should consider going ahead with Windows Server 2003 R2. The minimum supported configuration for Active Directory is Windows 2000 SP4 in Native Mode. Version 2 of the .NET Framework is required by OCS 2007, and any server running IIS must be running Version 6. The minimum version of SQL Server is SQL Server 2000 SP4 or SQL Server 2005 SP1. The recommended version is SQL Server 2005 SP2.

Planning an OCS 2007 Installation

We all know that planning is essential to successful deployment. In fact, it is always good to keep in mind the Seven Ps: Prior Planning and Practice Prevent Pretty Poor Performance. (For those of you familiar with the Seven Ps, I've modified the fifth *P* to make it suitable for a general audience.) The new OCS 2007 deployment tool, combined with new wizards for many of the more common, everyday tasks such as configuring pools and obtaining certificates, greatly simplifies the process of installing, configuring, and activating OCS 2007. But the deployment tool and wizards don't take the place of planning (keep in mind those Seven Ps); they simply make it much easier to carry out your plans. Microsoft's OCS Planning Guide suggests that you follow these steps when planning your installation:

1. **Determine key planning decisions** The first thing you and your staff need to consider before choosing your topology is your main decision points.

2. **Select your topology** You should probably consider several different sample deployments based on the size and functionality you're seeking. This process should guide you through the possible options available to you while planning your deployment.

3. **Plan your deployment path** Develop an overview of the deployment process and summarize all the important things you need to remember when you begin your OCS 2007 deployment.

4. **Prepare your infrastructure** What are your requirements for Active Directory Domain Services, certificates, DNS, automatic client sign-in, and ports? Make sure you've taken them into consideration.

5. **Review system and network requirements** Make a list of all your hardware and software requirements for all OCS 2007 server roles and clients.

6. **Plan for external user access** Develop a set of guidelines you will follow in deploying OCS 2007, especially when considering your perimeter network for the purpose of supporting messaging, presence, and conferencing with users connecting from outside your organization's firewall.

7. **Plan for deploying load balancers** Make sure you examine your hardware load-balancer requirements and configurations for an Enterprise pool. You should also evaluate the advantages of using hardware load balancers with edge server arrays.

8. **Plan for VoIP** Look at all the factors, requirements, and configuration tasks you'll need to consider to deploy Microsoft's software-powered VoIP solution.

9. **Plan for the Address Book Server** Examine the requirements of supporting the Address Book Server, including IIS, network file sharing, and required disk space.

10. **Plan for high availability and fault tolerance** Develop a set of guidelines to follow to ensure high availability. You should also determine which OCS 2007 features you'll need to optimize availability and fault tolerance.

11. **Plan for database storage** Determine your storage requirements for the databases and file shares that OCS 2007 will require. This should include all storage requirements for archiving and CDRs, databases, and new messaging support for rich text format. You'll also want to examine your requirements for Redundant Array of Inexpensive Disks (RAID; DAS), NAS, and SAN trade-offs, as well as basic calculations of disk space you'll need per meeting and per pool, based on the numbers of users.

12. **Plan for compliance and usage analysis** Finally, you'll need to determine how you're going to meet compliance requirements for archiving and CDR.

Let's take a few minutes now to discuss how to perform a new installation and an upgrade.

"Net-New" Installation

Let's discuss in a bit more depth what you need to do to prepare for a new installation. Microsoft says the first step is to *determine* what your key planning *decisions* are. What does that mean? Basically, it means you need to do two things: Determine what features you want in your installation and examine your business environment for specific needs.

The basic installation of the Standard Edition server or Enterprise pool will include IM, presence, and conferencing for users within your organization. Next, it's just a matter of deciding what bells and whistles you want to add. For instance, although no additional components are required for the Standard Edition should you want on-premises Web conferencing, A/V conferencing, or Address Book Server, you'll need the Web Conferencing Server and Web Components Server for Web conferencing, the A/V Conferencing Server for A/V conferencing, and the Web Components Server for Address Book Server in the Enterprise pool. If you want archiving and CDRs you'll need to install the Archiving and CDR Server. External user access, federation, and public IM connectivity will require installation of the Access Edge Server and an HTTP reverse proxy. If you want to include external users in your Web conferencing you're going to need both the Web Conferencing Edge Server and the HTTP reverse proxy, whereas A/V conferencing with external users will require an A/V Edge Server. If you want to provide IM with presence through a browser you'll need to install Communicator Web Access Server. Finally, if you want to use Enterprise Voice you'll need to install one of the following three options. Your first option is to install the Mediation Server and a basic media gateway. Your second option is the basic-hybrid media gateway where the Mediation Server is colocated with the basic media gateway. Your third option is the advanced media gateway, where the Mediation server logic is incorporated into the gateway design (not yet available at the time of this writing), and the A/V Edge Server (where the A/V authentication service is colocated).

Once you've decided what features of OCS you want to install, your next step is to evaluate your organization's requirements. The four main points you need to address regarding your organization's requirements are:

- How important is high availability to your organization?
- Where are the various components of your organization located?
- Do you plan to support external user access?
- Do you plan to deploy Enterprise Voice?

Let's look at the availability question first. Is high availability a requirement for your organization? Only you can make this call. Is this component of your business going to be mission-critical? If clients and customers are going to be using it, your answer should be "yes." If internal training is using it, you must decide how important internal training is. No book or high-priced consultant is going to answer this for you. This is your decision. If you need high availability, the Enterprise pool is appropriate. On the other hand, if high availability is not a requirement and simplicity and economy are more important, the Standard Edition server would be more appropriate. We discussed the differences between these two options earlier in this chapter, so we won't rehash the pros and cons of the two options here.

The next question you need to ask is where your staff is located. Microsoft recommends that if your organization is geographically dispersed and connected across various wide area networks

(WANs), you should place a Standard Edition server or an Enterprise pool in each local site. I agree. The addition of new and expanded audio and video features in OCS 2007 requires greater bandwidth. You can achieve a better user experience with a local server or pool than you can by using the centralized model servicing remote sites, as in Live Communications Server 2005.

Another reason you might want to go with local servers at your sites is if you have more than 100 users at each site. Again, bandwidth is the main consideration here, as it is if you want to allow external users access to internal Web conferences and A/V conferences. In this case, you should probably deploy a local Web Conferencing Edge Server and A/V Edge Server due to the higher bandwidth requirements of this traffic.

Keep in mind that anytime you allow external user access you're going to need an Access Edge Server. You will also need an HTTP reverse proxy for those external users to download Address Book files, expand distribution lists, and download meeting content for Web conferences. Supporting external user participation in Web conferencing requires a Web Conferencing Edge Server. Making media such as audio and video available to external users means that you need to deploy an A/V Edge Server. Of course, all three edge server roles can be colocated on a single computer for a small deployment, or you might want to use a load balancer with multiple servers to support even more users.

The last of our four major considerations is whether you are going to enable Enterprise Voice. If so, you'll need two things: a media (IP/PSTN) gateway to handle calls between users enabled for VoIP and the PSTN, and an OCS 2007 Mediation Server to handle the traffic between the gateway and your internal Communications Server infrastructure.

As discussed previously, there are three ways to deploy a Mediation Server and media gateway. Those three options are to install a basic media gateway and a separate Mediation Server; install a basic-hybrid gateway, in which the basic gateway and Mediation Server are colocated on a single computer; and install an advanced media gateway, where the Mediation Server logic is incorporated inside the gateway software.

You'll also need to plan for the normalization of the phone numbers you have stored in your Active Directory and then create dial plans for each location where your organization does business. To provide call answering, subscriber access, and auto-attendant services, you're also going to need to deploy Microsoft Exchange Server 2007 UM and then configure Exchange UM and Communications Server to work together. You have two main deployment scenarios when it comes to Enterprise Voice. You can choose stand-alone configurations in greenfield or departmental scenarios, or PBX coexistence.

The next step in your planning phase should be to select a topology. Microsoft, in its *Office Communications Server 2007 Planning Guide*, presents three examples of OCS 2007 topologies that provide IM and conferencing functionality and other features: small to medium-size deployment, centralized enterprise deployment, and global deployments. I won't discuss these in detail here. The point is that you should download the *Planning Guide* and carefully examine these three scenarios. Depending on your requirements, you can combine the different pieces of these example deployments to meet your company's needs.

The next step concerns how to plan your deployment path. There are three areas of concern:

- Things you need to know before deploying
- An overview of the deployment process
- Permissions required for deployment

There are some important things you need to know about the OCS 2007 requirements before you start. First, a PKI is required for OCS 2007. If you don't have an internal PKI, you'll need to use a public certificate authority (CA). Also, all domains where you deploy OCS 2007 require Windows 2000 native mode minimum (Windows Server 2003 native mode is strongly recommended). OCS 2007 can't be installed in a mixed-mode domain. You'll need a certificate issued by a public CA for federation and public IM connectivity; also, keep in mind that public IM connectivity is going to require an additional license.

If you are considering using voice, you need to know what to do in case of power, network, or telephone service outages. Remember than enterprise voice depends on server availability and voice client and hardware operability. You should also consider a secondary or backup method of contacting emergency services. Also remember that neither OCS 2007 nor any of its components provide a caller's physical location to emergency services when a caller dials emergency services. This may be required in some states or locations.

Things you should keep in mind when considering Web conferencing are fragmentation and virus scanning. You need to defrag the drives where meeting content is located from time to time. This is considered a best practice by Microsoft and just plain common sense by some of the rest of us. You also shouldn't run real-time antivirus scanning on the shares where meeting content, meeting content metadata, and meeting compliance data is stored. This can negatively impact performance for Web conferencing. Microsoft recommends scanning for viruses only when the server has little or no load and that antivirus protection be enabled on client computers at all times. Again, some might just call this common sense.

Edge servers have their own concerns. Face it. The biggest concern is that edge servers just don't scale well. You can't load-balance multiple edge servers at all in the consolidated topology. The only way you're going to load-balance your site is if you require one or more dedicated computers with colocated Access Edge Servers with Web Conferencing Edge Servers and one or more dedicated computers with A/V Edge Conferencing Servers. So, if you're going to deploy the consolidated edge topology at first and then later decide that you want to scale, you're going to have to deploy an entirely new edge topology. This is a major issue you need to think about before you start.

But that's not the only issue with edge servers. If you want to support public IM connectivity and federation, you need to make sure you have an external DNS SRV record for your Access Edge Server.

You can use only one Access Edge Server or array of Access Edge Servers for public IM connectivity and federation. This means that an Access Edge Server or an array of Access Edge Servers can be in only one physical location. Your remote sites can't deploy Access Edge Servers.

You'll need to make sure you have a reverse HTTP proxy for remote users to download Address Book files and expand distribution lists, and to allow external users access to meeting content for Web conferences.

The network interfaces of your A/V Edge Servers have to be directly addressable at the IP layer. You can't use NAT with them.

Finally, there are several other general concerns you need to be aware of. First, the Standard Edition server requires enough disk space on your local drive for any meeting content you may have. You can't install any OCS 2007 role on a domain controller. It's just not supported. There are also several general issues regarding fully qualified domain names (FQDNs) that you should familiarize yourself with. Microsoft lists many of these gotchas in its *Planning Guide*.

But as we're not going to get down and dirty here with a sample installation, but rather are going to continue to discuss general issues you need to be prepared for when deploying OCS 2007, let's turn our attention to the next area of concern: the deployment process. The first step of your deployment process should be to determine storage requirements, and to create file shares to store the following:

- Presentations to be downloaded or streamed by meeting attendees

- Information used internally by the pool's Web Conferencing Server

- Information used by the Address Book Server

- Content logged for any compliance requirements

Make sure you have the following already installed and ready to go:

- Microsoft Windows Server 2003 SP1 or R2 or later for OCS

- Microsoft Windows 2000 SP4 or later for Active Directory Domain Services

- Active Directory in Windows 2000 Server or later native mode in all domains involving OCS 2007 (Windows Server 2003 native mode is recommended)

- For Enterprise Edition, Microsoft SQL Server 2005 with SP2 (recommended) or SQL Server 2005 SP1, SQL Server 2000 with SP4 on the computer where the backend database will be deployed DNS

- An Enterprise (recommended), Standalone, or public CA

- IIS 6.0 on each computer where Standard Edition or Enterprise Edition Front-End Server will be installed (or, if deploying Enterprise Edition: Expanded Configuration on computers that are to serve as your Web farm)

- Active Server Pages components of IIS 6.0 on each computer where a Web Components Server will be installed (for Standard Edition, the computer running Standard Edition server; for Enterprise Edition: Consolidated Configuration, all Front-End Servers); for Expanded Configuration, all dedicated IIS servers)

The next step in your preparation should be to review your Active Directory infrastructure. The deployment tool is going to run Schema Prep, Forrest Prep, and Domain Prep as the first three steps in your installation and deployment. After your Active Directory infrastructure for OCS is ready, you'll need to create the DNS A records and SRV records that allow the OCS 2007 Standard Edition server or Enterprise Edition pool to be found.

You'll now be ready to begin the installation. The process of installing OCS 2007 will depend on what edition, configuration, and server roles you've chosen. The *Microsoft Office Communications Server 2007 Standard Edition Deployment Guide* and the *Enterprise Edition Deployment Guide* are available for download and provide easy-to-follow, step-by-step instructions on the setup tasks involved in deploying these two software applications. After the files are installed, the next step will be to configure the server or pool. Next, you must configure the certificates on each Standard Edition or Enterprise Edition server you're installing. The next step will be to verify that the Active Directory changes have been replicated, and after that you can start the services, making sure that your server or pool configuration performs as required.

Now will be the best time to install any front-end servers and other components, such as IIS for Web Component servers. Next, create your users and enable them, deploy the clients, and then install and configure your edge servers. The final phase of installation will be to install Enterprise Voice.

Make sure you have the required permissions to perform the installation before you start this process. Membership in the Domain Admins group is required to deploy or activate a server that is joined to an Active Directory domain.

The next phase in the planning process is to prepare the infrastructure. Before you start the deployment, you need to verify that your Active Directory is deployed with all the necessary prerequisites. You also need to make sure a certificate infrastructure is in place for all server-to-server and client-to-server communications. Make sure you know of all the DNS records that your installation will need for servers and pools to communicate and clients to locate their server or pool.

The fifth phase involves reviewing your systems and network requirements. After you've decided which features and components your OCS 2007 deployment will have, you need to decide whether your existing infrastructure will meet the platform requirements for OCS 2007 and, if not, what changes or additions you will need to make before you start installation. More than likely, you're going to have changes to make or things to add because OCS 2007 includes many new components that were not present in its predecessor, Live Communications Server 2005 with SP1.

You should examine the capacity planning section of the *Planning Guide*. The user model and network requirements are good topics to examine also. Network requirements will include things such as A/V and Web conferencing bandwidth requirements. Don't forget to look at your hardware, software, and operating system requirements too. The various types of servers to be installed may have different hardware and operating system requirements.

The next phase deals with planning for external users. Depending on your configuration's needs, you may or may not need to install edge servers. Remember that edge servers allow both internal and external users to communicate using Communicator or the Live Meeting 2007 client. Also remember that there are three basic types:

- Access Edge Server
- Web Conferencing Edge Server
- A/V Edge Server

So, anytime you are dealing with external users you are going to need one of these edge servers. The *Planning Guide* goes into detail about when each needs to be installed, and as I've suggested several times, you should spend considerable time during this phase becoming familiar with the information in this document.

The seventh phase of our planning scenario deals with planning for load balancing. Before you deploy OCS 2007, you need to have one or more hardware load balancers ready, in place, and configured appropriately. Again, we're not just talking about the primary servers but everything down to the edge servers.

Planning for VoIP is the eighth phase. This is a different type of consideration in that you must consider the impact on both your telephony and IP infrastructures. The one thing you won't have to consider here, though, is replacing your existing PBX.

Considerations you'll want to evaluate include:

- How many and where are your users?
- What deployment best suits your organization?
- How many media gateways are needed and where should they be located in your organization?
- What are the routing rules and user privileges for your Enterprise Voice deployment?
- Carefully develop your plan for call notification, voice mail, and other call services provided by Exchange UM.
- How will you migrate your users to Enterprise Voice?

The ninth phase in the planning process is to plan for the Address Book Server. Remember, the main reason the Address Book Server exists is to provide global address list information from Active Directory to the MOC 2007 client. If Communicator accessed Active Directory directly, it would affect your network performance. The Address Book Server is installed on every Front-End Server.

The tenth phase is to plan for high availability and fault tolerance. Remember that you can think of high availability as a system's capability to keep downtime to a minimum while continuing normal operation in the event of disruptions due to hardware, software, or service requirements. Fault tolerance, on the other hand, refers to reducing the risk of service disruption in the event of system or component failure. Earlier we talked about deciding whether high availability was important to your organization. If you chose to install the standard server, this question is moot to a certain degree. Then again, fault tolerance should be built into your systems to a certain degree, even for your workstations.

In the next phase, you should plan your database storage. Planning you database storage solution requires that you know what types of data are being generated and where each type is being stored. Spend some time on this aspect of your planning, as nothing can bring your OCS 2007 installation down as fast as poor storage planning. In your planning, make sure you balance three criteria: capacity, availability, and performance. The choices you make in this regard as you plan and implement your storage solution will affect the cost associated with administration and maintenance of your OCS 2007 environment.

The final phase is to plan for compliance and usage analysis. We all know how our companies and organizations are being required to retain more and more information, including both e-mail and IM conversations. And now these requirements are being extended to conferencing, and that includes meeting content. The OCS 2007 Archiving and CDR Server allows you to comply with any laws and/or policies that require retention of IM communications.

We've touched on some of the issues important to a new installation. Now let's take a look at upgrading.

Live Communications Server 2005 Upgrade

If you are running Live Communications Server 2003, you'll first need to migrate your installation to Live Communications Server 2005 with SP1. Microsoft has supplied a migration guide, which you can download at www.microsoft.com/downloads/details.aspx?familyid=20f67afc-6af5-4a03-99bf-4150def36457&displaylang=en. You can then complete your migration to OCS 2007.

When you have Live Communications Server 2005 with SP1 Access Proxies deployed, your only choice is to migrate your environment from the outside in. Think about it. OCS 2007 uses Access Edge Servers, not Access Proxies. To perform the upgrade you're going to have to start by upgrading the Access Proxies. So, the first thing you need to do is replace your Access Proxies with OCS 2007 Access Edge Servers, and only then can you migrate to OCS 2007 in your internal environment.

If you follow a phased approach such as described here in which you upgrade all the servers of a particular type at one time, you'll be able to save yourself a great deal of system downtime. The supported order is as follows:

1. Replace all your Access Proxies in the perimeter network with Access Edge Servers.

2. Replace the Directors.

3. Install Enterprise pools and Standard Edition servers.

4. Install Archiving and CDR Servers as necessary.

Why? Again, it's the logical progression. Replacing and installing servers in this order is supported. Not following this process means that files won't be installed in the proper order.

At this point, you should have some users test the behavior of IM and presence in the new environment. At this point, you have two operational installations: one Live Communications Server 2005 and one OCS 2007. Move the users from the Live Communications Server 2005 installation to the OCS 2007 and have them test IM and presence information in the MOC 2007 client. After you're sure that IM and presence are working correctly in your new environment, you can deploy Web Conferencing Edge Servers and A/V Edge Servers in your perimeter network. After you've made sure that Web conferencing and A/V conferencing are working properly, you can move the rest of your users to the new deployment and take the Live Communications Server offline.

Remember, planning your upgrade to OCS 2007 should include the following:

- Understanding the basic migration process

- Understanding coexistence issues

- Planning user migration

- Determining your requirements for additional hardware

Before you begin either your deployment or your upgrade, you need to spend some time with the OCS 2007 *Planning Guide*. It goes into considerable detail concerning each step for new installations. You can find the planning guide at www.microsoft.com/downloads/details.aspx?familyid=723347c6-fa1f-44d8-a7fa-8974c3b596f4&displaylang=en.

Summary

Microsoft OCS 2007 manages all real-time communications including IM, VoIP, and audio conferencing and videoconferencing. The system will work with your existing telecommunications systems so that you can deploy advanced VoIP and conferencing without tearing out your current telephone system.

Solutions Fast Track

What's New in OCS 2007?

- ☑ OCS 2007 builds on the foundations and services that Live Communications Server 2005 and MOC 2005 delivered.

- ☑ OCS 2007 is now integrated with Exchange Server distribution lists.

- ☑ OCS 2007 now supports the ICE framework of protocols, allowing users to take advantage of its new features wherever those users are located.

Comparing the Editions

- ☑ The Standard Edition provides full functionality for small organizations.

- ☑ The Enterprise Edition: Consolidated Configuration provides scalability and high availability while at the same time being relatively easy to plan, deploy, configure, and maintain.

- ☑ The Enterprise Edition: Expanded Configuration offers maximum capacity, performance, and availability for large organizations.

OCS 2007 Server Roles

- ☑ The Front-End Server is responsible for handling all signaling among and between servers and clients.

- ☑ The Edge Server resides in the perimeter network and provides connectivity for external users and public IM connections.

- ☑ The Mediation Server provides signaling and media translation between the VoIP infrastructure and a basic media gateway.

- ☑ The Archiving and CDR Server provides archiving for all IM conversations and for all CDRs for all users.

Planning an OCS 2007 Installation

- ☑ Determine your key planning decisions.
- ☑ Select your topology.
- ☑ Plan your deployment path.
- ☑ Prepare your infrastructure.
- ☑ Review your system and network requirements.
- ☑ Plan for your external users.
- ☑ Plan for deploying load balancers.
- ☑ Plan for VoIP.
- ☑ Plan for Address Book Server.
- ☑ Plan for high availability and fault tolerance.
- ☑ Plan for database storage.
- ☑ Plan for compliance and usage analysis.

Frequently Asked Questions

Q: What is Microsoft OCS 2007?

A: OCS 2007 is the latest version of Microsoft Live Communications Server 2005. This software group delivers enhanced communications to end-users, a software-powered VoIP infrastructure for organizations, and operational control for IT.

Q: How does the Web conferencing functionality in OCS 2007 compare with Microsoft Office Live Meeting?

A: The Web conferencing capabilities in OCS 2007 provide Web conferencing as an on-premises solution existing inside the corporate firewall. Both OCS 2007 and Live Meeting can be accessed using the same client. Whereas Live Meeting is offered as a hosted service, OCS 2007 is provided in-house by the enterprise.

Q: Will OCS 2007 interoperate with Live Communications Server 2005?

A: Yes. While organizations are in the process of migrating, OCS 2007 and Live Communications Server 2005 can interoperate.

Q: Can I upgrade from Live Communications Server 2005 to OCS 2007?

A: Yes. The migration process involves deploying some OCS 2007 infrastructure in parallel to a Live Communications Server 2005 deployment and then easily migrating the users across to the new infrastructure.

Q: How many servers do I need to run OCS 2007?

A: This depends on your organization's requirements. For smaller deployments, you could run your infrastructure on one server, but for environments where greater scale, geographical distribution, or fault tolerance is required, OCS 2007 has a flexible architecture to allow this kind of scaling in a multiserver environment.

Q: What are the system requirements for running OCS 2007?

A: Hardware requirements vary according to server role, configuration, and storage requirements. Operating system minimum requirements are Windows Server 2003 SP1R, but Windows Server 2003 R2 is recommended. For all servers requiring Active Directory, the minimum supported configuration is Windows 2000 SP4 in Windows 2000 Native Mode. OCS 2007 requires .NET Framework 2.0. For all servers running IIS, the required version is 6.0. For all servers requiring SQL Server, the minimum and recommended versions are as follows: minimum, SQL Server 2000 SP4 or SQL Server 2005, SP1

(32-bit or 64-bit versions of SQL Server SP1 or later are supported); recommended, SQL Server 2005, SP2.

Q: What version of MOC can I use with OCS 2007?

A: You can use MOC 2005 or MOC 2007 with OCS 2007. To use the new features offered by OCS 2007 you will need to use MOC 2007. For a specific user, once you have started using MOC 2007 with OCS 2007 you will no longer be able to sign in with MOC 2005.

Chapter 3

Installing the First OCS 2007 Front-End Server

Solutions in this chapter:

- **Addressing the Prerequisites**
- **Preparing Active Directory**
- **Installing and Configuring OCS 2007 Enterprise Edition**

☑ **Summary**

☑ **Solutions Fast Track**

☑ **Frequently Asked Questions**

Introduction

In the previous two chapters, we covered a variety of material to set the stage for implementing Microsoft Office Communications Server (OCS) 2007. Now, we will spend the next several chapters explaining a typical OCS implementation, and walking you through the installation process.

Many optional server roles can be put into action in an OCS 2007 implementation; however, one role in particular must exist to offer basic presence functionality within your environment: the front-end server. In this chapter, we will discuss the installation and configuration of not just the OCS bits, but also the prerequisite applications and services that must be in place. The key to a successful OCS implementation is to get the front-end server configuration right the first time, because this is where the user interaction with OCS takes place. Get this wrong, and the OCS implementation will always be suspect.

Addressing the Prerequisites

As mentioned, before you can begin to install OCS 2007, you first need to address some prerequisites. Before we get to the prerequisites, though, we need to discuss choosing the correct version of OCS for your environment. To that end, you have two options to choose from: Standard Edition and Enterprise Edition. Table 3.1 outlines the key differences between the two product versions.

Table 3.1 Comparison of Standard and Enterprise Editions

Feature	Standard	Enterprise
Presence	X	X
Instant messaging (including public IM and federation)	X	X
Conferencing	X	X
Voice	X	X
Archiving (off-box)	X	X
Load balancers		X
High availability		X
Multiple servers/pool		X
Sizing (estimated)	2,000 users	50,000 users

BEST PRACTICES ACCORDING TO MICROSOFT

Understanding exactly how Microsoft is handling licensing for OCS 2007 is important. For example, simply owning either Standard Edition or Enterprise Edition does not entitle you to all the features of that particular version. For instance, if you want to use the voice features of OCS, you must have an Enterprise Client Access License (eCAL). It's also important to note that if you already own Live Communications Server (LCS) 2005 with Software Assurance, you may be entitled to certain upgrade rights. Check with your licensing vendor for more details.

Although we will be generalizing most of our discussion within this chapter to address both the Standard and Enterprise editions, we will actually be performing an Enterprise Edition installation. Now that licensing is squared away, the first thing you need to do is verify that you are at the proper Active Directory level.

Forest/Domain Levels

As you are probably well aware, there are several functional levels of configuration for an Active Directory forest and domain. For forests, you can run in:

- Windows 2000 (supports Windows NT, 2000, and 2003 domains and domain controllers)

- Windows Server 2003 interim (supports Windows NT and 2003 domains and domain controllers)

- Windows Server 2003 (supports Windows 2003 domains and domain controllers only)

Similarly, domains have multiple functional levels under which they can function:

- Windows 2000 mixed (supports Windows NT, 2000, and 2003 domain controllers)

- Windows 2000 native (supports Windows 2000 and 2003 domain controllers)

- Windows 2003 interim (supports Windows NT and 2003 domain controllers)

- Windows Server 2003 (supports Windows 2003 domain controllers only)

For OCS 2003 and the internal certificate authority (CA) services to work, you will need to ensure that both the forest functional level and the domain functional level of your environment are set to Windows 2003 mode. Let's step through this process now.

First, you need to raise the domain functional level. To do this, complete the following steps:

1. From a domain controller, click **Start | Administrative Tools | Active Directory Users and Computers**.

2. Right-click on the name of your domain, and select **Raise Domain Functional Level** from the drop-down menu.

3. Under **Select an available domain functional level:**, choose **Windows Server 2003**.

4. Click the **Raise button** (Figure 3.1).

Figure 3.1 Raising the Domain Functional Level

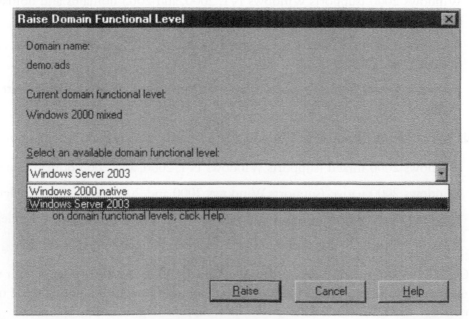

Next, you need to raise the forest functional level. You need to perform this task on a domain controller at the root of the forest. This may or may not be the same as your production domain, depending on how your Active Directory deployment is configured. To raise the forest functional level, you will need to perform the following steps:

1. From the domain controller, click **Start | Administrative Tools | Active Directory Domains and Trusts**.

2. Right-click on **Active Directory Domains and Trusts** from the management window, and select **Raise Forest Functional Level**.

3. Under **Select an available forest functional level:,** choose **Windows Server 2003**.

4. Click the **Raise button** (Figure 3.2).

Figure 3.2 Raising the Forest Functional Level

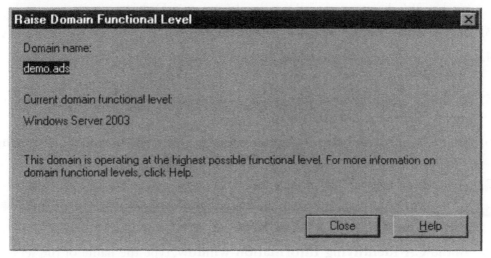

Now that your domain and forest levels are in their associated native modes, we can move on to the next step within the prerequisites: addressing the need for certificates within OCS 2007.

Certificate Authorities

You need certificates with OCS 2003 for a number of reasons, which we will discuss later in this book. The important thing to understand is that this has everything to do with the need to properly secure your presence engine to prevent the potential leak of confidential company information.

Although it would certainly be easier to use public certificates from an authorized CA such as VeriSign, Thawte, or a similar provider, we will be using an internal CA during most of this book. It is important to note that for certain features to function, such as federation, you will be required to use a third-party CA server because other parties (outside your corporate environment) need to authenticate communications with your OCS servers. Using a private CA to perform this function is far more complicated and ultimately more expensive than simply buying a certificate. However, I digress. At this point, we will walk through the steps of configuring a CA in Windows 2003. You can use just about any server within your environment to run as a CA, but your best bet is to keep it off the OCS server itself. Let's walk through the CA configuration process:

1. Click on **Start | Control Panel | Add/Remove Programs**.

2. When the **Add/Remove Programs window** opens, select **Add/Remove Windows Components**. Make sure you have either a Windows 2003 CD available, or the i386 directory copied to a local (or network) drive.

3. In the **Components window**, check the box next to **Certificate Services**.

4. If you are prompted with a warning window, read through the warning and click **Yes**.

5. In the **Components window**, click on the **Application Server option**, and then click on the **Details button**.

6. In the **Application Server details window**, check the box next to **Internet Information Services** and click **OK** (Figure 3.3).

7. Click **Next** to begin the installation.

8. In the **CA Type window**, you have a choice of multiple CA types. Click **Enterprise root CA**, and click **Next**.

9. In the **CA Identifying Information window**, type the name of the server into the box titled **Common name for this CA:** and click **Next** (Figure 3.4).

10. Unless you want to move the CA configuration files to another drive, accept the defaults in the next window, and click **Next**.

11. When the installation completes, click **Finish**.

Figure 3.3 Installing Internet Information Server (IIS)

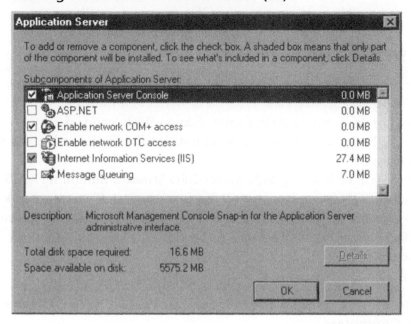

Figure 3.4 CA Identifying Information Window

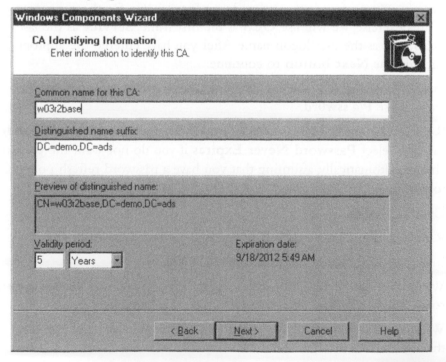

Now that the settings for the CA are ready, we can move on to installing our database which will be responsible for supporting the OCS front-end installation.

Database Server

OCS 2005 Enterprise Edition can support either SQL Server 2004 (with Service Pack 4) or SQL Server 2005 (with Service Pack 1, 32-bit or 64-bit). Of note, OCS 2005 Standard Edition will run on SQL Server 2005 Express Edition. With Standard Edition, if you do not already have SQL Server 2005 Express Edition installed, the OCS installer will install and configure it for you.

Although we will be installing SQL Server 2005 Standard Edition for OCS 2007, we will not be tuning SQL or configuring SQL for best practices. If you want to know more about how to configure and tune SQL Server 2005, we recommend that you read *Microsoft SQL Server 2005 Administrator's Companion* by Edward Whalen et al. (Microsoft Press). Let's install SQL Server 2005:

1. First, we will create a user account for the SQL Service to use. From a domain controller, click on **Start | Administrative Tools | Active Directory Users and Computers**.

2. Right-click on the name of your domain. From the drop-down menu that appears, select **New | User**.

3. Type in a first name, last name, and user logon name for the account you will use. In this exercise, we will use **OCS** as the first name, **Service** as the last name, and **OCSSQL** as the user logon name. After you have entered the appropriate fields, click on the **Next button** to continue.

4. Enter a password that meets your minimum password requirements. In our example, we will use **P@ssw0rd**.

5. Remove the checkmark from **User must change password at next logon**. You can also select **Password Never Expires** if you do not want the password to change automatically, assuming that you have a password refresh policy. Click **Next** to continue.

6. Click on **Finish**.

7. Return to the OCS server where you will be installing SQL.

8. Insert the SQL Server 2005 CD into the drive.

9. When the SQL Server 2005 splash screen appears, click on **Server components, tools Books Online, and samples** under the **Installs** area.

10. When the End User License Agreement (EULA) appears, make sure to read through the license agreement, take copious notes, and then click **Next**.

11.   On the **Installing Prerequisites page** (Figure 3.5), SQL will now verify that the SQL prerequisites have been met. If they have, click **Next**. If they haven't, click **Install** to begin installing the appropriate applications.

Figure 3.5 Installing Prerequisites Window

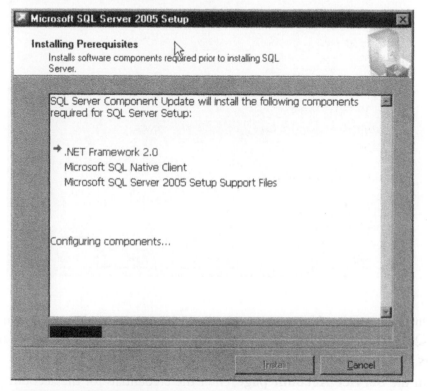

12.   When you reach the **Welcome screen**, click **Next**.

13.   On the **System Configuration Check (SCC) page** (Figure 3.5), SQL will now verify that the SQL prerequisites have been met. If they have, click **Next**. If they haven't, go back and address the missing prerequisites, and then restart the SQL installation.

14.   On the **Registration Information page**, enter your name and company information, and then click on **Next**.

15.   Select **SQL Server Database Services** and **Workstation components, Books Online, and development tools** from the **Components to Install page**, and click on **Next** (Figure 3.6).

Figure 3.6 Selecting SQL Server 2005 Components

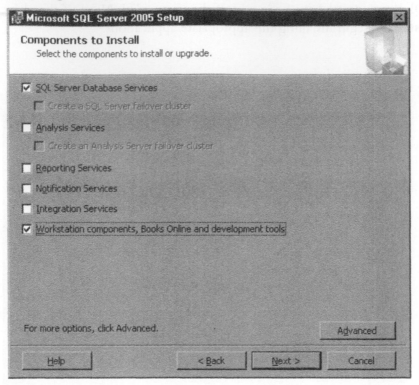

16. On the **Instance Name page**, you have the option of choosing a name for the SQL Server instance, or simply selecting the default. For the purposes of this book, we will be choosing the default instance name.

17. On the **Service Account page**, enter the credentials for the account you created earlier in this section, and click **Next**.

18. Next, you need to choose the authentication mode for SQL. We will be using **Windows Authentication**. Once you have chosen the authentication mode, click **Next**.

19. Click **Next** on the **Collation Settings page**.

20. Click **Next** on the **Reporting Settings page**.

21. On the **Ready to Install page**, verify the information, and click **Install** (Figure 3.7).

Figure 3.7 Ready to Install Page

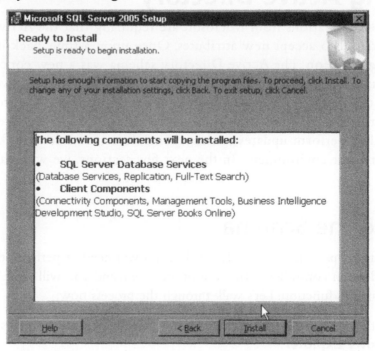

22.   When the installation of SQL is complete, click **Finish**.

Next, you will need to install Service Pack 1 or Service Pack 2 for SQL 2005. Depending on how and when you purchased SQL Server 2005, Service Pack 1 may have been bundled with the SQL Server DVD—this would likely be represented on the CD label. If not, you will need to download Service Pack 1 or Service Pack 2 (the latest SP as of the writing of this book). Service Pack 2 is available on the Microsoft Web site at http://technet.microsoft.com/en -us/sqlserver/bb426877.aspx. Because SP2 is the most recent update available, we will be using it for our configuration. The SQL Server 2005 Service Pack is fairly straightforward, so you can simply follow the defaults for upgrading. Please note that if the server you are using has other databases installed, upgrading to SP2 *will* stop any databases running on the server.

Now that your database server is humming along, you can begin to prepare Active Directory for the OCS attributes.

Preparing Active Directory

More and more applications from Microsoft are requiring that the Active Directory schema be modified to accept new attributes. Once upon a time, back in 2000, this was a pretty scary notion. The Active Directory schema was a new concept, and the general opinion of administrators was "don't touch my schema." However, as Active Directory and the applications requiring these types of changes have progressed, the chances of corruption or other issues have almost completely disappeared. With OCS 2007, you need to perform updates to the schema, forest, and domain for OCS to function within your environment. In the next few sections, we will walk you through this process.

Preparing the Schema

First, you need to prepare the schema. To do this, you will need to perform the following actions from a domain controller at the root of the forest, and you will need Schema Admin rights to perform this function. Let's walk through the process now:

1. From the domain controller, click **Start | All Programs | Accessories | Windows Explorer**.

2. If you are installing from a CD/DVD, navigate to the **<drive>:\Setup\i386** directory.

3. Double-click on **setup.exe**.

4. On the **Deployment Wizard page**, click on **Deploy Pools in an Expanded Topology**.

5. On the **Deploy Enterprise Edition Server page**, click **Prepare Active Directory**.

6. When the **Prepare Active Directory for Office Communications Server page** appears, click the **Run button** next to **Prep Schema** (Figure 3.8).

Figure 3.8 Preparing the Schema

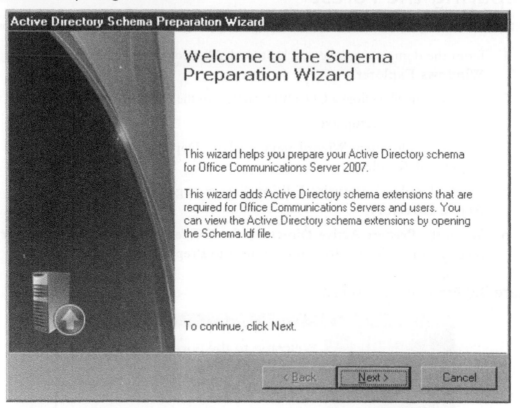

7. On the **Welcome page**, click **Next**.

8. We will use the default location for our schema files, so on the **Directory Location of Schema Files page**, click **Next**.

9. The schema is now ready to be prepared, so click **Next** again.

10. When the installation is complete, click **Finish**.

Preparing the Forest

Next, you need to prepare the forest for OCS. Let's get right into the configuration steps:

1. From the domain controller, click **Start | All Programs | Accessories | Windows Explorer**.

2. If you are installing from a CD/DVD, navigate to the **<drive>:\Setup\i386** directory.

3. Double-click on **setup.exe**.

4. On the **Deployment Wizard page**, click on **Deploy Pools in an Expanded Topology**.

5. On the **Deploy Enterprise Edition Server page**, click **Prepare Active Directory**.

6. When the **Prepare Active Directory for Office Communications Server page** appears, click the **Run button** next to **Prep Forest** (Figure 3.9).

Figure 3.9 Preparing the Forest

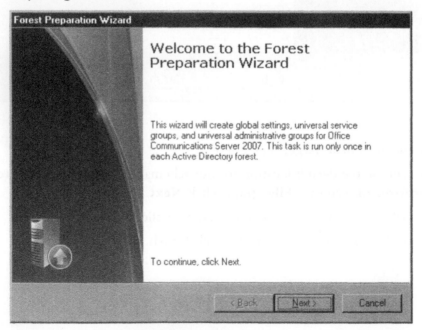

7. On the **Welcome page**, click **Next**.

8. We will use the default location for our Global setting, so on the **Directory Location of Global Settings page**, click **Next**.

9. On the **Location of Universal Groups page**, verify that the name of your domain is correct, and click **Next**.

10. On the **Specify the SIP domain to be used for default routing page**, verify the domain name again, and click **Next**.

11. Click **Next** to begin the process.

12. When the installation is complete, click **Finish**.

Preparing the Domain

We're almost at the end of the prerequisites for installing OCS 2007! The last step in the process is to prepare the production domain for OCS. Let's begin that process now:

1. From the domain controller, click **Start | All Programs | Accessories | Windows Explorer**.

2. If you are installing from a CD/DVD, navigate to the **<drive>:\Setup\i386** directory.

3. Double-click on **setup.exe**.

4. On the **Deployment Wizard page**, click on **Deploy Pools in an Expanded Topology**.

5. On the **Deploy Enterprise Edition Server page**, click **Prepare Active Directory**.

6. When the **Prepare Active Directory for Office Communications Server page** appears, click the **Run button** next to **Prep Domain** (Figure 3.10).

Figure 3.10 Preparing the Domain

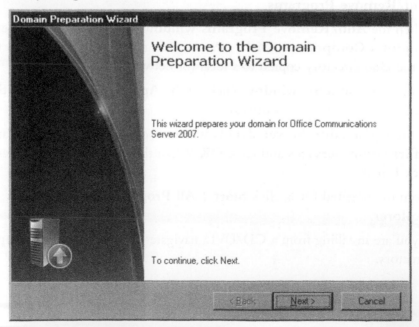

7. On the **Welcome page**, click **Next**.

8. Click **Next** to accept the next few default settings.

9. Click **Finish** once the prep process is complete.

10. Click on the **back arrow** on the **Prepare Active Directory page**; step 1
    is now complete!

Installing and Configuring OCS 2007 Enterprise Edition

The tension is building, excitement is in the air! You can cut the tension with a knife! Okay,
maybe we're overdoing it a bit, but this is, in fact, the moment we've all been waiting for.
Now that all of the prerequisites are out of the way, we can move on to the actual installation
of the OCS 2007 bits.

Installing the Software

Microsoft has done a fantastic job of simplifying the installation process of its products over
the past few years, and this still holds true with OCS 2007. At this stage, it's time to get that
front-end server up and running. Let's begin. The following steps will take place on the
server on which you have selected to run OCS 2007 as the front-end server.

1. First, you need to install IIS onto this machine. Click on **Start | Control Panel |
    Add/Remove Programs**.

2. When the **Add/Remove Programs window** opens, select **Add/Remove
    Windows Components**. Make sure you have either a Windows 2003 CD available,
    or the i386 directory copied to a local (or network) drive.

3. In the **Components window**, click on the **Application Server option**, and
    then click on the **Details button**.

4. In the **Application Server details window**, check the box next to **Internet
    Information Services** and click **OK**. When the installation completes,
    click **Finish**.

5. From the targeted OCS, click **Start | All Programs | Accessories | Windows
    Explorer**.

6. If you are installing from a CD/DVD, navigate to the **<drive>:\Setup\i386**
    directory.

7. Double-click on **setup.exe**.

8. On the **Deployment Wizard page**, click on **Deploy Pools in an Expanded Topology**.

9. Next, select **Step 2: Create Enterprise Pool** and click **Run**.

10. Click **Next** to get past the Welcome page.

11. Accept the license agreement, and click **Next**.

12. On the **Create Enterprise Pool Wizard**, enter a name for the pool, the pool's fully qualified domain name (FQDN), and enter the name of the SQL Server and instance. If you are using the default instance on the SQL server, simply enter the server name (Figure 3.11).

Figure 3.11 Enterprise Pool Wizard

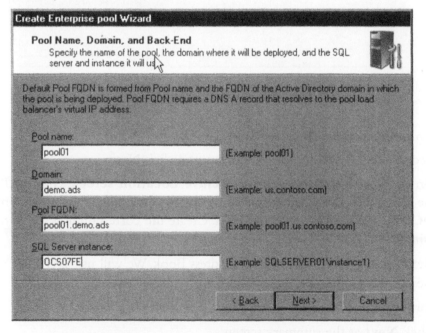

13. On the **Web Farm FQDN screen**, leave the field for **External Web Farm FQDN** blank (Figure 3.12), and click **Next**. This setting is used to allow external access to meetings hosted within the OCS infrastructure. You can change this feature post-installation.

Figure 3.12 External Web Farm FQDN

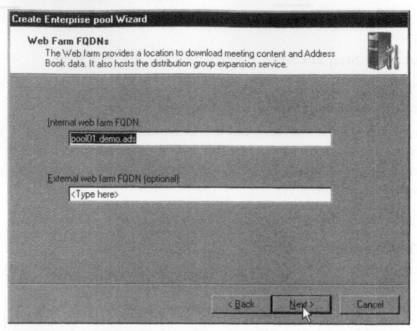

14. On the **Reuse existing database screen**, click **Next**.

15. Accept the defaults for the server files, and click **Next**.

16. On the **Meeting Content and Archive Location screen**, enter a UNC path on the server. For example, we will use **\\OCS07FE\share** for the content and **\\OCS07FE\share1** for the metadata. Create the corresponding shares on the server using Windows Explorer, and click **Next**.

17. Next, enter a UNC path for the Address Book. We will use **\\OCS07\AB**. Create the corresponding share using Windows Explorer, and click **Next**.

18. For now, leave the archiving options blank, and click **Next**.

19. Click **Next** at the summary screen.

20. Click **Finish** after installation has completed.

Configuring the Software

The installation of the OCS bits is complete, but we are still a long way from being ready to install the Microsoft Office Communicator (MOC) client and begin using the presence engine. First, we have to complete the configuration of the OCS server:

1. If you are installing from a CD/DVD, navigate to the **<drive>:\Setup\i386** directory.

2. Double-click on **setup.exe**.

3. On the **Deployment Wizard page**, click on **Deploy Pools in an Expanded Topology**.

4. Next, select **Step 3: Configure Pool** and click **Run**.

5. Click **Next** to get past the Welcome page.

6. On the **Administrative Tools Required page**, click **Next** to install the tools.

7. On the **Server or Pool to Configure page** (Figure 3.13), check to make sure that the name of the server is correct, and click **Next**.

Figure 3.13 Selecting a Server to Configure

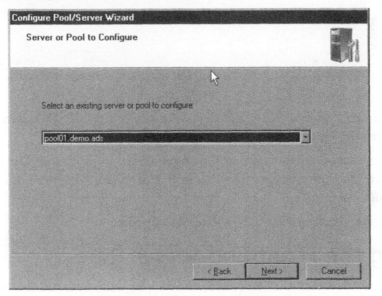

8. On the **Load Balancer Configuration Parameters page**, click **Next**.

9. On the **SIP domains page**, make sure your domain name is selected, and click **Next**. Notice that we are using a nonstandard domain name system (DNS) suffix. You will want to use an Internet standard such as .com, .net, and so on as an alternative.

10. On the **Client Logon Settings**, accept the defaults that state **Some or all clients will use a DNS SRV record for automatic logon** and **Use this server or pool as a Director for automatic logon** (Figure 3.14). Once you've accepted those defaults, click **Next**.

Figure 3.14 Client Logon Settings

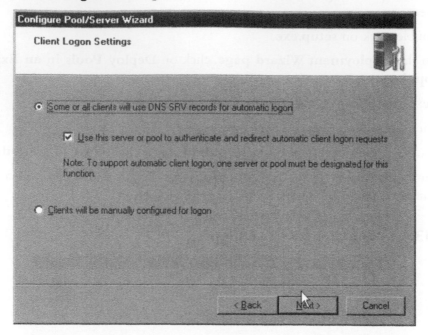

11.   Place a checkmark next to your domain name in the **SIP Domains for Automatic Logon page**, and click **Next**.

12.   On the **External User Access Configuration page**, choose **Do not configure for external user access now** (we will address this with the Edge server install) and click **Next** twice.

13.   When the configuration is complete, click **Finish**.

Installing the Front-End Server Role

You have the base configuration completed, so now you need to install the front-end server role bits onto this server. To complete this portion of the installation, follow these steps:

1.   If you are installing from a CD/DVD, navigate to the **<drive>:\Setup\i386** directory.

2.   Double-click on **setup.exe**.

3.   On the **Deployment Wizard page**, click on **Deploy Pools in an Expanded Topology**.

4.   Next, select **Step 5: Add Front End Server**.

5.   From the **Deploy Front End server screen**, choose **Step 1: Install files for Front End Server** and click **Install**.

6.   Click **Next** to get past the Welcome page.

7. Review and accept the EULA, and click **Next**.

8. Review and adjust the customer information as needed, and click **Next**.

9. Accept the defaults for file locations, and click **Next**.

10. Click **Next** to confirm the installation.

11. When the installation completes, click **Close**.

12. When you return to the **Deploy Front End server screen**, choose **Step 2: Activate Pool Front End Server**, and click **Run**.

13. Click **Next** to get past the Welcome page.

14. Verify the name of the domain, and click **Next**.

15. Under **Select Service Account**, enter and verify a password for the RTCService, and click **Next**.

16. Verify the settings you have chosen, and click **Next**.

17. When the installation completes, click **Finish**.

Working with Certificates

Now, you get to put your newly created certificate server to good use! You will be going back into the OCS Setup Wizard to initiate a certificate request so that you can use secure communications via the Transport Layer Security (TLS) protocol. Let's begin:

1. If you are installing from a CD/DVD, navigate to the **<drive>:\Setup\i386** directory.

2. Double-click on **setup.exe**.

3. On the **Deployment Wizard page**, click on **Deploy Pools in an Expanded Topology**.

4. Next, select **Step 5: Add Front End Server**.

5. From the **Deploy Front End server screen**, choose **Step 3: Configure Certificate** and click **Run**.

6. Click **Next** to get past the Welcome page.

7. Verify that **Create a new certificate** is checked, and then click **Next**.

8. Next, choose **Send the request immediately to an online certificate authority**, and click **Next**. You have the option of sending later, but because you already have your CA ready, there is no need to do this.

9. Next, verify that the name of your server is presented in the **Name box** of the **Name and Security Settings page**.

10. Remove the checkmark next to **Mark certificate as exportable** (Figure 3.15), and click **Next**.

Figure 3.15 Certificate Name and Security Settings

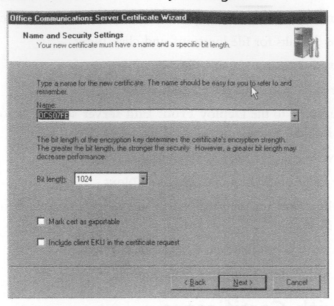

11. Next, fill in the **Organization** and **Organizational unit fields** with the name of your company and department, respectively, and then click **Next**.

12. In the **Subject name field**, enter the FQDN of the OCS pool.

13. Make sure that the **Subject Alternate Name** appears as **sip.<domain>.<com/ net/etc>** (Figure 3.16), and then click **Next**.

Figure 3.16 Subject Server Name Page

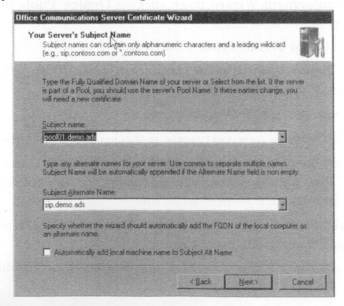

14. Now, enter the geographical information for the server (state/province and city/locality), and then click **Next**.

15. Verify that the name of your CA appears as in the **Choose Certificate Authority page** (Figure 3.17), and then click **Next**.

Figure 3.17 Choosing a CA

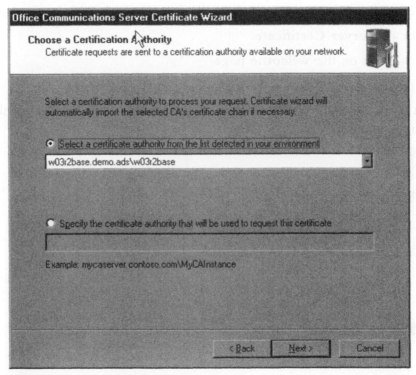

16. Click **Next** on the **Summary page**.

17. Click **Assign** on the **Completion page**.

18. Click **OK** on the **Communications Certificate Wizard page**.

19. Click **Finish**.

NOTE

If the certificate creation process fails, go back and make sure that the forest and domain levels are set for Windows Server 2003. This is a common issue.

Next, you need to go into the Internet Information Services Manager on the OCS server to begin to use the certificate that you just created:

1. Click **Start | Administrative Tools | Internet Information Services (IIS) Manager**.

2. Expand the server, expand the **Web Sites settings**, right-click on **Default Web Site**, and choose **Properties**.

3. Click on the **Directory Security tab** of the **Default Website Properties**.

4. Click on **Server Certificate**.

5. Click **Next** on the **Welcome page**.

6. Click **Assign an existing certificate**, and then click **Next**.

7. On the **Available Certificates page** (Figure 3.18), click the certificate that represents your server name, and click **Next**.

Figure 3.18 Available Certificates

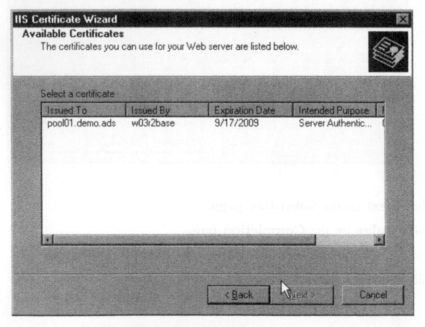

8. Click **Next** through the remaining screens, and then click **Finish** to complete the certificate configuration.

9. Close the IIS Management window.

Addressing DNS Requirements

As mentioned, OCS 2007 relies very heavily on DNS. For OCS to work as seamlessly as possible, especially for end-users, you need to make sure that you have the correct DNS records configured both internally and externally. The alternative to DNS records is that users would have to manually enter the name of their OCS server into the MOC client. Although this may not be a problem for users who will be using the product exclusively from inside the network, it is a major issue for people who will be travelling outside the network, as the Internet Protocol (IP) address (and FQDN, in some cases) will almost certainly be different from outside the network. In this section, we will walk you through the process of creating the proper DNS records for inside your network. Let's create those records now.

A user with administrative rights to the DNS will need to make the following changes. Furthermore, the DNS servers will need to be able to support SRV records for this to work properly. Windows 2003 DNS supports these types of records. If you are using a third-party (or legacy Microsoft) DNS product, verify that these records can be created, or you may need to upgrade to a newer DNS service.

1. From your DNS server, click **Start | Programs | Administrative Tools | DNS**.

2. Expand the DNS console until you get to the appropriate domain name for your internal network (Figure 3.19).

Figure 3.19 DNS Management

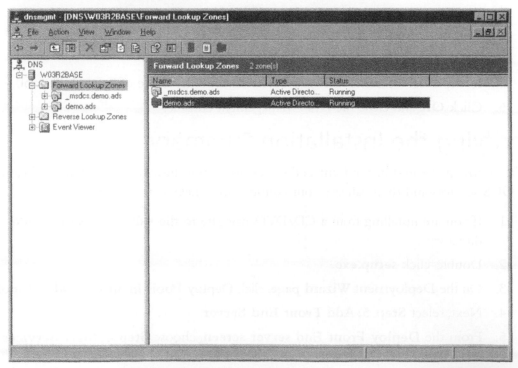

3. Right-click your domain name, and choose **Other New Records**.

4. Under **Select a Resource Type**, click **Service Location (SRV)** and click **Create Record**. Type **_sipinternaltls** in the **Service text field**, **_tcp** in the **Protocol field**, and **5061** in the **Port number field** (Figure 3.20).

Figure 3.20 SRV Record Settings

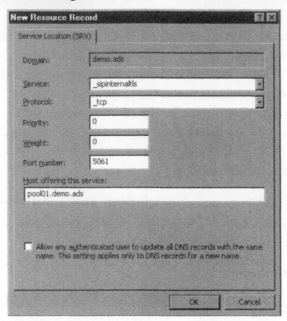

5. In the **Host offering this service field**, type the name of your OCS pool.

6. Click **OK** and close the DNS Management console.

Verifying the Installation Summary

We're almost at the end of the front-end server installation process! Next, you need to start the OCS services and then validate your configuration. Let's start the services now:

1. If you are installing from a CD/DVD, navigate to the **<drive>:\Setup\i386** directory.

2. Double-click **setup.exe**.

3. On the **Deployment Wizard page**, click **Deploy Pools in an Expanded Topology**.

4. Next, select **Step 5: Add Front End Server**.

5. From the **Deploy Front End server screen**, choose **Step 4: Start Services** and click **Run**.

6. Click **Next** to get past the Welcome page.

7. Click **Next** again to start the services.

8. Once the services have started, click **Finish**.

9. When you return to the Deployment screen, click on **Step 5: Validate Server Functionality** and click on **Run**.

10. Click **Next** to get past the Welcome page.

11. Choose **Validate Local Server Configuration** and **Validate Connectivity**. Make sure all other boxes are unchecked, and click **Next**.

12. Review the validation information (Figure 3.21), and click **Exit** to close the window.

13. If you are prompted with a validation issue, click through the information tree to figure out how to resolve the issue.

Figure 3.21 Sample Validation Information

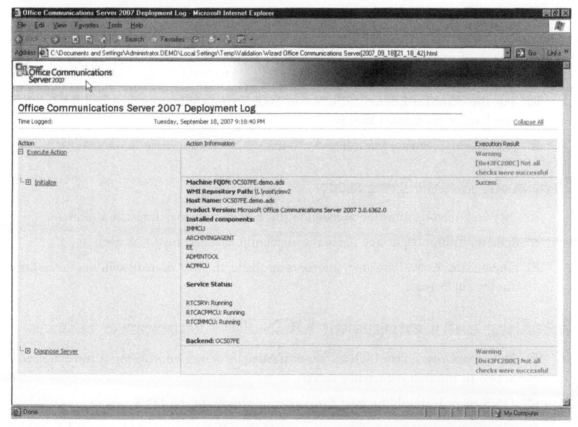

That's it for the server configuration! In the next chapter, we will discuss how the Communicator client is installed and configured, as well as how to set up a user to begin using OCS 2007.

Summary

Many optional server roles can be put into action in an OCS 2007 implementation; however, one role in particular must exist to offer basic presence functionality within your environment: the front-end server. The key to a successful OCS implementation is to get the front-end server configuration right the first time. After selecting the correct version of OCS for your environment (Standard or Enterprise Edition), you need to address the prerequisites and then prepare an Active Directory schema, forest, and domain. Once these steps have been completed, you can begin installing and configuring the software. Your final step involves starting the OCS services and validating your configuration.

Solutions Fast Track

Addressing the Prerequisites

☑ Make sure that the forest and domain functional levels are set to Windows Server 2003.

☑ For the Enterprise Edition of OCS, SQL Server 2000 SP4 or SQL Server 2005 SP1 is required.

☑ For the Standard Edition, SQL Server 2005 Express Edition is installed if you do not have it configured already.

☑ For internal security, you can use a Windows 2003 Enterprise Root CA.

Preparing Active Directory

☑ Active Directory must be prepared at three levels: schema, forest, and domain.

☑ Schema Admin rights are needed to make the changes for OCS 2007.

☑ During the Active Directory preparation phase, the SIP domain will be selected for use by OCS users.

Installing and Configuring OCS 2007 Enterprise Edition

☑ An external web farm FQDN is not needed; however, you can use it for external access to internal conference servers.

☑ DNS records should be used for user connectivity to the DNS servers.

☑ Certificates must be configured as part of the OCS server, but also must be configured in the IIS management console.

Frequently Asked Questions

Q: Does OCS 2007 support SQL Server 2005 SP2?

A: Yes.

Q: Can I use an external (third-party) CA server instead of an internal server?

A: Absolutely. The reason for using an internal server is based on trust (the fact that machines connecting internally are aware of the Enterprise Root CA) and cost.

Q: Why do I need to set my domain to Windows Server 2003 mode?

A: Unless you have a Windows 2000 or NT domain controller, there is no need to be in any Interim modes. Being in native mode also prevents issues with the certificate enrollment.

Q: Can I use a remote SQL server for OCS?

A: Yes, you will just need to point OCS to that server during installation.

Q: Will OCS 2007 be supported in Windows 2008?

A: At the time of this writing, there is no confirmation, but we believe it will be.

Chapter 4

Microsoft Office
Communicator 2007

Solutions in this chapter:

- What's New with MOC 2007?

- Installing MOC 2007

- Configuring a User for MOC 2007

- Working with the MOC 2007 Administrative Template

☑ Summary

☑ Solutions Fast Track

☑ Frequently Asked Questions

Introduction

Those of us who were early adapters as it were might remember that with the introduction of Live Communications Server (LCS) 2003, the default client was Windows Messenger 5.1. This client was sufficient for the first LCS release, and even for some users who needed no added functionality in LCS 2005. For those who wanted to be able to do more than send instant messages (IMs), share files, and use whiteboards, Microsoft released Office Communicator 2005 shortly after it released LCS 2005. With its enhancements to voice and video along with enrichments to the user interface, the roadmap for future clients was under way. This journey brings us to the newest client offering to go along with the newest LCS offering, Microsoft Office Communicator (MOC) 2007. So, it seems only right that we begin with an overview and discover just what has been added to this release.

What's New with MOC 2007?

With the advent of Office Communications Server (OCS) 2007 it would naturally make sense to introduce a new client as well. That is what Microsoft has done with the release of MOC 2007. Building on the already existing Office Communicator 2005, MOC 2007 takes greater advantage of the newest features of OCS 2007 and enhances the end-user experience. And building on the focus of unified communications along with a collaborative work environment, Microsoft has made those attributes the core of this newest client. As we review what's new, we will break down the improvements to MOC 2007 into two categories: overall user experience and Enterprise Voice.

The Overall User Experience

In MOC 2007, Microsoft has added features which are meant to enhance the overall user experience. These improvements build on the collaborative nature of MOC. Some have been in past clients, but we will focus here on what has been newly added. We'll begin with presence, a familiar past feature which has been improved.

Presence

Since the release of LCS 2003, Microsoft has included the concept of a user having *presence*. Of course, in MOC 2007 Microsoft has found ways to both improve and integrate new features. The idea of knowing that the person is actually there and able to communicate is not in itself a new technology, and let's face it, in all the major IM and communications software, the user's presence is determined by the user. With either a setting or a click of the mouse, we can easily become *unavailable* or *busy*. However, for the most part, presence awareness does work. When a user is signed in, he is there and available. When we talk about presence in messaging software we talk about user "states." This refers to the availability of the user you are trying to reach. We just need to believe that when a user's profile shows "busy" it means busy with work, not busy with World of Warcraft.

MOC 2007 offers users more granular control of their presence state. MOC 2007 uses a technology called *access levels* to determine who can view your presence state as well as how much of your personal information will be available to users. Access levels also grant users the ability to continue to send alerts to a user who is in a busy or away state. For instance, users assigned to a person's *Team access level* would be able to interrupt the user and communicate with him even when a "do not disturb" state is displayed on his contact. Figure 4.1 shows a full list of access levels and the information available to users assigned to particular levels.

Figure 4.1 MOC 2007 Access Levels

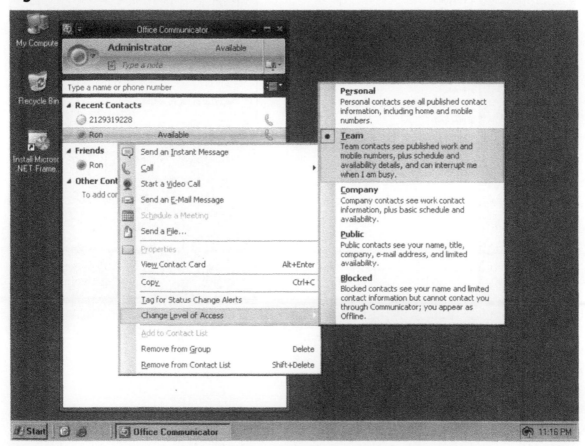

The newest area of presence in MOC 2007 is the new presence indicators. MOC users can manually change their presence state, choose from three preset locations or create custom locations, and even add a note that contacts can view. Figure 4.2 shows an example of user Ron's state set to "Be right back", with a note that he is out to lunch and will return at

1:00 P.M. In the right-hand corner, you can see that the Administrator's current location is "Clients Office" (this is a customized location set by the user).

Figure 4.2 Presence Indicators for MOC 2007 Showing the User's State and Location, and a Note

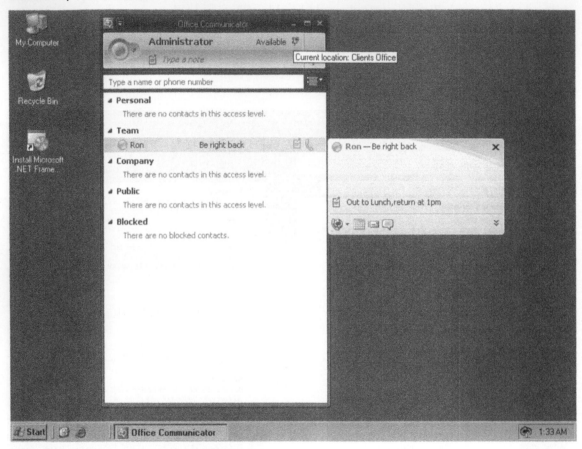

Along with states and access levels, you also have the ability to set your location. Several preset choices are available (as there were in MOC 2005), but MOC 2007 now offers the ability create custom locations. This is a tremendous advantage to those who are part of the mobile workforce and travel from office to office or from client to client.

Contact Management

New features for contact management include the ability to add Active Directory distribution lists to your contact list. You can then select a group for conversation, rather than just an individual. To further enhance contact management, you can now select multiple contacts and then choose to IM or conference them. Adding contacts is simpler than in past versions; just search for the user you want to add and drag and drop the user from the Search dialog into your contact list. This method works for users that are within your organization, federated users, and even users that are associated with public IM services. To further simplify you can now drag and drop contacts into the MOC 2007 contact list from the Outlook 2007 To: and CC: fields of an e-mail message. But perhaps the best drag-and-drop feature is the ability to add a contact into an active conversation window—in effect, dropping the contact into the conversation or conference instantly. In the reverse, you also have the option of taking a user from an active conversation and adding him to your contact list in MOC 2007 by simply dragging and dropping the user into your list of contacts. This level of simplicity makes it easier for users to find, add, and organize contacts in MOC 2007.

NOTE

Outlook 2007 also allows you to add a contact into MOC 2007, even without knowing the user's IM address. Simply open the user's contact information in Outlook and add an IM address (e.g., someone@rare-tech.net). As a placeholder, add the contact into your MOC 2007 client. You can later edit the user's IM address once you know the correct IM address for the contact.

Instant Messaging

IM has always been an important feature to Microsoft. In fact, with the release of Microsoft Exchange 2000, Microsoft released Exchange Instant Messenger Service. Microsoft removed this from Exchange 2003 and replaced it with LCS 2003. From the inception of LCS 2003, IM has been a core feature. Until the release of OCS 2007, Microsoft Messenger 5.1 was supported as an end-user client for LCS versions 2003 and 2005. So, it would make sense that we would continue to see new innovations in this aspect of the MOC client. In this newest client, users now have the ability to search for a contact by name and begin a conversation by simply choosing Enter after finding the person. Because MOC is enabled for rich text, you can now format IMs as well as copy and paste Word and Excel files into an IM.

Conversation History

With all these conversations going back and forth, it may become necessary to review past conversations, especially in this era of Sarbanes-Oxley and HIPAA. Integrating MOC with Outlook 2007, you now have the ability to right-click a contact(s) and check previous voice, conference, or IM conversations with the chosen contact(s). These are all logged in the Outlook Conversation History folder. Enabling the Conversation History folder is optional, and you set it in the **MOC 2007 Options** under the **Personal tab**. In the **Personal Information Manager section**, choose **Microsoft Outlook** from the drop-down menu and then check the following checkboxes:

- "Save my instant messages conversations in the Outlook Conversation History folder"
- "Save my call logs in the Outlook Conversation History folder"

The Conversation History folder keeps a history of all incoming and outgoing calls, as well as missed conversations. Links are used with the conversation history to rejoin conversations, embed notes taken with One Note, and view contextual information such as the e-mail or the calendar item that was used to start the conversation. Finally these items are archived by participants' names and methods of conversation.

Alerts

MOC 2007 comes with three types of alerts: actionable alerts, indicator alerts, and mini alerts. You use *actionable alerts* to reply to conversation alerts you've received. This allows you to respond to invitations via voice or IM, forward calls to another number, decline to join a conversation, or set a "do not disturb" for a set time. *Indicator alerts* display invitations to various types of conversations via visuals, to indicate the mode of communication and whether a user-to-user or conference invitation is being sent. You use *mini alerts*, which are expandable, to notify you of incoming calls or IMs.

Voice Features

MOC 2007 also includes some cool voice features. For instance, now you can choose how to handle incoming calls. MOC also offers several call forwarding features. You can forward a call to another phone, such as your home or mobile phone, forward a call to a user in your contact list, or have the phone call simultaneously ring your primary phone and a secondary phone. Of course, you need to configure the phone numbers in MOC (a process that we will review later in the chapter). Figure 4.3 shows the voice features in MOC 2007.

Figure 4.3 MOC 2007's Voice Features

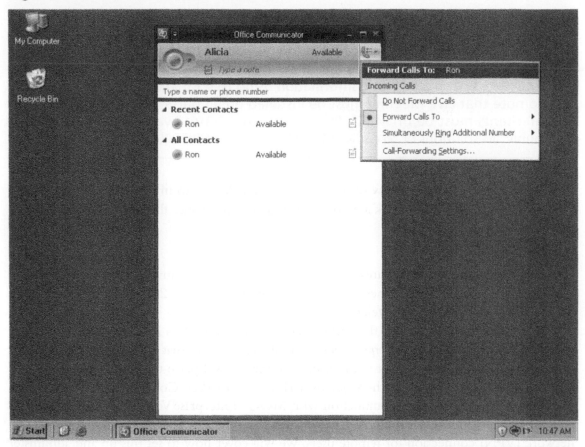

Other New Features in MOC 2007

MOC has several other great features, including the ability to create rich text IMs. This means you can now treat an IM the same way you would a document you are writing. This is a great addition, because as humans we do not tend to communicate in a flat, monotone way. The ability to use features such as italics and bold text, as well as change the color of the text, better reflects the way we communicate with each other, and if we are going to collaborate with others in an IM environment, we should be able to express our thoughts and inflections completely. So, although it may seem to somewhat trivial, rich text IMs really do have a big impact on how we work.

Another new feature is the ability to escalate a conference into a Live Meeting. With the Live Meeting client installed on all participants' machines, a user can simply right-click and choose **Share Information using Live Meeting** or click on the **Live Meeting icon**.

NOTE

The Live Meeting icon is available only when more than two people are in a conversation. To activate a Live Meeting with only two people, right-click a contact and choose **Share Information using Live Meeting**. It is also important to note that Live Meeting must be installed on all participants' machines, and all clients must be on MOC 2007; this feature is not available to third-party public IM solutions or to earlier MOC clients (e.g., MOC 2005 and Messenger 5.1).

This concludes our overview of what's new within MOC to improve the overall user experience. Next we'll take a look at what has been added to enhance the use of Enterprise Voice.

Enterprise Voice

The new Enterprise Voice features in MOC 2007 build on the unified communications infrastructure in OCS 2007. These newest components in MOC 2007 offer the ability to use the client as a full working telephone system.

The new items discussed in this section rely heavily on MOC's Enterprise Voice feature. Microsoft has used the term *enterprise voice* to emphasize the fact that this is an enterprise-level solution, available to anyone, but without the enterprise-level price tag. This latest version of MOC is making a big play in the Voice over IP (VoIP) market. Combining software with telephony, and when used in conjunction with MOC's Enterprise Voice feature, MOC 2007 is essentially an Internet Protocol (IP)-based softphone that doesn't require a virtual private network (VPN) connection for remote users. We will cover how to set this up and administer it a little later in the book. For now, let's look at what this means for the end-user.

TIP

Enterprise Voice is available to all users in the organization and works much the same way your regular phone does, with the obvious difference of not using a physical phone instrument, but rather a combination of software and hardware such as headsets or Universal Serial Bus (USB) phone devices. It is important to remember that users can take advantage of none of the features we're discussing here unless they are enabled for either Enterprise Voice or Remote Call Control (RCC) within OCS first. Also note that with these integrations, you can interchangeably use a traditional PBX phone or your MOC client. You also can have PBX/PSTN phone users call and receive calls from your MOC users.

With MOC becoming your primary means of communication, you have the ability to manage multiple phone calls, using options such as the following:

- **Call forwarding** The ability to forward voice calls

- **Call hold** The ability to put a voice call on hold

- **Call transfer** The ability to transfer voice calls

- **Call resume** The ability to resume a call put on hold

All calls are converted to VoIP calls to allow for enhanced properties within the call, such as added contextual information including call subject and urgency level. Using the presence feature, a phone call made to a user who has enabled "do not disturb" will be routed directly to voice mail if the caller is not a member of the Team access level. Calls can also be forwarded to voice mail from within MOC by using the Communications Server Auto Attendant, which is part of the Unified Messaging (UM) integration with Exchange 2007 (we will discuss this later in the book). Another method of forwarding is to use the Actionable Alerts option. Answering an inbound call will also put other active conversations on hold.

MOC also offers a host of forwarding options in this new release, including the following:

- **Forward call** Calls can be forwarded to another work phone, mobile phone, or contact, or, as mentioned earlier, to voice mail. You can also use redirection rules to forward calls after a predetermined time (the default is 20 seconds).

- **Simultaneously ring additional number** This will allow you to have a secondary number ring simultaneously with your default number. This is good provision to ensure that calls will not be lost if you are experiencing trouble logging into MOC 2007 or, in the case of an IT administrator, if you have a call that you urgently need to take but you are all over the office that day. This feature allows the call to go to your mobile phone or, perhaps, to the receptionist, who can then locate you and forward the call to you.

Calling Features

These features are available for Enterprise Voice users as well as users who have Remote Call Control (RCC is the ability to manipulate conversations and session-oriented dialogs, using the Session Initiation Protocol [SIP]). This means you can use RCC to integrate voice, video, and text sessions (IM), and integrate legacy phone systems such as PBX/PSTN. With either option enabled, these features will work across both telephony topologies. Users also can select Active Directory distribution groups and add them to their contact list in MOC 2007, and then choose this distribution list to start a multiparty call. Users can create their own groups from within the list of contacts and choose that group to start a conference call, or they can simply choose multiple contacts from within the disparate groups and lists of users and start a multiparty conference call.

> **NOTE**
>
> For a user to take advantage of conference and multiparty calling, the conferencing option must be enabled for the user from the OCS management console. You can set this in the OCS Global Properties under the Meetings tab, or within Active Directory Users and Computers by choosing the option to configure Office Communications Server and selecting a meeting policy for the users in the wizard.

Calls to other users have been simplified, allowing you to place VoIP calls to other PCs running MOC. Conversation windows now appear when a call is placed, and they automatically close when either party ends the call. Calls can be transferred to another number, device, or contact, and with improvements in call transfers you can now check with your co-worker before transferring a call and then transfer the call right from within the IM conversation window. Other features include the ability to place a call by entering the telephone number into the search box in MOC, as well as better readability for phone numbers formatted within the United States.

Conferencing

We touched on conferencing when we discussed new calling features. To review, you can create conference calls in several ways. But you can also now move from a person-to-person conversation to a multiparty conference, and collaborate further thanks to such improvements as Web, videoconferencing, and audio conferencing server roles. You can securely initiate a Web conference to other MOC users or escalate a conference to a Live Meeting conference. With improvements to the escalation feature, you can escalate an IM, phone, or audio conference into a Live Meeting session. You can also share files or start a Live Meeting session. With an Outlook add-in you can schedule Live Meeting conferences to your calendar (we will cover this in greater depth in Chapter 8). Another improvement is the ability to "dial out" to a contact. With this feature, you can dial out to a PSTN/PBX or to a mobile phone. This ability to conference a traditional phone user into a VoIP-based communications system truly enables a new level of collaboration and is continuing to foster "anytime, anywhere" productivity.

Switching Communication Modes

In MOC 2007, users can now switch *seamlessly* from person-to-person conversations to multiparty conversations (the key word is *seamless*, as this is where the improvement lies). Likewise, an IM session can become an IM conference, phone calls can become phone conferences, and if you need to share applications during a conference you can move easily into a Live Meeting session. Another enhancement concerns conference calls. In the past, users have been unable to add and remove conference call participants dynamically. With MOC 2007, you can add members to a conference call and call out to a participant, effectively *switching* communication methods.

Automatic Setup for Audio and Video Devices

Setting up audio and video devices is even easier now with automatic setup. With MOC 2007, you can disconnect, change, and reconnect an audio or video device without the need for any manual setup. MOC supports automatic setup for headsets, microphones, Web cameras, and USB handsets. Optionally, you can choose to have a headset or USB handset use the computer's speakers instead of the built-in earpieces for incoming audio.

USB Audio Devices

MOC now supports USB headsets and handsets, as well as audio devices with telephony-grade options such as caller information, call timers, and call subjects. For example, imagine a typical collaboration scenario in which two co-workers are preparing a presentation and contract for a potential client. Alicia needs to call Rosa to discuss a contract negotiation, but she knows Rosa has been working on her presentation, so her MOC client is set to "do not disturb". Being part of Rosa's team and using the Subject and Importance features, Alicia can flag the call so that as MOC 2007 rings in Rosa's office, Rosa can see by the Subject line that the call has to do with her presentation and she can see that the issue is urgent.

Rosa answers the call from Alicia, and as they discuss the contract issue, they realize that the legal department needs to be involved. They invite Jenny from legal into a conference. As they begin to talk, they realize they need to start a Live Meeting so that they can collaborate on rewording the contract. Alicia escalates the conference into a Live Meeting session. When they come across the page in question, they realize it was edited by Emma, one of the department managers. So, they try to reach Emma via MOC. Emma is not at her desk; she is headed to a client's office. But she has turned on the "Simultaneously ring additional number" feature, so her mobile phone rings. Emma explains that the change was made per the prospective client's requirements. Jenny from legal reviews company policy and legal procedure, and finds that the change doesn't expose the company to any risk. So, with the problem corrected and the issue resolved, Rosa can make the necessary changes to her presentation so that the meeting will run smoothly.

This concludes our look at what is new in MOC 2007. Next, we will discuss how to install the client and ways to configure a single client and multiple clients, as well as how to use client templates for MOC 2007.

Installing MOC 2007

Before we install the MOC 2007 client, we will want to plan our deployment. Let's consider several factors. First, the installation file for MOC 2007 is a Windows installer package (.msi); therefore, we have the option of using single-system installation methods, Group Policy software installation, or other third-party installation software deployment tools. Because software installation through Group Policy is free, we will discuss deployment via Group Policy and single-user installation techniques.

Single-User Installation

We will begin with a single-user install. To install MOC 2007 begin by clicking on the **communicator.msi file** and choosing **Next**; the license agreement screen will appear. Accept the licensing terms and click **Next**. On the next screen, you can choose the default install location or you can click the **Browse radio button** to change the location. Once you've decided where to install the client, click the **Next button**. On the final installation screen, click the checkbox to review the online notes for MOC 2007.

Group Policy Installation

In this section, we'll discuss how to install MOC 2007 using the Group Policy software installation feature. A Group Policy Object (GPO) is a virtual container for Group Policy settings. This container is attached or applied to objects within Active Directory, such as the Site, Domain, or Organizational Unit (OU). Using GPOs to install software affords some flexibility that you do not necessarily get with single-user installation. To set up the Group Policy installation open **Active Directory Users and Computers**, right-click the **OU** to which you want to apply the installation policy, and choose **Properties**. From the **Properties page** choose the **Group Policy tab** and click the **Open radio button** to launch the **Group Policy Management Console (GPMC)**. Another way to launch the GPMC is to select **Start | Run**, type **gpmc.msc**, and click **OK**. Once you select where you want to place this policy, you can choose to create a new Group Policy or edit an existing Group Policy.

TIP

Because you are installing a software package, you can create a new Group Policy or perhaps edit an existing one. In most instances, depending on your organization's size and complexity, you also want to try not to apply the Group Policy to the default domain policy. Rather, you should apply the Group Policy to an OU. The real trick is to balance not having too many Group Policies while trying to segregate domain activities at the same time. Some large organizations that use Group Policy installation will have an Installation Group Policy where they will create and manage all their installation packages. Ultimately, there is no wrong way, but managing these gets a bit hairy when there are too many of them. So, consider these factors when deciding to install the client via Group Policy.

Figure 4.4 shows an OU named OCS Users; this is where we will create our new MOC 2007 installation GPO.

Figure 4.4 Creating a Software Installation GPO Using the GPMC

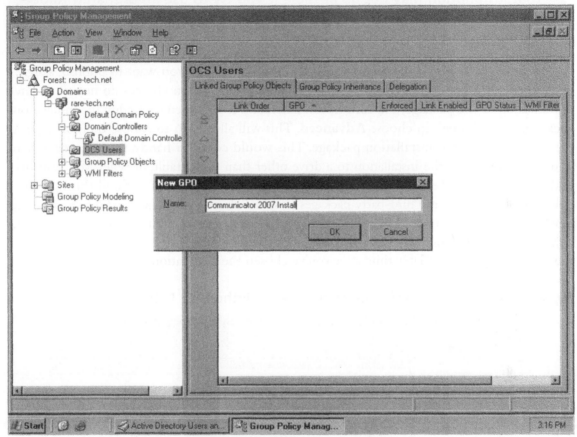

Once you have created your new Group Policy, you need to decide whether you will apply the GPO to the computer configuration or to the user configuration. Perhaps users do not always sit at the same system, or maybe temporary workers fill in at workstations where staff members are on vacation or are ill. In these cases, applying the GPO to the user is advantageous. Or maybe you have users who work from laptops out of the office and you do not use MOC outside the perimeter network; in this case, a computer-based installation might work better. For our example, we will use the user configuration. Click on the **Software Settings folder** and then on **Software Installation**. Right-click and choose **New Package**. From here, you need to navigate to where your installation (.msi) file is located.

> **WARNING**
>
> You should place the installation package in a network share to ensure that users will have the proper permissions to install MOC 2007. GPMC will warn that installation may not be possible if you try to use an unshared folder location.

As shown in Figure 4.5, you now need to choose whether you want to publish, assign, or customize the package to be deployed. The publish and assign choices do not allow any modification to the package, and each installs differently. If you need to modify the installation package, you will need to choose **Advanced**. This will allow you to choose transform (.mst) files to customize the installation package. This would come in handy, for instance, when you want to redirect the installation to a drive other than the default, or when you want to make changes to a Registry setting for the package that cannot be defined through the Administrative template. Third-party packages exist to help you create transform files, but note that anytime you create such files you should do so with extreme care, as you are, in effect, changing the installation file directly. You are not able to modify the installation, or apply transform packages, at a later time after you've chosen the installation method.

Figure 4.5 Choosing a Software Deployment Method for MOC

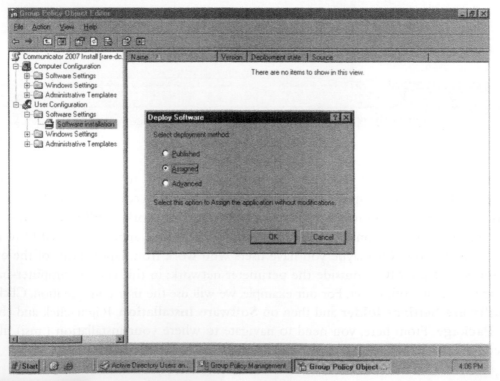

For our deployment, we will use the *Assigned* deployment method. So, we will choose **Assigned** and click **OK**. After the screen refreshes, we will see that the deployment package is ready. Because we have chosen to assign the application, it will install automatically to the users in the OCS OU the next time they log in.

Now, let's take a moment to discuss deploying MOC 2007 where a Group Policy installation for MOC 2005 is already implemented. Go to your **GPO** where MOC 2005 is set to be deployed and choose to **Edit that policy**. In the **Software Installation section**, create a new installation package in the GPO; however, after you choose your method of deployment, check the **Properties** to see that the settings are in place. Click the **MOC 2007 installation package** and the **Properties screen** will open. Click on the **Upgrades tab** and the screen in Figure 4.6 will appear.

Figure 4.6 The Upgrades Tab, Which Shows Client Packages That Will Be Upgraded

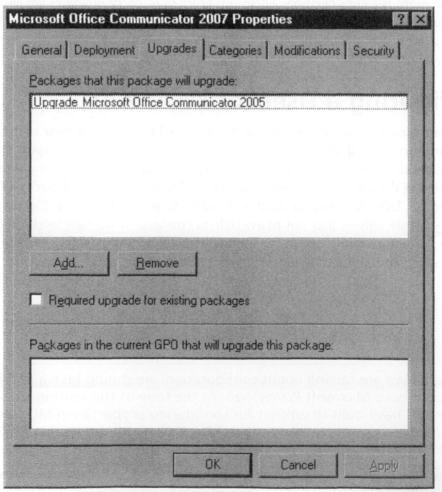

Checking the **Required upgrade for existing packages** checkbox will force the upgrade of the end-user client to MOC 2007, for all users linked to the GPO. You may not want to remove the old MOC 2005 client on certain end-users. But to make a correct assessment, you should consider the list of changes and differences between the 2005 and 2007 Group Policy deployments, which you can review in the *Communicator 2007 Deployment Guide*.

Other Installation Methods

In addition to traditional and Group Policy installs, you have other options for installing the MOC client. For instance, you can install MOC using Windows login scripts (which you can do silently using command-line options to suppress user intervention). Or you can use software such as Systems Management Server (SMS) 2003 or System Center Configuration Manager 2007, which was in beta at the time of this writing. These programs are good for installations in which scheduling of network traffic or of wide area network (WAN) implementations is a consideration. These and other third-party programs are also effective when complex implementations are necessary.

Now that we have the client installed, we need to configure our end-users before they can sign in and use MOC.

Configuring a User for MOC 2007

Before your users can sign in and use MOC, you need to configure their accounts in Active Directory. You can do this in both Active Directory Users and Computers and the Communications Server Administrative Console. However, there is one step you must perform first by running the Communications Server Users Wizard from Active Directory Users and Computers. So, let's take a look at what we need to do to enable users in Communications Server. Some user settings may not be available to configure at the user level if the Global and Voice Properties are not enabled or configured to allow for end-user configuration. We will look at these properties in detail later in the chapter.

NOTE

Because we are talking about configuration, we should take a moment to talk about Microsoft PowerShell. At the time of this writing, OCS 2007 does not have built-in support for configuring properties in MOC using PowerShell. However, third-party tools are available for managing Group Policies in PowerShell.

WARNING

Certain settings also require that you set up a server role for the settings to work. For example, you need to install archiving services to allow message archiving, and Access Edge Servers are required to allow public IM connectivity and federation.

Let's walk through the steps of enabling and configuring user objects in Active Directory.

Configuring Active Directory User Objects

One of the great aspects of deploying MOC is that you can handle most of the user configuration in Active Directory Users and Computers. The Active Directory User Objects also use wizards to help guide you through the enabling and configuration of MOC users. Because configuring user properties in Active Directory Users and Computers is a familiar task, the process is much easier to master.

Enabling Users

In this section, we will discuss how to enable and configure single users and multiple users for MOC access; we'll begin with setting up a single user object in Active Directory Users and Computers. You can access this on a machine where the Active Directory Administration tools are installed. By default, these tools are installed on all domain controllers. However, you can use a Windows XP or Vista workstation with the Windows Administrative tools installed. So, browse to your **Administrative tools**, or launch it from **Start | Run** or the command line by typing **dsa.msc**:

1. Open **Active Directory Users and Computers**.

2. Go to the **OU** where the user is located.

3. Right-click the **selected user** and choose **Enable users for Communications Server**.

4. The Enable Office Communications Server Users Wizard launches. Click **Next**.

5. Choose a **standard server** or **enterprise server pool** in which to assign your user, and click **Next**.

6. Choose a sign-in name for the user. You can use an e-mail address, a User Principal Name (UPN), a first name - last name *@somedomain.com, or* sAMAccoutName *@somedomain.com.* After you have chosen a sign-in name, click **Next** (see Figure 4.7).

Figure 4.7 Choosing How the Username Is Generated for MOC Sign-in

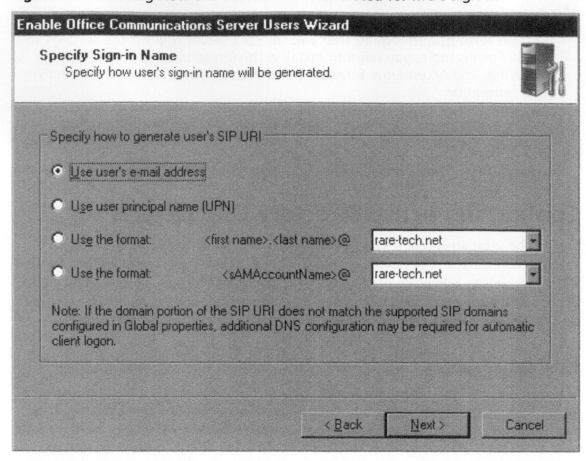

After you complete step 6, an operation status screen will appear, telling you whether the operation succeeded or failed.

Using the Configuration Wizard

Now that you have enabled the user for MOC let's look at the configuration. Again, from the user object within Active Directory Users and Computers, **right-click** and choose **Configure Communications Server Users**. Now you will see the **Configure User Wizard**; click **Next**, and then you will see a display of the user settings you can configure from this wizard. Table 4.1 shows which settings are available and what Global or Voice Properties are required to allow individual user configuration.

Table 4.1 User Configuration Wizard Settings

User Configuration	Available Settings	Tab	Global and Voice Properties
Federation	Enabled/disabled	Federation	Fully qualified domain name (FQDN) of director or Access Edge Server for internal and external access
Public IM connectivity	Enabled/disabled	Federation	FQDN of director or Access Edge Server for internal and external access
Enhanced presence	Enabled/disabled	User	Enable to allow users to see presence information for noncontacts
Archive internal messages	Enabled/disabled	Archiving	Set to **Archiving** according to user settings to override global settings
Archive federated messages	Enabled/disabled	Archiving	Set to **Archiving** according to user settings to override global settings
Organize meetings with anonymous participants	Allow/disallow	Meetings	Set to **Enforce per user** to override global settings
Change meeting policy	Check whether to change meeting policies and choose a policy template	Meetings	Set to **Use per user policy** to set the features allowed in a Web conference
Change Enterprise Voice settings	Check to allow changes, choose **Enable Voice**, and select a voice policy for the user	Policy tab in the Voice Properties	Set voice dialing properties for users. Set to **Use per user policy** to modify settings per user

Using the Properties page in the Communications Server Administration Console, or the Communications tab in Active Directory Users and Computers, you can configure more user settings. So now, let's look at the User Options page.

Tools & Traps...

Be Wary When Allowing Public IM

Although public IM is a great tool, you need to be wary of whom you let inside your network. The ability to exploit a user via IM is another of a list of growing threats we face each day. Remember that MOC is not simply IM software. The ability to transfer files, retrieve groups and contacts from Active Directory, and conference and collaborate means you need to be careful whom you allow to use this service.

Setting Individual User Properties

In the User Options page, you can change individual user properties. Many of these are options we considered before for forest, domain, and group-level configuration. The options we can set here are the username, the domain, which MOC server or pool to set for meetings (this is an option only when global settings allow for configuration), and additional options. Figure 4.8 shows the additional options.

Figure 4.8 The User Options Page Found under Additional Options

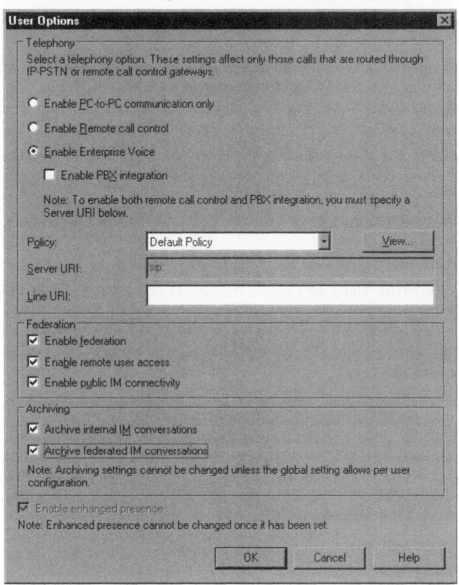

Additional Options

In this page, you can configure IP/PSTN or RCC telephony options for the user. These include the following:

- **Enable PC-to-PC communication only** The user can make PC-to-PC voice calls only. There is no integration with phone systems.

- **Enable Remote call control** You can use your phone line to make PC-to-PC or PC-to-phone calls.

- **Enable Enterprise Voice** MOC is used to route all inbound and outbound calls for the user, and can be used to make these calls. Enterprise Voice also offers enhanced features not available in RCC.

- **Enable PBX integration** Users can receive calls from their legacy phone system or the MOC client.

- **Policy** This is where you can define what call privileges are available to the user.

- **Server URI** This is the Uniform Resource Identifier (URI) of the RCC server, and it is required to integrate RCC with PBX (it is not necessary to provide this to enable RCC; you need it for RCC to interact with a PBX system).

- **Line URI** This is the URI of the user's telephone. RCC and Enterprise Voice use it for call routing.

You can also choose federation options for users with more granularity. In the Federation section of User Options you can change the options of a single user. For instance, your company policy may be that all departments by default have public IM connectivity and the ability to ederate with other organizations that use MOC with federation enabled. However, the marketing department may be employing several summer interns that need internal IM access, but that will not need to communicate outside the local office or with public IM clients. Here, you have the option to change that setting for a single user. The options are:

- Enable federation

- Enable remote user access

- Enable public IM connectivity

NOTE

Public IM connectivity requires additional licensing, so you should use this sparingly as it can become an expensive addition if not moderated closely. These licenses are available from Microsoft through volume licensing programs, starting with Open Value for five or more licenses, Select for 25 or more licenses, and Enterprise agreements for 250 or more licenses. The public IM connectivity license is a per-user, per-month subscription, and this is in addition to the use CAL. The average retail price for the per-month subscription is about $1.49 per user.

Next, you can set up archiving options for the user. You can configure the available options only if the global properties are set to **Archive according to user**. The options are:

- Archive internal IM conversations
- Archive federated IM conversations

Using the Group Policy Administrative template for MOC, you can choose to have these conversations archived to the user's Outlook mailbox.

The last option is the **Enable enhanced presence** option, which you cannot change once set. You can leave this configuration option alone when setting up the default configuration of users in Active Directory (which we will discuss shortly). You also can set it on an individual user basis.

We have considered how to configure individual user settings using the Active Directory user object. Now let's look at what we can do to configure multiple users.

Configuring Multiple Users

One of the most compelling reasons for multiuser configuration is the control of feature sets within MOC. Due to the costs associated with Live Meeting and public IM connectivity licensing, users within certain departments may not be configured for public IM connectivity or Live Meeting usage. Or perhaps corporate policy or standards such as HIPAA or Sarbanes-Oxley dictate that federation should not be allowed and that archiving is a must. So, let's look at where we can configure user settings and what properties are affected. We will begin by discussing the forest-wide settings, which affect all users in the SIP domain.

Global Properties and Voice Properties

Both Global Properties and Voice Properties are available in multiuser configurations. To configure the Global and Voice Properties for your forest, open the **Office Communicator Administration Console**. Choose your **forest**, **right-click**, go to **Properties**, and choose **Global Properties** or **Voice Properties**, as seen in Figure 4.9.

Figure 4.9 Navigating to the Global and Voice Properties Pages in the MOC Console

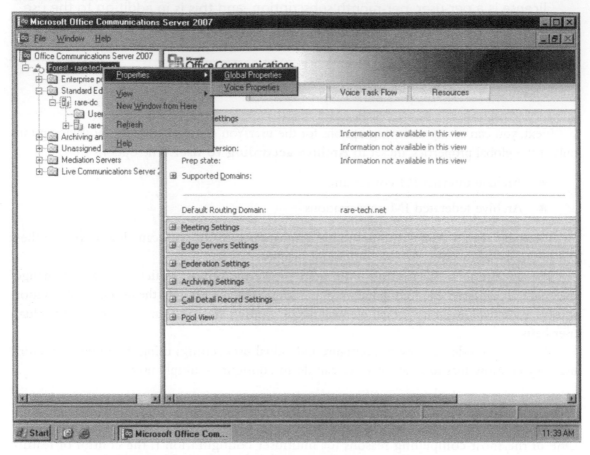

The Global Properties page includes eight tabs, listed here and shown in Figure 4.10:

- **General** Specifies the supported SIP domains in your organization

- **Search** Specifies how MOC handles search queries

- **User** Specifies the maximum subscribers and devices (points of presence) for each SIP domain

- **Meetings** Specifies the allowance of anonymous users and the meeting policy settings

- **Edge Servers** Specifies the *internal* FQDN of Access Edge Servers as well as Web conference and audio/video conference servers

- **Federation** Specifies the FQDN of the director or Access Edge Server that internal users will use to route outbound traffic

- **Archiving** Specifies the settings for archiving internal and federated communications

- **Call Detail Records** Specifies the use of call detail records (CDRs) for peer-to-peer, conferencing, or voice calls

Figure 4.10 Global Properties Page in the MOC Admin Module

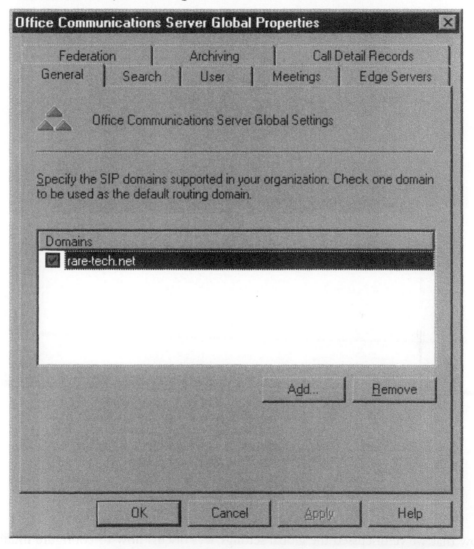

The Voice Properties page includes four tabs, listed here and shown in Figure 4.11:

- **Location Profiles** Defines how numbers are translated when dialed from a specific location

- **Phone Usages** Defines how to manage phone usage records
- **Policy** Specifies the Enterprise Voice policy for users
- **Routes** Defines the routing parameters for a voice call

Figure 4.11 Voice Properties Page in the MOC Admin Module

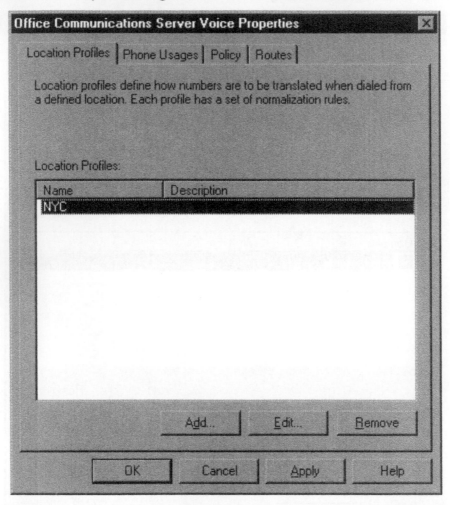

Now that we've discussed the global settings, let's discuss how to configure multiple users in a domain. To do so we will go back to Active Directory Users and Computers.

Enabling Multiple Users in Active Directory

You can enable and configure multiple user settings in three ways: enable a group, enable an OU, or choose random users within Active Directory Users and Computers. Just as with individual users, to enable multiple users you **right-click** and choose **Enable users for Communications Server**. Then follow these steps:

1. Open **Active Directory Users and Computers**.

2. Go to the OU, group, or highlighted individual users to be enabled.

3. Right-click and choose **Enable users for Communications Server**.

4. The Enable Office Communications Server Users Wizard launches. Click **Next**.

5. Choose a standard server or enterprise server pool in which to assign your users, and click **Next**.

6. Choose a sign-in name for the users. You may choose an e-mail address, a User Principal Name (UPN), first name - last name *@somedomain.com, or* sAMAccoutName *@somedomain.com.* After you have chosen a sign-in name, click **Next**. Refer to Figure 4.6 for the sign-in naming conventions.

After you complete step 6, you will receive an operation status screen telling you whether the operation succeeded or failed, and letting you know which users have been enabled and which haven't. Figure 4.12 shows both successful and failed operations.

Figure 4.12 The Success and Failure Operations in the Enable Office Communications Server Users Wizard

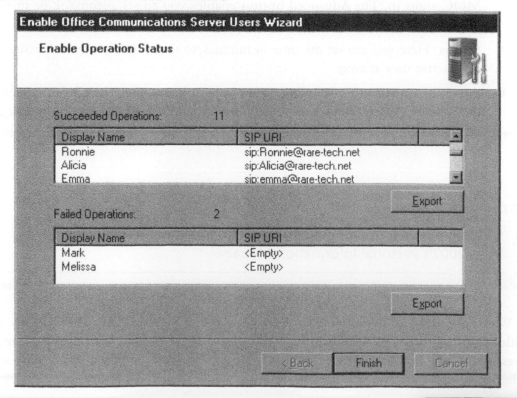

Configuration Wizard

Now let's discuss how to configure multiple users. Open **Active Directory Users and Computers**, **right-click**, and choose **Configure Communications Server Users**. This launches the **Configure User Wizard**; click **Next**. As discussed earlier, here we can set up federation, public IM connectivity, enhanced presence, and archiving (both internal and federated messages); set meeting options (including policy settings); and set Enterprise Voice options.

Configuring the MOC Client

Now we will look at the configuration options available in the MOC 2007 client. To configure the MOC client go to the **Status** button or menu button on the **Communicator client** and choose **Options** in the menu. Here you will see four tabs: Personal, Phones, Alerts, and General. We will discuss each tab in the sections that follow.

Configuring Personal Options

From the Personal tab, you can configure the following:

- **My Account** Here you can configure the sign-in address, choose to allow MOC to start when Windows starts, and choose to automatically open the contact list when MOC signs in. The Advanced option enables you to set automatic or manual configuration for the connection.

- **Status** Here you can set the time in minutes, to show an idle user as inactive and an inactive user as away.

- **Personal Information Manager** Here you can set up integration with Outlook or the Windows Address Book, or set it for no integration at all. You need Outlook 2007 for full integration with MOC 2007.

NOTE

You may need an update to Outlook 2007 to allow for integration with MOC 2007's Personal Information Manager.

When choosing Outlook you have the option to check or uncheck the **Display my Outlook out of office information to contacts in my Personal, Team, and Company access levels** option. When **Out of office** is enabled, your status is updated and a note shows up in MOC displaying your out of office message. Figure 4.13 shows an example.

Figure 4.13 A Contact's Out of Office Message Displayed in MOC

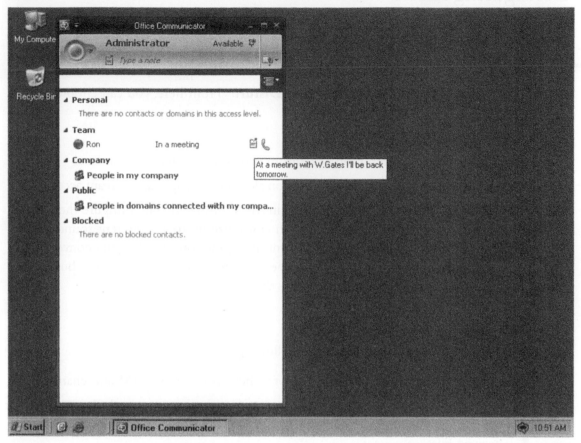

Additional options include the following:

- Update my presence based on my Outlook calendar information
- Show meeting subject and location to contacts in my Team access level
- Save my instant message conversations in the Outlook Conversation History folder
- Save my call logs in the Outlook Conversation History folder

Configuring Phone Options

From the Phones tab, you can configure the following:

- **My phone numbers** Here you can add phone numbers for Work, Mobile, Home, and Other, and you can choose which of these numbers to publish to your presence profile.

- **Phone integration** Here you can choose to integrate MOC with your phone system. The Advanced options let you configure the Remote Call Control and phone URI.

Configuring Alerts

From the Alerts tab, you can configure the following:

- **General alerts** These notify you when someone adds you to their contact list, and they display the subject or message in conversation alerts.

- **When my status is set to Do Not Disturb** From here, you can choose one of the following:

  - Do not display alerts

  - Display only conversation alerts from people in my Team access level

  - Display all alerts, but only conversation alerts from people in my Team access level

  - **Sounds** This lets you play sounds in MOC. You can also configure the sounds that are used in MOC, and you can customize up to 17 different sound alerts. For example, you can suspend instant messaging sounds when the conversation window is in the foreground; suspend sounds when your status is busy; or suspend sounds when your status is do not disturb.

Configuring General Options

From the Options tab, you can configure the following:

- **Instant Message Settings** This lets you show emoticons in IM and change fonts.

- **File Transfer** From here, you can choose where to store received files. The default location is C:\Documents and Settings\All Users\WINDOWS\Documents\My Received Files.

- **Windows Media Player** From here, you can pause Windows Media Player for calls, video calls, and conferences

- **Language** Here you can choose the communicator language (to switch languages you must have a Multilanguage User Interface [MUI] package installed).

- **Quality** This lets Microsoft collect information about how you use MOC.

- **Logging** From here, you can turn on logging as well as event logging for MOC.

More Customization Options

MOC also allows more complex customization options for end-users. Here is a short list of some of the more common capabilities you have available:

- Customize presence states

- Add context-sensitive tabs

- Customize the Help menu

- Add custom text to the IM pane

- Add commands to the MOC menu

With these options, you can really adjust MOC for your organization's needs. However, many of the additional options available depend on a combination of XML files and Registry edits, and they are out of scope for our discussion. For more information, refer to Appendix B at the end of this book. There you will find examples of the XML files and Registry edits used to customize MOC 2007.

Working with the MOC 2007 Administrative Template

As IT professionals, we have control issues. We love to be able to keep a tight grip on things running in our environment, and MOC 2007 allows us to do that. We spoke earlier about pushing out an installation of MOC 2007 via Group Policy. To close out this chapter, let's look at how to control what users can do and what is configured once MOC is installed.

We'll begin with installing the MOC Administrative template, and we'll look at what you can *control* once it is installed. The communicator.adm file should be located in the MOC 2007 installation folder. You can find the Administrative template at www.microsoft.com/downloads/details.aspx?familyid=DD3CAE08-3153-4C6A-A314-DAA79D616248&displaylang=en or you can search the Microsoft Web site for the "Office Communicator 2007: Communicator 2007 Policies" documentation. Installing the documentation will create an Excel spreadsheet and the communicator.adm file.

To install the Administrative templates, launch the GPMC by selecting **Start | Run**, typing **gpmc.msc**, and clicking **OK**. Browse to the GPO where you want to apply the Administrative template.

TIP

It is a best practice to apply the template to the GPO that was used for the MOC installation if you used the Group Policy installation method. If you used a single-user install, scripting, or third-party tools, you will want to apply the template at the OU level rather than at the domain policy level. This gives you the ability to customize MOC logically, by department, hierarchy, or geographical location.

Next, **right-click** and choose **Edit**; the **Group Policy Object Editor** will open. Choose whether to apply the template to the user or the computer, and then choose **Administrative templates** under that object (we will apply the templates to the user object in our example). From the **Action menu** choose **Add/remove templates**. The **Current Policy Templates dialog box** will appear. Click **Add**, choose the **communicator.adm file**, and click **Open**; you will now see MOC in the current policy templates. Choose **Close** on the dialog box and you will see a folder named Microsoft Office Communicator Policy Settings (see Figure 4.14).

Figure 4.14 The MOC Administrative Policy Settings in the Group Policy Object Editor

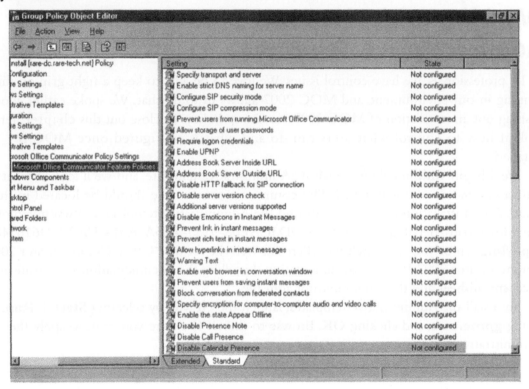

The template controls more than 60 different items (Appendix B lists all the available settings). Here is a broad overview of some of them:

- **Security** We can configure the SIP security level, storage of passwords, and the need for logon credentials. We can also configure whether users can even run MOC. For instance, interns or temporary employees in an office may not require MOC. It is easier to disable usage than to uninstall the client or to allow usage to a transient employee. Remember, every hole you open in your network puts you that much closer to risk.

- **User experience** We can control the use of emoticons, disable several presence features, and prevent the saving of IMs. But be prudent when considering use of this feature. In an organization of 1,500 employees, saving IMs in archives can be resource-intensive and may require the services of two or three extra admins, which in today's business climate can be considered a luxury that is not easily afforded.

- **Bandwidth usage** We can configure SIP compression and control data as well as audio conferencing and videoconferencing. This could be useful for smaller offices, where Internet access may be less affordable, or in offices with many users where bandwidth is being sucked dry because employees are holding videoconferences to decide what to do about lunch.

- **Application integration** MOC allows integration with Outlook 2007 and One Note (there is limited support for integration with earlier versions of Outlook, such as Outlook 2003). Features such as enabling or disabling automatic archiving of IMs or calls to Outlook can be useful. Again, you need to determine what works for your organization.

Notes from the Underground…

The Dangers of Spim (Spam Messages)

A new growing segment of danger comes from spim. You can think of spim as spam's ugly cousin. Spim sends out random messages to users in the hopes of accessing their contact lists. Many spim messages contain links to unsavory pieces of spyware or to Web sites that would be considered outside an organization's Acceptable Web Usage Policy. As the protectors of information technology, we need to protect our users from themselves sometimes. The ability to disallow hyperlinks in IMs can save you time and prevent headaches for your users and you.

As I said earlier, as IT professionals we want control, and specifically, we want control over the flow of information. We do not want to stop it; we just want to make sure it doesn't come crumbling down around us. MOC gives you that control. This useful tool make your job easier, and can save you time that you no doubt will need for other IT issues.

Summary

In this chapter, we discussed MOC 2007 and its many new and exciting features which continue to build on the unified and collaborative framework that has become synonymous with many of Microsoft's Office products. Enhancements to presence information, the ability to integrate MOC with your existing phone system, and the ability to integrate MOC with Office products allow you to be more productive. Easy installation and simplified control of feature sets via Group Policy mean you can control the user experience and limit unnecessary risk, while also customizing the MOC client for your organization. Adding to that the ability to interact with partners and clients to collaborate in real time and to escalate these real-time conferences into a Live Meeting makes MOC 2007 a no-brainer for any organization.

Solutions Fast Track

What's New with MOC 2007?

☑ Enhanced presence provides the ability to create custom presence states and locations.

☑ Contact management uses access levels to manage presence information available to users. Team options allow interruptions when a user state is set to "do not disturb".

☑ Enterprise Voice is a full-featured softphone that includes call forwarding, the ability to simultaneously ring an additional number, and conferencing capability.

Installing MOC 2007

☑ MOC 2007 installs easily with minimal upfront configuration, and auto-discovers audio, video, and USB telephony devices.

☑ You can use Group Policy to deploy MOC 2007 to an organization and to control upgrades of previous versions of MOC.

☑ You can choose from several methods of generating a user's SIP URI.

☑ MOC 2007 supports quiet install modes via logon scripts, and it uses the Windows Installer .msi extension. MOC can be packaged easily within third-party installers for more complex deployments.

Configuring a User for MOC 2007

☑ MOC 2007 supports Outlook 2007 out of office messages and publishing of free/busy calendar information.

☑ You can easily configure most MOC user settings from within Active Directory Users and Computers.

☑ MOC 2007 allows you to configure the client at the domain, server, and client levels; additional configuration is available via the Administrative template.

Working with the MOC 2007 Administrative Template

☑ You can install Administrative templates under the Computers or User object in the Group Policy Object Editor.

☑ Templates allow enhanced administrative control that is not allowed in the standard installation.

☑ Along with enabling and disabling features, the template allows further configuration for users, including specifying transport methods and internal and external SIP domains.

Frequently Asked Questions

Q: Can Enterprise Voice integrate with all PSTN/PBX phone systems?

A: Yes. Several systems are directly supported by OCS. Those that do not support OCS directly can be configured to work with a mediation server and a PSTN/SIP gateway device. More information on mediation servers is available in Chapter 6.

Q: Where can I get details regarding why a user fails to be enabled in MOC?

A: You can get this information from the **Operations success/failure section** of the **Enable User Wizard**. You can export this information to an XML file which will provide details about the failure.

Q: Can I configure my MOC client's audio and video devices manually?

A: Yes, although MOC installs and configures these automatically. Under the Tools menu item is the option to adjust and change audio and video settings for individual clients. Alternatively, you can disable them altogether.

Q: After configuring an OU, a user is added and configured individually. Which setting will take priority?

A: As in Windows Server, the OU setting will take priority over the individual settings and the global properties settings will take priority over OU or group settings, unless the global properties are set to enforce the user settings.

Q: Can I dial phone numbers of people not in my contact list?

A: Yes. You can directly enter a phone number in the **Search box** and press **Enter** or **right-click** and choose **Call**.

Q: Can I create my own groups in MOC?

A: Yes. Go to **Menu | Tools** and choose **Create groups**.

Q: Are these groups viewable when MOC is sorted by access level group?

A: No. Access level groups are predefined and cannot be viewed; however, contacts from the user-created group will be viewed in an access level group.

Q: What does it mean to tag a contact for status change alerts?

A: This option exists to alert you when a contact that has presence set to Busy, Be Right Back, Do Not Disturb, or Away returns to an available state.

Q: Can Communicator be configured to make a user appear to be offline rather than busy or away?

A: Yes. You can do this through the Administrative template. It appears as an option for users if this administrative policy is enabled.

Chapter 5

Configuring the Edge Server

Solutions in this chapter:

- Installing the Edge Server
- Working with Certificates
- Dealing with Security Issues
- Testing the Edge Server

☑ Summary

☑ Solutions Fast Track

☑ Frequently Asked Questions

Introduction

The Edge Server seems to be one of the least understood Office Communications Server (OCS) components, and one that causes the most confusion. The Edge Server installation is straightforward; the wizard makes things easy. Most of the confusion comes from not understanding the underlying network requirements, having problems with certificates, or improper security configuration. In the following sections, I will clear up some of the mystery by walking you through an Edge Server deployment, step by step. To start, I'll give you some background on the Edge Server.

The Edge Server connects your OCS deployment to the outside world. There are four main reasons for you to deploy the Edge Server. You need the Edge Server if your organization requires:

- Users to access OCS from outside the firewall without a virtual private network (VPN) connection

- Users to send and receive instant messages (IMs) with public IM providers (MSN, Yahoo!, or AOL)

- External parties to participate in your OCS-hosted Live Meetings

- The ability to federate with other organizations that are using OCS or Live Communications Server (LCS)

To accomplish this functionality, the Edge Server has main three services (also called roles): the Access Edge, A/V Edge, and Web Conferencing Edge. The Access Edge service is responsible for external user authentication allowing home or mobile users to connect. The A/V Edge service gives remote users the ability to utilize OCS audio and video capabilities. And the Web Conferencing Edge service allows external users to connect to the Live Meeting service hosted by OCS.

You can choose to enable all of this functionality, or just a subset; it's not an "all or nothing" proposition. For example, if you want your users to be able to connect to OCS from home but not to use voice or video, you would simply not activate the A/V Edge service on your Edge Server. The Edge Server is flexible, and you can tailor it to meet your needs.

Installing the Edge Server

In this section, we will discuss how to install all three services on a single server—the "consolidated" approach. If you are looking for maximum scalability, you can also install each service separately on three different servers. Most of the concepts in the consolidated approach apply to the distributed approach as well.

Before I move on to the actual installation, it is worth spending some time planning for the Edge Server. As I mentioned in the introduction, the installation is easy; it's the planning and understanding that take time and attention.

Planning Edge Server Hardware

I recommend using a dedicated server for the Edge Server—don't try to put it on an existing machine that is already running applications in your perimeter network. Even though this is technically possible, you will save yourself hours of troubleshooting by giving the Edge Server its own server with dedicated hardware. It's also worth noting that Microsoft doesn't recommend or support the Edge Server on a virtual server. One of the main reasons is performance: If you are using your Edge Server as an A/V Edge service, it will be handling voice and video streams, and virtual servers are notoriously bad at handling real-time communications such as these. Another reason to avoid virtualization is the complexity of the network requirements, which I will address in the next section.

Planning for Network Interface Cards

To configure your consolidated Edge Server with all three services, you will need at least four network interface cards (NICs) in your server: one for each of the three services, and a fourth "internal" interface for communications with the OCS front-end. Although it is possible to use fewer than four NICs, I have found that configuration is much simpler when you allocate a separate NIC to each function. I'll explain why it's a bad idea to try to assign multiple Internet Protocol (IP) addresses to the same NIC later in this section.

Planning DNS and IP Addressing

Planning for domain name system (DNS) and IP addresses ahead of time will save you major headaches. Because the Edge Server requires so many different addresses and fully qualified domain names (FQDNs), you will find yourself forgetting which address does what.

Creating DNS Entries

Each of the three services in the Edge Server needs an FQDN, such as *sip.contoso.com* for the Access Edge service, *conference.contoso.com* for the Web Conferencing Edge service, and *av.contoso.com* for the A/V Edge service. These are the names that external clients and servers use to reach each service. Once you decide on FQDNs for your three services, create the corresponding "A records" in your external DNS server.

TIP

When deciding on a name for the FQDN for each service, try to use something that describes the service rather than the actual server name. This makes the Edge services more "portable" to a new server when you need to upgrade hardware or move an Edge service to its own server. By choosing a name such as *sip.company.com* rather than *server01.company.com* for the Access Edge service, you will be making it much easier on yourself in the future.

If you want your external clients to be able to automatically connect to your Edge Server without manually specifying a server name, you need to create an external DNS SRV record. The SRV record that the OCS clients look for is *_sip._tls.contoso.com* pointing to *sip.contoso. com* on port 443. If you are using a Windows DNS server to manage your external DNS, the entry would look like the screenshot in Figure 5.1.

Figure 5.1 External DNS Entry for Auto-Configuration

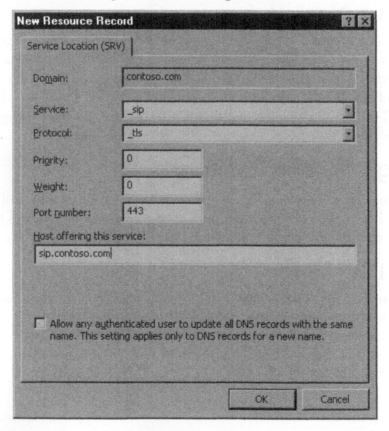

If you are planning to federate with other companies, you may want to consider an SRV record that enables "enhanced" federation. This record will automatically direct federated partners to your Edge Server without them having to know the name of your Edge Server. The record for enhanced federation would be *_sipfederationtls._tcp.contoso.com* pointing to *sip contoso.com* on port 5061.

You will create only one internal DNS record for the Edge Server: the record for the internal interface. This should be a record with the FQDN in your internal DNS namespace, such as *edge01.company.local*, and it should resolve to an internal, private IP address. Even though the Edge Server will *not* be installed in your domain, it does require a DNS record, as shown in Figure 5.2.

Figure 5.2 Internal DNS Record for the Edge Server

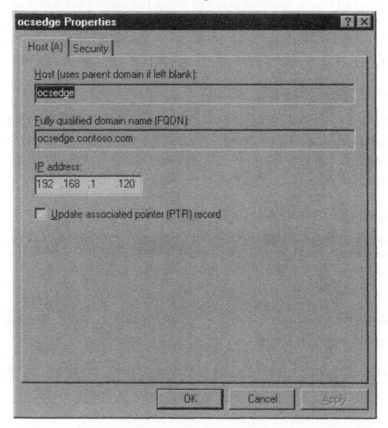

Obtaining Public IP Addresses

Each of your three FQDNs needs a publicly routable IP address, because external users will be accessing all three external services: Access Edge, A/V Edge, and Web Conferencing Edge. Your Internet service provider (ISP) assigns these publicly routable IP addresses. In most networks, the public IP addresses typically will terminate on your firewall.

Some people have complained that the Edge Server requires too many public IP addresses, too many FQDNs, and consequently, too many Secure Sockets Layer (SSL) certificates. You could use just one FQDN and public IP address for all three Edge services, but I don't recommend this unless you really have a good grasp of the Transmission Control Protocol/ Internet Protocol (TCP/IP), OCS, certificates, and firewalls. Departing from the default ports requires you to change these port numbers in several locations, making your deployment more complex than it needs to be. It becomes difficult to troubleshoot when you aren't sure which ports are supposed to be in use and which are not.

Why all the fuss? Under normal circumstances, using a single IP address would create TCP port conflicts. All three of the Edge services use TCP port 443; if you are using only on IP address, you can't have multiple services using the same port. OCS does allow you to specify different ports for different services, but this will lead you astray from most of the published OCS documentation. I have heard of people getting this to work successfully, but it is certainly not the most straightforward and easily supported method.

Assigning IP Addresses

Our OCS deployment will have three different networks. The Edge Server will touch each one.

As noted earlier, an Edge Server with all three roles installed needs four NICs. Each NIC should have a single IP address bound to it. Your Edge Server Network Connections window should look something like the screen shown in Figure 5.3.

Figure 5.3 Network Connections on the Edge

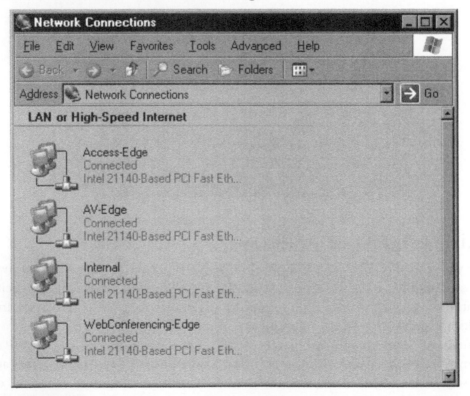

I recommend renaming all your connections the way I have in Figure 5.4. You will be working with the network connections quite a bit, and it will help to have more descriptive names than the default "LAN Connection 1" and so forth.

> **WARNING**
>
> Do not try to assign multiple IP addresses to the same NIC; this can have strange and unpredictable results on the Edge Server. Although many other applications seem to have no trouble using several IP addresses bound to the same NIC, many times I have seen OCS in general and the Edge Server in particular not functioning reliably with this configuration.
>
> For example, if you assign the internal and external IP addresses to the same NIC, the Edge Server will not allow any external OCS clients to log in. Save yourself the time and effort by sticking to the Microsoft-recommended (and supported!) method of assigning only one IP address to each NIC.

I will explain this further in the "Dealing with Security Issues" section later in this chapter, but for now it's important to know that the A/V Edge service must have a public IP address assigned to it.

Some people will want to put the "internal" interface in the DMZ segment; others will be fine with having it connect directly to the internal network. In our setup, I have the Access Edge and Web Conferencing NICs in the DMZ, with the Internal NIC connected directly to the internal network segment.

When you assign IP addresses, you are also prompted to enter a default gateway for each IP address. On the Edge Server, enter a default gateway only on your A/V Edge service. For the rest of your addresses, do not add a default gateway; this will cause the Windows routing table to behave erratically and you will definitely have problems getting the Edge Server to work.

To be able to route to the rest of your segments, you will need to create static routes on the Edge Server.

Creating Static Routes on the Edge Server

Because the Edge Server will use addresses on three networks but will have only one default gateway, you will need to configure a couple of static routes on your Edge Server for it to be able to reach all the necessary networks.

As I said in the prior section, the A/V Edge will have a default gateway, so it's the other two networks that need the static routes. In our scenario, these networks are in the 192.168.1.0 and 172.16.1.0 range. To configure static routes to these networks follow these steps:

1. Open a command prompt on your Edge Server by selecting **Start | Run** and typing **cmd**.

2. Once the command window opens, type the following command:

```
C:\route add -p 192.168.0.0 MASK 255.255.0.0 192.168.1.1
C:\route add -p 172.16.0.0 MASK 255.255.0.0 172.16.1.1
```

3. Once the routes are added, type the following command:

```
C:\route print
```

> You will see that the routes we have added appear at the bottom of the route table. They show up as persistent routes (that's what the *-p* switch in the command does) because they will remain even after a server reboot.

4. Once you add the static routes, reboot the server for the changes to take effect. When the server comes back, be sure you can connect to servers on all three networks.

Installing the Software

Now that we've taken great pains to ensure that our underlying networking components are set up correctly, we can move to the installation of the Edge Server. Note that you should install the Edge only after you have deployed your OCS front-end and back-end servers internally. (The only exception to this rule is if you happen to be migrating from LCS to OCS. In that case, the Edge Server is typically deployed first.)

Install the Edge Server on a Windows Server 2003 or Windows Server 2003 R2 platform. The machine on which you install the Edge Server should not be a member of the domain, but rather a stand-alone workgroup.

TIP

You can install OCS Edge into a domain, but it just should not be the same domain where the rest of your OCS servers exist. If you make the mistake of installing the Edge Server into your primary domain, be sure to deactivate the server before removing or rebuilding it. You can deactivate the server by right-clicking on it in the OCS admin interface and selecting **Deactivate**. This removes all the Active Directory objects and configurations associated with the server.

Installing Edge Server Program Files

You can install the Edge Server using either the OCS Enterprise Edition or the OCS Standard Edition server. In either case, you will need to copy the OCS installation files to the Edge and run setup.exe.

The Deployment Wizard will prompt you to install the Microsoft Visual C++ 2005 SP1 Redistributable. Click **Yes** to install the file and proceed. You will also be prompted to install the Microsoft .NET Framework 2.0. Click **Yes** to install the .NET Framework.

Once these installations complete, the OCS Wizard will begin. Click on **Deploy Other Server Roles**. This will bring up the screen with options for installing other server roles besides the front-end server. Click **Deploy Edge Server**. This starts the Edge Server deployment process.

In the **Step 1: Install Files for Edge Server** section, click **Install** (see Figure 5.4).

Figure 5.4 Initial OCS Deployment Screen

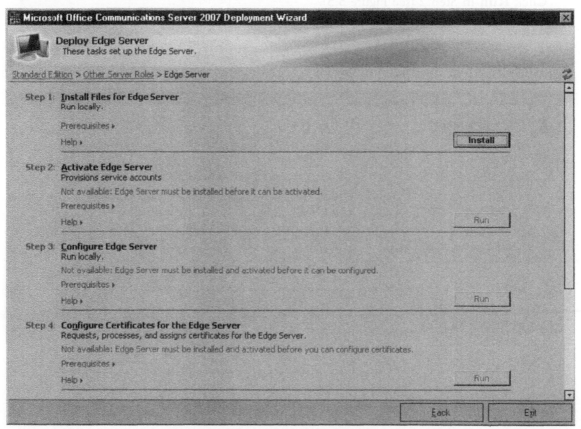

After starting the installation, a Welcome screen greets you. Click **Next** to proceed. The wizard prompts you to accept the license agreement. Click **Next** once you've read the agreement and accept the terms.

The next screen asks you for your username and organization. Fill these out as appropriate and click **Next**.

The default directory for OCS Edge Server files is C:\Program Files\Microsoft Office Communications Server 2007\Server\—under most circumstances, you won't need to change this. Click **Next** to install the Edge Server program files. As the wizard executes, you will notice that this step also creates a number of security groups and sets all relevant permissions needed by the Edge Server. Click **Close** to finish.

Activating the Edge Server

You are now ready to activate the Edge Server. The Activation step determines which Edge Server roles you will deploy on this server. As I mentioned at the beginning of the chapter, you will be installing all the roles on this server; this is known as the "consolidated" topology.

Click **Run** in Step 2 (see Figure 5.5).

Figure 5.5 Activating the Edge Server

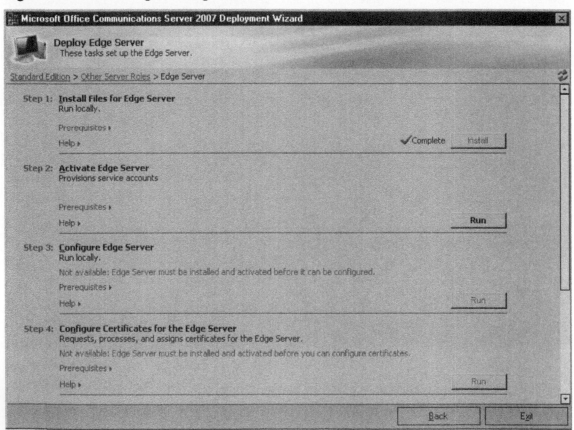

A Welcome screen greets you; click **Next** to proceed (see Figure 5.6).

Figure 5.6 Enabling the Different Edge Roles

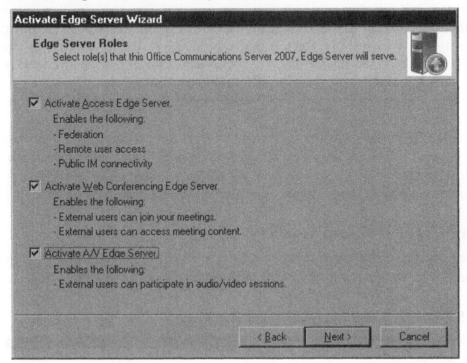

Check all the roles that you want to activate on this machine, then click **Next**.

> **NOTE**
>
> If you are planning to use separate servers for each Edge role, select only one role at this point. You can always rerun this wizard at a later date to add additional roles.

The next screen prompts you for a service account and password. Remember, this machine is not part of your domain, so you will most likely need to create a new account here. The default name for the account is RTCProxyService. I recommend keeping this name. Enter a password for this account and click **Next**.

WARNING

The OCS Installation Wizard will fail to install the Edge Server properly (or any of the roles, for that matter) if you choose a password with any quotation marks (" ", ' ') or spaces. For some reason, the wizard does not handle this and the services will not start. If you would like to use one of these characters, you can always go back after the installation and change the password through the Users and Groups administrative snap-in.

The wizard then gives you an opportunity to review the settings you have chosen. Click **Next** to proceed. Once the activation completes, the wizard will ask whether you would like to view the log file. Be sure to check the log file if the wizard completes with any warnings or failures. Click **Finish** to return to the main OCS installation page.

Configuring the Edge Server

Once the Edge Server activation completes, you are ready to configure all the necessary components. To continue with the process, click **Run** in Step 3 (see Figure 5.7).

Figure 5.7 Running the Edge Configuration Wizard

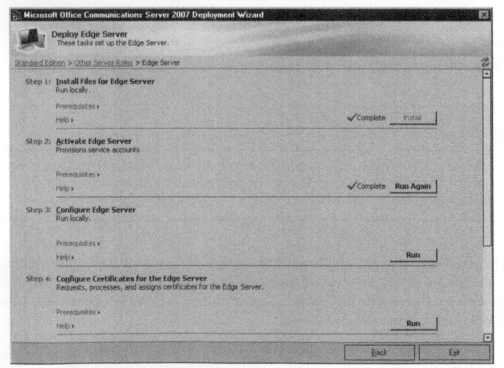

The Welcome Wizard greets you at the first screen. Click **Next** to continue.

The next screen asks you whether you are importing Edge Server settings from a previous install; assuming this is your first Edge Server, do not check the box. Click **Next** to continue.

You now must configure the internal interface of the Edge Server.

In the first drop-down menu, select the IP address of your Edge Server that sits in your internal network. You will see that the wizard recognizes all IP addresses assigned to your server. In this example, the 192.168.1.120 address is in my internal network (see Figure 5.8).

Figure 5.8 Configuring the Internal Interface

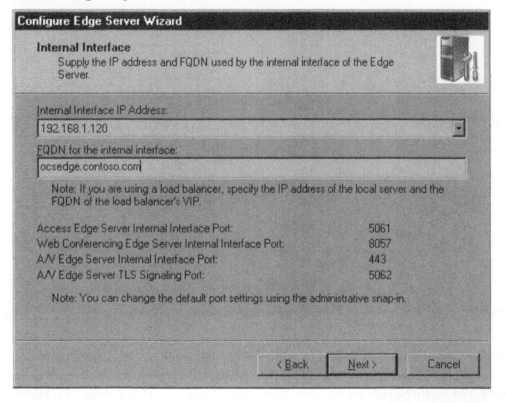

Here you also need to enter the internal FQDN of your Edge Server. Because I am using *contoso.com* for my internal and external domain names, I've entered **ocsedge.contoso.com**. That is the actual server name (*ocsedge*) plus my internal domain name. If you are using something such as *contoso.internal* or *contoso.local* for your internal domain, you must use that suffix here. Notice that the wizard shows you all the ports that this IP address will use and the different functions for each port. Click **Next** to continue.

The next page contains the external interface configuration.

The Access Edge and the Web Conferencing NICs will sit in my DMZ network; here I've assigned them 172.16.1.*x* addresses (see Figure 5.9). The A/V Edge, however, sits in my public segment and therefore has a public IP address. I explain the reasons for this later in the chapter, in the section "Using Network Address Translation (NAT)."

Figure 5.9 Configuring the External Interfaces

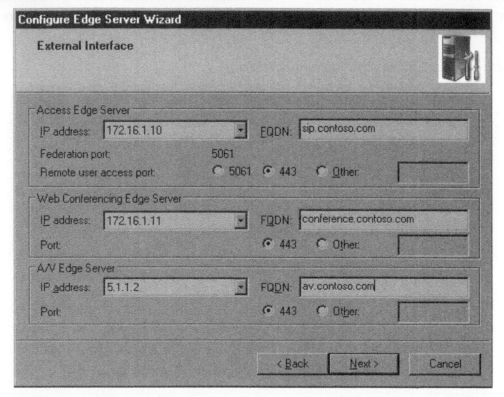

You are also assigning the external FQDNs for each service here. These names must have corresponding DNS entries on a public DNS server and be reachable from outside your network. For further detail on this, see the section "Creating DNS Entries," earlier in this chapter. Click **Next** to continue.

Now you need to enable features on your Edge Server.

Checking the first box, **Allow remote user to access your network**, enables users to connect their OCS clients from home, from hotels, or from any other outside location without requiring a VPN connection.

If you check the second box, **Allow anonymous user to join meetings**, people outside your organization (i.e., any non-employee without an Active Directory account) will be able to join Live Meetings hosted by your OCS server (see Figure 5.10).

Figure 5.10 Enabling Features

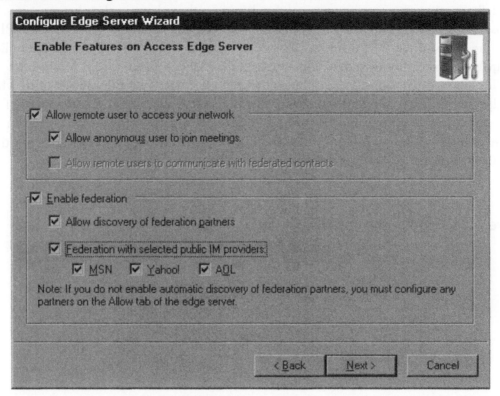

> **NOTE**
>
> By selecting this checkbox, you are not enabling all Live Meetings to be accessible to anonymous participants; you are really only saying that you want users to be able to invite anonymous users to *some* meetings. You can enable or disable this feature on a per-user or per-meeting basis.

Check the box labeled **Enable federation** to allow your users to communicate with other organizations that run LCS and OCS. Federation normally requires you to define explicitly the partners with whom you would like to federate in a separate list.

However, you also have a second method to enable federation: "open" federation. When you select the checkbox that says **Allow discovery of federation partners**, this allows companies to use your DNS record to automatically locate your Access Edge Server and connect to you without needing to explicitly define them as a federated partner. This was known as unrestricted enhanced federation in LCS 2005 SP1. Allowing automatic discovery potentially raises some security concerns. I will address those later in the chapter.

Lastly, this screen gives you the opportunity to enable Public IM Connectivity (PIC). Check the boxes of the IM providers with whom you plan to federate. You will need to license this capability separately by purchasing an external connector license from Microsoft.

Click **Next** to continue. Enter the name of the OCS Standard Edition server to which the Edge will be connecting. If you are using Enterprise Edition, enter the name of the OCS pool rather than the name of a front-end server. If you are using an OCS director, enter its name here. Note that you need the entire FQDN (*OCSFE02.contoso.com*), not just the NetBIOS name (*OCSFE02*) of the server (see Figure 5.11).

Figure 5.11 Configuring the Next Hop

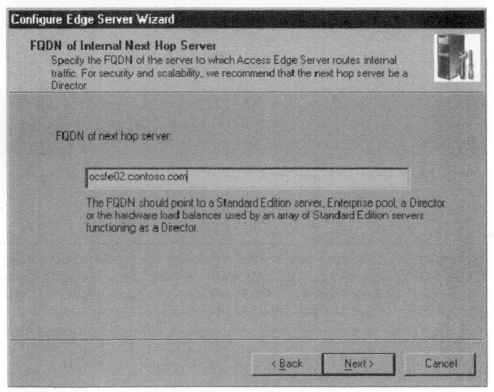

Click **Next** to continue.

Enter the name of the Session Initiation Protocol (SIP) domain that your Edge Server will be using (see Figure 5.12). If the Edge is routing SIP requests for more than one domain, enter the additional domains here.

Figure 5.12 Adding SIP Domains

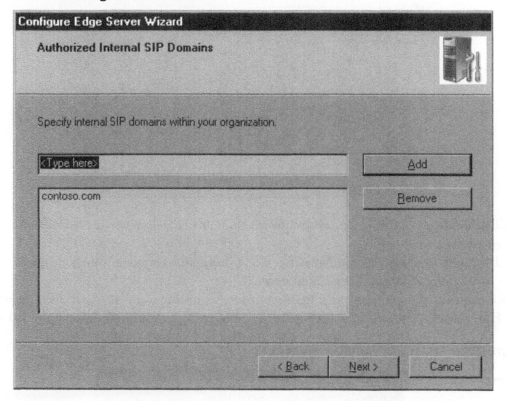

Click **Next** to continue.

Enter the FQDNs of the servers authorized to connect to the Edge Server (see Figure 5.13). This includes all Standard Edition servers and Enterprise Edition front-end pools. If you are migrating from LCS 2005, enter the name of the legacy LCS pool.

Figure 5.13 Adding Authorized Internal Servers

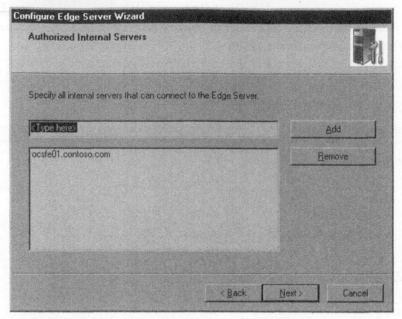

Click **Next** to continue. The wizard gives you a chance to review the settings in the configuration.

Click **Next** to apply the configuration. The wizard will complete shortly; if there are any errors or warnings, you will be notified here.

You may want to export your Edge Server settings in the event that you need to rebuild your Edge Server. To do so, click **Export** now. Otherwise, click **Finish** (see Figure 5.14).

Figure 5.14 Finishing the Configuration

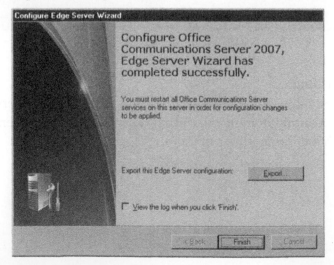

Configuring the Front-End Server for Communication with the Edge

The main OCS wizard appears again. The next step in the wizard is to work with certificates. But before you do this, leave the Edge Server for the moment. This is a good time to configure the front-end server to work with the Edge. Once we complete that, you can return to the Edge Server configuration.

Browse to your OCS 2007 installation directory and rerun setup.exe on your front-end server. This will launch the OCS Installation Wizard. Click on **Deploy Standard Edition Server**. If you are using Enterprise Edition, choose the corresponding option. You will then see the wizard with the steps you completed when you originally installed the front-end server (see Figure 5.15).

Figure 5.15 Configuring the Front-End Server with the OCS Deployment Wizard

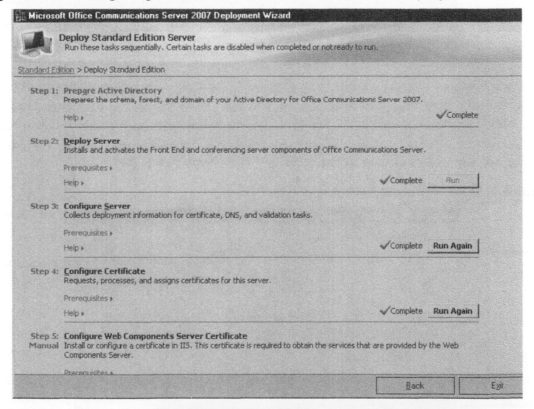

Now you need to reconfigure the front-end server. Click **Run Again** in Step 3. This launches the Front End Configuration Wizard.

Click **Next** at the Welcome screen. Then choose the front-end server or pool that you want to configure for external connectivity (see Figure 5.16).

Figure 5.16 Selecting a Pool to Configure

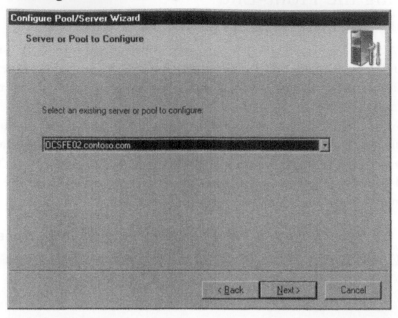

Click **Next** to continue. Leave the existing SIP domains in the next screen and click **Next**. In the Client Logon Settings screen, you can leave the options unchanged and click **Next**. The same goes for the SIP Domains for Automatic Logon screen. Click **Next**.

The wizard prompts you to configure external access. Select the radio button that says **Configure for external user access now** and click **Next** (see Figure 5.17).

Figure 5.17 Configuring External User Access

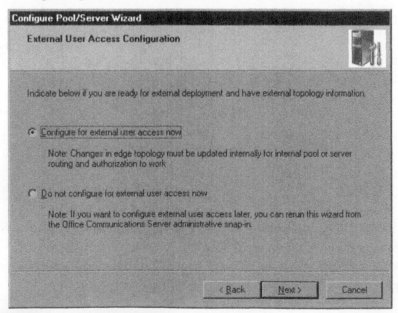

Next, select the method you would like to use to route incoming traffic from the Edge Server. If you have an OCS director role installed, choose that method. If you do not have a director installed, choose **Route directly to and from internal pools and servers** (see Figure 5.18).

Figure 5.18 Configuring SIP Routing

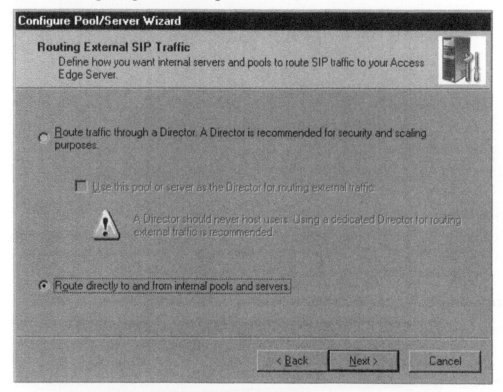

Click **Next** to continue.

Now you need to enter the name of the Edge Server as a trusted server. You need to enter only one name here, because our Edge Server is both an Access Edge and a Web Conferencing Edge. If we had broken the Edge into multiple servers, each with a different role, you would enter both server names here. Notice that I have entered the *internal* interface name here, even though the wizard is asking for Access Edge and Web Conferencing Edge FQDNs (see Figure 5.19). Do not enter the external names here; enter only the internal FQDN.

Figure 5.19 Adding the Edge to the Front-End Server

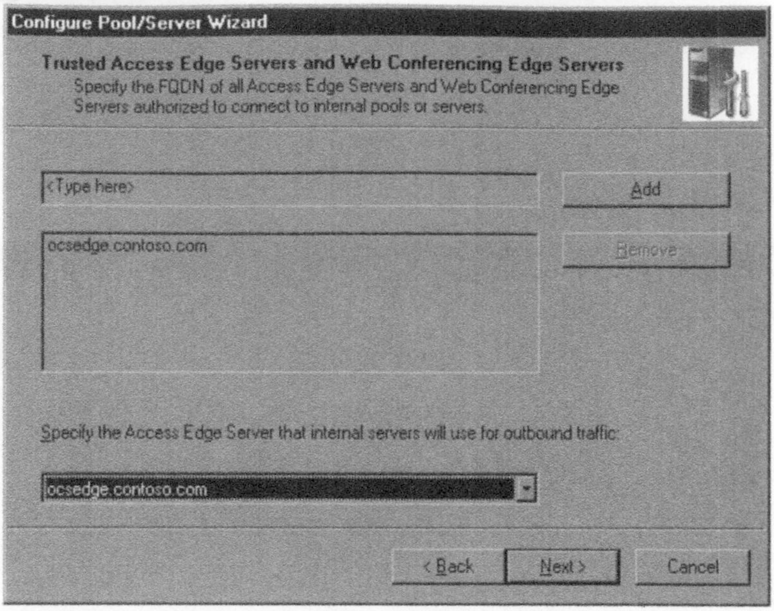

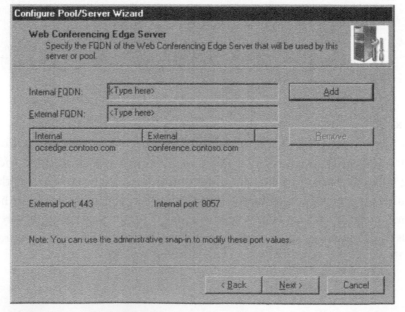

Click **Next** to continue.

Configure the internal and external names of your Web Conferencing Edge server. For the internal FQDN, enter the internal name of the Edge Server: **ocsedge.contoso.com**. Externally, users will connect to *conference.contoso.com* (see Figure 5.20).

Figure 5.20 Adding the Web Conferencing Servers to the Edge

Click **Next** to continue.

At the next screen, you need to enter the name and port of your A/V Edge server (see Figure 5.21).

Figure 5.21 Adding the A/V Edge Server

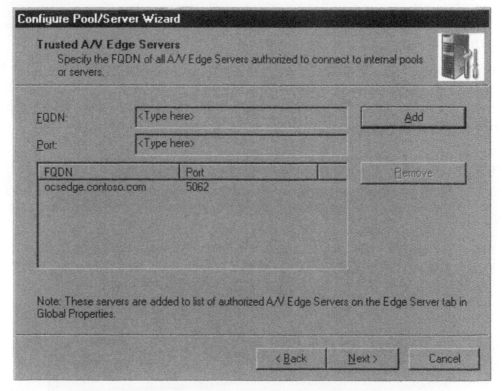

Unlike the previous screen, this is asking only for the internal name of the Edge Server hosting the A/V Edge service. Enter the FQDN: **OCSEDGE.contoso.com**. The A/V Edge service listens on port 5062 by default.

WARNING

Do not enter the A/V Edge's external name here; the wizard is only looking for the internal FQDN of the Edge Server.

You can always change this value at a later date by viewing the Global Properties page in the OCS Administrative Console. Click **Next** to continue.

If you specified multiple A/V Edge servers here, the next screen will ask you for one server. Because we have only the one A/V Edge server, you can accept the default and click **Next**.

The wizard now gives you a chance to review your settings. Click **Next** to apply the settings. The wizard should complete successfully. Check the log file for details if you received any warnings or failures.

Stop and start the Front-End Services for these changes to take effect.

Finishing the Front-End Configuration

The front-end server has a few other settings that you need to configure for full Edge Server functionality. The first is to enable users to be able to invite external anonymous participants to meetings. Go to the OCS Administrative Console and right-click on the **forest**. Choose **Properties | Global Properties**. Click on the **Meetings tab** (see Figure 5.22).

Figure 5.22 Allowing Anonymous Users to Join Live Meetings

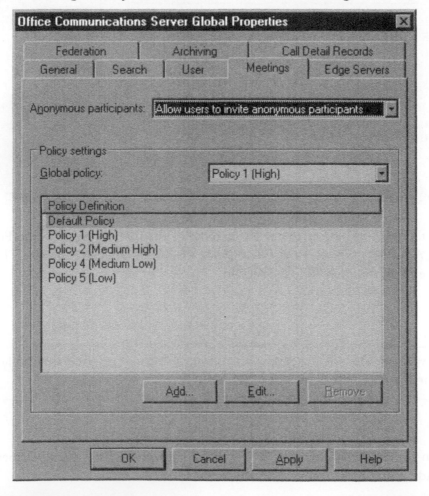

The drop-down menu at the top of the page gives you three options:

- Allow users to invite anonymous participants.

- Disallow users to invite anonymous participants.

- Enforce per user.

Select **Allow users to invite anonymous participants**. Click **OK**.

Next, you need to enable users to utilize the Edge services. Open a user in the OCS Administrator Console. In the section called **Additional Options** click **Configure**.

Check **Enable federation**, **Enable remote user access**, and **Enable public IM connectivity** to enable these features for a user (see Figure 5.23). You can choose to enable or not enable any combination of these features for each user. Click **OK**. Users will need to log out and log back in for these settings to take effect.

Figure 5.23 Enabling User Features

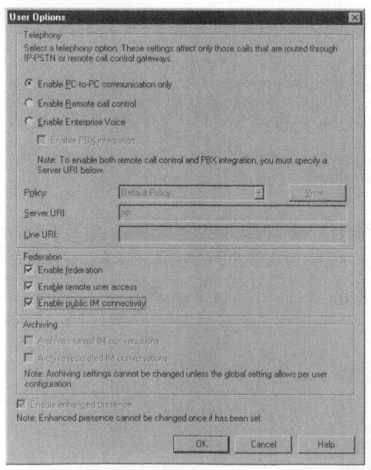

Finishing the Edge Deployment

At this point, we have configured all the features and functions in both the Edge Server and the front-end server. The only task remaining is to configure certificates on the Edge Server.

Working with Certificates

As with the other OCS roles, the Edge Server requires SSL certificates for all communications. This chapter assumes that you have installed and configured an Enterprise Root certificate authority (CA) in your Active Directory domain as part of your front-end server deployment. All OCS internal server-to-server communications are encrypted using SSL certificates issued by your internal Enterprise Root CA.

However, unlike the other OCS roles, the Edge also requires a few certificates issued by public CAs. Public certificates issued by trusted CAs are generally required for any secure communication with external users. And because the Edge Server is responsible for all communication with external users and public IM providers, the Edge Server therefore requires public certificates. If you wanted to use an internal CA for this, everyone connecting to your OCS server would need to add the CA's root certificate to their local machines' list of trusted roots. You may be able to get your users to do this, but it's unlikely that anyone outside your organization will want to just join a Live Meeting or federate. Not using a public CA for the Access Edge cert would also prevent you from connecting to any of the public IM providers.

You can obtain public certificates from many different vendors. VeriSign and Entrust are among the most common.

Configuring the Internal Interface Certificate

To configure Edge Server certificates for the first time we must go back to the Edge Server installation wizard.

Click **Run** in Step 4 to proceed with the certificate configuration (see Figure 5.24).

Figure 5.24 Configuring Certificates with the OCS Deployment Wizard

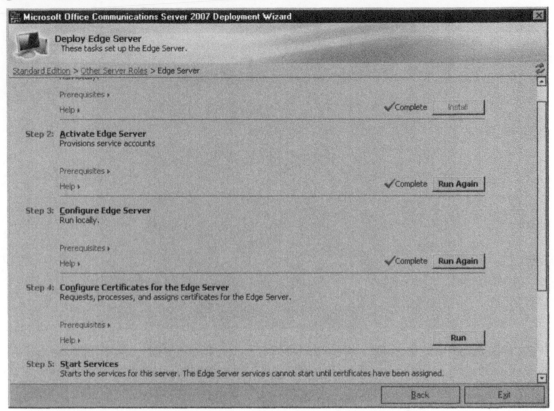

Requesting the Certificate

The Certificate Wizard will greet you with a Welcome screen; click **Next** to continue. At the first screen, select **Create a new certificate** and click **Next**.

The wizard prompts you to select the component to which you will be assigning a certificate. Choose **Edge Server Private Interface**. You can process only one certificate at a time, so we will start with the internal interface first. Click **Next** (see Figure 5.25).

Figure 5.25 Configuring the Certificate for the Internal Interface

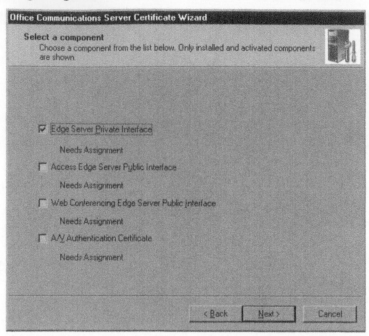

Choose **Send the request immediately to an online certification authority**; we will be sending the request to our Enterprise CA. Click **Next** to continue (see Figure 5.26).

Figure 5.26 Sending the Certificate Request

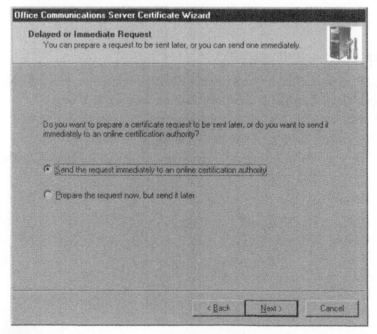

Give the certificate a name and mark it as exportable. Click **Next** to continue. When prompted, enter your relevant organization, department, and geographic information. Click **Next** to continue. You now need to enter the subject name (see Figure 5.27).

Figure 5.27 Adding the Subject Name to the Certificate

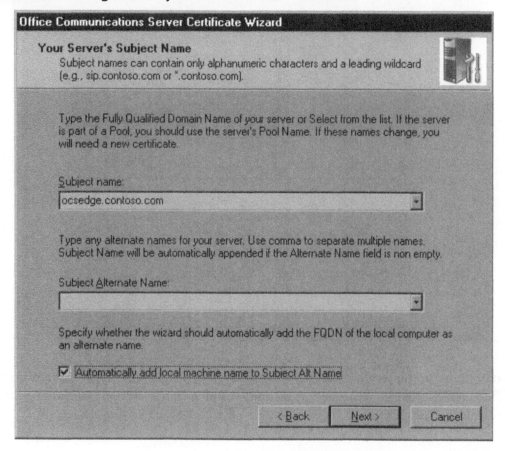

Enter the full *internal* FQDN of your Edge Server. This name needs to match what you entered during the Edge Server setup for the internal interface name. You can also check the box for **Automatically add local machine name to Subject Alt Name**. Click **Next**.

Enter the relevant geographic information about your organization and click **Next**.

You now are prompted for the name of the CA to which you are sending the request. We are using the CA that I've installed on my OCS front-end server. In production environments, the CA would never be installed on an OCS server. Enter your CA's information and click **Next** (see Figure 5.28).

Figure 5.28 Sending the Request to Your CA

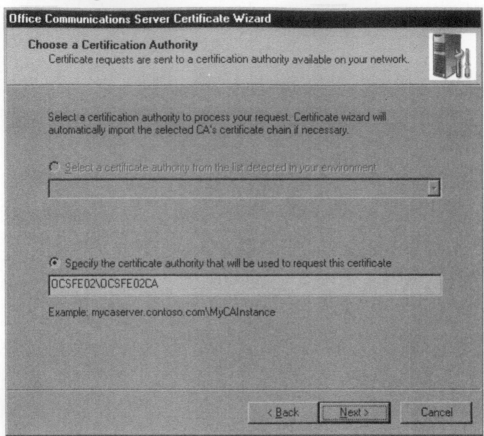

You will be prompted for credentials to log in to your CA server. Enter them in the dialog box. Click **Next** to proceed. The wizard will then finish and let you know whether your request was successful.

TIP

If your request was not successful, make sure you spelled the name of your CA server correctly and that you have the right name for the CA service on your server. Also check to make sure you can ping the CA server from the Edge Server. If not, check your firewall to make sure communication between the Edge and CA server is open.

If all else fails, you can run through the wizard again, this time preparing your certificate as a text file and copying it over to the CA server manually.

Assigning the Internal Certificate

Your CA should automatically issue the certificate based on the request you sent it. If not, you need to go to the CA and manually issue the certificate from the Pending Certificates container.

Once the CA issues the certificate, you need to assign the certificate. To do this, click **Run** in Step 4 of the Edge Server installation wizard (Configure Certificates for the Edge Server). This time, choose **Assign existing certificate** in the Certificate Wizard. Click **Next** to view a list of the available certificates.

Choose the certificate that was just issued by the CA and click **Next** (see Figure 5.29).

Figure 5.29 Viewing the Certificate

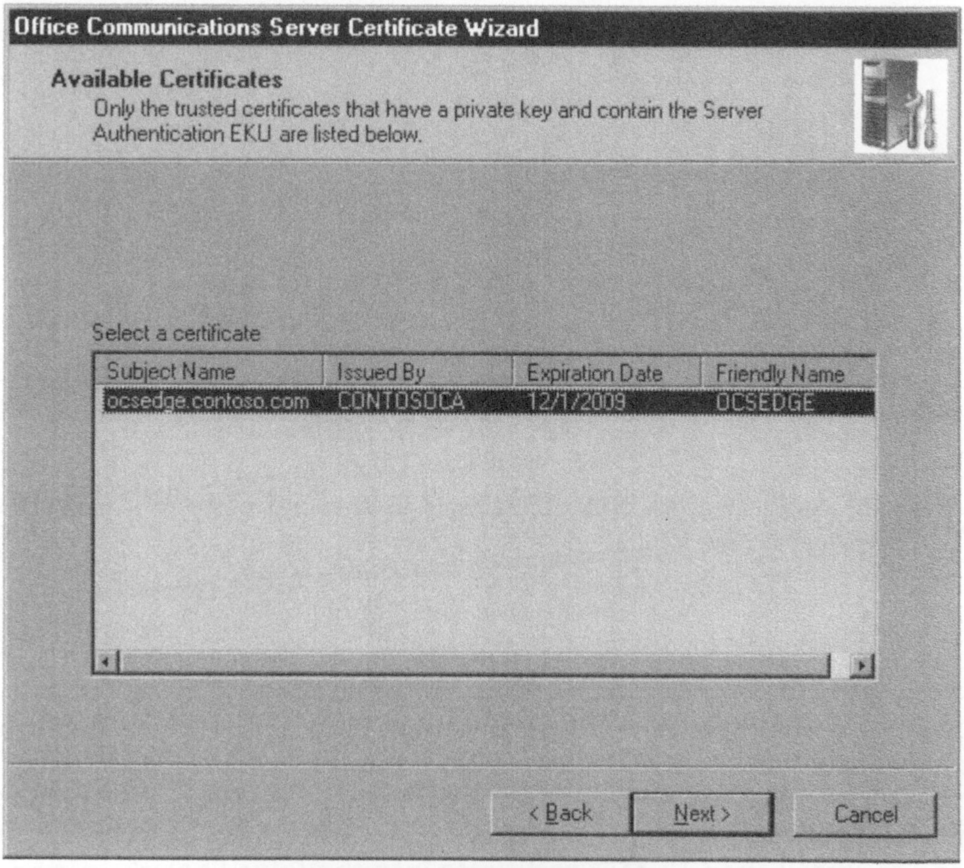

Now check the box that says **Edge Server Private Interface** and click **Next** (see Figure 5.30).

Figure 5.30 Assigning the Certificate

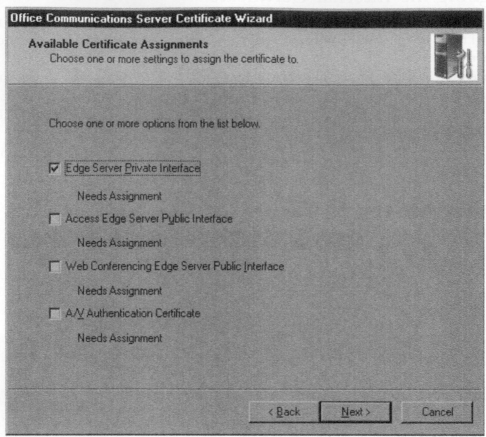

To assign the certificate, click **Next**. The wizard finishes and warns you of any problems.

TIP

If you were unable to send the certificate request to the CA automatically, you may also need to add the CA's root certificate to your Edge Server. Because the Edge Server is not a member of the domain, the certificate issued by the internal CA may not be trusted by default. To remedy the problem, we need to install the CA's root certificate into the Edge Server's trusted root container.

This problem won't occur if you were able to send the certificate request to the CA automatically.

Requesting and Assigning the External Certificates

The external certificate process is the same as the internal process we just used for the internal certificate.

Run through the process three more times: once each for the Access Edge, A/V Edge, and Web Conferencing Edge. The main difference with the public certificates is that you won't be sending your certificate requests to your internal CA, you'll be sending them to a public CA. Most public CAs ask that you send the request in a text file. The CA will then process the text file and send you a secure certificate in return. (Each vendor handles the request and processing differently; you will need to follow the instructions on the CA vendor's Web site.)

Install the public certificates into your Edge Server's certificate store using the MMC Certificates snap-in. Once you install the certificates, run through the Edge Server Certificate Wizard to assign them. Note that you can assign only one certificate at a time.

Dealing with Security Issues

Because the Edge interacts with the outside world, you need to pay special attention to security. In this section, we'll cover some of the most important aspects of a secure Edge deployment.

Firewall Setup

The Edge Server communicates extensively with the OCS front-end server components as well as with the outside world; most of this communication will traverse your firewall. Correctly configuring your firewall will ensure that your OCS deployment is both secure and functional.

In the simplest configuration, your network will have a single perimeter firewall that terminates your Internet connections. You could deploy multiple firewalls (one on each side of your OCS Edge), but I will concentrate on a single-firewall configuration here.

External Connectivity

You need to open TCP port 443 for each one of your Edge roles, along with port 5061 for federation and public IM connectivity.

The Edge Server also requires you to open a large range of User Datagram Protocol (UDP) ports for A/V connectivity: ports 50,000 through 59,999. This is quite a span and may cause some concern. However, OCS is not actively listening on these ports—in other words, they are not open all the time waiting for someone (an attacker or otherwise) to connect to them. A port is opened only when an external client has established an A/V session. When the session is finished, the port is closed and is no longer actively listening.

DMZ Connectivity

Your Access Edge service and your Web Conferencing Edge service sit in the DMZ segment. These services must be able to communicate with the outside world as well as with your internal network. Make sure your internal network is able to reach the internal interface of your Edge Server on all the required ports.

Using Network Address Translation (NAT)

DMZ segments are commonly assigned their own range of private IP addresses. The firewall then uses NAT to translate the public IP addresses to private ones. The Access Edge and Web Conferencing IP addresses can be configured using NAT in this fashion.

However, *the A/V Edge address cannot use NAT.* This means the IP address you assign to the Edge Server's NIC dedicated to the A/V service must be the same as the public IP address assigned to the external interface on your firewall.

NOTE

OCS *requires* a public IP address on the A/V Edge service and will not work properly without it. OCS uses Simple Traversal of UDP over NAT (STUN) to make the VPN-less connection, and STUN requires a public IP address for public-facing applications. This is called out in STUN RFC 3489, Section 6. Any application using STUN has the same requirements. For further information on STUN, view the entire STUN RFC at www.faqs.org/rfcs/rfc3489.html.

This often can cause security administrators to panic. But don't let them forget that having a public IP address does not mean the firewall isn't protecting the server. Most firewalls will support this kind of firewalling.

To do this securely you must configure your firewall to route requests "transparently" to the NIC dedicated to the A/V service. Different firewall vendors support transparent firewalling in different ways, so consult your vendor for details on how to configure transparent firewalling.

If your firewall doesn't support a transparent mode, you will need to find a different way to secure your server. Under no circumstances should you put your Edge Server's A/V NIC on your public Internet segment without protection; this would be a major security risk. Instead, you may want to consider some other form of protection, such as a software-based firewall.

It is critical that you use a publicly routable IP address for the A/V service; using a private address via NAT will cause unpredictable results with external users and voice/video calls as well as Live Meeting audio and video. I have tested a private IP address for the A/V service and encountered issues each time. In fact, I opened a support case with Microsoft Support and the first thing the engineer told me was that I needed to change the IP address to a public one. I protested to him that it shouldn't matter, but he correctly pointed out that the requirements are the requirements. I took his suggestion and within minutes of changing to a public IP, all of my A/V Edge problems disappeared.

Using ISA Server

OCS 2007 uses ISA to publish the address book to external users. The front-end server compiles an address book that contains a list of all the users in your organization. Each time users log in to their OCS clients, they receive a new copy of the address book from the server. The front-end server stores the master copy of the address book in a secure Web site hosted in Internet Information Server (IIS). The OCS clients retrieve copies by automatically connecting to this site using SSL.

For internal clients, the connections to the front-end server use the internal FQDN of the pool, such as *https://ocspool.company.internal*. And logically, it follows that the certificate that is bound to this site has the subject name *ocspool.company.internal*. In this way, clients make secure connections to retrieve the address book.

However, external users trying to download the address book will have trouble unless you are publishing the address book with ISA (or any other reverse-proxy server). As I mentioned earlier, the front-end server stores the master copy of the address book, and the front-end server, unlike the Edge Server, does not sit in the perimeter network. It should not be accessible to external users, and therefore, external users will not be able to retrieve the address book without going through ISA.

To avoid using ISA, you may be tempted to just open a port on your firewall to allow access into the front-end server. That is a bad idea for two reasons. First, it unnecessarily exposes your front-end server to the outside world and this poses a security risk. But also, and more important, this method won't work. The reason comes back to SSL and certificates: Because the directory where the address book is stored must use SSL, it must have a certificate bound to it. And because this directory must be accessible to internal as well as external users, it must have a certificate with the internal FQDN as the subject *and* the external FQDN as a subject alternate name. Unfortunately, subject alternate name certificates are not supported for this use: You must pick either the internal name or the external name.

This is where the ISA server comes in. The ISA server sits in your perimeter network and securely publishes your address book to the outside world. You can assign an external FQDN such as *addressbook.contoso.com* and have ISA publish your internal address book to the outside with the new name.

> **TIP**
>
> You set the URL that clients use to download the address book during the Standard Server configuration (or front-end pool, if you are using Enterprise Edition). Misleadingly, the wizard calls this the External Web Farm FQDN. This is really the external URL for the address book download as well as a few other components. Many people breeze right through this step without understanding exactly what it is. The unfortunate part is that once you've set this parameter in the wizard, you can't change it through any method on the OCS administrative console. You can't even change it by rerunning the setup! I recommend that you use the command-line utility lcscmd.exe for this purpose.

Testing the Edge Server

The best way to test the Access Edge Server is to log in to your OCS client from a machine outside your firewall and test as many features as possible. This section walks you through the way to test most aspects of the Edge Server.

Testing the Access Edge

Log in to the client and make sure all your contacts, including federated or public contacts, appear. If the client logs in successfully, the Access Edge Server is working properly. Send IMs to your contacts and make sure their presence appears correctly in your client. Test to see whether your public and federated contacts can send you IMs.

If you are unable to log in to the OCS server from outside the firewall, you most likely have a problem with either the Edge Server or the underlying network components. You should test the network components first before poking around with your Edge configuration.

The first thing you should do is make sure name resolution is working from the outside. Try to ping *sip.company.com* from a command prompt. Make sure it resolves to the right IP address. If the correct public IP address comes back, you know DNS is working. Oftentimes, firewall administrators will not allow ping or other ICMP traffic through, so your ping may fail even if the name resolved to the correct public IP address.

If you are using NAT on your firewall, make sure you have the correct NAT rule set up to translate from your public IP address to your private IP address. Also make sure the firewall is configured to allow port 443 traffic into your private IP address.

The way to verify that your server is online and listening for requests is to use the command-line utility telnet to connect to *sip.company.com* on port 443. The Edge Server is listening for client connections on port 443 and by using telnet, we can test to see whether any connections are allowed through the firewall to the Edge Server.

TIP

Windows Vista no longer enables the Telnet client by default. To enable the client, go to the Control Panel and click on **Programs and Features**. Click on the link for **Turn Windows Features On or Off**. Check the box next to **Telnet Client** and click **OK**.

A successful Telnet connection will show a blank screen with a blinking cursor. An unsuccessful Telnet connection will look like Figure 5.31.

Figure 5.31 Failed Telnet Connection

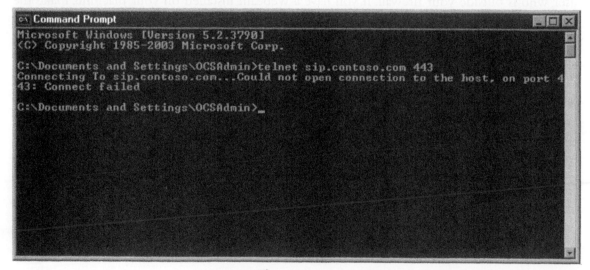

```
Microsoft Windows [Version 5.2.3790]
(C) Copyright 1985-2003 Microsoft Corp.

C:\Documents and Settings\OCSAdmin>telnet sip.contoso.com 443
Connecting To sip.contoso.com...Could not open connection to the host, on port 4
43: Connect failed

C:\Documents and Settings\OCSAdmin>_
```

However, if you are able to telnet to your Edge Server on port 443, it is likely that the Edge Server is unable to pass the authentication through to your front-end server or directors. Run the Edge Server Validation Wizard to make sure it makes all the proper connections back to the front-end server.

If the Validation Wizard comes back with no errors, run the Front End Server Validation Wizard to make sure it can connect to the Edge Server.

TIP

The command-line tool NBTSTAT is your friend. If you are having problems connecting, run *NBTSTAT –ab* from a command prompt on the Edge. Its output will tell you whether the server is listening on the correct ports.

If all else fails, don't forget to use the Windows event logs. The application log and the OCS log provide lots of good information about any errors that occur. Check both the Edge Server event logs as well as those on the front-end server.

Testing the A/V Service

To test the A/V service log in to a client from outside the firewall and make a communicator-to-communicator call to another user who is inside the firewall. Try making a call to another user who is outside your firewall. If you have a Webcam installed on your machine, make the same calls again, but this time use video. Ensure that the A/V conferencing service works by making a voice call to another user, then conferencing in a third party.

Testing the Web Conferencing Service

And finally, test the Web Conferencing Edge by launching a Live Meeting from a client that is outside your firewall. Make sure that both internal and external clients can connect and that they are able to hear voice and see video.

Summary

The Edge Server is a required component if you plan to have your OCS deployment connected with the outside world. The Edge has multiple roles that handle different types of external connectivity; you can choose to enable some or all of the roles on your Edge Server.

The Edge requires the use of several IP addresses, FQDNs, certificates, and several available ports on your firewall. Planning these underlying network and security components will be important to ensure a successful Edge deployment. Once you have settled on these components, the actual installation of the Edge Server will be straightforward.

Solutions Fast Track

Installing the Edge Server

☑ Make sure you have all public IP addresses and DNS entries ready.

☑ Install the Edge into a server that is *not a member of the domain.*

☑ Pay attention to port numbers and FQDNs during the configuration.

Working with Certificates

☑ Be sure to have an Enterprise Root CA in your Windows Active Directory domain.

☑ Be prepared to purchase certificates from a public CA for your Edge Server's externally facing roles.

☑ Make sure you install the certificates to your computer's certificate store before trying to apply them to the Edge Server.

Testing the Edge Server

☑ Test the Access Edge by logging in to OCS from a client outside your firewall.

☑ Test voice and video calls from outside your network.

☑ Test Live Meeting with voice and video from several clients outside the firewall.

Frequently Asked Questions

Q: Should I install the Edge Server in my domain?

A: No, you should install the Edge Server in a stand-alone workgroup.

Q: Do I really need to use a publicly routable IP address on my A/V Edge NIC?

A: Yes! Absolutely use a public IP address on your NIC for this role. You will not have a properly functioning Edge Server without it.

Q: Can I assign multiple IP addresses to the same NIC?

A: It is not recommended to use multiple IP addresses on the same NIC. In many cases, this will cause your Edge Server to stop functioning properly.

Q: Can I just use a single public IP address for all my Edge Server roles?

A: I do not recommend using a single IP address for all your Edge Server roles. It is possible, though. Under the right circumstances, and if you are willing to spend time and effort to stray from the recommended path, you may be able to get things working properly.

Q: Can the Edge Server be installed on another machine that I have in the DMZ?

A: I do not recommend installing the Edge Server on a server that has other applications running. The Edge Server has a lot of distinct networking requirements and having it share hardware with another application is likely to cause more problems than it is worth.

Q: Why shouldn't I just install the Edge on the same server as my Exchange 2007 Edge?

A: Aside from the answer to the preceding question, Exchange 2007 runs on 64-bit hardware and requires the 64-bit version of Windows Server. OCS, on the other hand, is a 32-bit application.

Q: Can I install the Edge on virtual server or VMWare?

A: I do not recommend installing the Edge as a virtual machine, but yes, it is possible to install it as such.

Chapter 6

Configuring the Mediation Server

Solutions in this chapter:

- **Installing the Configuration Server**
- **Configuring Dialing Rules**
- **Configuring Users for Voice Functionality**
- **Testing Voice Functionality**

☑ **Summary**

☑ **Solutions Fast Track**

☑ **Frequently Asked Questions**

Introduction

The Mediation Server is an additional role in the Office Communications Server (OCS) 2007 deployment that allows connectivity to legacy private branch exchange (PBX) systems as well as Public Switched Telephone Network (PSTN). The Mediation Server provides media translation and signaling between a media gateway such as the Audiocodes MP-114 in the sample configuration in this chapter and your Enterprise Voice infrastructure. The Mediation Server is deployed inside your network, behind the firewall. The Mediation Server requires two network interface cards (NIC) because one listens on one NIC secured with mutual Transport Layer Security (TLS) that is connected to your OCS environment and a second NIC that is connected to your gateway over an unsecured connection. Both NICs require a separate IP (Internet Protocol) address. Because traffic from the Mediation Server to the gateway is unsecured, you may want to consider a VLAN or a separate network that provides more security on the unsecured connection.

The Mediation Server's main functions are to translate SIP over the Transmission Control Protocol (TCP) on the gateway side, and over mutual TLS on the Enterprise Voice side. It also encrypts and decrypts the Secure Real-time Transport Protocol (SRTP) on the Communications Server side, translates media streams between the media gateway and the Communications Server, connects clients from outside the network to the internal Interactive Connectivity Establishment components which enable media traversal firewalls, and acts as a connector for calls from remote workers on the Enterprise Voice client.

OCS supports three different gateways: the Basic Gateway, which requires the use of a separate Mediation Server; and the Basic Hybrid Media Gateway and Advanced Media Gateway, which offer the Mediation Server built into a SIP-based Voice over IP (VoIP) gateway. This helps to provide a solution for interfacing your OCS environment with your legacy PBX system that doesn't require another server to be deployed.

As you begin to think about deploying Enterprise Voice solutions with OCS, you need to consider the type of gateway you'll be using, the number of gateways required, what configuration will be required for the gateways, and where you should place the gateways. Although the gateway deployment options you have may be vast, the option you choose can increase the required investment of your voice solution.

You can go with a distributed gateway solution, a data center deployment, or a hybrid distributed/data center deployment. Your answers to the following questions can help you to make the correct choice:

- How many locations do you have to support?
- What is the estimated traffic at each location?

In a distributed environment, such as that shown in Figure 6.1, you would place gateways in the outlying offices. Calls between users at each office and between the offices are routed over the company's intranet. Calls made to people outside the company will be routed over the gateway that is closest to the location of the destination number. This configuration may be complex depending on the number of offices you have to support. In this situation, it might be best to have a few strategically located data centers.

Figure 6.1 A Distributed Topology

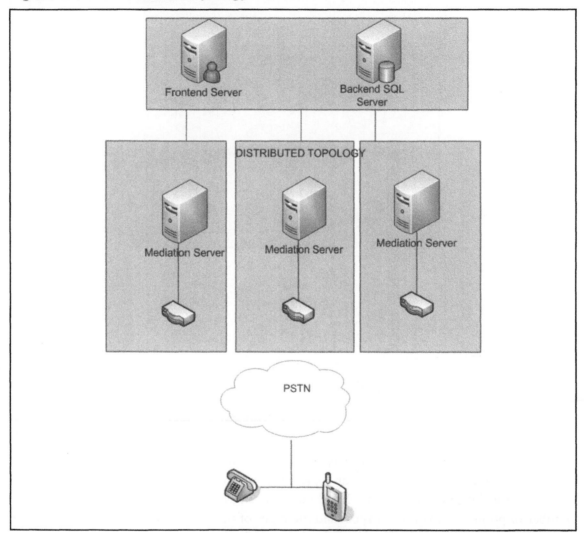

In a data center configuration such as that shown in Figure 6.2, you would deploy several large gateways to support the traffic for each data center. Calls that are bound for the outside are routed over the data center gateways and calls that are bound for internal users are routed over the PSTN to the data center gateway. Call routing at the data center will determine how to route calls to the targeted users.

Figure 6.2 A Data Center Configuration

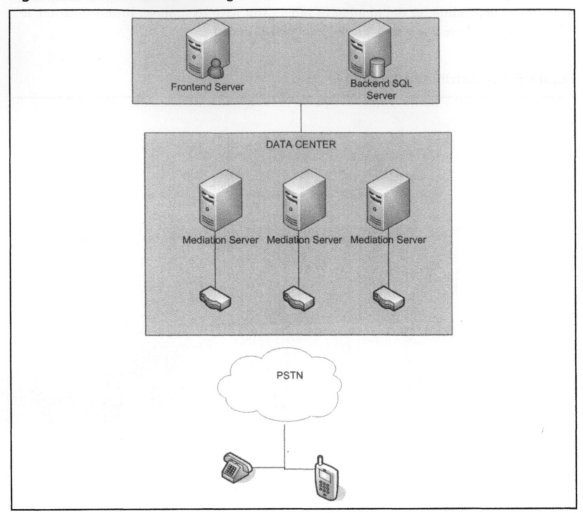

You can deploy gateways in a variety of ways, each with its advantages and disadvantages. You need to consider the goals of your deployment when choosing your locations.

Sizing for the gateways can vary based on traffic and location. You need to consider the number of phone calls you can expect and the types of users in each location where you are placing gateways. Microsoft offers the following guidelines:

- A light telephone user (one PSTN call per hour) should allocate one port per 15 users.

- A moderate telephone user (two or more PSTN calls per hour) should allocate one port per 10 users.

- A heavy telephone user (three or more PSTN calls per hour) should allocate one port per five users.

You have a choice of deploying fewer large gateways or more small gateways for any number of users you have to support. It is a good idea to have at least two gateways to provide some level of fault tolerance.

Each basic media gateway you deploy needs to have one Mediation Server. You can point a single gateway at more than one Mediation Server but you can point only one Mediation Server at one gateway.

As a general rule, if you are deploying a hybrid gateway, the Mediation Server is collocated and should not be pointed at any other Mediation Server.

Hardware sizing for the Mediation Server will depend on the number of E1 or T1 cards that are in the media gateways you will support. A single-processor, dual-core 2 GHz machine with 2 GB of RAM and two 1 GB network interface cards (NICs) will support four T1 or three E1 interfaces. A single-processor, dual-core 3 GHz machine with 2 GB of RAM and two 1 GB NICs will support five T1 or four E1 interfaces. A dual-processor, dual-core 3 GHz machine with 2 GB of RAM and two 1 GB NICs will support 10 T1 or eight E1 interfaces. A dual-processor, quad-core 2.66 GHz machine with 2 GB of RAM and two 1 GB NICs will support 18 T1 or 14 E1 interfaces.

NOTE

E1 is a European equivalent of the North American T1. It differs slightly from T1, as it does not take bits, so all eight bits are used to code the signal on each channel. This enables the E1 (2.048 million bits per second) to carry more data than the T1 (1.544 million bits per second). You can interconnect the two for international use.

The Mediation Server we will configure in this chapter will use two NICs. One NIC will interface to the gateway and the other will interface to the OCS and will provide the internal next hop for the Mediation Server. The media gateway is creating a security loophole, as the gateway does not support master key identifiers (MKIs), TLS, or SRTP, so you should not trust it. The two NICs in the Mediation Server create a separation between the two networks, with one NIC accepting traffic from the internal network and the other accepting traffic from the media gateway. (In the exercises in this chapter, we will configure each card with a separate listening address so that there is a separation between trusted and untrusted network traffic). The internal edge port defaults to 5061 and the external edge port defaults to 5060.

When you install the Mediation Server role using the Deployment Wizard, it will detect both network cards and will write their addresses to the OCS listening IP addresses and to the gateway listening address. You will find both on the General tab of the Mediation Server properties.

The media bandwidth for the basic gateway is 64,000 bps for each concurrent call. If you multiply the number of ports by this number, you will get an estimate of the required bandwidth on the gateway side of the Mediation Server. The default port range is 60,000–64,000, which enables the server to handle up to 1,000 simultaneous voice calls.

Encryption is used for traffic flowing in both directions between the OCS and the Mediation Server. Traffic is encrypted using SRTP. You are encouraged to create an exception for the media port range if you have deployed IP Security (IPSec) for packet security, as it will slow down traffic.

Installing the Configuration Server

In this chapter, we will be installing and activating the Mediation Server. We will use the Mediation Server role to connect our OCS environment with the existing PBX. Our Mediation Server name for this exercise will be NWN-OCS-MED.

Download the evaluation version of OCS and extract the files for installing onto the C: drive into a folder called Office Communications Server_Eval. You will need to navigate to the folder c:\Office Communications Server_Eval\se-eval\setup\i386.

1. Double-click the **setup.exe file**. This will launch the Deployment Wizard (see Figure 6.3).

Figure 6.3 The Deployment Wizard

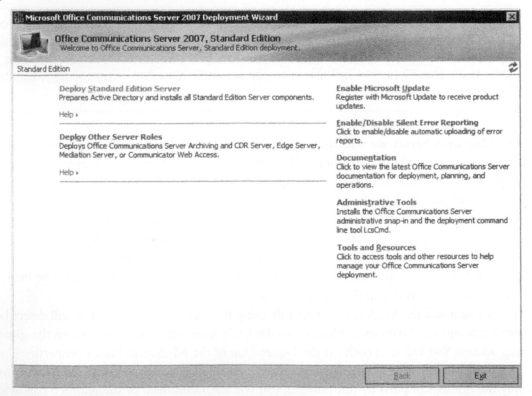

2. In the **Deployment Wizard**, click **Deploy Other Server Roles**. On the **Deploy Other Server Roles screen**, click **Deploy Mediation Server**. In the **Deploy Mediation Server Deployment Wizard**, next to Step 1: Install Files for Mediation Server, click **Install**.

3. On the **Welcome page**, click **Next** (see Figure 6.4).

Figure 6.4 The Welcome Screen

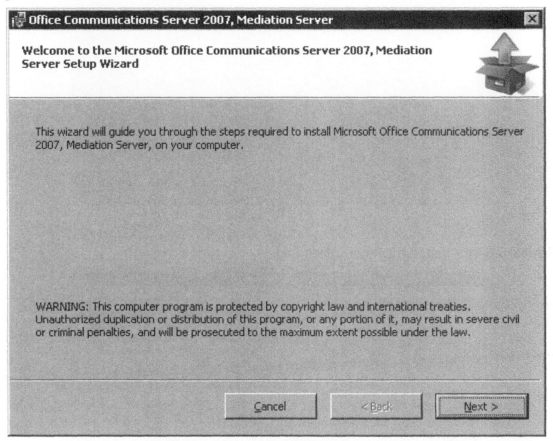

4. On the **License Agreement page**, click **I accept the terms in the licensing agreement** if you agree to the terms.

5. On the **Install Location page**, select the location for installing OCS (see Figure 6.5).

6. On the **Confirm Installation page**, click **Next**.

7. On the **Installation Complete page**, click **Close** (see Figure 6.6).

Figure 6.5 The Mediation Server File Location

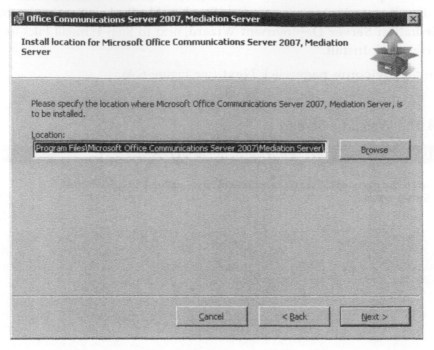

Figure 6.6 The Installation Complete Page

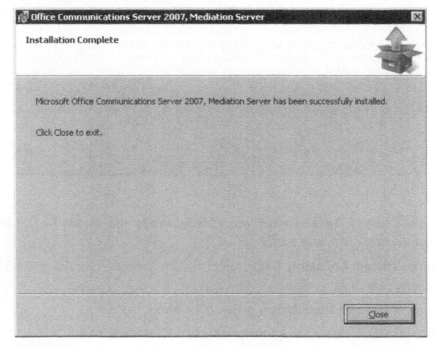

You have installed the files for the Mediation Server. Next, you need to activate the server. You will do this from the Deploy Mediation Server Deployment Wizard (see Figure 6.7).

1. To activate the Mediation Server, click **Run** next to Step 2: Activate Mediation Server.

Figure 6.7 The Deployment Wizard

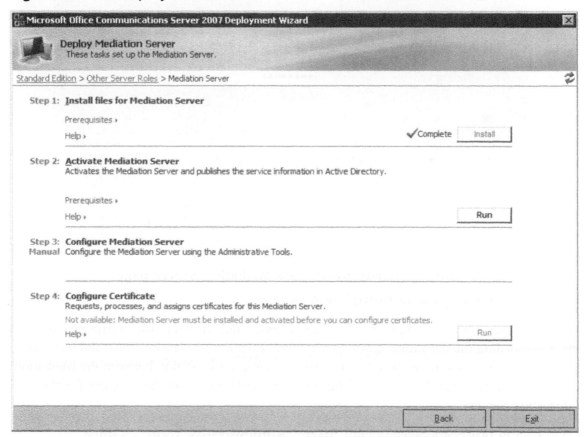

2. Click **Next** on the **Welcome page** of the **Activation Wizard**.

3. Type your password in the **Password text box** on the **Service Account** page, and then click **Next** (see Figure 6.8).

Figure 6.8 Selecting a Service Account

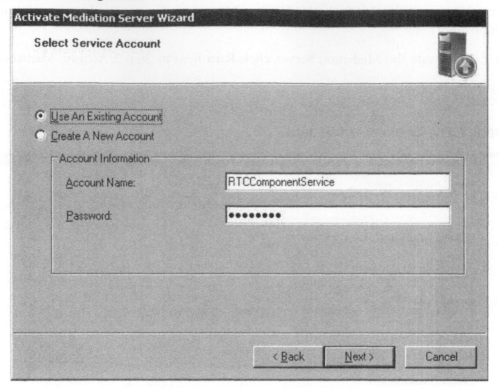

4. Click **Next** on the **Ready to Activate Mediation Server page**.

5. Click **Finish** on the **Completion page**.

Now you need to configure the Mediation Server and configure the certificates. You will be downloading the certificates from your internal certificate authority (CA), and requesting and assigning a certificate on the server to enable secure communication between the Mediation Server and your OCS 2007 server. The final step will be to start the services for the Mediation Server.

1. On NWN-OCS-MED, click **Start | Administrative Tools | Office Communications Server 2007** to launch the Admin tool for OCS.

2. Expand **Forest – domainname.com**, expand **Mediation servers**, and then click on your Mediation Server (**NWN-OCS-MED**).

3. Right-click **NWN-OCS-MED.domainname.com** and click **Properties**.

4. Click the **General tab**.

5. In the **Communications Server listening IP address drop-down list**, select the IP address on the Mediation Server that interfaces to the OCS server. This tells the server to listen on this IP for OCS communications.

6. In the **Gateway listening IP address drop-down list**, select the IP address on the Mediation Server that interfaces to the SIP-PSTN gateway device. This tells the server to listen on this interface for communication from the SIP-PSTN gateway.

7. Select the **A/V Edge Server list**, and verify that **(None)**. See Figure 6.9.

Figure 6.9 The General Tab in Mediation Server Properties

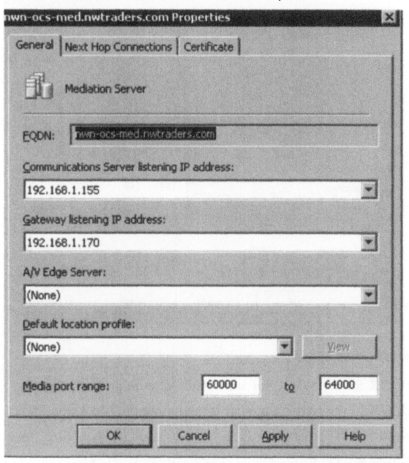

8. Click the Next Hop Connections tab.

9. Under the Office Communications Server next hop, in the FQDN drop-down list, select the OCS Server (NWN-OCS.domainname.com).

10. Under the **PSTN Gateway next hop**, in the **IP address box**, type the IP address of your gateway. Then in the **Port box**, accept the default of 5060 and click **OK** (see Figure 6.10).

Figure 6.10 The Next Hop Connections Tab in Mediation Server Properties

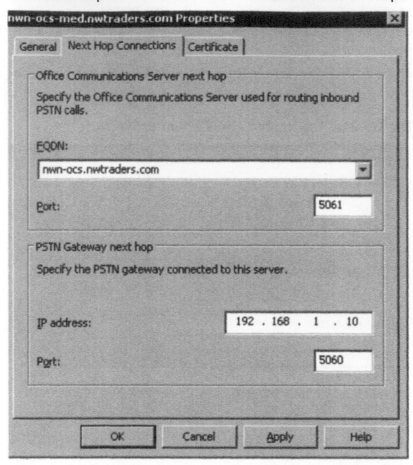

11.   Click **OK** for the A/V server and default location profile setting.

12.   Click **OK** to the warning prompt for restarting the Mediation Server.

13.   Close the OCS 2007 console.

This completes the Mediation Server configuration process. Now you need to download the certificate:

1.   On the Mediation Server (NWN-OCS-MED), click **Start**, click **Run**, type **http://servernameforCA/certsrv**, and then click **OK**.

2.   Microsoft Internet Explorer launches and displays the CA web page. Under **Select a Task**, click **Download a CA certificate, certificate chain, or CRL** (see Figure 6.11).

Figure 6.11 The CA Web Page

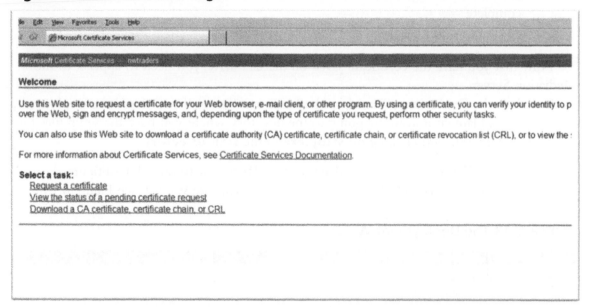

3. Under **Download a CA certificate, certificate chain, or CRL**, click **Download CA certificate chain**.

4. In the **File Download box**, click **Save** (see Figure 6.12).

Figure 6.12 The Save As Screen

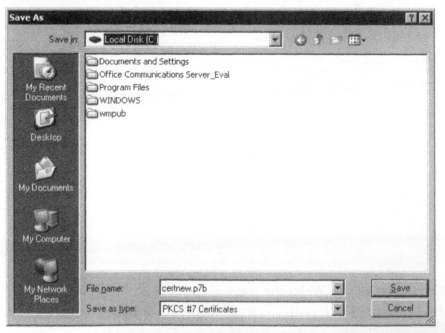

5. Save the certnew.p7b file to the C:\ drive and click **Close** when the download is complete.

6. Close Internet Explorer.

Now that you have the certificate saved on the C:\ drive, you need to apply it to the Mediation Server.

Switch to the Deployment Wizard on the Mediation Server. If you closed the Deployment Wizard you can launch it again by going to the directory where you have the setup files for Microsoft OCS 2007 and clicking on **setup.exe** in the **i386 directory**.

1. On the **Deployment Wizard page**, click **Run** next to Step 4: Configure Certificate, to launch the Communications Certificate Wizard (see Figure 6.13).

Figure 6.13 The Deployment Wizard

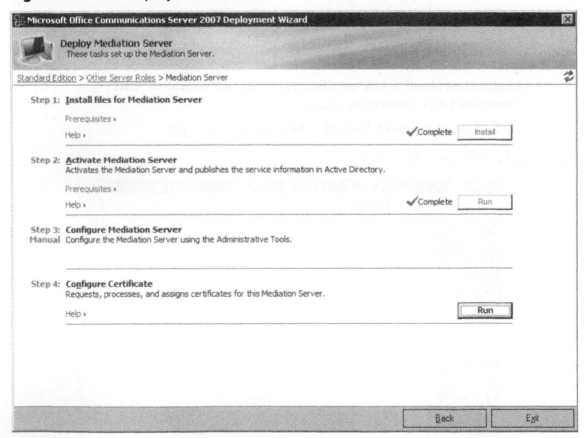

2. Click **Next** on the **Welcome page**.

3. On the **Available Certificate Task page**, click **Import a certificate chain from a .p7b file** and then click **Next** (see Figure 6.14).

4. Click **Browse** on the **Import Certificate Chain page**.

Figure 6.14 The Certificate Wizard

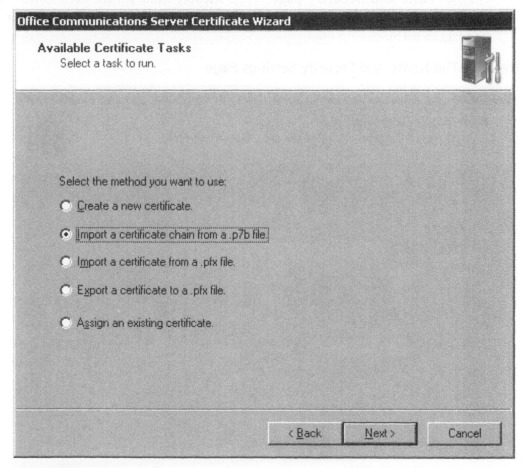

5. Navigate to the C:\ drive, click on the **certnew.p7b file**, and then click **Open**.

6. Click **Next** on the **Import Certificate Chain page**.

7. Click **Finish**.

Now it's time to request a certificate for the Mediation Server. Switch to the Deployment Wizard on the Mediation Server. If you closed the Deployment Wizard, you can launch it again by going to the directory where you have the setup files for Microsoft OCS 2007 and clicking **setup.exe** in the **i386 directory**.

1. On the **Deployment Wizard page**, click **Run** next to Step 4: Configure Certificate, to launch the Communication Certificate Wizard.

2. Click **Next** on the **Welcome page**.

3. On the **Available Certificate Task page**, create a new certificate and then click **Next**.

4. On the **Name and Security page**, type a friendly name for the certificate, verify that the **Mark cert as exportable box** is checked, and then click **Next** (see Figure 6.15).

Figure 6.15 The Name and Security Settings Page

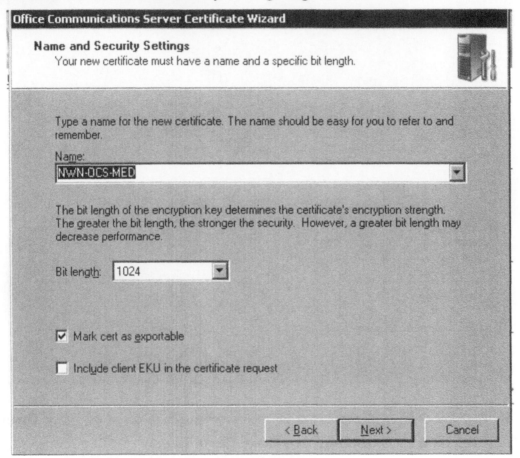

5. On the **Organization Information page**, enter your organization name and your Organizational Unit name (OU), and then click **Next**.

6. On your server's **Subject Name page**, in the **Subject Name box**, verify that your Mediation Server name is selected. The subject name should match the fully qualified domain name (FDQN) of the Mediation Server.

7. Click **Next**.

8. On the **Geographical Information page**, type in your city and state in the appropriate boxes, and then click **Next**.

9. On the Choose a Certificate Authority page, verify that your CA server is selected and then click Next.

10. Click **Next** on the **Request Summary page**.

11. Click **Assign** on the **Certificate Wizard Complete page**.

12. In the **Communication Certificate Wizard prompt**, click **OK** and then click **Finish**.

13. Click **Exit** to close the Deployment Wizard.

To start the Mediation Server services, follow these steps:

1. On the Mediation Server (NWN-OCS-MED), click **Start | Administrative Tools | Services**.

2. Make sure that "Office Communications Server Mediation" appears in the list of services.

3. Right-click **Office Communication Server Mediation** and then click **Start** (see Figure 6.16).

Figure 6.16 Starting the Mediation Server Services

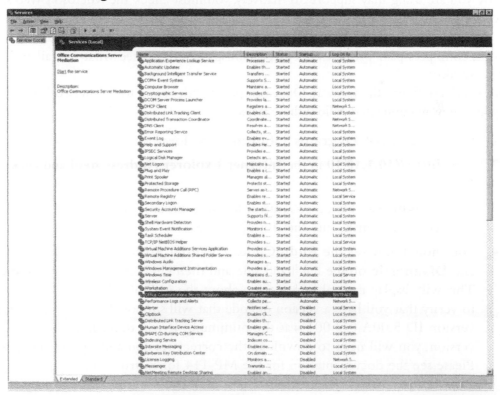

4. After the service starts, close Services.

Configuring the Gateway

In the configuration we are using in these exercises, we have an AudioCodes MP-114 gateway (www.audiocodes.com) which has two FXO ports and two FXS ports. We will plug an analog handset into FXO port 1, and we will configure the gateway for endpoint phone numbers, routing and manipulation tables, and hunt groups. When we finish with this setup our gateway will be ready to send calls from the analog handset to OCS and will be ready to receive calls from OCS. An optional connection to FXS port 3 will allow us to send calls to the PSTN.

Although we are using a gateway from AudioCodes, other companies also offer certified gateways for use with OCS. Among them are Dialogic (www.dialogic.com), Cisco (www.cisco.com), and Quintum (www.quintum.com). The gateways come with various port configurations and protocol support. Your configuration requirements will depend on which PBX you are interfacing with, the number of ports required, and the locations where you want to place your gateways.

Some PBX companies are building SIP functionality into their products. For instance, Cisco has built SIP functionality into its Call Manager product, as has Nortel with various models of its Communication Server line of products. It is important to remember that although the PBX you are using may support SIP natively, you must check the Microsoft Web site for a list of approved hardware if you expect to receive support from Microsoft should you have issues. You can check out the vendor list for Microsoft Unified Communications at www.microsoft.com/presspass/presskits/uc/partners.mspx#EOH to see what is available from different vendors.

Now let's configure the gateway. On a computer with access to the network where you have your gateway connected, follow these steps:

1. Click **Start | All Programs | Internet Explorer**.

2. Type **http://10.1.10.10** in the **Internet Explorer Address field** and click **Enter**.

3. In the **Login text box**, type **Admin** for the username and password. Both are case-sensitive, so make sure the *A* is uppercase.

4. You should now see the **AudioCodes Channel Status page**. Click on **Status** and **Diagnostic** on the left-hand side and then click on **Device Information**. This will display general information about the AudioCodes MP-114. You want to verify that you have a version of code that will support OCS. As of this writing, version ID 5.00A.033.001 was the minimum. If you don't have the correct version, you will need to download the correct version and update the gateway. Please see the documentation for the MP-114 for instructions on updating the gateway.

Now that you have verified that you have the correct version, it's time to configure the MP-114 to support your environment. If you had to update your gateway and reset the box, you'll need to get back into the gateway as Admin.

We'll start by defining the endpoints:

1. Click **Protocol Management** and then **Endpoint Phone Numbers** on the toolbar.

2. Configure endpoints 1 and 2 with phone numbers to ring the handset that is plugged into FXO ports 1 and 2. In Figure 6.17, we are using 3365551201 and 3365551202.

Figure 6.17 Endpoint Phone Number Table

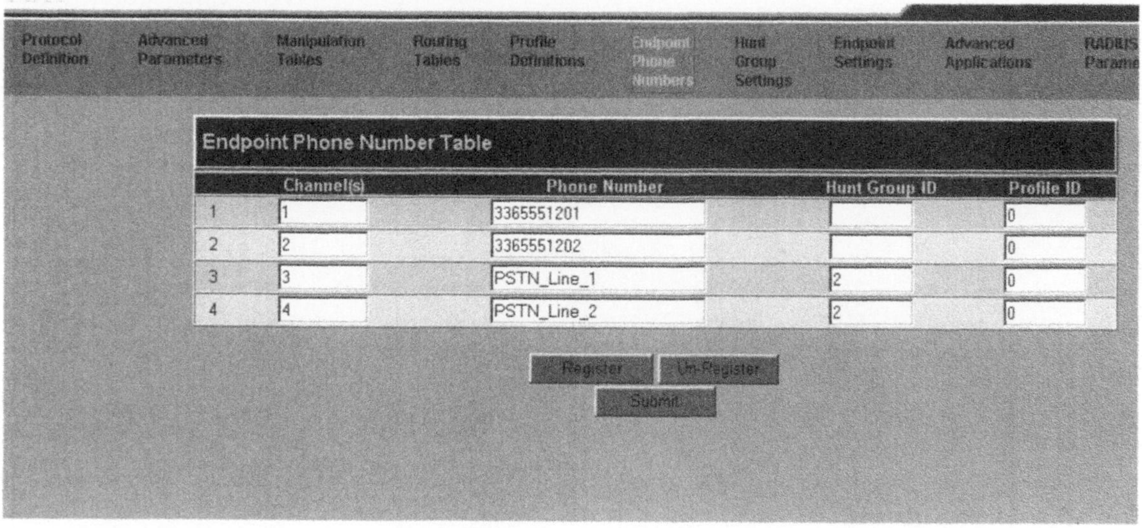

3. Once you have the endpoints configured, click **Submit**.

Now let's configure the routing tables:

1. Click **Routing Tables** on the toolbar then click **Tel to IP Routing**.

2. Configure the routing tables to match your environment. In our example, we want to route calls for +13365551201 and +13365551202 to the MP-114 gateway address of 10.1.10.10. So, we will route calls for +133655512 to the OCS Mediation Server gateway address of 10.1.10.25, and we will route all other calls to the MP-114 address of 10.1.10.10. Also, make sure you have the **Route calls after Manipulation** set in the **Tel to IP Routing** mode. See Figure 6.18 for an example of the configuration.

Figure 6.18 Tel to IP Routing

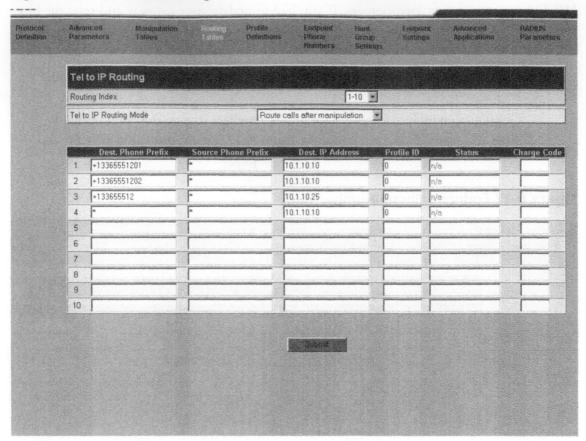

3. Click **Submit**.

Now we'll configure the manipulation tables:

1. Click **Manipulation Tables** on the toolbar, and then click **IP → Tel Destination Numbers**.

2. Configure lines 1–5 to match the table shown in Figure 6.19. In this step, you are manipulating calls to match the number you need to successfully complete calls. Notice how, in the figure, we are stripping or adding digits based on what is dialed.

Figure 6.19 The Tel Destination Number Table for IP → Tel Calls

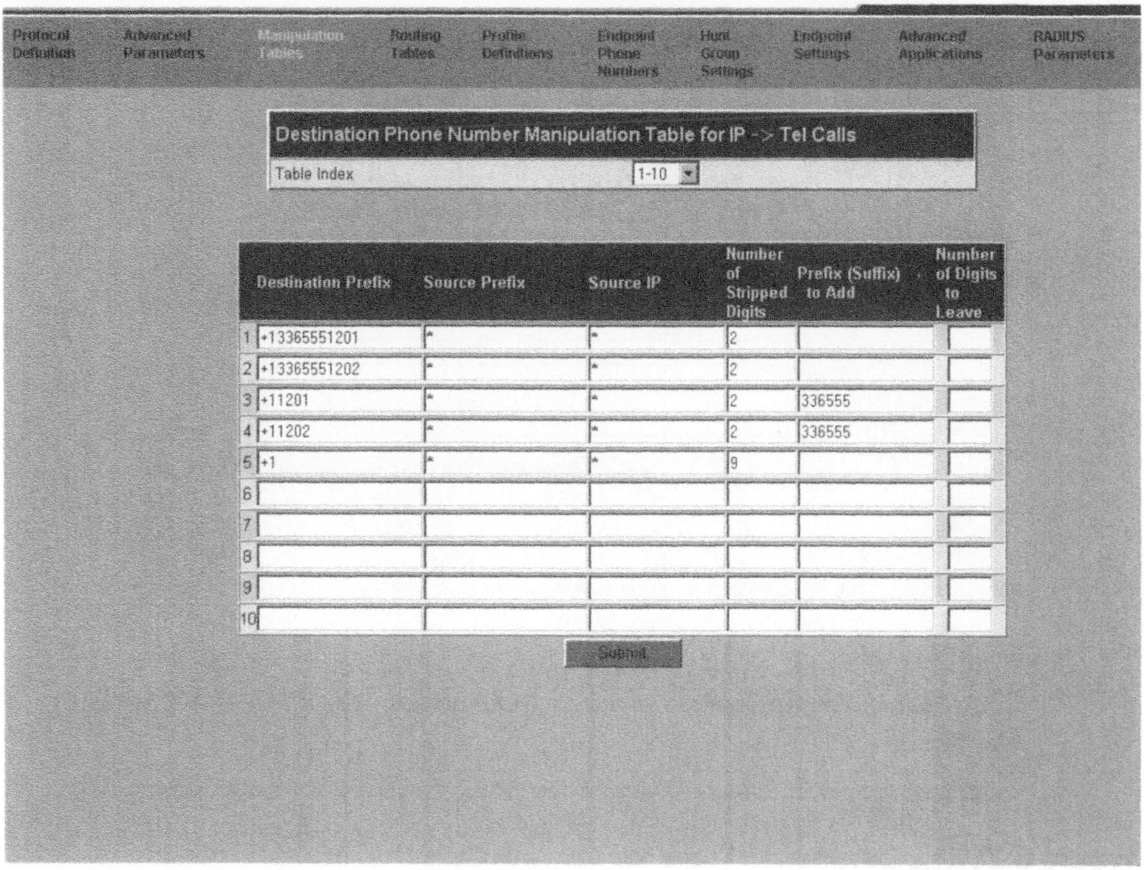

Protocol Definition	Advanced Parameters	Manipulation Tables	Routing Tables	Profile Definitions	Endpoint Phone Numbers	Hunt Group Settings	Endpoint Settings	Advanced Applications	RADIUS Parameters

Destination Phone Number Manipulation Table for IP -> Tel Calls

Table Index [1-10 ▾]

	Destination Prefix	Source Prefix	Source IP	Number of Stripped Digits	Prefix (Suffix) to Add	Number of Digits to Leave
1	+13365551201	*	*	2		
2	+13365551202	*	*	2		
3	+11201	*	*	2	336555	
4	+11202	*	*	2	336555	
5	+1	*	*	9		
6						
7						
8						
9						
10						

Submit

3. Click **Submit**.

4. Click **Manipulation Tables** on the toolbar, and then click **Tel → IP Destination Numbers**.

5. Configure the Destination Phone Number Manipulation Table for Tel → IP Calls to match the table shown in Figure 6.20.

Figure 6.20 The Destination Table for Tel → IP Calls

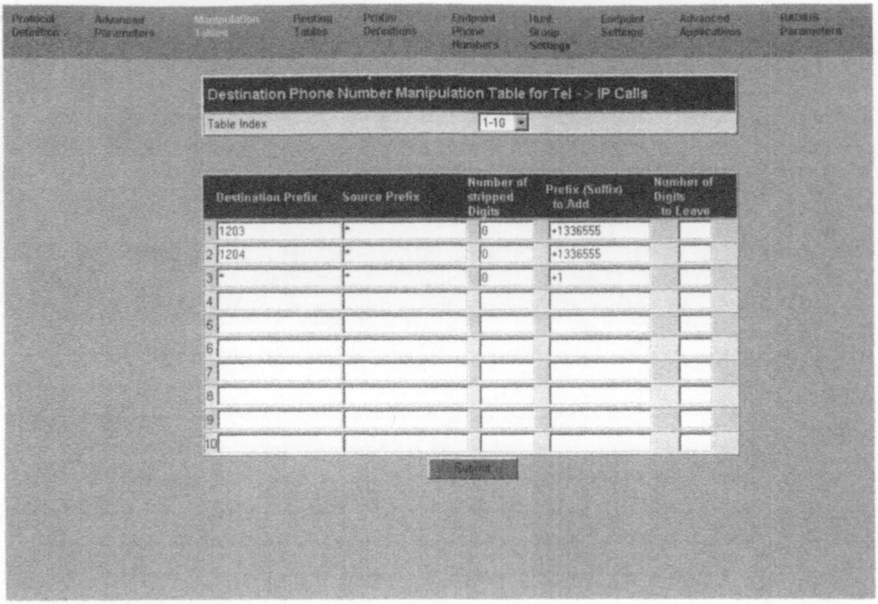

6. Click **Submit**.

7. Click **Manipulation Tables** on the toolbar, and then click **Tel → IP Source Numbers**.

8. Configure Tel → IP Source Numbers to match the table shown in Figure 6.21.

Figure 6.21 The Destination Table for Tel → IP Calls

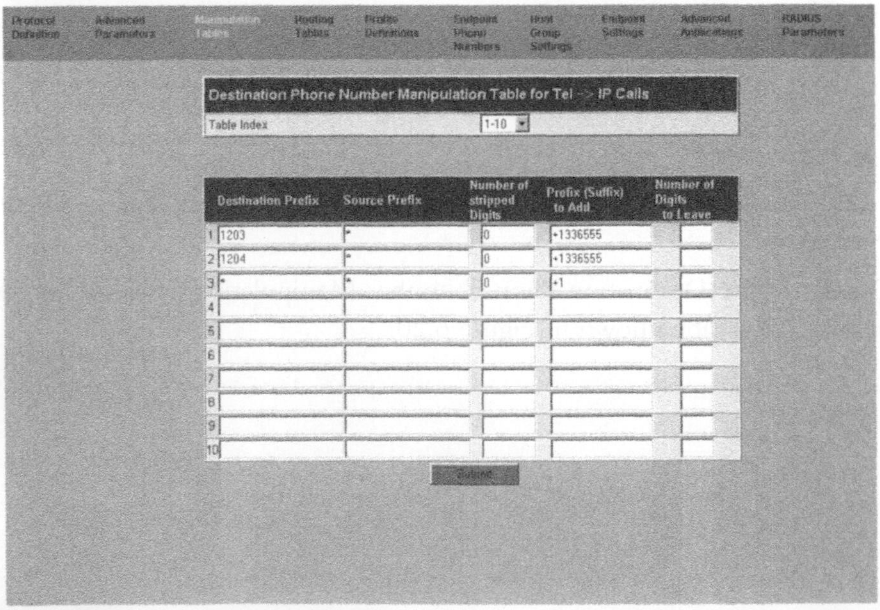

9. Click **Submit**.

Now it's time to configure the hunt groups:

1. Click **Hunt Group Settings** on the toolbar.
2. Configure the hunt groups to match the table shown in Figure 6.22.

Figure 6.22 The Hunt Group Settings

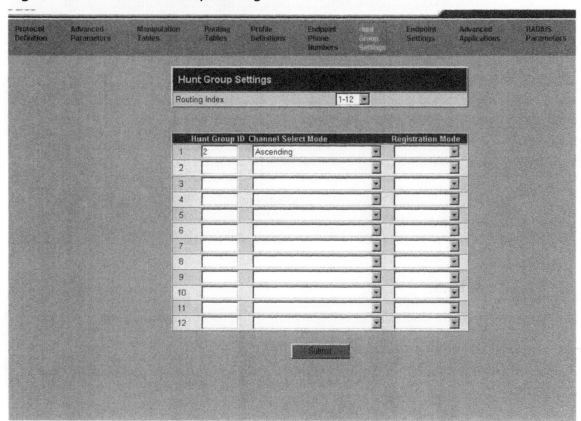

3. Click **Submit**.
4. Click **Routing Tables** on the toolbar, and then click on **IP to Trunk Group Routing**.
5. In the drop-down list for IP to Tel Routing mode, make sure **Route calls after Manipulation** is set. If it isn't, select it.
6. Configure the IP to Hunt Group Routing to match the table shown in Figure 6.23.

Figure 6.23 The IP to Hunt Group Routing Table

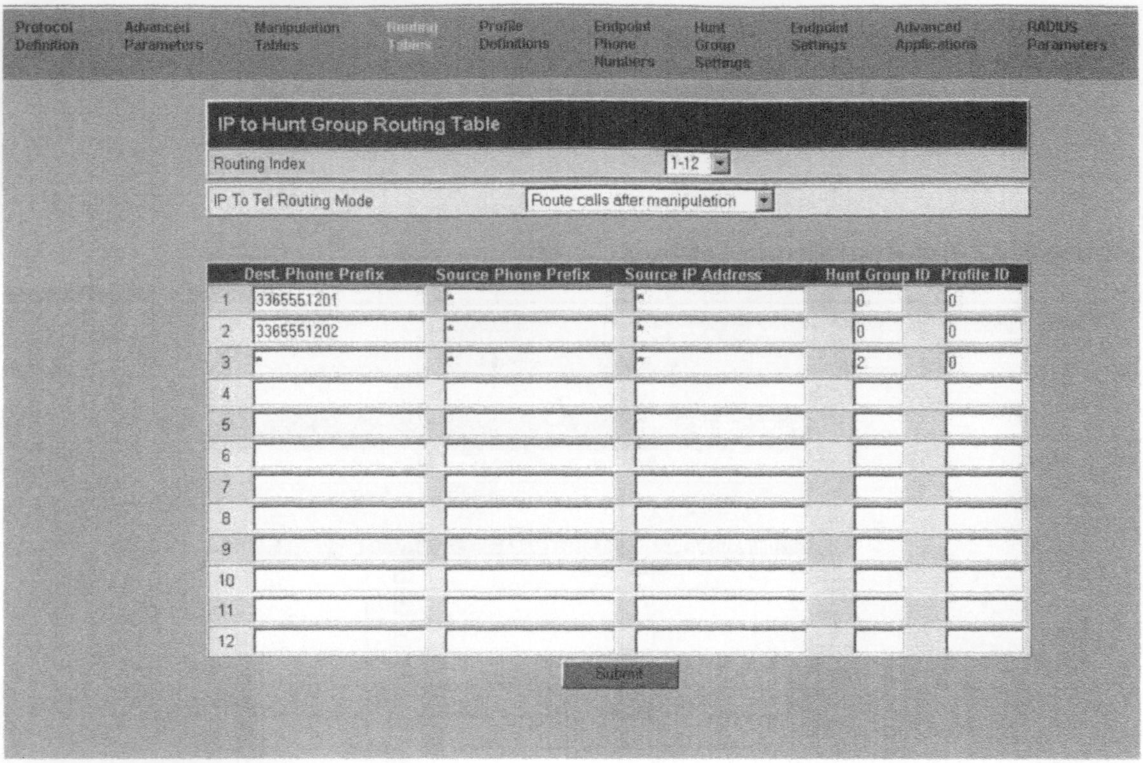

7. Click **Submit**.

Now that you have done all this configuration work, you need to make sure you save it:

1. Click **Maintenance** on the left-hand side of the screen.

2. Click **Burn** under the **Save Configuration section** (see Figure 6.24).

Figure 6.24 Maintenance Actions

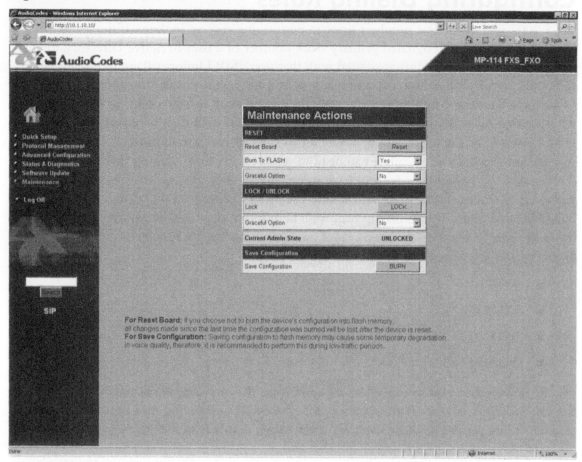

3. Once the new configuration has been saved you can exit Internet Explorer.

Configuring Dialing Rules

OCS 2007 will normalize numbers prior to performing reverse lookups. If the normalized number matches the designated primary work number of a user in Active Directory, the call will be sent to the endpoints associated with that user's SIP Uniform Resource Identifier (URI). If no match is found, that number will be considered outside the enterprise. The Outbound Routing component will check the caller's phone usage policy to determine whether that caller is authorized to make the call. The call will then be directed to the media gateway, or the caller will be notified that the call was not authorized. This is a great way to deny long distance calls if you need to restrict users from making such calls.

As we've discussed thus far, you have some control over how calls are handled, so now you need to determine an outbound dialing plan. Your dialing plan will define how the server handles dialed digits. In the dialing plan we'll be using in this exercise, we will look at how the server handles numbers that members of our Greensboro, North Carolina, team call. Common numbers that the Greensboro team calls are:

- 1234
- 93365551212
- 95551212
- 913365551212

We will create a plan to normalize the numbers in the preceding list to use the E.164 format for OCS dialing. Normalizing numbers is a process of converting numbers dialed into a standard E.164 pattern. Because users will enter phone numbers in various formats, normalizing the numbers enables call routing and authorization.

The normalization rules we use may need to account for the following fields: Dial Plan, Country Code, Area Code, Site Prefix, and Length of Extension.

You create normalization rules using .NET regular expressions. When creating normalization rules you may need to understand regular expressions. You can find a guide to regular expressions at www.amk.ca/python/howto/regex/ and a detailed guide to regular expression syntax at http://docs.python.org/lib/re-syntax.html.

Let's create a location profile and define phone number normalization rules for outbound calls:

1. On the OCS server, click **Start | Administrative Tool | Office Communications Server 2007**. On **Forest – yourdomainname.com**, right-click and point to **Properties**, and then click **Voice Properties** (see Figure 6.25).

Figure 6.25 Clicking Voice Properties

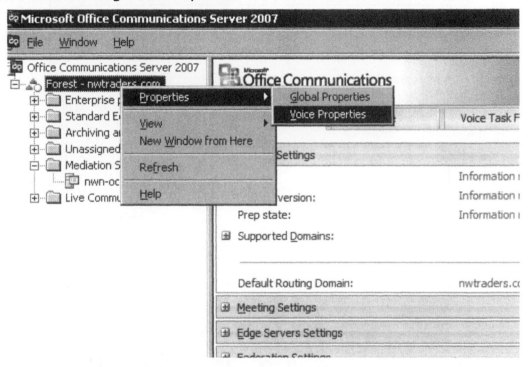

2. On the **Location Profiles tab**, click **Add**. In this step, you are creating a location profile for your office.

3. Type in a name for your profile in the **Add Location Profile box**, and then type in a description for your location profile, as shown in Figure 6.26.

Figure 6.26 Adding a Location Profile for the Main Office

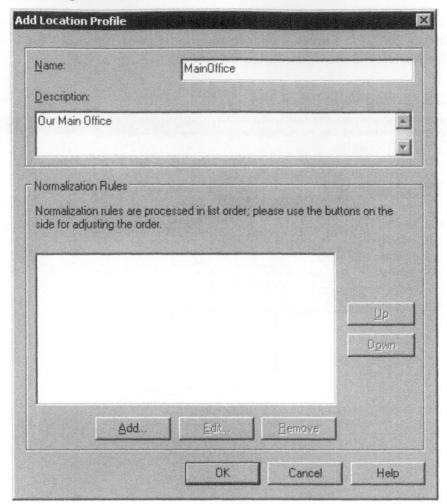

4. Click **Add** under **Normalization Rules**. Perform the following steps in the Add Phone Number Normalization Rule, as shown in Figure 6.27:

- Type in a descriptive name for four-digit dialing in the **Name box**.

- Type in a description for the rule.

- Type in (don't use spaces) **^1(\d{3})$** in the **Phone pattern regular expression box**.

- Type in **+13365551$1** in the **Translation pattern regular expression box** and click **OK**.

Figure 6.27 Adding a Normalization Rule for Four-Digit Calling

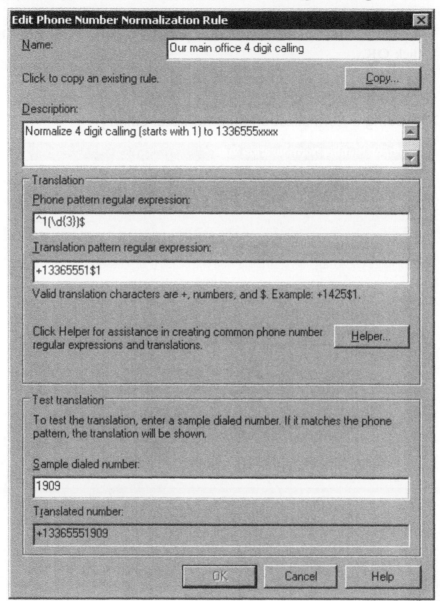

5. Click **Add** under **Normalization Rules** to add a second normalization rule. Perform the following steps in the Add Phone Number Normalization Rule, as shown in Figure 6.28:

   ■ Type in a descriptive name for seven–digit dialing in the **Name box**.

   ■ Type in a description for the rule.

- Type in (don't use spaces) **^9([2–9]\d{6})$** in the **Phone pattern regular expression box**.

- Type in **+1336$1** in the **Translation pattern regular expression box** and click **OK**.

Figure 6.28 Adding a Normalization Rule for Local Calling

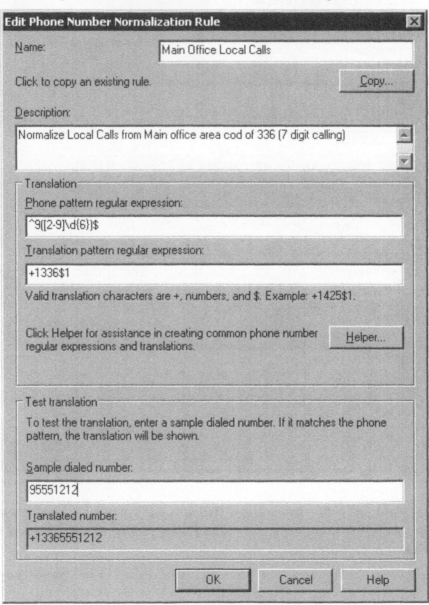

6. Click **Add** under **Normalization Rules** to add a third normalization rule. Perform the following steps in the Add Phone Number Normalization Rule:

- Type in a descriptive name for 1 + 10-digit dialing in the **Name box**.

- Type in a description for the rule.

- Type in (don't use spaces) **^9(\d{10})$** in the **Phone pattern regular expression box**.

- Type in **+1$1** in the **Translation pattern regular expression box** and click **OK**.

7. Click **Add** under **Normalization Rules** to add a fourth normalization rule. Perform the following steps in the Add Phone Number Normalization Rule:

- Type in a descriptive name for 9, 1 + 10-digit dialing in the **Name box**.

- Type in a description for the rule.

- Type in (don't use spaces) **^91(\d{10})$** in the **Phone pattern regular expression box**.

- Type in **+1$1** in the **Translation pattern regular expression box** and click **OK**.

Now let's create the phone usage record:

1. Click the **Phone Usages** tab and then click **Add**. Type a descriptive name for the phone usage record for local calling. Type a description for the record for local calling only (see Figure 6.29).

Figure 6.29 Adding a Phone Usage Record

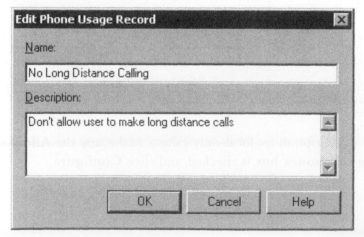

2. Click **Add** on the **Phone Usages tab**. Type a descriptive name for the phone usage record for allowing local and long distance calling. Type a description for the record for allowing local and long distance calling.

Now we need to define our policies:

1. Click the **Policy tab** and then click **Add**, as shown in Figure 6.30.

Figure 6.30 The Policy Tab in the Voice Properties

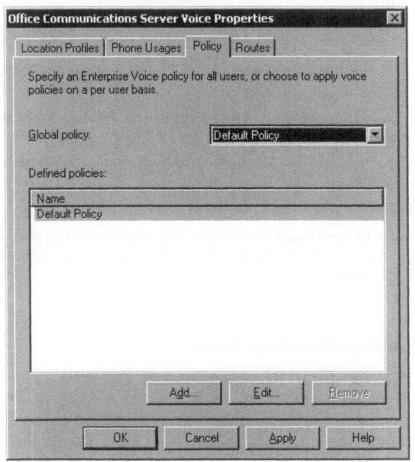

2. Type in a description for local-only calling. Make sure the **Allow simultaneous ringing of phones box** is checked, and click **Configure**.

3. In the **Configure Phone Usage Records dialog box**, in the **Available** phone usage records list, select your local calls only phone usage record and then click the **Right Arrow button** (>) to select this usage record, as shown in Figure 6.31.

Figure 6.31 Configuring Phone Usage Records

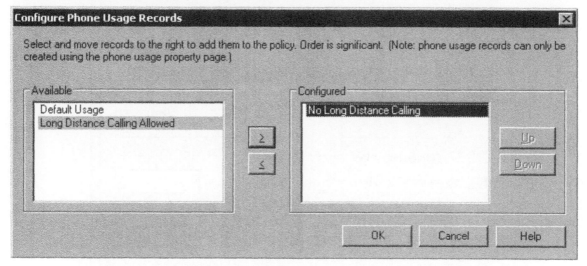

4. Click **OK** two times. Click the **Policy tab** and then click **Add**.

5. Type in a description for local and long distance calling. Make sure the **Allow simultaneous ringing of phones box** is checked, and click **Configure**.

6. In the **Configure Phone Usage Records dialog box**, in the **Available** phone usage records list, select your local and long distance calls phone usage record and then click the **Right Arrow button** (>) to select this usage record.

7. Click **OK** two times. In the **Global Policy drop-down list**, select **Use per user policy**, click **Apply**, and then click **OK**.

Now you can define the default location profile for the pool. Expand **Standard Edition Servers** and click your OCS standard server. Then, follow these steps:

1. Right-click the server, click **Properties**, and then click **Front End Properties**.

2. On the **Voice tab**, under **Location Profile**, select the location profile for the main office, as shown in Figure 6.32.

3. Click **OK**.

Figure 6.32 The Voice Tab on the Front-End Properties Page

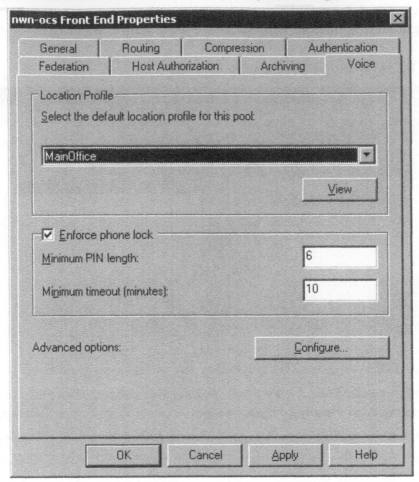

Now you can define the default location profile for the Mediation Server:

1. Expand **Mediation Servers** and click your Mediation Server.

2. Right-click the server and click **Properties**. On the **General tab**, under **Default Location Profile**, select your location profile for the main office.

3. Click **OK** to the warning prompts.

Now you will define the outbound call route. This will help OCS to determine the optimal gateway for calls that need to be routed to the PSTN.

1. Right-click **Forest – yourdomainname.com**, point to **Properties**, and then click **Voice Properties**.

2. Click the **Routes** tab and then click **Add**. In the dialog box for **Add Routes**, type the following information:

    ■   Type in a description for the route for all calls.

    ■   Type in a description.

    ■   Type .* (a period followed by an asterisk). Make sure there are no spaces.

3. Under **Gateways**, click **Add**. Under **Select the Gateway**, select **yourservername. yourdomainname.com:5061** and then click **OK**, as shown in Figure 6.33.

Figure 6.33 Adding a Route

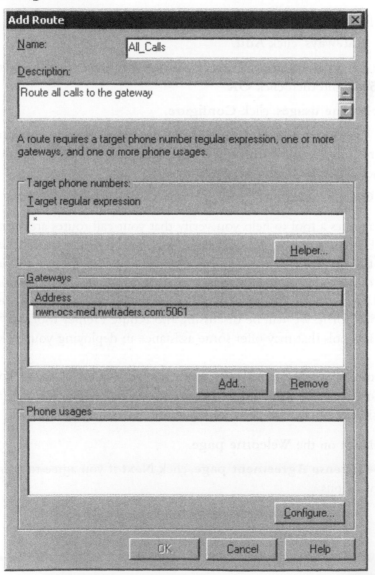

4. Under **Phone usages**, click **Configure**.

5. In the **Configure Phone Usage Records dialog box**, in the **Available** phone usage records list, select the policy you configured that allowed local and long distance calling, and then click the **Right Arrow** button (>).

6. Click **OK** two times.

7. Click the **Routes tab** and then click **Add**. In the dialog box for **Add Routes**, type the following information:

   ■ Type in a description for the route for local calls.

   ■ Type in a description.

   ■ Type **^(\+1336)**.

8. Under **Gateways**, click **Add**.

9. Under **Select the Gateway**, select **yourservername.yourdomainname. com:5061** and then click **OK**.

10. Under **Phone usages**, click **Configure**.

11. In the **Configure Phone Usage Records dialog box**, in the **Available** phone usage records list, select the policy you configured that allowed only local calling, and then click the **Right Arrow** button (>).

12. Click **OK** two times.

Microsoft provides a tool to help you verify that your call routes are working correctly. It is called the Enterprise Voice Route Helper and you can find it in the Resource Kit for OCS 2007. At the time of this writing, you could download the Resource Kit at www. microsoft.com/downloads/details.aspx?familyid=B9BF4F71-FB0B-4DE9-962F-C56B70A8 AECD&displaylang=en. If the download is no longer there, you may want to use your favorite search site to look for it. We will be discussing the Route Helper tool, but you can find many other useful tools that may offer some assistance in deploying your next OCS installation.

In this exercise, you will install the Resource Kit on your OCS server. You will need to download the tool to the server. To start the installation process, launch the .msi file called OCSResKit.msi.

1. Click **Next** on the **Welcome page**.

2. On the **License Agreement page**, click **Next** if you agree to the licensing terms and conditions.

3. Select a location for the installation of the Resource Kit for OCS (see Figure 6.34).

Figure 6.34 The Resource Kit Tools Install Location

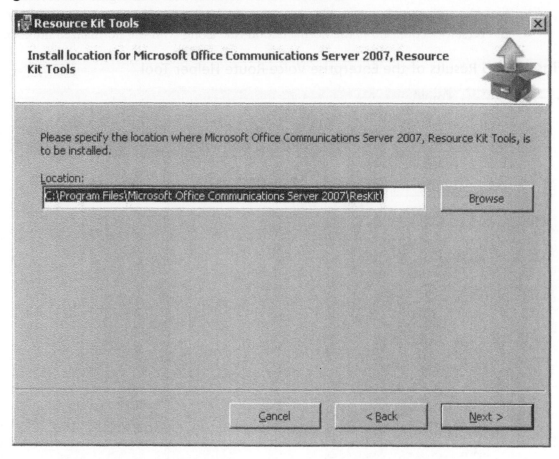

4. Click **Next** on the **Confirm Installation page**.

5. Click **Close**.

Now that you have the Resource Kit installed, you can test your dial plans. In this exercise, we will test only four-digit dialing; however, you can test the remaining numbers and policies to verify that all is well.

1. On the OCS server where you installed the resource kit, click **Start | Run | Office Communications Server 2007 | Resource Kit | Enterprise Voice Route Helper**.

2. You should see your location profile and your normalization rules, which have been automatically imported. Click on the **Ad-hoc Test tab**.

3. Type in **1234** in the **Dialed Number box**, select the **MainOffice location profile**, and select the **Local Only policy**.

4. Click **Test** and you should see results similar to those shown in Figure 6.35. Notice how the corresponding normalization rule is highlighted in the center box and how the Results section shows the normalization rule along with the normalized number.

Figure 6.35 Results of the Enterprise Voice Route Helper Tool

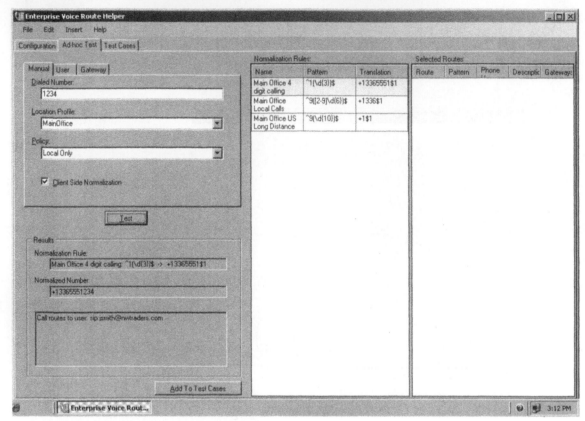

You can test additional numbers by repeating steps 3 and 4. In our example, we used the Ad-Hoc Test tab, but you can use the Test Cases tab to test numerous dial patterns to verify that the results you are getting are the results you expect. This is a great tool for testing prior to rolling out a dial plan for your Enterprise Voice solution.

Configuring Users for Voice Functionality

In this section, we will configure users for voice. We will enable and update the voice information on a couple of users we have defined in Active Directory. We will use the OCS 2007 console to make these changes.

1. Expand **Forest – Yourdomainname.com** and then expand **Standard Servers.**

2. Expand your **standard server name.**

3. Right-click **Users,** and then click **Configure Users.** The Configure Users Wizard will launch.

4. On the **Welcome page,** click **Next.**

5. On the **Configure User Setting bulk configuration page,** click **Next** to leave the current settings in place. On the **Configure User Setting organize meeting page,** click **Next** to leave the current settings in place.

6. On the **Configure User Setting specify meeting policy page,** click **Next** to leave the current settings in place.

7. On the **Configure User Setting enable users for VOIP** page, click **Enable Voice** and then select a **Voice Policy** for the Users drop-down list. Select the **Local Only Policy,** and then click **Next.**

8. On the **Configuration Operations Status page,** click **Finish.**

9. In the **User window,** right-click on a user that you want to enable for local and long distance calls and click **Configure User.**

10. On the **Welcome page**, click **Next.**

11. On the **Configure User Setting bulk configuration page**, click **Next** to leave the current settings in place. On the **Configure User Setting organize meeting page**, click **Next** to leave the current settings in place. On the **Configure User Setting specify meeting policy page**, click **Next** to leave the current settings in place.

12. On the **Configure User Setting enable users for VOIP** page, click **Enable Voice** and then select a **Voice Policy** for the Users drop-down list. Select the **Local and Long Distance calling policy**, and then click **Next.**

13. On the **Configuration Operations Status page**, click **Finish**.

Now you need to define user extensions for your users. Here we will select only a couple of users on which to perform these tasks.

1. In **Users**, right-click on your users and then click **Properties**.

2. On the **Properties page**, next to Additional Options, click **Configure**.

3. Under **Telephony**, in the **Line URI box**, type **tel:+13365551234**.

4. Click **OK** twice.

Testing Voice Functionality

When testing voice it's important to understand how OCS will process a call coming from a Communicator client to the PSTN. In Figure 6.36, you can see how the components connect and what protocols pass through the OCS environment to complete a call.

Figure 6.36 Enterprise Voice Component Diagram

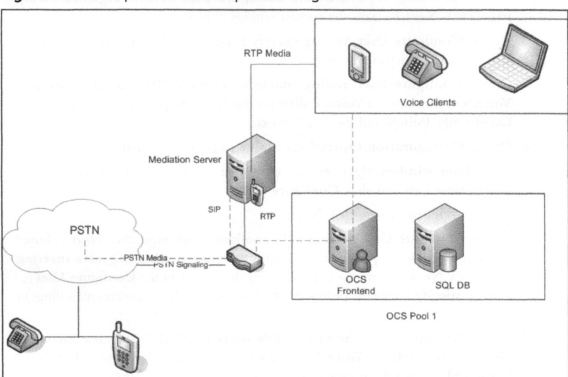

When you place a call from your voice client to the PSTN, the call will travel through the OCS environment as follows:

1. The user will place a call from the Communicator client.

2. The server will normalize the number and will check for routing rules based on the location profiles and the user policy, and then will send the call to the appropriate Mediation Server.

3. The Mediation Server will perform necessary media transcoding and will send the call to the PSTN gateway.

4. The gateway will apply any local dialing rules and will pass the call to the PSTN or the PBX.

In this final exercise, you will make a call from the Communicator to the analog phone you configured earlier. You will also make calls from the analog phone to the user you just set up. You will work from Microsoft Office Communicator (MOC) to make a call to the analog handset.

1. Launch your MOC.
2. Type in **3365551201**.
3. Answer the analog phone.
4. Pick up the analog handset.
5. Dial **3365551234**.
6. Answer the call on your Communicator client.

Summary

The Mediation Server enables voice connectivity between an existing PBX and an OCS solution. When you are designing your solution you have to choose between different types of gateways that may require a physical server to play the Mediation Server or role, or that may incorporate that role into the appliance. The Mediation Server will enable you to maintain a secure connection between your OCS environment and your PBX while providing SIP integration that is secured for OCS and SIP integration that is over basic TCP for your PBX connection.

The Mediation Server will provide:

- Encryption/decryption for communication with OCS and the gateway
- Media translation
- A call flow that the gateway doesn't support
- Remote access for users outside the network to allow for firewall traversal

Solutions Fast Track

Installing the Configuration Server

☑ Use the Deployment Wizard to install the Mediation Server role.

☑ Activate the Mediation Server.

☑ Configure certificates.

Configuring Dialing Rules

☑ Create location profiles. Create rules for normalizing numbers to the E.164 standard based on numbers dialed.

☑ Create phone usage records to configure calling permissions. Create routes to define optimal gateway usage.

Configuring Users for Voice Functionality

☑ Enable users for voice using the Administration tool for OCS.

☑ The policy for the user.

☑ Add telephone information for the user.

Testing Voice Functionality

☑ Using MOC, place a call to a user.

☑ Using MOC, place a call to a phone extension.

☑ Using MOC, place a call to an outside user.

Frequently Asked Questions

Q: Can the Mediation Server be virtualized?

A: No. Microsoft does not currently support virtualization with OCS. If you do decide to virtualize the Mediation Server, you will see a drop in voice quality.

Q: Is there a way to report on voice quality?

A: Yes. Microsoft offers a Quality of Experience (QOE) capability that enables you to report on calls being made and on voice quality. This is a great way to spot issues with devices so that you can resolve problems.

Q: How do I know I am configuring the Mediation Server following Microsoft's best practices?

A: You can run the Microsoft Best Practice Analyzer. It will report on all aspects of your OCS configuration and help you to resolve any issues it may find.

Q: What is a good gateway for building a small voice lab with OCS?

A: The AudioCodes MP-114 is a great small gateway to help you build and understand voice integration. The MP-114 comes with two FXO ports and two FXS ports, which will enable you to configure internal handsets and integrate to the local PSTN.

Q: When I am configuring certificates, I don't get the Assign button per the instructions.

A: This can happen. However, if you restart your certificate service and step back through the certification process, you should see the Assign button.

Q: Is there a way to test dialing plans on the server?

A: Yes. You can download and install the OCS Resource Toolkit. You will find an Enterprise Route Helper Toolkit that will help you visualize and test your voice configuration.

Chapter 7

Configuring Archiving

Solutions in this chapter:

- Addressing Compliance Requirements
- How OCS Addresses Compliance
- Archiving Topology
- Installing the Archiving Server

☑ Summary

☑ Solutions Fast Track

☑ Frequently Asked Questions

Introduction

As part of your Office Communications Server (OCS) deployment, you will need to consider whether your organization requires the archiving of instant messages (IMs) and meetings or the recording of call detail records (CDRs) and other usage information. This will depend on your organization's policies as well as on government legislation and professional bodies which may also require the archiving of these messages.

Addressing Compliance Requirements

To address compliance requirements you need to determine which government legislation you must follow. For example, healthcare organizations need to take into account the requirements of the Health Insurance Portability and Accountability Act of 1996 (HIPAA). Some professional bodies also advise or require that communications are archived, so you will also need to know to which professional bodies your organization belongs.

Although there are external influences on archiving requirements, your organization may also have internal policies that you need to take into account when planning your archiving requirements for OCS. In general, the requirements for the archiving of IMs tend to be the same as for e-mail and other forms of electronic communication. If you are unsure of your organization's requirements, you should discuss it with your colleagues.

Types of Compliance

Each form of government legislation has its own compliance requirements; some of these may require long-term storage of IMs, and others may require that IMs are randomly sampled to ensure compliance.

HIPAA

HIPAA requires that any organization that handles protected health information (PHI) follow the rules set down in the Act; the Security Rule contains a Security Safeguard that requires all electronic transmission of PHI be audit-logged. Therefore, it is advisable that you archive IMs to ensure compliance.

Sarbanes–Oxley Act

Since the Sarbanes-Oxley Act of 2002 was signed, it has caused major reform of business practices within the organizations that are required to follow it. Part of this reform is the requirement to archive all incoming and outgoing electronic communication. IMs fall under this requirement; therefore, you are required to archive all the IMs your organization generates.

Other Compliance Requirements

Your organization may be subject to many other compliance requirements. For example, the U.S. Securities and Exchange Commission requires IMs to be stored for at least three years; the National Association of Securities Dealers requires that all IMs be treated the same as e-mail and other electronic forms of communication.

How OCS Addresses Compliance

Compliance in OCS is handled via an Archiving and CDR Server that allows you to configure OCS to archive all IMs and meetings to a dedicated database. Due to the scalable nature of OCS, the Archiving and CDR Server can scale from a single server to multiple servers to ensure that compliancy requirements are met. Microsoft Message Queuing (MSMQ) is used to transport the messages from the front-end server to the Archiving and CDR Server.

NOTE

MSMQ is a Windows component that allows applications to send and receive messages to each other. If the receiving application is not running, messages are stored on the receiving file system until the application is started.

MSMQ is a transactional system that ensures that resources are available to accept messages to the MSMQ service for transmission. These mechanisms in MSMQ are used to ensure that compliance requirements are met and messages are not lost.

OCS can archive only IMs and meetings. If you need to store the contents of audio/video calls, Live Meetings, and Enterprise Voice calls, you will need to find alternative ways to do this.

Another aspect of the Archiving and CDR Server is the ability to generate CDRs; *CDR* in OCS is a generic term used to capture and store usage information for IMs and meetings, audio/video calls, Live Meetings, and Enterprise Voice calls. This information allows you to perform extensive data mining using SQL Reporting Services or any other SQL reporting tools.

The Archiving and CDR Server is one of the few resources that you can share across multiple pools. This means the same archiving infrastructure and database can be used by multiple pools to provide a single database for data mining and reporting. Sharing the infrastructure among multiple pools allows for better utilization of the Archiving and CDR Server for companies that have multiple pools for business reasons. For example, one pool may require the archiving of only 30 staff members; therefore, it is not worth setting up dedicated Archiving and CDR Servers for such a small number when other servers can be used.

Archiving Conversations and Instant Messages

Archiving in OCS allows you to archive *IMs*, which basically are conversations between two parties. Conversations among three or more parties are called *meetings*. Archiving is configured differently for IMs and meetings because conversations among three or more parties are handled by the IM Conferencing Service, whereas conversations between two parties are handled by the Front-End Service.

IM Archiving

IM archives are configured at the forest level, which means that these settings affect all the pools in your organization. A number of options are available to you when you configure IM archives, as shown in Figure 7.1. Although the IM archiving options are configured at the forest level, archiving is enabled on a per-pool basis, allowing users in one pool to be archived while users in another pool are not.

Figure 7.1 Configuring Forest-Level Archiving

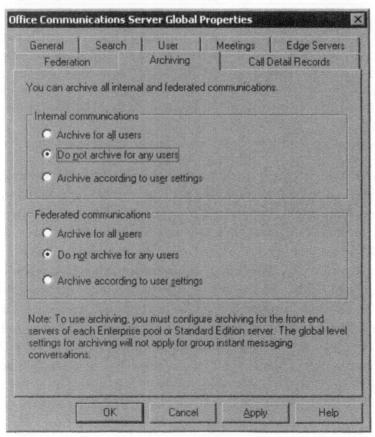

If you configure archiving on a per-user basis, archiving is disabled by default for each user, and you will need to enable it for each user for which you require archiving. You do this through the OCS Administration Tool. Configuration of federated communication also covers Public Internet Connectivity (PIC) connections used when connecting to public IM networks.

Meeting Archiving

Because of the way meetings are handled, archiving options are limited; archiving is enabled when archiving for the pool in enabled, and all settings at the forest level are ignored. Meetings are also archived regardless of whether they have internal or federated participants.

If your organization has multiple pools, to ensure that all meetings are archived you will need to enable archiving on every pool. Meetings are hosted in the pool in which the initiating user is located.

Call Detail Records

CDR in OCS is used to generate usage information. This is configured at the forest level in terms of the information logged, but is enabled on a per-pool basis. Figure 7.2 shows the available options.

Figure 7.2 Configuring CDR

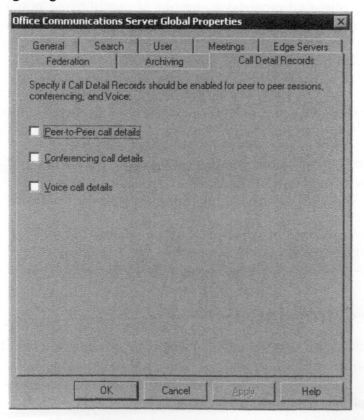

You can use the CDR information you collect to analyze OCS usage; in addition, companies can use this information to recharge costs to individuals or departments. Some possible uses are as follows:

- Recharge costs based on conference minutes used
- Recharge costs for phone calls when using Enterprise Voice
- View the most active users
- View users who have not used OCS to allow for training to be arranged
- Report on users who used Remote Assistance or Application Sharing

There are many other possible uses for the information, depending on what your organization requires. If you are planning to report against the CDR information, you will need to write your own queries to extract the information from the database.

SOME INDEPENDENT ADVICE

The OCS resource kit provides a number of useful tools; many of these tools were written by the OCS development team but were not mature enough to make it into the actual product. Two tools are useful for archiving: the ArchivingCDR Reporter and LCSError.

The ArchivingCDR Reporter provides a number of predefined SQL queries which allow you to easily view the CDR information collected; these queries are stored in an XML file, so you can easily view them and either modify them or use them in other applications. You can add additional queries to the XML file and view them through the ArchivingCDR Reporter.

LCSError allows you to translate error codes into a description of the error; it also may provide additional details regarding possible error causes and solutions. This tool can be useful when log files list only error codes and no descriptive text.

You can use both of these tools on machines that are not running OCS, allowing them to be used by support teams and analysts.

Ensuring Compliance

With OCS archiving you have the ability to archive all meetings and IMs. This is referred to as *Critical Mode archiving*. When archiving is running in this mode and a front-end server is unable to archive messages, it will shut down, ensuring that no further messages can be passed and compliancy requirements are maintained.

An additional aspect of the archiving capabilities in OCS allows the messages to be encrypted between the front-end server and the Archiving and CDR Server, which may be part of your compliancy requirements. If your setup includes use of a database on a remote server, you will need to use SQL SSL encryption to secure the traffic between the Archiving and CDR Server and the database server; as an alternative, you can use Windows IP Security (IPSec) encryption.

Handling Failure

Archiving can fail in OCS in a number of ways, and all of these failures are handled in the same way if you are running in Critical Mode. In such a scenario, an error is written to the Windows Event Log and the Front-End Service is shut down. If you are not in Critical Mode, an error is written to the Event Log but the Front-End Service continues to function.

Because MSMQ is used as the underlying transport mechanism for archiving, failure may not happen instantly, as messages can be queued on the front-end server if the Archiving and CDR Server is not accessible. This helps to ensure that temporary network outages or a reboot of the Archiving and CDR Server does not result in an archiving failure.

If the archiving agent is unable to submit messages to the MSMQ queue on the front-end server, a failure will be instant. These failures are usually due to a configuration issue or to the Message Queuing Service not running.

If messages cannot be sent to the Archiving and CDR Server, the messages will sit in the message queue for 30 minutes until a failure is issued. If messages are sent to the Archiving and CDR Server but the archiving service is not running or is unable to process the messages for any reason, after 45 minutes a failure will occur; you can configure both of these timeout periods through Windows Management Instrumentation (WMI).

If the archiving service is unable to write messages to the database for any reason other than the SQL server being unavailable, the messages are written to a log file which is then processed when it becomes possible to write to the database again; if it is not possible to write to the log file, the messages are returned to the MSMQ queue to be reprocessed when possible. A failure will be issued if the database is not available again within 45 minutes. This value is configurable via WMI.

If the SQL server is unavailable, the archiving role server will try to connect for 45 minutes. In this time, the messages will remain in the message queue. If after 45 minutes the archiving role server is unable to connect, a failure is issued. This timeout value is configurable via WMI.

Modifying WMI Settings for Archiving

Archiving and CDR Server settings are stored in WMI. Although most of these settings are configurable through the OCS Administration Tool, the settings used to configure failure times need to be configured outside of this tool. You will need to change these settings on all servers running the front-end server and the Archiving and CDR Server.

To change WMI settings you can use the *wbemtest* tool which comes with Windows 2003; with this tool you can change the WMI settings on both the local and remote machines. The two settings are:

- **TimeToBeReceived** This is the number of minutes a message will wait on the Archiving and CDR Server before a failure is issued. By default, this is 45 minutes.

- **TimeToReachQueue** This is the number of minutes a message will wait on the front-end server before a failure is issued. By default, this is 30 minutes.

The maximum value is 1,440 minutes, and the minimum value is 0 minutes.

To change the WMI settings follow these steps (it is assumed that you are logged in as an administrator):

1. Click **Start | Run** and enter **wbemtest** in the **Open dialog**. Then click **OK**.
2. Once the Windows Management Instrumentation Tester loads, click **Connect**.
3. In the **Namespace field** enter **root\cimv2**. Click **Connect**.
4. Select **Open Instance**.
5. In **Object Path**, enter **MSFT_SIPLogSetting** and click **OK**.
6. In the **Properties field**, select either **TimeToBeReceived** or **TimeToReachQueue** and then select **Edit Property**.
7. Under **Value**, select **Not Null** and enter a value between 0 and 1440.
8. Click **Save Property**.
9. Once you have edited all the properties you need to change, click **Save Object**.
10. Click **Exit**.

Archive Retention

The database used for archiving is not designed for long-term data retention. It is designed to be a holding area until the archived data can be moved to a more permanent location. For a system with 65,000 users, it is recommended that the data be moved every three days. Although this may not seem like an ideal solution, there are a number of reasons for this:

- The database was designed to optimize writes to ensure that there is not a backlog of messages to be archived.
- There is no audit history on who views the archived information.
- There is no easy way to view the archived information.
- The data could be easily modified.

Third-party products are available that allow for long-term data archival. These products let you store, search, and retrieve the archived data so that you can fulfill compliance requirements regarding online instant access to archived messages. Two of these products are IMSecurity from Symantec, which uses Enterprise Vault for archiving; and FaceTime Enterprise Edition. Each product provides its own collection mechanism, making the Archiving and CDR Server useful only for CDR collection and as a secondary source of data collection when using these products.

The Archiving and CDR Server can purge data after a certain number of days, if required; this is configured on a per-server basis through the OCS Administration Tool. The maximum days logged can range from 0 to 2,562, with the recommended value being seven days; if you are using a third-party product for long-term storage, you should set this to a value that ensures that data is collected for long-term storage. Third-party products may take care of removing old data themselves.

To configure the maximum number of days logged follow these steps:

1. Click **Start | All Programs | Administrative Tools | Office Communication Server 2007**.

2. Once the administration tool has loaded, expand the **Forest tree**.

3. Expand **Archiving and CDR Servers**.

4. Right-click the **Archiving and CDR Server** and select **Properties**.

5. Check the **Maximum Days Logged checkbox** and enter the number of days in the **Number of Days box**.

6. Click **Apply** followed by **OK**.

7. Restart the Archiving and CDR Service for these settings to take effect.

It is possible to restrict purging to off-peak hours to try to prevent a performance impact; you can configure off-peak hours through WMI in the same way you modify other WMI archival settings. These settings are stored under the *MSFT_SIPLogServiceSetting* class, in the *PurgeTime* property. The *PurgeTime* property specifies the hour that the purge should start. The value can be between 0 and 23.

You should modify these settings on each Archiving and CDR Server on which you have configured purging; it is a good idea to stagger these times if the servers are all using the same database. Once you have changed this setting, you should restart the Archiving and CDR Service.

Archiving Topology

The topology for archiving varies depending on your compliance requirements and the version of OCS you are using. This section will discuss the topology for a Standard Edition deployment and an Enterprise Edition deployment.

Archiving in OCS is split into two components. The first is the archiving agent, which is installed with the front-end server. The second is the Archiving and CDR Server, which you can install on multiple machines and which can accept archiving traffic from multiple agents.

Standard Edition Topology

A Standard Edition deployment allows for a single OCS server running the Front-End and Conferencing Server roles; within a Standard Edition setup there are two options for archiving, depending on the number of users and the archiving traffic generated.

The first option is to colocate the Archiving and CDR Server on the Standard Edition server. This is not a recommended route, as it can create a high server load and therefore cause performance issues, but you could use it in a small deployment. Ideally, the database should be on a separate machine, but if necessary, you could use the same database you used for the OCS configuration database; this is not advised, however.

The second solution is to use a dedicated server for the Archiving and CDR Server. This is the recommended route for a Standard Edition deployment. With this setup there are two options for the database. You can either place the database on the same machine or use a dedicated or shared database server. Figure 7.3 shows a Standard Edition deployment using a dedicated server for the Archiving and CDR Server and a dedicated database server.

Figure 7.3 Standard Edition Archiving Topology

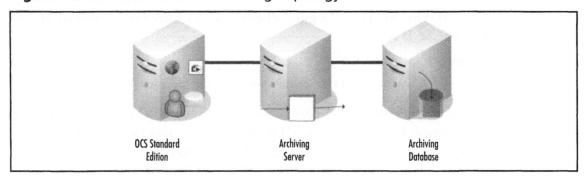

OCS Standard Edition	Archiving Server	Archiving Database

To ensure compliance in this environment you can set the Front-End Service to shut down if archiving or encryption fails. Because a Standard Edition setup can have only a single front-end, if the Front-End Service does shut down OCS will effectively shut down as well. If you require high availability and you need to be able to ensure compliance, you will need to consider an Enterprise Edition deployment.

WARNING

When you set the front-end server to shut down due to an encryption failure, this will be triggered only if the encryption fails as part of the MSMQ process that is between the archiving agent and the Archiving and CDR Server.

If you are using encryption between the archiving and database servers and it fails, causing a link failure, this failure will be logged as an archiving failure, not as an encryption failure. Therefore, you should monitor for failures in archiving and encryption to ensure that compliance requirements are met.

Enterprise Edition Topology

In an Enterprise Edition deployment, you can deploy multiple front-end servers. This increases the number of users OCS can support, and it allows for high availability, which enables you to use Critical Mode archiving while still maintaining availability to users.

When you are deciding on a topology for an Enterprise Edition deployment, you should consider the following three factors:

- Do you require Critical Mode archiving?
- Do you need to ensure that MSMQ encryption is used?
- Is loss of service acceptable to ensure compliancy?

These go hand in hand, as loss of service will generally occur only when using Critical Mode archiving or when you want to ensure that MSMQ encryption is used. Figure 7.4 shows a topology that allows for the failure of an Archiving and CDR Server, but still prevents a loss of service due to the front-end servers being split across two Archiving and CDR Servers; to mitigate failure of the database a clustered database solution is used.

Figure 7.4 Enterprise Edition Archiving Topology

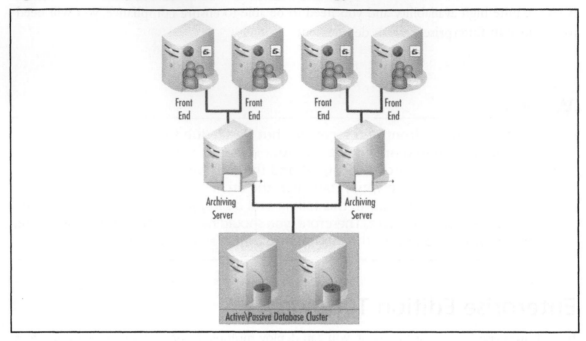

Although this solution may appear complex, it helps to ensure that compliancy is maintained, along with serviceability which is a key requirement for many organizations. If you are planning to implement a solution such as this, there should be enough spare capacity to allow for the loss of two front-end servers.

The recommended maximum number of users per Archiving and CDR Server is 65,000, allowing each server to support six front-end servers. For environments where you do not have to ensure compliancy, this may be suitable, but if you are running in Critical Mode, this could result in the loss of six front-end servers, resulting in a very high load on the remaining servers and the possible loss of service to some users.

Your topology should take into account your compliancy requirements along with the service level you want to offer to your users. The Archiving and CDR Server should run on dedicated servers and use a dedicated database server to that ensure you are getting the best performance.

Because organizations have different compliancy requirements and service levels, it is not possible to provide a one-size-fits-all solution for archiving. Therefore, you should use this information as a guideline for designing your OCS solution. Archiving should not be an afterthought; you should consider it throughout the design stage.

Installing the Archiving Server

This section covers installation, activation, and configuration of the archiving server. Each process is distinct and is sometimes performed by different people in an organization. In this section, we will discuss installing the Archiving and CDR Server onto a dedicated server in an existing enterprise pool, using a SQL server on a dedicated server.

Installation

You need to install the Archiving and CDR Server on a Windows 2003 SP1 or later server which is a member of the same domain as the front-end server. Before you install the Archiving and CDR Server, you must install MSMQ with the Active Directory Integration subcomponent. This subcomponent is usually selected by default when installing MSMQ; you should install it on all servers running the Archiving and CDR Server and front-end server.

To install MSMQ follow these steps:

1. Log in to the machine using a domain account that has local administrator permissions.
2. Click **Start** and then select **Control Panel**.
3. Select **Add or Remove Programs**.
4. Select **Add/Remove Windows Components**.
5. Select **Application Settings** and click on **Details**.
6. Select the checkbox next to **Message Queuing**. This should become checked with a gray background.
7. Select **Details** and ensure that **Active Directory Integration** is selected.
8. Click on **OK** twice and then click **Next**, followed by **Finish**.

Once MSMQ is installed you will be able to install the Archiving and CDR Server; if all the prerequisites are not met, the options to install the server are disabled.

Before you start the installation, you will need to know what you want to call the MSMQ queue. By default, it is called *LCSLog*, but you can change it if you want.

To install the Archiving and CDR Server follow these steps:

1. Log in to the machine using a domain account that has local administrator permissions.
2. Insert the OCS installation media into the machine. The Deployment Wizard should run automatically. If it doesn't, you can start it from **My Computer**.
3. From the wizard, select **Deploy Other Server Roles**.

4. Select **Deploy Archiving and CDR Server**.

5. Click the **Install button** under **Install Files for Archiving and CDR Server**; if this is grayed out, ensure that the prerequisites are met.

6. The Install Wizard should now be loaded. Click **Next**, accept the terms and conditions, and click **Next** again.

7. You will be prompted for the installation path. Change this if required and click **Next**.

8. You will be prompted to specify the MSMQ queue name. If you do not need to change this, click **Next**. If you do need to change this, enter the new name and click **Next**.

9. Click **Next** to start the installation, followed by **Close**.

The installation should now be complete and you can continue to the activation stage. If the installation fails you can view the log files in your Temporary Files location. Two files should be created: LCSSetup_Commands.log and caArchService.msi-[*today's date and time*]; the Windows Event Log may also contain useful information.

Activation

During the activation phase you perform the initial configuration of the Archiving and CDR Server and make it available for use. At this point, you will need to either create a service account or specify an existing one. If you intend to install multiple archiving servers you should use the same account for all of them. If you intend to create a new account during the activation process you will need a password that conforms to your organization's password policies; by default, this account is called *RTCArchivingService*, but you can change it to conform to your organization's policies.

NOTE

If your organization forces passwords to expire, you will need to ensure that you change the password regularly and update it for the OCS Archiving and CDR Service on each server running the Archiving and CDR Server; failure to do this will result in archiving failure.

Another option is to set the service account so that the password never expires, although setting this can break your security policies.

The final requirements relate to the SQL server and database you will be using. You can use either SQL 2000 SP4 or later, or SQL Server 2005.

The first requirement is to install SQL Distributed Management Objects (SQL-DMOs) onto the Archiving and CDR Server. If you are using SQL 2000, you can install this from the SQL 2000 installation media by installing the client tools. If you are using SQL Server 2005, you will need to install the Microsoft SQL Server 2005 Backwards Compatibility Components. These are available on the SQL 2005 installation media.

If this is the first Archiving and CDR Server install you will probably be creating the database during the activation process. If you already have an existing database that you want to use you can specify it during the activation; if you are creating a database you will require the following information:

- Database server name

- Database name to use

- Path for the database data files

- Path for the transaction log files

To activate the Archiving and CDR Server role you will need an account with permissions to perform the tasks that occur during activation. If you are creating the service account during the activation process you will need an account that has permissions to perform this task on the domain. If you are using an existing account you will need to be a member of *RTCUniversalServerAdmins* role and of the local administrator group on the Archiving and CDR Server and the SQL server.

To activate the Archiving and CDR Server role follow these steps:

1. Log in to the machine using an account that has the appropriate permissions.

2. Insert the OCS installation media into the machine. The Deployment Wizard should run automatically. If it doesn't, you can start it from **My Computer**.

3. From the wizard, select **Deploy Other Server Roles**.

4. Select **Deploy Archiving and CDR Server**.

5. Click the **Run button** under **Activate Archiving and CDR Server**; if this is grayed out ensure that the install was completed successfully.

6. The Activation Wizard should now load. Click **Next**.

7. If you are using an existing account select the **Use an Existing Account radio button** and enter the **Account Name** and **Password** fields; if you want to create a new account select the **Create a New Account radio button** and fill in the **Account Name**, **Password**, and **Confirm Password** fields and click **Next**.

8. Enter the **SQL server** to be used. You can specify an **Instance** if required. If you want to change the database name you can specify it under **Database Name**; then click **Next** to continue.

9.   You will have the choice of overriding an existing database if it exists or reusing an existing database (you will receive this warning even if there are no existing databases). If you are adding an additional archiving server ensure that you *do not* check the checkbox labeled **Replace any existing database**; otherwise, you will lose all existing data. Click **Next** to continue.

10. You will be prompted to enter the location where you want the database files to reside. The paths you specify are local to the SQL server; click **Next** to continue.

11. If you do not want to start the service after activation, uncheck the checkbox labeled **Start the service after activation** and then click **Next** to continue.

12. Once you have confirmed all of the settings, click **Next** to continue.

13. If the activation completes successfully, you should need to view the log only if the activation fails.

Once the activation is complete, restart the Archiving and CDR Server to ensure that the Archiving and CDR Service starts and that there are no errors in the Windows Event Log.

Configuration

You perform the configuration through the OCS Administration Tool. This tool is not installed on the Archiving and CDR Server by default, but you can install it from the OCS installation media if required, using the tool installed on the front-end server or on an administration machine.

Forest Configuration

Forest-level configuration allows you to specify which types of messages are archived and who is archived; we outlined these options earlier in the chapter, along with the forest CDR configuration options.

To modify the forest configuration follow these steps:

1.   Click **Start | All Programs | Administrative Tools | Office Communication Server 2007**.

2.   Once the administration tool has loaded right-click **Forest – *domain name***, select **Properties**, and then select **Global Properties**.

3. On the **Archiving** and **Call Detail Records tab** select the options you require.

4. Click **Apply** and then **OK**.

Front-End Configuration

You perform front-end configuration on a per-pool basis. It allows you to enable the Archiving and CDR Server for the pool and to associate each front-end server to an archiving server.

To enable archiving follow these steps:

1. Click **Start | All Programs | Administrative Tools | Office Communication Server 2007**.

2. Once the administration tool has loaded expand the **Forest tree**.

3. If you're running the Enterprise Edition, expand **Enterprise pools**, expand the pool you want to configure, right-click **Front Ends** and select **Properties**.

4. If you're running the Standard Edition, expand **Standard Edition Servers**, right-click the **pool**, select **Properties**, and then select **Front End Properties**.

5. Select the **Archiving tab**, as shown in Figure 7.5.

6. To enable message archiving, check the **Archive content archiving box** (if you receive an error indicating that archiving is disabled, ensure that you have configured archiving at the forest level).

7. If you want to enable Critical Mode archiving check the **Shut down server if archiving fails box**.

8. If you want to enable encryption failure, check the **Shut down server if Message Queuing encryption fails box**.

9. If you want to capture usage information check the **Activate call details recording box**.

10. To associate each front-end server with an Archiving and CDR Server, for each front-end server select the front-end server name and click **Associate**. The **Associate Queue Path window** will open (see Figure 7.6). In the first box enter the **Archiving and CDR Server Hostname**. In the second box enter the **MSMQ Queue Name**; this was specified when you installed the archiving server. Click **OK**.

11. Click **Apply** followed by **OK**.

Figure 7.5 Configuring Front-End Archiving

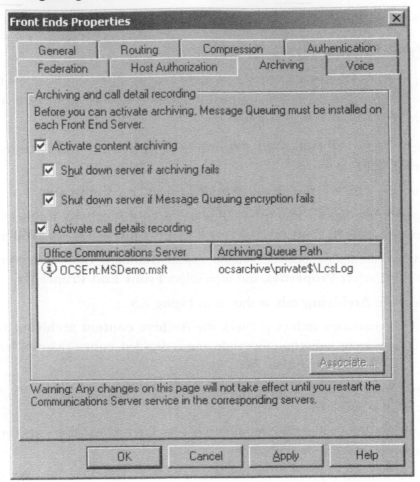

Figure 7.6 Associating the Queue Path for Front-End Archiving

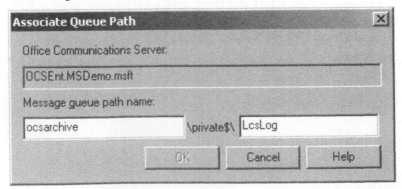

Once you have configured archiving for the front-end servers, you should restart each front-end server to ensure that they start correctly and that no errors appear in the Windows Error Log; archiving will not be enabled until after the OCS Front-End Service is restarted.

If you add additional front-end servers in the future you will need to remember to associate them with an Archiving and CDR Server.

User Configuration

User configuration is required only if you have configured archiving on a per-user basis. If you have chosen to either archive all users in your forest or not to archive them, these configuration options will be disabled. To configure users you will need to be either a domain administrator or a member of the *RTCUniversalUserAdmins* group; the configuration is performed through the OCS Administration Tool.

To configure users for archiving via the Configure Users Wizard follow these steps:

1. Click **Start | All Programs | Administrative Tools | Office Communication Server 2007**.

2. Once the administration tool has loaded expand the **Forest tree**.

3. If you're running the Enterprise Edition, expand **Enterprise pools**, expand the pool you want to configure, and click **Users**.

4. If you're running the Standard Edition, expand **Standard Edition Servers**, expand the **pool**, and click **Users**.

5. Select the users you want to configure from the right-hand pane (multiselect is possible).

6. Right-click the selected users and select **Configure users**.

7. The Office Communications Server Users Wizard will load. Click **Next**.

8. You will be presented with the **Configure User Settings screen**, as shown in Figure 7.7. From this screen, you can modify the archiving settings. If the archiving checkboxes are grayed out, per-user archiving is not enabled. This screen will not indicate any current archiving settings. To modify the archiving settings you will need to check the **Archive internal messages** and **Archive federated messages checkboxes** and then choose either **Enable** or **Disable**.

9. Click **Next** four times to perform the change. You will see a screen that shows the success or failure for each user; failures usually occur due to permissions issued.

10. Click **Finish** to exit the wizard.

Figure 7.7 The Configure Users Wizard

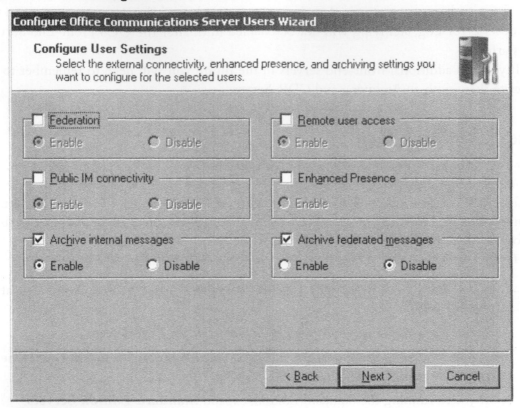

You can also change the archiving settings through the properties for each user; this also allows you to view the current archiving settings for each user.

To configure users for archiving via user properties follow these steps:

1. Click **Start | All Programs | Administrative Tools | Office Communication Server 2007**.

2. Once the administration tool has loaded expand the **Forest tree**.

3. If you're running the Enterprise Edition, expand **Enterprise pools**, expand the pool you want to configure, and click **Users**.

4. If you're running the Standard Edition, expand **Standard Edition Servers**, expand the **pool**, and click **Users**.

5. Select the user you want to configure from the right-hand pane, right-click, and select **Properties**.

6. Click **Configure**.

7. The advanced options will open, as shown in Figure 7.8.

8. Under **Archiving** you can configure the internal and federated archiving options. If these are grayed out, per-user archiving is not enabled. Click **OK** to continue.

9. Click **Apply** followed by **OK** to complete the configuration.

Figure 7.8 Advanced User Options

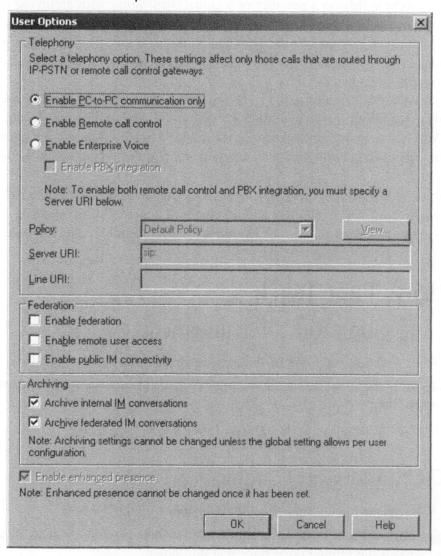

Any changes you have made to these settings will not take effect until the user either signs out and back in to OCS or the user's registration is refreshed; registration is refreshed every two hours for internal users and every 10 minutes for external users.

Summary

Compliancy is a major requirement for a lot of organizations. This is made possible in OCS by the use of archiving. When designing your topology you should take into account the compliancy requirements for your organization and how you can implement them. When you need to ensure compliancy you should use Critical Mode archiving.

OCS can archive IMs on a per-user or a global basis, along with archiving meetings. If you require the archiving of other aspects of OCS you should use third-party products. If you need long-term storage of messages along with the ability to easily search and retrieve these messages you will need to use third-party products as the OCS database is designed to store messages for only a few days.

When installing and activating the archiving server you should ensure that you install it on a machine that fulfills the prerequisites and that you have the information required, such as the MSMQ queue name and database server to use. When configuring archiving you should ensure that if you configure per-user archiving you should configure the users you want to archive.

Within many organizations, compliancy is often seen as an obstacle and is often left as an afterthought. Your OCS topology should take into account all of your organization's compliancy requirements from the start to ensure that your topology provides the compliancy you require.

Solutions Fast Track

Addressing Compliance Requirements

- ☑ Ensure that you are aware of all government legislation that affects IMs.
- ☑ Ensure that you are aware of any professional and internal requirements to archive IMs.
- ☑ As a rule of thumb, you should treat IMs the same as e-mail.

How OCS Addresses Compliance

- ☑ OCS addresses compliance via the Archiving and CDR Server.
- ☑ You can use Critical Mode to ensure that no messages are lost. If an archiving server fails the Front-End Service will shut down.
- ☑ You can capture usage information in the form of call detail records.

Archiving Topology

☑ If you're using the Standard Edition, you can install the archiving server on either the front-end server or a dedicated server.

☑ If you're using the Enterprise Edition, you should use dedicated servers.

☑ If you're using the Enterprise Edition and Critical Mode archiving, you should spread the front-end servers over multiple archiving servers to ensure uptime.

☑ Use a dedicated SQL server to prevent performance issues.

Installing the Archiving Server

☑ Install MSMQ on the front-end servers and archiving servers.

☑ Using a Domain Administrator account, install the archiving server. During the install, you will need to specify the MSMQ queue name.

☑ Activate the archiving server. During the activation, you will need the database server name, file paths, and either details of an existing service account or a password for a new one.

☑ Configure archiving at the forest level and enable archiving on the pool level.

Frequently Asked Questions

Q: During activation, I get an error that says "Failed to start SQL service or invalid SQL instance." I am running the Standard Edition and I am trying to use the SQL server installed by OCS. What is wrong?

A: When OCS is installed, it installs a specific SQL instance, called *hostname*\rtc. When you specify the SQL server for archiving, you will need to enter *hostname*rtc instead of entering only the hostname.

Q: What should I do if I have configured archiving, but nothing is appearing in the SQL database?

A: Make sure that you have restarted the Front-End Service after configuring archiving. If you have multiple front-end servers, ensure that you restart the service on all of them.

Q: My Front-End Service keeps shutting down. How can I fix the problem?

A: If you are using archiving, check whether you have Critical Mode enabled. If you do and archiving is failing, your Front-End Service will keep shutting down. If this is the case, check your Event Logs for errors that may indicate why archiving is failing.

Chapter 8

Configuring Conferencing Servers

Solutions in this chapter:

- **Understanding On-Premises Conferencing**
- **Using On-Premises Conferencing**
- **Microsoft RoundTable**
- **Installing Conferencing**

☑ **Summary**

☑ **Solutions Fast Track**

☑ **Frequently Asked Questions**

Introduction

Video, audio, instant messaging (IM), and *Web conferencing* have quickly become common terms in today's workplace. Regional, national, and international companies use these forms of conferencing as a way to better collaborate with coworkers and customers who often reside in separate geographic locations. With the ability to more actively share slide presentations, whiteboards, and even applications, companies are rapidly deeming these forms of communication *mission critical*. Office Communications Server (OCS) 2007 delivers an easy-to-use video, audio, IM, and Web conferencing solution that offers rich integration with other Microsoft Office applications. OCS provides reliable conferencing with just a few clicks of the mouse from within applications with which most people are already familiar.

In addition to offering a full set of traditional conferencing features in OCS 2007, Microsoft has also announced a videoconferencing device named RoundTable. RoundTable brings Web conferencing to a new level by providing a 360-degree panoramic video experience to meeting participants.

After reading this chapter, you should have a clear understanding of the new conferencing features in OCS 2007 and be ready to configure and use those features in your organization.

Understanding On-Premises Conferencing

Web conferencing is one of the fastest-growing collaboration applications available today. Web-based conferencing provides an easy-to-use interface that enables users to quickly learn how to use the application and begin to host meetings. Typically, Web conferencing is a hosted solution provided by a third party outside your company's firewall. Microsoft began to offer its own Web conferencing solution, known as Live Meeting, just a few years ago. Live Meeting was instantly a success and is now the Web conferencing tool of choice for thousands of organizations. OCS 2007 delivers *on-premises conferencing*, giving your company the capabilities and features of a hosted conferencing solution, but allowing you to maintain the service within your corporate network.

OCS delivers three main conferencing solutions:

- **On-Premises Live Meeting Web conferencing** This service provides a more secure and possibly more cost-effective way to host Web conferences. Most of the features of the Hosted Live Meeting service are now available through OCS.

- **Audio and videoconferencing** By using the Microsoft Office Communicator (MOC) 2007 client, you can contact another OCS user(s) via an audio or video call. OCS even allows you to invite multiple parties to the audio/videoconference within MOC.

- **IM conferencing using MOC** OCS also provides an easy way to conduct IM conferences via MOC. With MOC 2007 you can now instantly start a group chat that includes other users inside your organization as well as users outside your company. You can even invite members from public IM networks such as AOL, MSN, and Yahoo! to the conference.

Both Live Meeting and IM conferencing using MOC include the ability to use audio and video within conferences. Because on-premises conferencing moves video, IM, and Web conferencing to your network, you need a good understanding of what it takes to support a conferencing infrastructure in-house.

Before you begin any implementation or proof of concept, you should plan to evaluate and review features and limitations of competing products. During your OCS evaluation, you may want to check out other Web conferencing solutions such as Adobe Acrobat Connect and IBM Lotus Sametime. Both products offer a version for on-premises meetings:

- Adobe Acrobat Connect is a Web and videoconferencing solution built on Adobe's Flash technology. Acrobat Connect provides good performance of both Web and video features due in part to the fact that Flash is an established platform that has proven itself reliable. Acrobat Connect provides integration features with Microsoft Outlook and other applications in the Microsoft Office suite; however, you may find that this integration is not as rich as OCS to Office integration. Acrobat Connect also offers a hosted conferencing option.

- IBM Lotus Sametime provides an on-premises conferencing solution that integrates heavily with Lotus Domino and Lotus Sametime Instant Messaging. IBM's conferencing solution provides a similar experience to an OCS Live Meeting. A key difference is that IBM relies on Java that is downloaded and run on the client when the user first enters the meeting, whereas OCS uses the installed Live Meeting client.

On-Premises vs. Hosted Live Meeting

Before deploying the conferencing features in OCS 2007, it is important that you understand the differences between the traditional Hosted Live Meeting and the new On-Premises Live Meeting. Hosted Live Meeting is a service provided and managed by Microsoft, and On-Premises Live Meeting is a service supported by OCS. Sometimes you will need to use one instead of the other due to some distinct differences in security, features, and the number of conference attendees.

On-Premises Live Meeting

On-Premises Live Meeting uses OCS to provide a feature-rich Web conferencing solution that has a familiar look and feel to end users (see Figure 8.1). On-Premises Live Meeting uses the Live Meeting client that must be installed on all participants' workstations. This lightweight application provides the interface in which attendees can start, interact with, and take part in a Web conference meeting. The client connects to the OCS conferencing server when a meeting is started or joined. The conference is then managed by services running on the OCS server. A few key features of On-Premises Live Meeting that the hosted solution does not provide are:

- **Active Directory integration** You can control security and admittance into conferences via Active Directory. You can set up conferences to allow only Active Directory users who receive the invitation, any Active Directory user, or anonymous users who have a meeting code. You can also use Active Directory to control who can initiate Web conference sessions via Live Meeting.

- **Federation** Using On-Premises Live Meeting, you can also take advantage of OCS federation features to allow federated partners to join and take part in the conference. If you want to enable federated users to join a Live Meeting, you will want to deploy an OCS edge server in your perimeter network.

- **Local storage of archived and recorded sessions** On-Premises Live Meeting also allows you to record and archive meetings on your servers instead of storing them on Hosted Live Meeting servers. This may be a requirement for regulatory and compliance purposes.

Figure 8.1 Live Meeting Client with Whiteboard Session Open

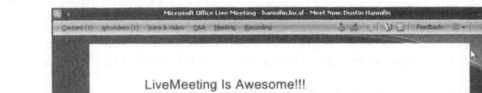

On-Premises Live Meeting requires that you set up and configure the supporting infrastructure during your OCS deployment. On-Premises Live Meeting also requires the initial cost of deployment of OCS, but there are no monthly or per-use fees for using the in-house conferencing service. You should also keep in mind that On-Premises Live Meeting supports a limit of 250 users per meeting.

NOTE

If you plan to deploy OCS Standard Edition, you should keep in mind that each Standard Edition server can support upward of 2,000–5,000 users, depending on hardware. If you plan to do a lot of Web conferencing with thousands of concurrent meeting attendees, you may want to consider deploying OCS Enterprise Edition, which can support upward of 50,000 users per pool. The maximum number of simultaneous Web conferences depends on the features used, the number of meetings using those features, and the number of users per meeting. A lot of small conferences that use audio and video in each will support a smaller number of total users than a few large conferences using the same features.

Hosted Live Meeting

Hosted Live Meeting uses Microsoft's servers for establishing and hosting conferences. This approach to Web conferencing has been around for a few years now and has become very popular in the corporate world. Microsoft itself uses the Hosted Live Meeting service to deliver Webcasts and presentations to thousands of customers on a daily basis. Hosted Live Meeting is a pay-per-use or per-month service. Hosted Live Meeting conferences provide the following benefits over On-Premises Live Meeting conferences:

- **Support for thousands of attendees** Hosted Live Meeting can support up to 2,500 attendees. This obviously allows you to provide conferences for target audiences much larger than the 250-attendee limit of OCS.

- **Web client option** If meeting attendees do not have the Live Meeting client installed or are unable to install the client, Hosted Live Meeting offers the choice to use a Web client to attend the meeting.

- **Breakout rooms** If you are hosting a large training event, you can set up breakout rooms for attendees to collaborate within smaller groups.

If you are a smaller business looking for a Web conferencing solution but you have limited resources, you may want to consider the Hosted Live Meeting offering from Microsoft.

The initial cost of Hosted Live Meeting is very small because you are paying using a subscription model and there is no infrastructure to deploy. Most companies that plan to deploy OCS should probably consider a hybrid approach to Live Meeting. In this approach, you can use On-Premises Live Meeting for internal conferences and smaller conferences with customers and federated partners. Then, if you need to support a very large number of attendees, you can use the Hosted Live Meeting solution. You can use the same Live Meeting client in either situation. This provides end users with a common, easy-to-use interface for both services. Consider this scenario. Your company currently employees 2,000 people with offices located in six large cities throughout the United States. You have thousands of customers in five countries. Every Monday, sales teams have planning meetings for the coming week. Each sales team is composed of 10–20 members. During the meeting, the preceding week's sales figures and goals for the coming week are presented. This situation is a perfect example of when you can use OCS to host On-Premises Live Meetings. By using OCS, the sales teams can conduct their weekly meetings without paying for a hosted solution. Using Hosted Live Meetings in this situation would prove to be very costly over time. Now consider this situation. Your company's CEO is planning a corporate presentation that needs to be broadcast via a Web conference that every person in the company and several hundred external partners can view. Because this is a high-profile meeting that could have far more than 2,000 attendees, Hosted Live Meeting would be the better option.

You should now have a good understanding of the differences between Hosted Live Meeting and On-Premises Live Meeting. You can now determine in which situations you should use Hosted Live Meeting services and On-Premises Live Meeting provided by OCS. Table 8.1 provides a summary of key differences between the two Live Meeting options.

Table 8.1 On-Premises Live Meeting and Hosted Live Meeting Comparison

Features	On-Premises Live Meeting	Hosted Live Meeting
Requires OCS 2007	X	
Requires Active Directory integrated security model*	X	
Archived sessions stored on local network	X	
Up to 250 conference attendees	X	X
Up to 2,500 conference attendees		X
Optional Web client		X

* External users are not required to have an AD account.

Using On-Premises Conferencing

Now that you have a good understanding of what on-premises conferencing is, let's jump right in and learn how to use the different conferencing features provided by OCS 2007. On-premises conferencing has traditionally been reserved for very large enterprises due to complexity and cost. OCS 2007 now makes it feasible for medium-size and even some smaller businesses to deploy on-premises Web and videoconferencing.

MOC-Based Videoconferencing

Chapter 4 provided you with details on setting up and configuring MOC 2007. This section focuses on using the videoconferencing features of MOC. Earlier in this chapter, you learned that OCS provides the ability to have videoconferences. Users can instantly start a MOC-based videoconference with any other MOC user.

Setting Up Audio and Video

Before you can start a videoconference with other MOC users, you need to set up the audio and video features in the MOC client. A simple wizard will guide you through this process, but there are a few requirements before running the Set Up Audio and Video Wizard.

- **Audio output device** If you plan to hear the person on the other end of the call you need a sound card and speakers or headphones. Just about any modern computer should come with a sound card and at least built-in speakers. It is highly recommended that you purchase a conferencing headset for better-quality audio.

- **Audio input device** Just as you need to hear audio, others need to hear you. As such, you need some sort of microphone to plug into your sound card to capture your voice. Again, it is highly recommended that you purchase a conferencing headset for a better-quality conferencing experience. These days, headsets are easy to find and are reasonably priced.

- **Videoconferencing camera** If you want others to see you in the videoconference, you obviously need a videoconferencing camera, also known as a Webcam. Microsoft recently released some very nice cameras in its LifeCam product line.

Let's go ahead and set up the audio and video for MOC. Before you begin to set up audio and video, follow these steps to install the software and drivers for your audio and Webcam devices:

1. Make sure are you logged on to your MOC client and the contact list is open and visible.

2. Select **MOC menu | Tools | Set Up Audio and Video** (see Figure 8.2). This will launch the **Set Up Audio and Video Wizard** (see Figure 8.3).

3. The default speaker and microphone for audio/videoconferencing should be selected. If you want to change these settings, select the **Custom** choice from the **drop-down menu**. You can then choose the speaker and microphone you want to use from each respective drop-down menu. After you have selected the speaker and microphone you want to use for audio and videoconferences, click **Next**.

4. Select the speaker you want to use for **audio alerts** such as new IM messages. In most cases, this will be the same speaker you selected in the preceding step. After you select the speaker you want to use for audio alerts, click **Next**.

5. Select the Webcam of your choice. This is the camera you use for videoconferences in MOC. Your Webcam should turn on and display video in the **wizard window** (see Figure 8.4). If you need to make any Webcam adjustments such as color, contrast, or zoom, you can do so on this screen. After you have confirmed that your smile is well presented by the Webcam go ahead and click **Finish**. You have now successfully set up and configured your audio and video for MOC. Let's start videoconferencing!

Figure 8.2 Launching the Set Up Audio and Video Wizard

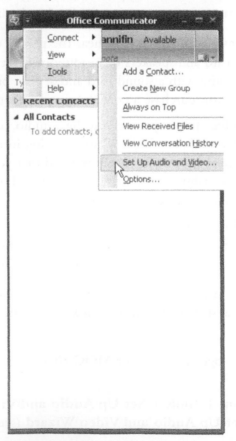

Figure 8.3 Configuring the Speaker and Microphone

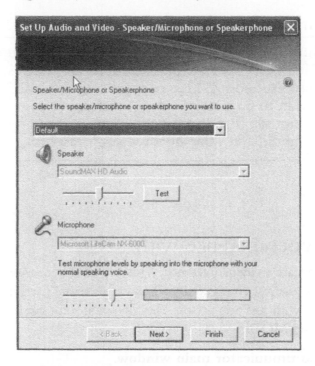

Figure 8.4 Configuring the Webcam

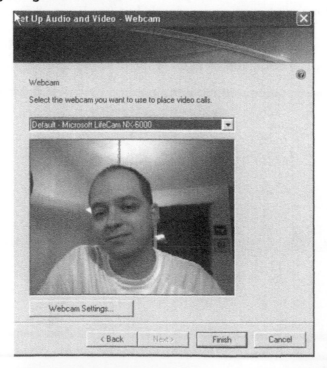

Some Independent Advice

Before deploying OCS video and audio conferencing features, be sure to plan for the added load on your network infrastructure. Microsoft recommends that network links support 45 Kbps per audio stream and 300 Kbps per video stream. If you plan to do a lot of videoconferencing you may need to plan for a network upgrade first. In most situations, it is not recommended that you to attempt audio and video over wireless networks.

Starting a Videoconference with MOC

You are now ready to start a videoconference. With any conference we need two things: a conferencing medium (we just configured that) and conference participants. It's somewhat difficult to conference with just one person. The following steps guide you through starting a videoconference using MOC:

1. Open the **Communicator main window**.

2. Locate someone in your **contact list** with whom you want to have a conference, or search for a contact using the **search bar** (see Figure 8.5).

Figure 8.5 MOC User Search

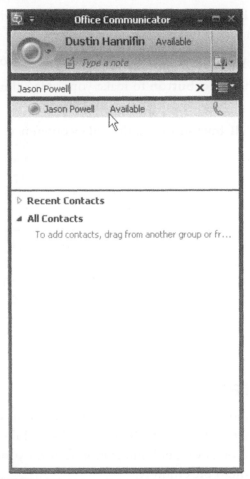

3. Right-click the name of the person you want to invite to a videoconference and click **Start a Video Call** from the pop-up menu.

4. MOC will initiate a call to the other user. The other user will receive a pop-up window from the System Tray on his computer. From the pop-up, he can click **Answer** and the two of you will be instantly bridged into a videoconference. You should see the other person in the conversation window and yourself in the picture-in-picture window.

Now that you have started the videoconference you can see and talk to the person on the other end. You can also take advantage of the following options within the conversation window:

- Use the **Invite button** to invite other attendees to the videoconference.

- Click the **Show instant message window button** to display an IM window to chat with the other person.

- Click the **Pause picture-in-picture button** to pause your Webcam.

- Click the **Switch Video button** to make your video the main window and the other person the picture-in-picture window.

- Click the **End Call button** to end the videoconference.

NOTE

All parties in the MOC-based videoconference do not need to have a Webcam or microphone. For example, the presenter or main speaker may have a Webcam and microphone, but other participants in the conference may use only text-based chat to engage others in the conference.

Outlook Integration

MOC and Live Meeting both provide integration with Microsoft Outlook. This integration enables you to easily interact with other MOC users and schedule Live Meetings within Outlook. To take advantage of all Outlook integration features you will need to install the Conferencing add-in for Microsoft Outlook.

BEST PRACTICES ACCORDING TO MICROSOFT

Microsoft offers a free Web scheduling add-on to OCS 2007. The add-on allows you to schedule new and review current Live Meetings via a Web site. This feature is useful if you do not have access to your Outlook client. This is similar to the online experience that Microsoft's Hosted Live Meeting solution offers. You can download the Web scheduler from Microsoft's Web site.

MOC Integration with Outlook

The MOC integration with Outlook allows you to see presence information regarding other OCS users beside their names in e-mail messages. You can start an IM session simply by locating the person's name in the e-mail message and right-clicking on the name of the user you want to IM. Then choose the **Reply with Instant Message** option. You can also schedule a MOC-based conference call from your Outlook Calendar.

Live Meeting Integration with Outlook

Outlook's integration with Live Meeting allows you to easily schedule a Web conference within the Outlook Calendar. To schedule a Live Meeting from Outlook follow these steps:

1. Open your Outlook Calendar.
2. Locate and click the date and time you want to schedule the Live Meeting.
3. Click the **Schedule a Live Meeting button** in the Live Meeting toolbar.
4. Add the requested attendees in the **To: field**.
5. Click the **Presenters button** if you want to add other presenters to the meeting.
6. Click the **Audio button** to customize the audio options for the meeting.
7. Click the **Access button** to set the access level for the meeting.
8. Confirm that the date and time are correct for the meeting and click the **Send button**.

The meeting request will be sent to all invited attendees via e-mail. By using the **Access button** in step 7 you can choose whether you want to limit the meeting to particular users. Selecting **Open Authenticated** will allow anyone with an account in your Active Directory domain. Open Authenticated also allows any federated user to join the Live Meeting. If you select **Closed Authenticated**, only those whom you have invited and who have Active Directory accounts will be allowed to join the meeting. Choosing **Anonymous** will allow anyone who receives the meeting invitation to join.

Ad Hoc Escalation

Live Meeting provides the ability to create a meeting on demand instantly, without prescheduling in Outlook. The Live Meeting client can connect to OCS or Hosted Live Meeting and can connect meeting users within seconds. The following section guides you through setting up the Live Meeting client for hosted or on-premises ad hoc Live Meetings as well as introduces you to some of the Live Meeting features.

Configuring the Live Meeting Client

Before you begin to use Live Meeting, you will want to configure the client. As mentioned earlier in this chapter, you can configure the Live Meeting client to use both Hosted and On-Premises Live Meeting sessions. The client can be configured for either service in just a few easy steps.

Configuring the Live Meeting Client for Hosted Live Meetings

The Live Meeting client is easy to set up and configure; however, in most deployments you will want to preconfigure these settings via Group Policy or your software deployment system. Complete the following steps to set up the Live Meeting client:

1. Select **Start | All Programs | Microsoft Office Live Meeting 2007 | Microsoft Office Live Meeting 2007**.

2. After the application launches and the main window is displayed, click **Live Meeting menu | Open User Accounts** (see Figure 8.6).

Figure 8.6 Opening the User Accounts Option via the Live Meeting Menu

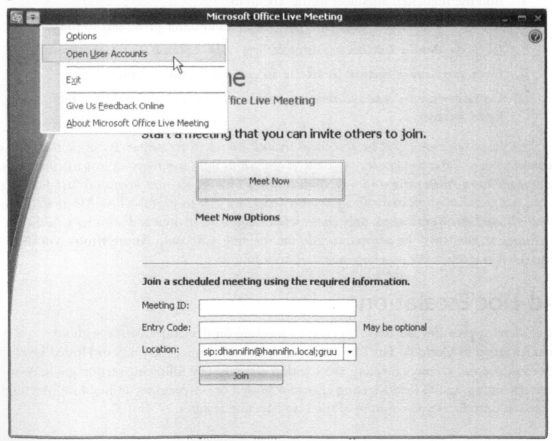

3. The **User Accounts** window will open. Locate the **Live Meeting Service** section.

4. Enter the **Hosted Live Meeting Service URL**, your **Live Meeting username**, and your **password**. Your Hosted Live Meeting administrator should have provided these to you when your Live Meeting account was created (see Figure 8.7).

Figure 8.7 Configuring Live Meeting for Hosted Conferencing

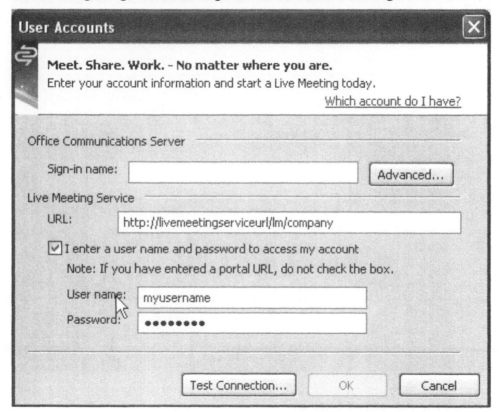

5. Click **Test Connection** to ensure that the information you entered is correct. Then click **OK**.

Configuring the Live Meeting Client for On-Premises Live Meetings

1. Select **Start | All Programs | Microsoft Office Live Meeting 2007 | Microsoft Office Live Meeting 2007**.

2. After the application launches and the main window is displayed, click **Live Meeting menu | Open User Accounts** (see Figure 8.6).

3. The **User Accounts** window will open. Locate the **Office Communications Server** section.

4. Enter your **OCS sign-in name** (see Figure 8.8).

Figure 8.8 Configuring Live Meeting for On-Premises Conferences

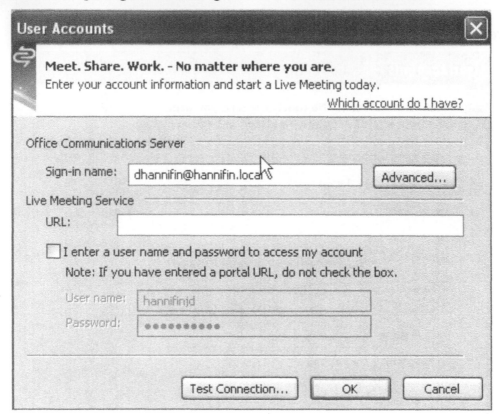

5. Click the **Advanced button**.

6. If you have not configured SIP Service records in the domain name system (DNS), you will need to enter the internal and external names of your OCS server in their respective text boxes. Note that these names must match the fully qualified domain name (FQDN) of the Secure Sockets Layer (SSL) certificate assigned to these servers (see Figure 8.9).

7. Select **TLS** as the connection protocol.

8. Optionally, you can check the **Use the following user name and password** checkbox. Enter your domain username and password in the corresponding text box and click the **OK button**. This option is useful if you are logged on to an

untrusted domain or logged on to your computer with a different user account than the one you use for Live Meeting.

9. Click the **Test Connection button** to ensure that you have properly entered server names and logon information.

10. After a successful test, click the **OK button**.

Figure 8.9 Configuring Live Meeting Advanced Connection Settings

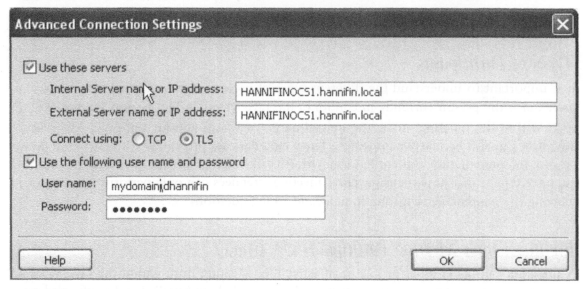

You now have successfully configured the Live Meeting client for either hosted or on-premises Live Meetings. Next, you will use the Meet Now option to initiate an ad hoc Live Meeting.

Using the Live Meeting Client's Meet Now Option

The Live Meeting client offers an option which provides ad hoc escalation of Web conferences. When you open the client and click the **Meet Now button**, a Web conference is instantly established and you are placed in the meeting as the presenter. After being placed in the meeting, you can invite other attendees via e-mail or MOC. Ad hoc, or on-demand Live Meetings, can be particularly useful in situations when you are struggling to demonstrate something on a phone call. Using Live Meeting, you can instantly invite all members on the phone and demonstrate to them visually what you couldn't describe in words. A great example of this would be in tech support situations. Let's say Mary is receiving an error message while trying to save a document within her word processing application. Mary calls the help desk and requests assistance; however, she's not sure how to describe the exact error she receives. The help desk technician can instantly initiate a Live Meeting session and ask Mary to share her screen. The technician can then see the error message for himself and more quickly resolve her problem.

Overview of Live Meeting Features

Live Meeting offers a wide variety of features to enable people to better collaborate in real time. In this section, I will provide a partial list of these features and explain how to use them.

Types of Participants

It is important to understand the different types of users within a meeting. The active presenter is the person currently in control of the Live Meeting. This person can perform all tasks within the meeting, including uploading content and conducting polls. Meeting attendees can also be inactive presenters. These attendees are presenters who currently do not control the presentation content but can perform tasks such as answer questions. The third attendee type is that of participant. These meeting attendees can only perform tasks such as viewing the content, participating in polls, and asking questions.

Inviting Other Meeting Participants via E-mail

A presenter can invite other people to an active Live Meeting from within the Live Meeting client. To invite meeting participants you need an e-mail client installed and configured on the same computer as the Live Meeting client. To invite other participants from an active Live Meeting simply select **Attendees menu | Invite | By Email**. A preformatted e-mail is created within your default e-mail client. Simply type in the e-mail address of the person you want to invite and click the **Send button**.

Sharing Content

Live Meeting provides the ability to share content including documents, Web sites, and presentation slides. To share content within a Live Meeting first start a new Live Meeting session and then select **Content menu | Share | Upload File (View Only)**, as shown in Figure 8.10. From within the open file window, browse to the file you want to share and click the **Open button**. The file uploads and is displayed within the Live Meeting window.

Figure 8.10 Live Meeting Console Uploading a File

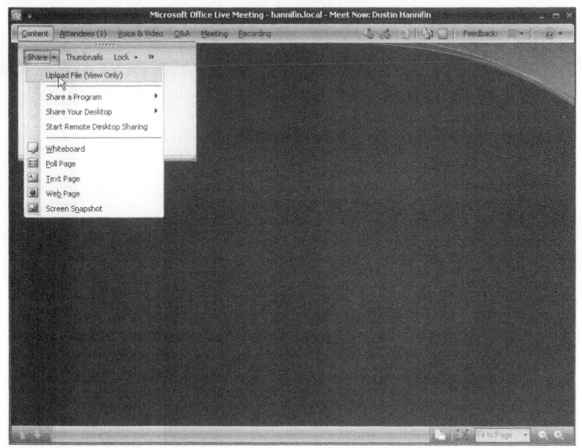

Sharing Applications and Desktops

You can use Live Meeting to display to other participants applications running on your computer or your entire desktop. To share an application or your desktop select **Content menu | Share | Share a program** or **Share your desktop**. This displays the selected application or your entire desktop to other meeting participants.

Sharing a Whiteboard

You can use Live Meeting to display a shared digital whiteboard. The whiteboard feature allows you to draw freeform shapes, include text, and embed other images. To use the whiteboard feature, you select **Content menu | Whiteboard**. This displays the digital whiteboard on the screen, as shown in Figure 8.11.

Figure 8.11 A Live Meeting Whiteboard Session

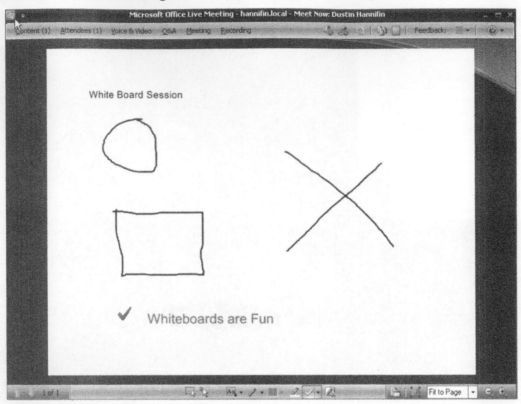

Conducting Polls and Displaying Results during the Session

Live Meeting allows you poll all meeting participants and display the results in the session. This feature allows you to quickly get the opinions of all other meeting participants. To set up a poll, you simply select **Content menu | Share | Poll Page**. The **Create Poll** dialog box is displayed. Type your question and choices in the appropriate fields (see Figure 8.12) and click **OK**. Your poll is now displayed and is open for participants to respond (see Figure 8.13). The meeting presenter can, at any time, choose to close the poll, display results, or update the poll question and choices. After all participants have had an opportunity to vote, the presenter should click the **Close Poll button** and then click the **Display Results button** at the bottom of the poll page.

Figure 8.12 Creating a Poll

Figure 8.13 An Active Poll in Live Meeting

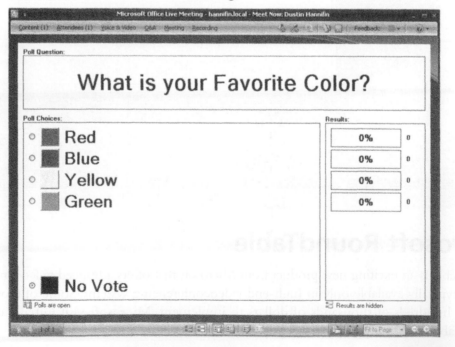

Allowing Attendees to Ask Questions

Throughout the meeting, participants can ask the presenter(s) questions. Participants can do this via the **Q&A menu option**. To ask a question select **Q&A menu | Q&A tab**. During the Live Meeting, the presenter(s) can answer questions at any time via the Q&A reply option. You access this by selecting **Q&A menu | Manage tab** (see Figure 8.14). The presenter can choose to answer the question publicly to all participants, or privately to the person that asked the question.

Figure 8.14 The Live Meeting Console Displaying the Q&A Feature

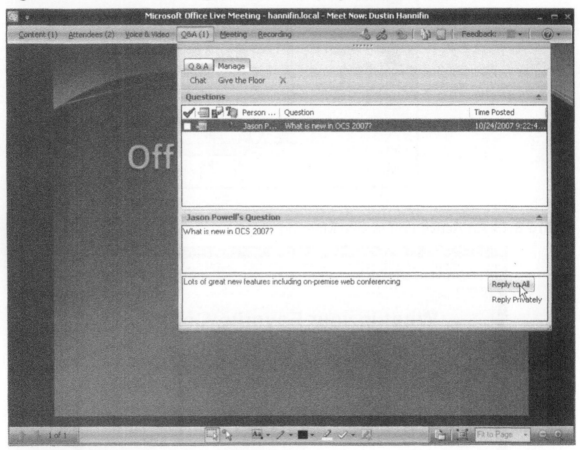

Microsoft RoundTable

RoundTable is an exciting new product from Microsoft that offers advanced videoconferencing features typically available only in high-end videoconferencing systems. Some of those systems can cost hundreds of thousands of dollars to implement. Microsoft will initially offer RoundTable with a suggested retail price of around $3,000.

What Is RoundTable?

Microsoft RoundTable is a new hardware device that provides a rich videoconferencing experience by delivering a 360-degree view of the meeting. RoundTable takes a panoramic image of all attendees within a conference room and displays this image within Live Meeting. RoundTable then adjusts instantly to focus on the current speaker in the room. RoundTable is easy to set up and works with both Hosted and On-Premises Live Meeting.

How Does RoundTable Work?

It is important to understand how the RoundTable device works to be able to properly integrate it into your Live Meetings. First, you place the device in the center of a conference room table. It is important that RoundTable has a clear line of sight to each meeting participant. Next, you plug the device into a computer that will participate in or host a Live Meeting Web conference. After you turn on the RoundTable device, the embedded camera performs a 360-degree scan of the conference room and gathers an image of each participant. After performing the scan, RoundTable constructs a panoramic image of all meeting participants and displays this image within the Live Meeting client. Other users participating in the Live Meeting can see the panoramic display. As a participant in the conference room begins to speak, the RoundTable microphone detects that person's voice and instantly displays live video of that person in a separate window within the Live Meeting. If another person in the conference room begins to speak, the camera jumps to that person and displays him or her in the main video window. This process continues throughout the meeting as different participants speak.

Why Use RoundTable?

You may be asking yourself, "Why should I use RoundTable? It's just another Webcam." In a sense, this is true, but there are several compelling reasons why you may want to consider using RoundTable:

- RoundTable costs about the same as today's high-quality speaker phones. Most well-made, high-quality speaker phones that businesses use today can cost upward of $3,000. This price varies, of course, depending on features.

- RoundTable provides a better experience than traditional videoconferencing systems in the same price range. RoundTable allows remote users to feel more engaged in the meeting by seeing all other users in the conference room.

- RoundTable is easy to set up and integrates seamlessly with Live Meeting. Most modern-day videoconferencing systems require IT staff involvement to set up and configure, whereas typically any user who has basic knowledge of Live Meeting can set up RoundTable.

Installing Conferencing

Conferencing capabilities are installed by default when you install OCS. However, you must perform several configurations post-setup. You can configure OCS Live Meeting features either globally or on a per-user basis. In this section, we will discuss how to set up these features.

Configuring Global Settings

Global Live Meeting settings are set up at the forest level and impact all OCS users in that forest. To configure global settings perform the following:

1. Select **Start | All Programs | Administrative Tools | Office Communications Server 2007**.

2. Locate and right-click the Active Directory forest and choose **Properties | Global Properties** (see Figure 8.15).

Figure 8.15 The Forest Properties Menu

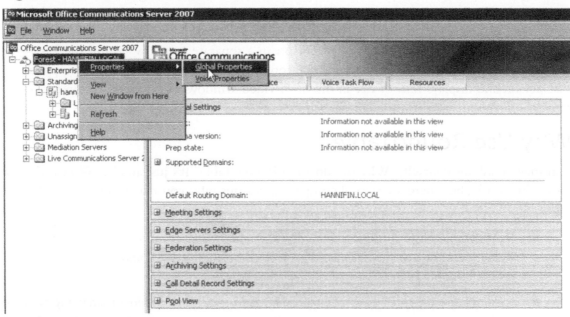

3. Click the **Meetings tab** in the **Office Communications Server Global Properties window**.

You should now see several options on the Global Configurations tab. The following is a brief description of each:

- **Anonymous Participants** This allows you to decide whether you want to allow participants to join a Live Meeting via a meeting code. By allowing anonymous participants, you enable users without an Active Directory account in the OCS domain to join meetings via a passcode. You can also choose whether you want to **Enforce this policy at the user level**, which would allow you to set up different options for different user accounts.

- **Global Policy** This option allows you to choose or customize several Live Meeting options, including the color depth of the meeting, permission to record meetings, and whether IP audio and video are enabled for users. You can also determine whether you want to force this same policy to all users or configure the policy on a per-user basis (see Figure 8.16). You can also edit existing and create new policy definitions in this window. Policy definitions define different sets of rules that can be applied globally or per user. For example, you can edit the default policy and disable the ability to record a Live Meeting session (see Figure 8.17). You can then edit **Policy 1 (High)** and allow recording of Live Meetings. After editing both policies, you can apply either one globally, or if you select **Use per user policy** you can assign the default policy to some users and Policy 1 (High) to others (see Figure 8.18). This gives you more granular control over who has what abilities within Live Meeting Web conferences.

Figure 8.16 OCS Global Properties

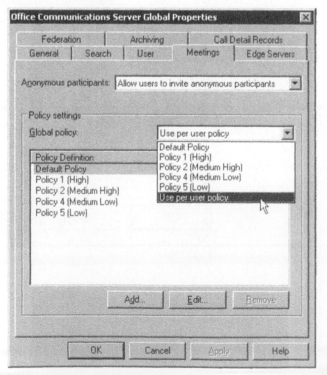

Figure 8.17 The Edit Policy Window

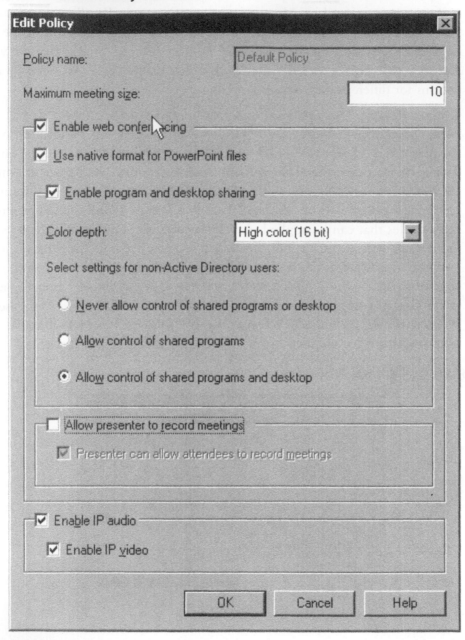

Figure 8.18 The User Properties Window

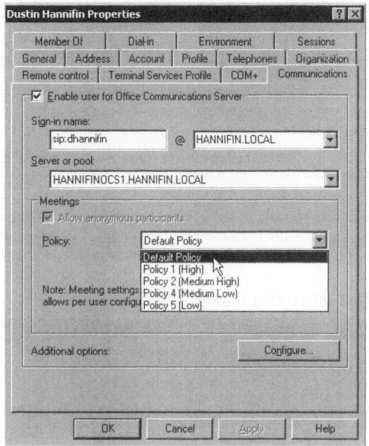

Configuring Server Settings

After you configure the forest-level settings, you need to configure server settings. You must configure and set up these settings in each server in your OCS deployment. Let's take a look at configuring server settings.

1. Open the OCS 2007 Microsoft Management Console (MMC).

2. Expand the **Standard Edition Servers or Enterprise Pools folder**, depending on which version of OCS you have deployed.

3. Find the name of the server you want to configure and right-click on that server. From the pop-up menu, choose **Properties | Web Conferencing Properties**. The Web Conferencing Properties window will be displayed.

4. The Meeting Compliance tab will be displayed. Meeting compliance allows you to archive all Live Meeting sessions. This feature is necessary for organizations that

need to archive sessions for regulatory compliance. Check the box next to **Enable Meeting Compliance** if you want to archive Live Meeting Web conferences.

5. You can also optionally choose to shut down Live Meetings if they cannot be archived for some reason. Check the box **Shutdown Meetings, if compliance fails** to enable this option.

6. If you choose to **Enable Meeting Compliance** you must specify a folder location to store the Live Meeting archives. The Web conferencing service account *must* have write access to this folder.

7. After configuring meeting compliance settings, click the **Web Conferencing Edge Server** tab. You will need to configure options on this tab only if you have an edge server in your OCS deployment.

8. Click the **Add button** and enter the internal and external FQDNs of the edge server (see Figure 8.19). Do not change the port numbers unless you changed them on your edge server. After entering the FQDNs of your edge server, click **OK**.

Figure 8.19 Web Conferencing Edge Server Settings

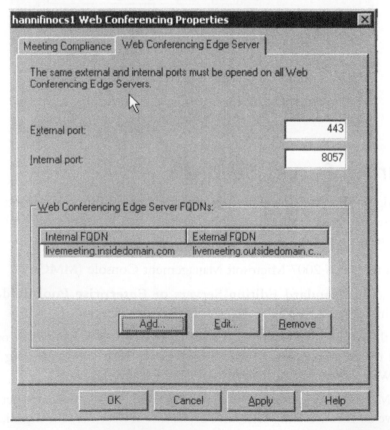

9. If you configured the edge server settings in the preceding step, you will need to configure the audio visual (A/V) conferencing settings for the same server. To configure these settings right-click on the same OCS server as you did in step 2. Select **A/V Conferencing Properties** from the pop-up menu.

10. Choose the internal FQDN of your edge server from the drop-down menu. If you want to encrypt A/V traffic, ensure that the **Require encryption** option is selected, as seen in Figure 8.20, and then click **OK**.

Figure 8.20 The A/V Conferencing Properties Dialog Box

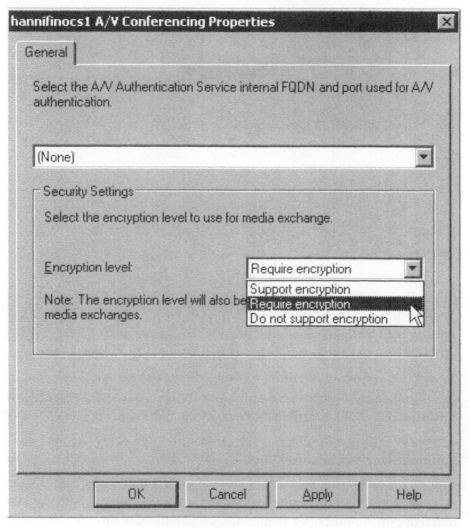

11. Now let's expand the server tree in the OCS MMC and locate the same server name displayed as the FQDN (see Figure 8.21). Right-click the server name and select **Properties | Web Conferencing Properties** from the pop-up menu.

Figure 8.21 The OCS MMC

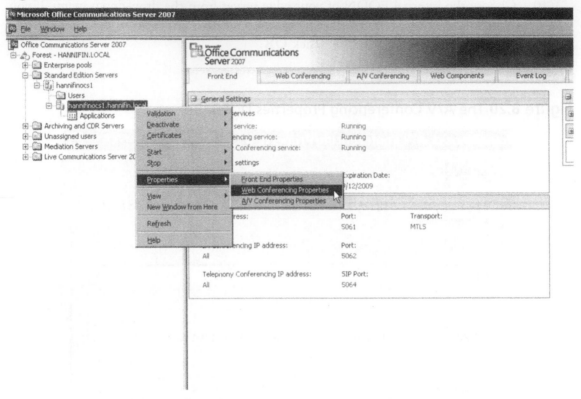

12. In the **Web Server Conferencing Properties** window, ensure that the correct listening IP address and port are specified. In most cases, you can leave the default options of **All** IP addresses and a **Media listening port** of 8057 selected. Port 8057 is used for outgoing Live Meeting traffic being sent to the edge server.

13. Click the **Certificate** tab. Ensure that the certificate you selected in the initial setup of OCS is chosen. If that certificate is not shown, click the **Select Certificate button** to choose the certificate assigned to the OCS server. Then click **OK**.

14. Right-click the same FQDN server name in the OCS MMC and choose **A/V Conferencing Properties** from the pop-up menu.

15. The A/V Conferencing Server properties window will be displayed. Again you do not need to change any settings on this tab unless you have configured OCS to use different port numbers (see Figure 8.22). Click the **Certificate** tab. Ensure that the certificate assigned to this server during initial setup is selected, and then click **OK**.

NOTE

Port 5063 is the default SIP port used to listen for incoming requests. These requests are made over the Transmission Control Protocol (TCP).

Figure 8.22 The A/V Conferencing Server Properties Window

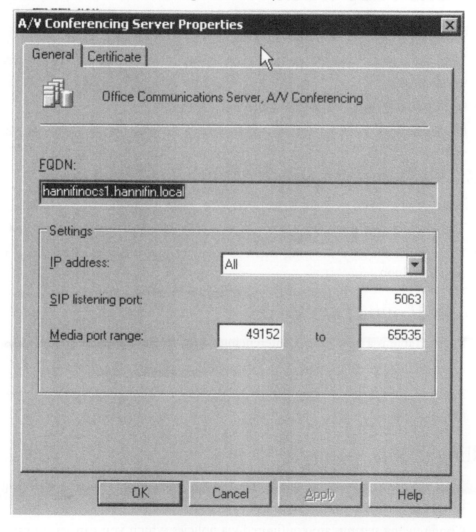

Summary

This chapter provided you with an overview of the conferencing capabilities of Office Communications Server 2007. After reading this chapter, you should have a good understanding of IM, Web, and videoconference services offered by OCS and Microsoft's Hosted Live Meeting solution. You should also now be ready to set up, configure, and host your own video and Web conferences via OCS. Happy conferencing!

Solutions Fast Track

Understanding On-Premises Conferencing

☑ Web, audio, video, and IM conferencing services are available in on-premises conferencing.

☑ OCS provides on-premises conferencing services.

☑ Microsoft offers hosted conferencing services on a subscription or per-use basis.

Using On-Premises Conferencing

☑ You can use MOC to hold an IM, video, or audio conference with others.

☑ The Outlook add-in allows you to schedule Live Meetings within Microsoft Outlook.

☑ You can use the Live Meeting client to instantly start a Web conference in an ad hoc fashion.

Microsoft RoundTable

☑ RoundTable is a new videoconferencing hardware device offered by Microsoft.

☑ RoundTable provides a 360-degree view of the meeting room.

☑ RoundTable pricing is reasonable enough for even smaller companies to take advantage of it.

Installing Conferencing

☑ Most conferencing settings are installed and automatically configured during the initial OCS setup.

☑ Conferencing settings are configured via policies which you can set up on a global or per-user basis.

☑ You must configure each front-end server that will be used for Web conferencing to allow end users to access conferencing features on that server.

Frequently Asked Questions

Q: How do I resolve an "Invalid Certificate" error when trying to connect to OCS via MOC or Live Meeting?

A: Ensure that you refer to the server by its FQDN specified in the server's SSL certificate.

Q: What purpose does the edge server role play in conferencing?

A: The edge server allows OCS users, federated users, and anonymous users to connect to conferences from outside the corporate firewall.

Q: Is there a way to troubleshoot and validate the OCS conferencing configuration?

A: Yes, Microsoft offers several free downloadable tools for OCS, including the OCS 2007 Best Practice Analyzer (BPA).

Q: What should I do if I am unable to record my Live Meeting session?

A: Ensure that your account is configured to use a Web conferencing policy that allows you to record Live Meeting sessions.

Chapter 9

Integration with PBX and IP-PBX Systems

Solutions in this chapter:

- Using a Gateway
- CSTA/SIP Gateways

☑ Solutions Fast Track

☑ Frequently Asked Questions

Introduction

Office Communications Server (OCS), by default, enables users to make PC-to-PC voice and video calls. Although PC-to-PC calls are a handy way for users within an organization to talk, they don't address the need to communicate with non-OCS users with devices such as home phones, cell phones, and Private Branch Exchange (PBX) phones. OCS 2007 provides a few ways to do this, and these methods are the subject of this chapter.

OCS has two major categories of integration with non-OCS voice solutions: Enterprise Voice and Remote Call Control. The rest of the chapter will explain how and why you may want to integrate OCS using one of these two methods.

Gateway Access to Non-OCS Solutions

The Enterprise Voice option turns your OCS client into a "soft phone" by using your PC's microphone and speakers like a telephone. (You can also use a headset plugged into your PC). To call a person using Enterprise Voice, you click on the person's contact name in the OC client and select **Dial**, or you type the person's phone number into the OC client. OCS then will send the call to the remote phone system and establish a call between the two phone systems.

Most PBXs support analog lines and digital lines for connectivity, whereas OCS supports only Voice over IP (VoIP). To make these two different systems talk, you need a third-party voice gateway. The gateways can translate between OCS's VoIP communication and the PBX's analog or digital communication. A typical gateway will have an Ethernet port configured to talk VoIP to OCS and one or more digital or analog ports to be connected to a PBX.

This solution treats OCS and the PBX like two different phone systems: You may have several people whose phone numbers are homed to OCS and several people whose phone numbers are homed to a PBX. The gateway solution allows users from either system to place calls to each other. In this scenario, it would be impossible for a user to have the extension 2100 on OCS *and* have the extension 2100 on the PBX.

Remote Call Control

Remote Call Control (RCC) is a different form of integration with a PBX. It allows you to dial a phone number from your OC client and have your OCS client make your PBX phone dial the number. In this case, the OC client *does not* act like a phone—no audio will be going through your PC. The OC client is simply sending the digits to your PBX phone and letting your PBX phone handle the rest.

RCC is useful for people who want to be able to use their Communicator client to display their contacts and phone numbers, and to be able to click on a contact to dial them, but who want the voice calls to be routed through to their PCs. If your users don't have sound cards, microphones, or headsets, RCC is a good option. Likewise, if some users are not ready to adopt what they see as "cutting-edge" technology, they may feel more comfortable making calls from a traditional-looking phone.

An additional benefit of this type of integration is that you will be able to receive phone-related presence information regarding users. In other words, with RCC, you can see when a user is on his or her PBX phone.

> **NOTE**
>
> At this time, the presence information sent out by OCS is not readable by many, if any, third-party PBXs. This means OCS users can see the status of a user's PBX phone, but any PBX presence applications will not be able to see a user's OCS status.

Using a Gateway

When choosing a gateway for your integration, you will need to know what kind of connectivity your PBX supports. Most modern PBXs support T1/PRI connections, which are digital connections that provide 23 voice channels over a single line. Some older PBXs may not support T1/PRI, but an older version of T1 signaling: either T1/CAS (channel associated signaling) or T1/E&M signaling. In any case, make sure you know what your PBX can support and choose your gateway accordingly. Another thing to consider is whether your PBX has an available port or ports for connectivity to your OCS gateway. If you are planning to use two T1/PRIs to connect to OCS, your PBX will need two available PRI ports. If you don't have an available port, you will need to order a new card or module for your PBX that provides the extra capacity. This is important to determine prior to moving forward with your OCS planning and deployment.

If you do not require more than a few connections into OCS, handling only a few calls at a time, you will want to look at a gateway that uses FXO ports. I've never heard of any PBXs that would require using an FXS port for integration, so unless you have specific ideas for connecting analog devices to your gateway (such as a fax machine), you probably don't need a gateway with FXS ports.

FXO ports allow one phone call at a time, so you will need a gateway that has as many FXO ports as you plan to have simultaneous calls between OCS and your PBX. FXO ports usually don't support the extra features that a T1/PRI does, such as caller ID. This information is usually carried in the digital signaling channel on a PRI. Because FXO ports are analog, they can't easily send this information. Some PBXs do have the ability to send this kind of signaling over FXO ports, and some gateways do have the ability to decode this signaling. But this will vary widely among PBX vendors and gateway vendors.

Supported Gateways

At this time, Microsoft supports three vendors' gateways: AudioCodes, Dialogic, and Quintum. As vendors have more time to become certified with OCS, you can look for more supported gateways. It is Microsoft's intention to be able to support direct integration via the Session Initiation Protocol (SIP) with Internet Protocol (IP) PBXs such as Cisco's CallManager and Nortel's CX1000; however, at the time of this writing, no such integrations are supported.

I will spend some time describing the direct SIP integration with Cisco's CallManager because it does work, but keep in mind that it is not supported yet. Until Microsoft officially supports the integration, certain aspects of the integration may not function properly. I've heard that features such as third-party transfers, conferencing, and caller ID may not always function as intended. The same holds true for any direct-SIP integration. Likewise, neither Microsoft nor Cisco offers any support for integration with the Cisco Unified Presence Server (CUPS), even though it is possible to get this to work as well. It's worth noting, however, that Live Communications Server (LCS) 2005 SP1 integrated to CUPS has been supported for some.

Configuring an AudioCodes Gateway

AudioCodes offers several different gateways for integration with OCS. In general, you will need to decide between an AudioCodes gateway that has T1/PRI ports and a gateway that has analog FXO ports only.

In this example, I will cover how to configure an AudioCodes MP-114—a gateway that has two FXO ports. The MP-114 also has two FXS ports; I will not be using the FXS ports and therefore won't be configuring them.

Configuring Cisco CallManager As a Gateway

Cisco CallManager Version 5.x and later support SIP trunking. This means you can connect to other SIP-capable phone systems over your IP network; you don't need to configure a PRI or FXO connection, nor do you need a separate hardware-based gateway. If both systems support SIP trunking you can make a direct connection through your network.

OCS 2007 supports SIP trunking and Cisco CallManager 5.x and later support SIP trunking. They are natural candidates for a direct integration. However, not all vendors choose to implement SIP in exactly the same way. This may be because SIP is a relatively new protocol and certain fields in the protocol are either optional or interpreted differently by different vendors. Because of this, you can't assume that two phone systems will interoperate just because they both support SIP.

In the case of OCS and CallManager 5.x and later, both Microsoft and Cisco implement SIP in a similar manner. You can configure the two systems to talk to each other without requiring a third-party gateway, as I discussed earlier. However, because neither vendor has given the official stamp of approval to the integration, you may not have all the features you expect.

If you are willing to accept the risk of not being supported by either Cisco or Microsoft, you can integrate directly with SIP. If this is not a risk you are willing to tolerate, you must use one of the third-party gateways listed on the Microsoft Web site. If that is the route you choose, you will need to provision a PRI port or FXO port on your Cisco voice gateway and connect it to the AudioCodes, Dialogic, or Quintum gateway. Although this is a somewhat more expensive and convoluted scenario, it is supported by both Cisco and Microsoft.

Understanding Partitions and Calling Search Spaces

You will find entire books dedicated to creating and implementing dial plans in Cisco CallManager. I won't attempt to squeeze hundreds of pages of knowledge into a single subsection, but it is important to understand the basics of how CallManager routes calls. Partitions and calling search spaces make up the two basic components of a dial plan in CallManager.

When you create a phone number in CallManager, you need to assign it to a partition. In a sense, partitions are almost like phone books—containers that have phone numbers listed in them. So, for example, you could create phone numbers 1000–2000 and put them in a partition called Chicago Extensions. Then you could create phone numbers 3000–4000 and put them in a partition called Springfield Extensions. Partitions are a logical way to organize phone numbers.

If one of my users wanted to be able to call anyone in Chicago, I would assign him rights, or a calling search space that included the Chicago Extensions partition. If that were the only partition in his calling search space, he would only be able to dial numbers 1000–2000. If he tried to dial the number 3100, his call would fail. If I wanted to give him the ability to dial people in both Chicago and Springfield, I would assign him a calling search space that included both Chicago Extensions and Springfield Extensions. My test user would now be able to dial 3100 and have the call go through.

Table 9.1 shows the way partitions and calling search spaces work.

Table 9.1 Partitions and Calling Search

Calling Search Space Name	Partitions in Calling Search Space	User Can Call	Pattern/Extension User Can Dial
CSS-Chicago-Only	Chicago	Only Chicago extensions	1000–2000
CSS-Springfield-Only	Springfield	Only Springfield extensions	2001–3000
CSS-Chicago-and-Springfield	Chicago; Springfield	Any extension	1000–3000

Table 9.1 shows which calling search space to assign a user based on who the user should be able to dial. You will notice, though, that I've only shown how to assign permissions to users to make internal calls. If a user tried to make an outside call (e.g., 312-555-1212) with any of the calling search spaces listed in the table, the call would fail because there is no pattern that matches "3125551212" or anything like it.

Understanding Route Patterns

The way to resolve this issue in CallManager is to create route patterns. Route patterns are entries in the CallManager dial plan that let you dial other numbers besides extensions in your organization. For example, I could create a route pattern in the format 9.312XXXXXXX and put it in a partition called Chicago Local Numbers. The 9 is to signify "outside line," the dot is just a marker which I'll discuss later, the 312 represents a local area code in Chicago, and the seven Xs mean any seven-digit number.

Now I create a new calling search space called CSS-Chicago-and-Local-Calls and add the Chicago-Local-Numbers partition to it. Our table now looks like Table 9.2.

Table 9.2 New Partitions and Calling Search

Calling Search Space Name	Partitions in Calling Search Space	User Can Call	Pattern/ Extension User Can Dial
CSS-Chicago-Only	Chicago Extensions	Only Chicago extensions	1000–2000
CSS-Springfield-Only	Springfield Extensions	Only Springfield extensions	2001–3000
CSS-Chicago-and-Springfield	Chicago Extensions; Springfield Extensions	Any extension	1000–3000
CSS-Chicago-and-Local-Calls	Chicago Extensions; Chicago Local Numbers	Chicago extensions and 10-digit numbers that start with 312	1000–2000 312XXXXXXX

Another useful route pattern is one that allows you to dial digits on another PBX. Let's say, for example, that all the phones on the remote PBX were in the range of 6000 to 6999. I can create a route pattern that would let me dial an "access code" and then four digits to dial a user on the remote PBX. A pattern to do that would look something like "77.6XXX". So a user would dial 77 to signify a call to a remote PBX (the access code could really be any number, but I picked 77 at random) and then the extension of the user on the PBX, as long as it begins with 6—for example, 77.6600. In my route pattern, I will choose the option "strip digits pre-dot" so that CallManager will send over just the four-digit extension to the remote PBX and ring 6600.

For a user to be able to dial this pattern, we need to put it into a partition, Remote PBX Extensions, and then add that partition to a calling search space, CSS-Chicago-and-PBX-Calls. With this addition to the dial plan, the table now has five entries (see Table 9.3).

Table 9.3 New Partitions and Calling Search

Calling Search Space Name	Partitions in Calling Search Space	User Can Call	Pattern/ Extension User Can Dial
CSS-Chicago-Only	Chicago Extensions	Only Chicago extensions	1000–2000
CSS-Springfield-Only	Springfield Extensions	Only Springfield extensions	2001–3000
CSS-Chicago-and-Springfield	Chicago Extensions; Springfield Extensions	Any extension	1000–3000
CSS-Chicago-and-Local-Calls	Chicago Extensions; Chicago Local Numbers	Chicago extensions and 10-digit numbers that start with 312	1000–2000 312XXXXXXX
CSS-Chicago-and-PBX-Calls	Chicago Extensions; PBX Extensions	Chicago extensions and remote PBX extension	1000–2000 77XXXX

Understanding Gateways

I have left out one important aspect: how CallManager knows where to route such route patterns as 9.312XXXXXXX and 77.6XXX once a user has dialed them. The answer is that we specify a *gateway* in our route pattern. In the case of outside numbers such as 9.312XXXXXXX, the gateway will usually be a Cisco router with a voice card in it.

However, with CallManager 5.*x* and later you can specify a SIP trunk as the gateway, instead of a router. This means any number that matches a pattern (such as 77.6XXX) gets routed over the network to a server that speaks SIP. Because OCS 2007 is SIP-compliant, we can successfully route calls from CallManager to OCS using this method. All we need on the Cisco side (in addition to what we've already created) is a SIP trunk.

Understanding SIP Trunks

A SIP trunk in CallManager is just a logical gateway that tells CallManager where to send phone calls bound for a remote destination. The trunk is really an IP address of a remote system

(OCS, in our case) along with some parameters that specify how to send and receive calls with the remote system. By far, the most important part of the configuration is getting the IP address of your OCS Mediation Server entered properly.

Once you've created the SIP trunk and assigned it to your route pattern, phone calls will be able to flow between OCS and CallManager. The next section looks at how to configure CallManager to make this possible.

Configuring Cisco CallManager

You will need an administrative login for CallManager to perform the tasks in this section. Also, as I've noted before, you should be working with Cisco CallManager Version 5.0 or later, preferably Version 5.1 or later. In these examples, I am using CallManager 5.1.

Configuring a Partition and Calling Search Spaces

I will first show you how to create a partition called Chicago Extensions. This is the partition where all the users' extensions will live. Once you've logged in to CallManager via the Web interface, go to **Call Routing | Class of Control | Partition** and click **Add New** (see Figure 9.1).

Figure 9.1 Cisco Unified CallManager Administration

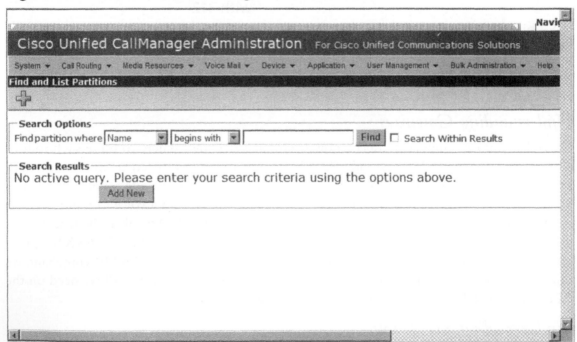

Enter **Chicago Extensions** and click **Save** (see Figure 9.2). All phone numbers that you create for your Cisco IP phones should be placed in this partition.

Figure 9.2 Partition Information

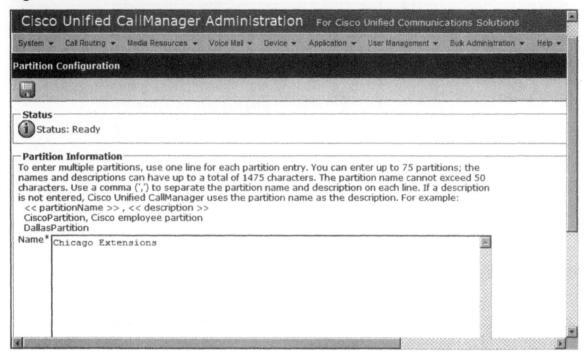

In this same way, create another partition called **CCM Calls to OCS** and click **Save**. We will use this partition for the route pattern that will send calls to our SIP gateway and over to OCS.

Next, create a calling search space that includes both the Chicago Extensions and the CCM Calls to OCS partitions. Do this by going to **Call Routing | Class of Control | Calling Search Space** and clicking **Add New** (see Figure 9.3).

Figure 9.3 Find and List Calling Search Spaces

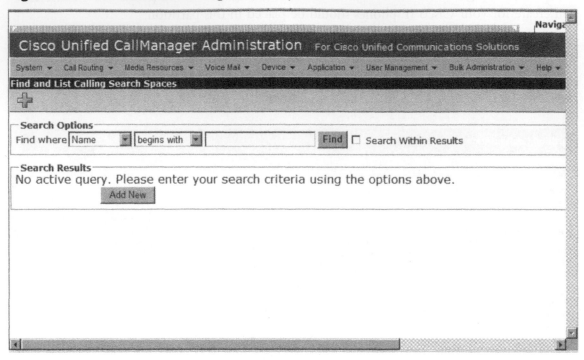

In the **Name field**, enter **CSS-ChicagoExtensions-and-OCS-calls**. Add a description as appropriate. Highlight the **CCM to OCS Calls** and **Chicago Extensions** partitions in the **Available Partitions** section (see Figure 9.4).

Figure 9.4 Calling Search Space Configuration

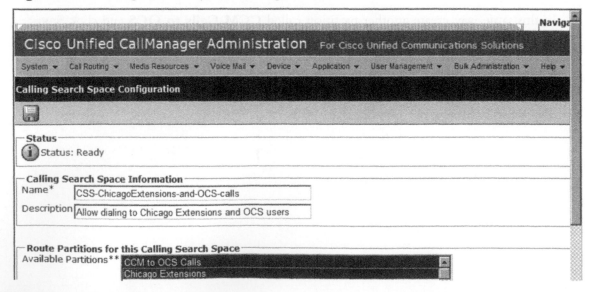

Click the **Down arrow** icon to add these partitions to the Selected Partitions space (see Figure 9.5). Then click **Save**.

Figure 9.5 Selected Partitions

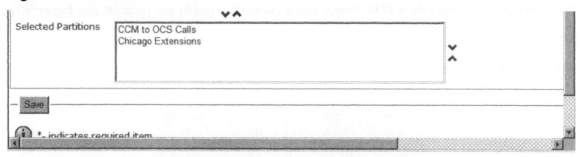

Next, create a new calling search space called **CSS-ChicagoExtensions**. Add only the Chicago Extensions partition to this calling search space (see Figure 9.6). Then click the **Save** icon.

Figure 9.6 Calling Search Space Configuration

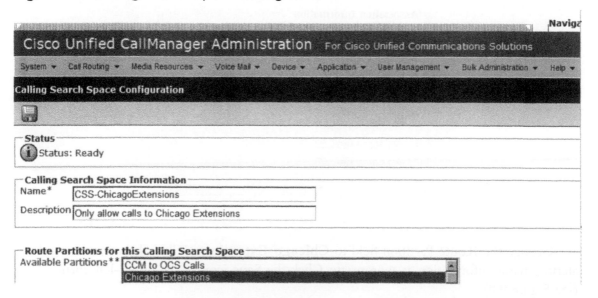

Assigning Phone Numbers to a Partition

I won't go into great detail on how to configure phones in CallManager. There are too many options and too many settings to cover in a book about OCS. I will assume that you have a phone or two already created in CallManager. What we need to do now is make sure our phones are in the Chicago Extensions partition.

Go to **Device | Phone** in the CallManager administrative Web site. In the search options, search for a phone that already exists in the system. When the search returns your phone, click on the phone to configure it. On the left side, you will see the Directory Number (DN) settings. Click on the **DN** in line 1.

In this example, the DN is **4736**. Notice that it currently is not in any partition (see Figure 9.7).

Figure 9.7 Phone Configuration

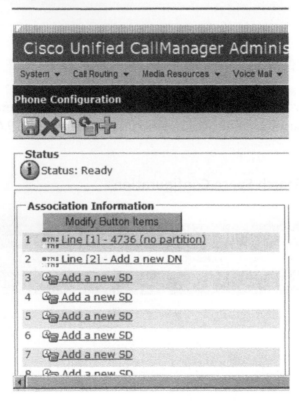

Change the Route Partition field to **Chicago Extensions**. Fill in the username and alerting name information as appropriate. Click the **Save** icon in the upper-left corner (see Figure 9.8).

Figure 9.8 Directory Number Configuration

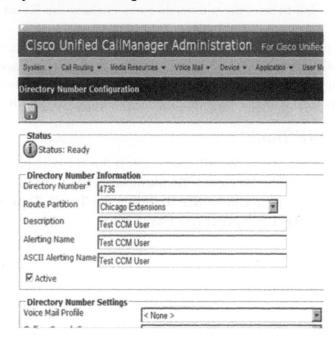

Return to editing your phone. While we are here, set the calling search space to **ChicagoExtensions–and–OCS–Calls** (see Figure 9.9).

Figure 9.9 Device Information

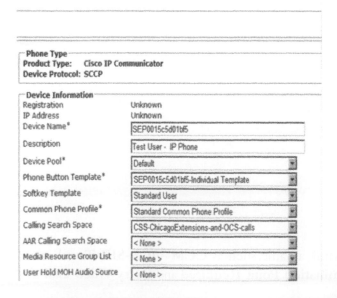

Save the phone's configuration by clicking the **Save** icon in the upper-left corner. When CallManager prompts you to reset the phone, do so by clicking the **Reset** button in the upper-left corner.

We now have a phone with a number in the Chicago Extensions partition and we've assigned it the CSS-ChicagoExtensions-and-OCS-calls calling search space. The phone now has permissions to call other phones in the Chicago Extensions partition. Once we are done with the rest of the CallManager configuration, this phone will be able to call OCS users as well.

Configuring the SIP Trunk

We now can turn our attention to the SIP trunk; this is the key configuration that allows us to send calls to OCS. Go to the **Device | Trunk** menu in the CallManager administrative Web site. Click **Add New**. Then choose **SIP Trunk** in the **Trunk Type field**. The device protocol will default to **SIP**. Click **Next** (see Figure 9.10).

Figure 9.10 Trunk Information

Give the SIP trunk a name, such as **CCM-OCS-SIP-Trunk**, and provide a description. Check **Media Termination Point Required** and **Retry Video Call as Audio** (see Figure 9.11).

Figure 9.11 Device Information

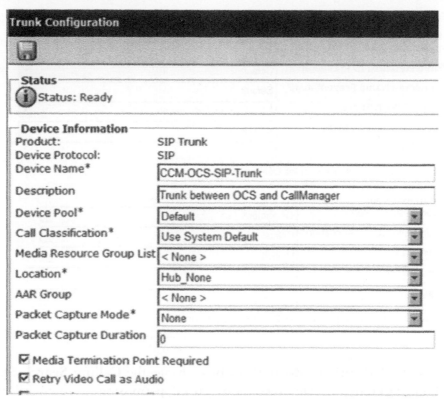

Farther down the list, notice the **Significant Digits field**. As I described in an earlier section, this field allows you to limit the number of digits that CallManager sees when receiving an incoming call. This is how we strip out the leading digits of the fully normalized E.164 numbers that OCS sends to CallManager. Set this to **4**; this will change a call from going to +13125554736 to just 4736. This is important because CallManager can't recognize the + sign (see Figure 9.12).

NOTE

It's true that when we change this to four digits, OCS users won't be able to send calls to outside numbers such as +18005551212. In the example I provide, all we are concerned about is routing calls from OCS users to CallManager users. In real life, you need to use some tricky routing in CallManager with translation patterns to be able to send calls to both internal extensions and outside numbers. This advanced routing is beyond the scope of this book.

Figure 9.12 Call Routing Information

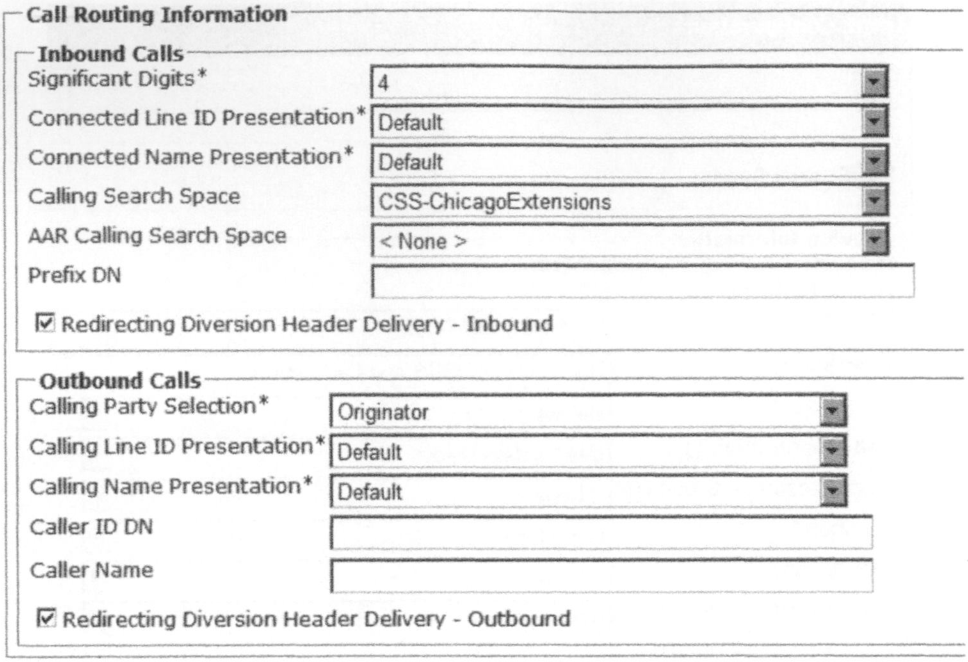

Also in the **Call Routing Information box**, change the **Calling Search Space field** to **CSS-ChicagoExtensions**. This gives the SIP trunk permissions to route calls from OCS to any DNs in the Chicago Extensions partition.

TIP

Not configuring the calling search space properly is one of the most common mistakes I see when people are trying to make the OCS-CallManager integration work. The inbound calling search space determines what numbers OCS users will be able to call. Leaving this setting blank will prevent any calls from routing to CallManager.

Be sure to check the **Redirecting Diversion Header Delivery** boxes in both the **Inbound Calls** and **Outbound Calls** sections. This will send additional signaling information along with inbound and outbound calls.

The most important section of the SIP trunk is the **SIP Information** section. Enter the IP address of your Mediation Server's gateway listening address in the **Destination IP Address box**. In this example, the Mediation Server's IP address is **192.168.100.100**. Remember that the Mediation Server has two IP addresses: one for talking to OCS and one for talking to a gateway. CallManager will be talking to the Mediation Server on the gateway side. Enter **5060** as the destination port (see Figure 9.13). This is the port that the Mediation Server's gateway side will use to listen for SIP connections.

Figure 9.13 SIP Information

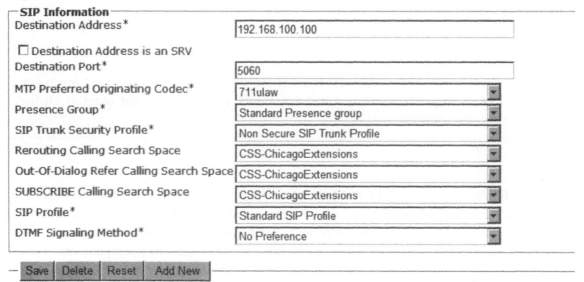

I've configured the Rerouting Calling Search Space, Out-of-Dialog Refer Calling Search Space, and SUBSCRIBE Calling Search Space boxes with **CSS-ChicagoExtensions**. These fields aren't necessary to establish basic connectivity between OCS and CallManager. However, I have found that in most circumstances, it is a good idea to assign a calling search space to all fields in the event of something going awry with the trunk.

Click **Save** to apply the settings.

> **WARNING**
>
> When making changes to your SIP trunk, you will always need to reset the trunk for the changes to take effect. However, resetting the trunk will cause any active calls between OCS and CallManager to drop immediately!

With the SIP trunk now configured, all we'll need to do is set up a route pattern to send calls over to OCS.

Configuring the Route Pattern

Create a new route pattern by going to **Call Routing | Route/Hunt | Route Pattern** in the CallManager administrative Web site. Click **Add New**.

> **NOTE**
>
> Do not select SIP Route Pattern from the Call Routing | Route/Hunt menu. It looks like it might be exactly what you need, but alas, it's not used at all for OCS interoperability.

In the Route Pattern field, we need to define the digits that users will dial when placing calls to OCS users. It's a good idea to use a "routing code" to help send calls to a remote system. Many organizations use routing codes to send calls to other sites—for example, "Dial 5 and then the extension to reach a user in New York". This helps to keep your dial plan clean by having a simple, consistent way to dial users on other systems.

I should mention that you don't *have* to use a routing code. If you know that all OCS users have extensions that start with 6 (6000–6999), you could simply use a routing pattern of 6XXX. Anyone on the Cisco side dialing an extension that starts with 6 will match this and route to OCS. The trouble is that you will often have some users with noncontiguous numbers on each system. In other words, you may have extensions 6001, 6004, and 6602 on OCS, but extensions 6002, 6005, and 6606 on CallManager. This makes it difficult to write a single route pattern that captures all OCS extensions.

I've chosen 77 as our routing code here. This means a user with a Cisco IP phone who is trying to call extension 6600 on OCS would first dial 77 and then 6600. I also have inserted a dot in between the routing code and the extension range. You will see how we can use that dot to our advantage in a moment. For now, make sure you choose **CCM-OCS-SIP-Trunk** as the gateway/route list. Also, be sure that **Route this pattern** is selected (see Figure 9.14).

Figure 9.14 Route Pattern Configuration

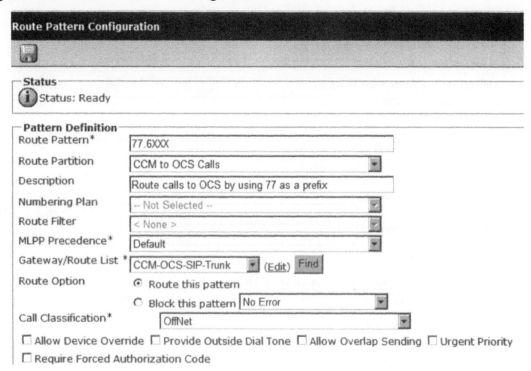

Farther down in the SIP trunk properties, fill in the Calling Party Transform Mask field with **XXXXXXXXXX**—this will send over all 10 digits of the IP phone's calling number when an IP phone calls an OCS user. This assumes that all your phones have 10-digit numbers and that you've configured them to display the full 10 digits to callers. Leave all the rest of the information in Calling Party Transformations at their defaults, as shown.

In the Called Party Transformations box, however, notice the Discard Digits field. I have set this to **PreDot** (see Figure 9.15). This will cause CallManager to drop the 77 routing code from the dialed digits string and only send over the remaining digits. This is critical; if you do not strip the 77 OCS will not know what to do with a call destined for extension 776600, and your call will fail.

You can leave the remainder of the fields at their defaults.

Figure 9.15 Calling Party Transformations

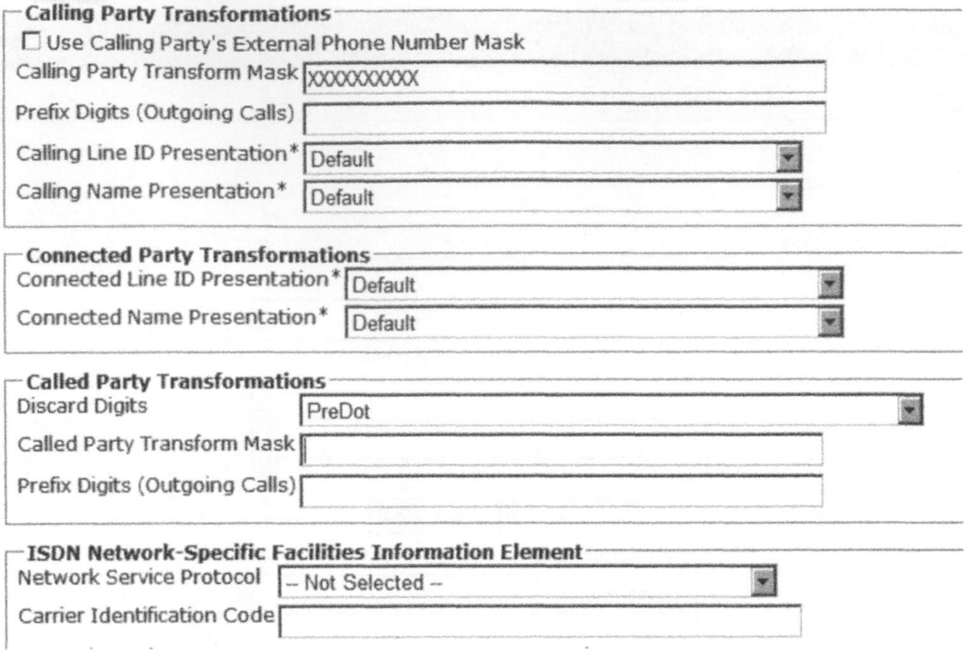

Click **Save** to apply the settings. You will be warned that any changes to this route pattern will reset the associated gateway. In our case, this means the SIP trunk. Be sure that your SIP trunk is not in use when you make changes to this route pattern because when the trunk resets, CallManager will drop all active calls.

Testing the Configuration

If you have already configured OCS as part of an earlier deployment, you should now be able to route calls from CallManager to OCS. This assumes, of course, that you have a user with an extension that starts with 6 in OCS and that you've configured normalization rules to expand the four-digit extension to the full E.164 format (+13125556602). If this is the case, dial **776602** from any IP phone that has the calling search space CSS-ChicagoExtensions-and-OCS-calls. You will see the incoming call pop up on the screen of the user with extension 6602.

If you haven't configured OCS yet, you will have a little more work to do. Plus, we also need to configure OCS to be able to route calls to users on the CallManager side.

Configuring OCS

Because other sections of this book deal more extensively with configuring the OCS dial plan, I will move through this rather quickly.

Configuring a Normalization Rule for Four-Digit Numbers

OCS requires us to assign a full E.164 number to all users. This is a + followed by a country code (1 for the United States), and then followed by the rest of the phone number. In our example, these numbers are in the format **+13125556602**.

From our OCS clients, we can type in the fully normalized number and make a successful call. But because we want to also dial other users by their four-digit numbers from within our OCS clients, we'll need to create a normalization rule to expand a four-digit number to the full E.164 number.

To create a normalization rule, first open the OCS administrative console. Right-click on the **Forest** object and select **Properties | Voice Properties**. Edit your location profile (assuming you've already created one). Then click **Add** in the **Normalization Rules** section (see Figure 9.16).

Figure 9.16 Add Location Profile

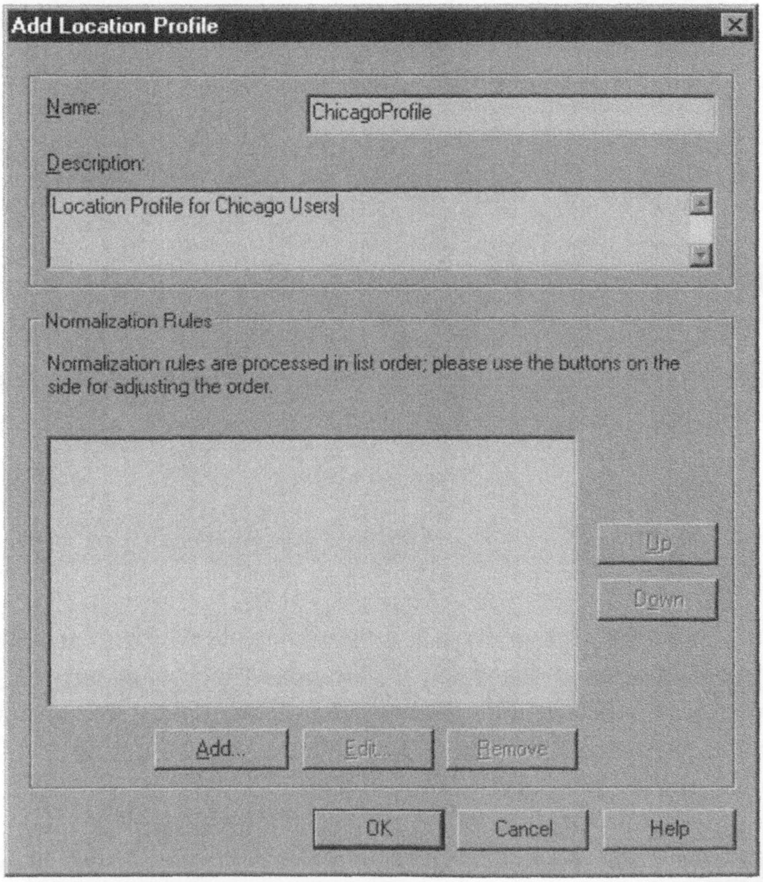

Create a rule that looks like the one shown in Figure 9.17.

Figure 9.17 Edit Phone Number Normalization Rule

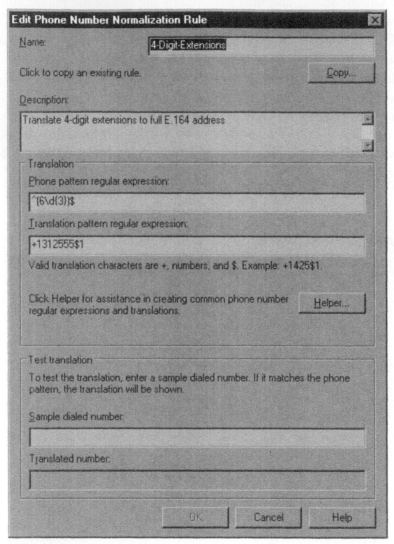

Again, I won't spend much time describing how the rule works (that's the subject of a different section), but understand that this will allow two things to happen: 1) an OCS user can now dial another user with only four digits; but more important to this chapter 2) incoming calls from CallManager destined for a user's four-digit extension will now be converted to the full number and successfully routed to the end-user.

One thing to note: Your OCS users must be enabled for Enterprise Voice to receive incoming calls made to their extensions. To double-check that a user is enabled, open the user in the OCS administrative console and click **Configure** in the **Additional Options** section.

Make sure **Enterprise Voice** is checked and that you have filled out the **Line URI:** field with a number that resembles the one shown in Figure 9.18.

Figure 9.18 User Options

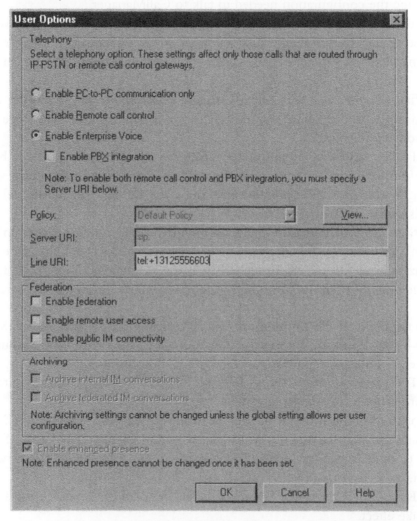

TIP

Be aware that the Line URI field must contain the word *tel:* before the E.164 address. This field, rather than any other "phone" field in the user's Active Directory properties, controls the phone number used by OCS.

Configuring the Mediation Server

The Mediation Server is the link between OCS and CallManager. One of the Mediation Server's IP addresses needs to be configured to talk to OCS, and one needs to be configured to talk to CallManager.

Because this book already covered the Mediation Server in a separate chapter, I will quickly describe the configuration needed to talk to CallManager.

Open your OCS administrative console. Expand the container called **Mediation Servers**. You should see the Mediation Server that you've already installed (see Chapter 6 if you have not already installed a Mediation Server). Right-click on the **Mediation Server** and select **Properties**.

On the first tab, you see a field called **Communication Server Listening IP Address**. Make sure to choose the IP address on the Mediation Server that is on the same network as your OCS front-end server.

The field called **Gateway Listening IP Address** is the IP address that will be talking to CallManager. Earlier in this chapter, you configured a SIP trunk in CallManager and specified a destination IP address of **192.168.100.100**. This is the address you should select for the **Gateway Listening IP Address**.

The **Default Location Profile** field is an important one. Choose **ChicagoProfile**, as configured in a prior step in this chapter. The location profile that you enter here is what ties your normalization rules to the Mediation Server. If you don't enter a location profile here that can normalize four-digit numbers into E.164 addresses, your calls from CallManager to OCS will fail.

Click on the **Next Hop Connections tab**. The **Office Communications Server Next Hop** should be filled in with the fully qualified domain name (FQDN) of your Standard Edition Server or Enterprise Edition front-end pool and using port 5061.

The **PSTN Gateway Next Hop** needs the IP address of CallManager. Enter the **IP** of your CallManager here and enter port **5060**.

Note that if you would like to be able to route calls to more than one CallManager (for redundancy or load balancing), you need to install another Mediation Server and configure it to point to the secondary CallManager here in the **PSTN Gateway Next Hop** section.

Click **OK** to apply the settings. Then restart your Mediation Server's services for the changes to take effect.

If you didn't try to make a call from a Cisco IP phone in the last section, try it now. You should be able to successfully dial an OCS user's four-digit extension and have it ring.

Configuring a Route to CallManager via the Mediation Server

Now we need to configure OCS to be able to route outbound calls to CallManager. The key to this step is to create a route in OCS. To do this, open the OCS administrative console. Right-click on the **Forest** object and select **Properties | Voice Properties**. Click on the **Routes tab** (see Figure 9.19).

Figure 9.19 Voice Properties

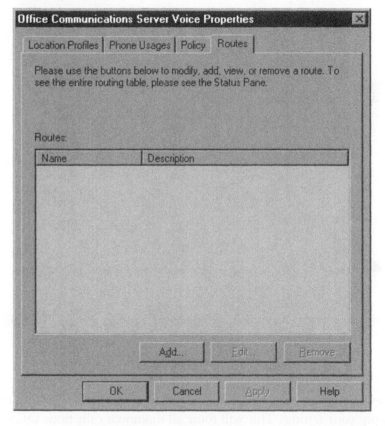

Click **Add**, and add a new route that looks something like the one shown in Figure 9.20.

Figure 9.20 Add Route

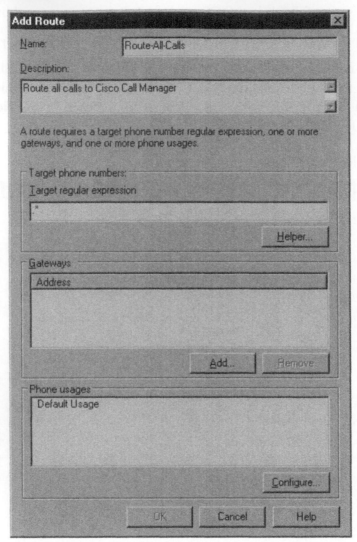

In the **Gateways** section, click **Add**. Select your Mediation Server and click **OK**. Click **OK** again to apply your settings. This will route all unknown calls from OCS to CallManager. This is, of course, a simplistic route and you probably wouldn't want to use it in real life. In our case, it does what we want it to by sending any calls over to CallManager that don't match an OCS user's phone number.

Restart your OCS server's Front-End Services for the changes to the dial plan to take effect.

Testing and Call Flow

From an OCS client, type in the extension of an IP phone user and watch the number normalize to **+1 (312)555-4736**. Click the **phone icon** to the right of the normalized number to make the call. The call will be sent from your client to the Mediation Server. The Mediation Server will then send the call to CallManager's SIP trunk. CallManager will strip off all the leading digits, leaving just 4736, and will route the call to extension 4736.

Routing to the PSTN via CallManager

In the example we've just walked through, CallManager can now route calls to OCS users and OCS users can now route calls to CallManager users. I haven't addressed the possibility of OCS users being able to route calls to the Public Switched Telephone Network (PSTN) via CallManager because the routing to be able to do this (while also routing to users' extensions on CallManager) is complex and beyond the scope of this book.

However, I'll give you a couple of ideas to use on your own system so that you can see how this can be done. Note that by doing this you will most likely break the routing to IP phone extensions that we've set up already.

For CallManager to handle this kind of number (the + sign isn't something CallManager is designed to handle), you will need to adjust your significant digits in the SIP trunk to **11**. This will strip out the + sign and route the remaining 11 digits: 1 plus the full 10-digit number. If this is an outside call, you will want to configure your SIP trunk to automatically prepend a **9** to your calls, assuming that 9 is your outside access code. Lastly, you will need to change the calling search space on your SIP trunk to one that has permissions to make outside calls.

If you really want to be able to route all calls to all destinations via CallManager, I suggest that you create several translation patterns and put them in a special **OCS to CCM Calls** partition that only the SIP trunk is allowed to access. Each translation pattern should be manipulating a particular type of call: internal calls, long distance calls, 911 calls, and so on. Once the calls have been stripped of their + signs and prepended with 9s (for outside calls when appropriate), the translation patterns should route the calls to their destinations.

CSTA/SIP Gateways

I mentioned this at the beginning of the chapter, but it's worth repeating: At the time of this writing, Microsoft does not support any direct SIP or Computer Supported Telecommunications Application (CSTA) integrations with OCS 2007. Both Microsoft and Cisco are expected to support integrations in the near future (as they both currently support LCS 2005 SP1 integrated to CUPS today), but any attempt to integrate with OCS 2007 will not be supported at present.

What Does CSTA Do?

CSTA integrations make Remote Call Control possible and enable OCS users to see PBX presence information. Few vendors today support OCS 2007 via CSTA integration. Two of the better-known integrations, however, are with Genesis Labs and CUPS. These integrations are fairly complex and require a good amount of configuration on both the OCS side and the Genesis or Cisco side.

In the remainder of this chapter, I will cover only the CUPS integration.

Cisco Unified Presence Server

CUPS is designed to integrate with CallManager. Whereas CallManager is an IP-PBX that is the core component of an IP telephony deployment, CUPS is an instant messaging (IM) and presence server that adds additional functionality to your environment. Cisco sells a client application for CUPS, called CUPS-C (CUPS Client), that allows users to send and receive internal IMs and see each other's presence. The CUPS client can also be used like a remote control; giving users the ability to click on a name in the CUPS client and having their Cisco IP phone automatically dial the number.

It is important to understand that you must install and configure CUPS to work with CallManager if you want to get OCS Remote Call Control working. OCS integrated directly with CallManager will allow you to enable Enterprise Voice for your OCS users, but CallManager alone cannot provide presence or Remote Call Control. CUPS is required for these features to work.

The CUPS server uses SIP as the protocol to exchange presence and IM information, and because OCS 2007 also supports SIP, we can integrate the two products. CUPS also uses CSTA to allow a client application to remotely control an IP phone, giving users the ability to "click-to-dial". OCS 2007 also uses CSTA and therefore, through some careful configuration, we can make it so that we can use an OCS client to have a Cisco IP phone make a call.

For OCS to integrate to CUPS, you need to configure three elements: OCS, CUPS, and CallManager. These configurations will make up the remainder of this chapter.

Configuring CallManager for a CUPS Integration

You need to integrate CallManager with both CUPS and OCS. I am not going to spend any time talking about the CUPS installation, nor the integration with CallManager. Cisco provides detailed documentation for this purpose and I will not attempt to reinvent that wheel.

Instead, I will focus on the pieces of CallManager configuration that are important for getting OCS integrated to the Cisco environment. The major objects to configure are:

1. The SIP trunk
2. The users
3. The application dial rules

Configuring a SIP Trunk

The SIP trunk that we will configure for CUPS/Remote Call Control integration will look like the one we configured for Enterprise Voice/SIP integration, except for one major difference: The destination IP address of our SIP trunk is that of your CallManager.

To create the new trunk, open the CallManager administrative Web site. Click on **Device | Trunk** and then click **Add New**. Give the trunk a name and description that will differentiate it from the SIP trunk we created in the previous sections (see Figure 9.21).

Figure 9.21 Trunk Configuration

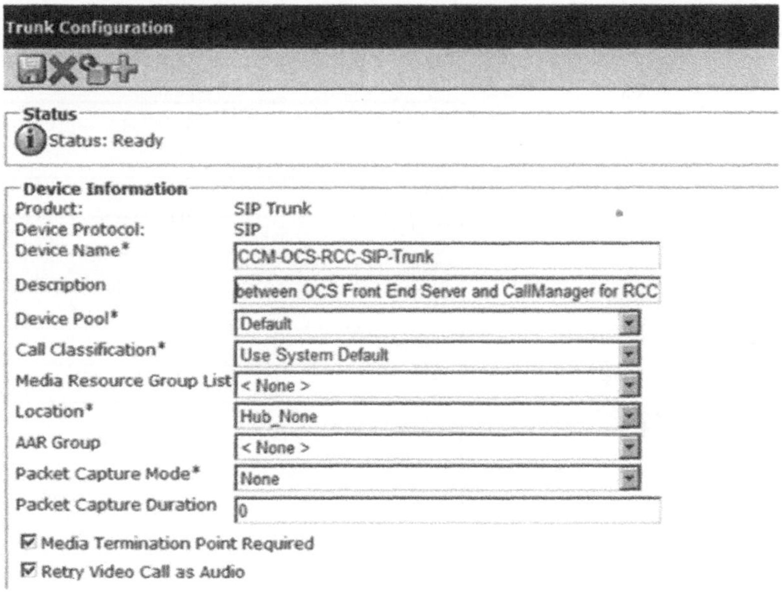

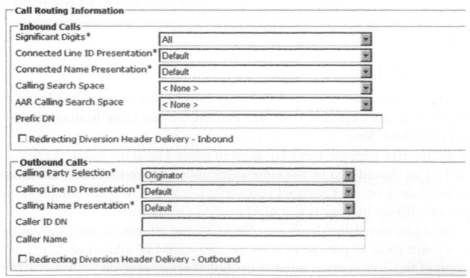

You can leave the **Call Routing Information** section at its defaults (see Figure 9.22).

Figure 9.22 Call Routing Information

The **SIP Information** section, once again, is the most important. Notice in the example shown in Figure 9.23 that the destination IP address is **192.168.100.200**—which is my **CallManager**. This may seem strange, but you do not configure a SIP trunk to OCS in any way here. OCS only pulls status information from CUPS, which gets its information from CallManager.

Figure 9.23 SIP Information

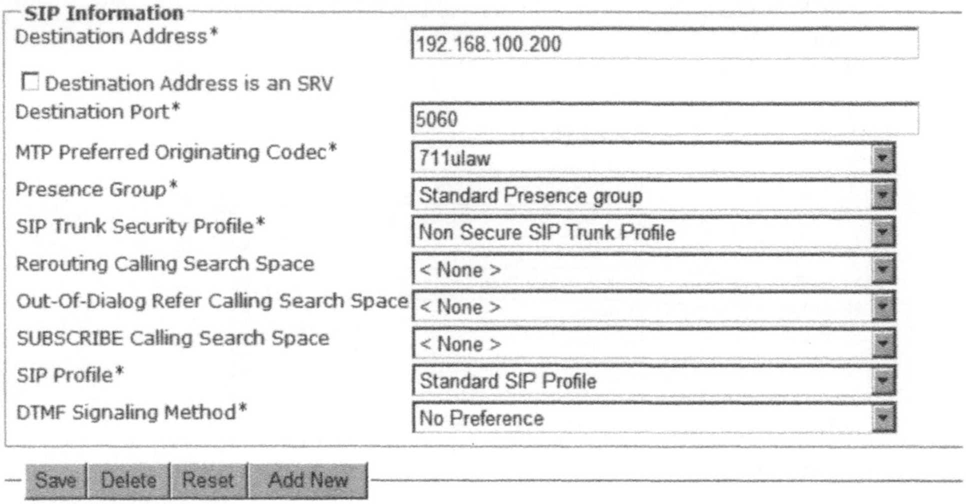

```
┌─SIP Information──────────────────────────────────────────┐
  Destination Address*              ┌────────────────────────────┐
                                    │ 192.168.100.200            │
                                    └────────────────────────────┘
    □ Destination Address is an SRV
  Destination Port*                 ┌────────────────────────────┐
                                    │ 5060                       │
                                    └────────────────────────────┘
  MTP Preferred Originating Codec*  │ 711ulaw                 ▼ │
  Presence Group*                   │ Standard Presence group ▼ │
  SIP Trunk Security Profile*       │ Non Secure SIP Trunk Profile ▼ │
  Rerouting Calling Search Space    │ < None >                ▼ │
  Out-Of-Dialog Refer Calling Search Space │ < None >         ▼ │
  SUBSCRIBE Calling Search Space    │ < None >                ▼ │
  SIP Profile*                      │ Standard SIP Profile    ▼ │
  DTMF Signaling Method*            │ No Preference           ▼ │

  ─ Save │ Delete │ Reset │ Add New ─────────────────────────────
```

Notice also that I haven't filled in any information in the **Calling Search Space** section. This is because we won't actually be using the SIP trunk to route calls; it will only be sending signaling and presence information to and from CUPS. Remember, with Remote Call Control, the Cisco IP phone is the device that does the actual calling, not OCS. OCS is just sending digits to the IP phone for it to dial.

Click **Save**.

Configuring CallManager Users

The next step is to configure users in CallManager. Add a new user to CallManager by opening the CallManager administrative Web site and clicking **User Management | End User**. Then click **Add New**.

Fill in the **userID** with the user's SIP account name. This must match the SIP account name exactly. This should also be the same as the user's Active Directory account name (SAMAccount name), but isn't required necessarily. It is recommended, though, to minimize the number of different usernames that users need to remember.

In this example, user Patty Doe has an OCS login of pdoe@contoso.com, an Active Directory account name of pdoe@contoso.com, and an SMTP address of pdoe@contoso.com. Because of this, I must enter **pdoe** as her CallManager user ID.

You are also required to enter a password and a PIN; neither of these needs to match the user's Active Directory password (see Figure 9.24).

Figure 9.24 User Information

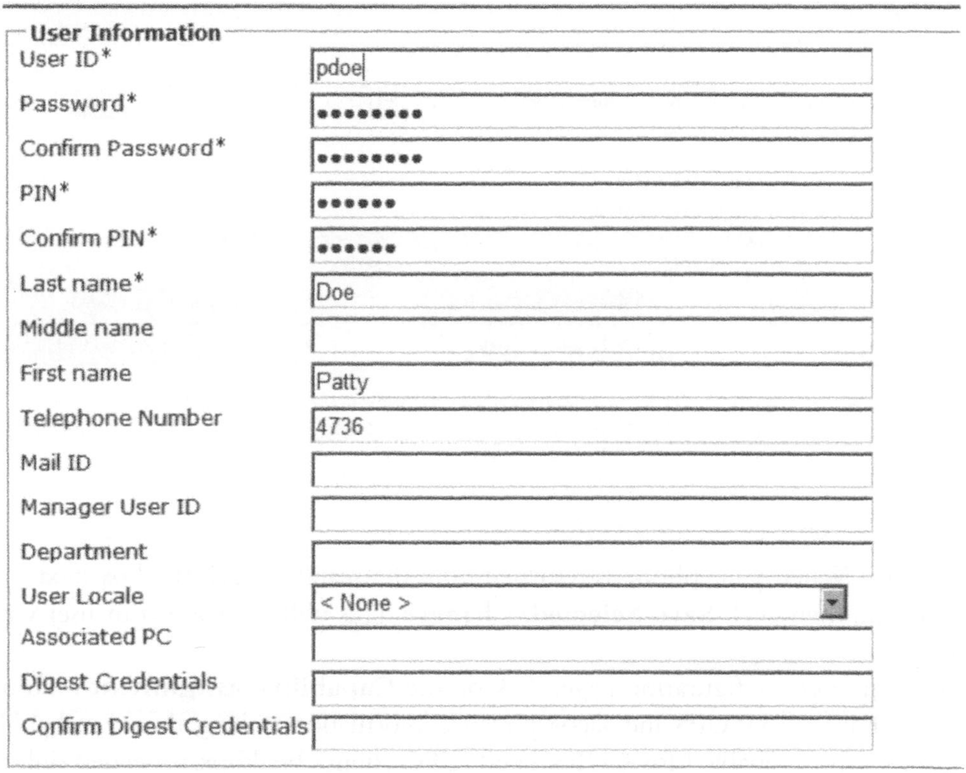

```
┌─ User Information ──────────────────────────────────────────┐
│ User ID*              [pdoe                            ]     │
│ Password*             [••••••••                        ]     │
│ Confirm Password*     [••••••••                        ]     │
│ PIN*                  [••••••                          ]     │
│ Confirm PIN*          [••••••                          ]     │
│ Last name*            [Doe                             ]     │
│ Middle name           [                                ]     │
│ First name            [Patty                           ]     │
│ Telephone Number      [4736                            ]     │
│ Mail ID               [                                ]     │
│ Manager User ID       [                                ]     │
│ Department            [                                ]     │
│ User Locale           [< None >                     ▼]       │
│ Associated PC         [                                ]     │
│ Digest Credentials    [                                ]     │
│ Confirm Digest Credentials [                           ]     │
└─────────────────────────────────────────────────────────────┘
```

Click **Save**. Then scroll down to the **Device Associations** section of the user screen. You should now see a button in the section called **Device Association**. Click that button.

Choose **Directory Number Begins With** and enter the extension of the user's phone. In this case, the user's number is **4736** (see Figure 9.25).

Figure 9.25 User Device Association

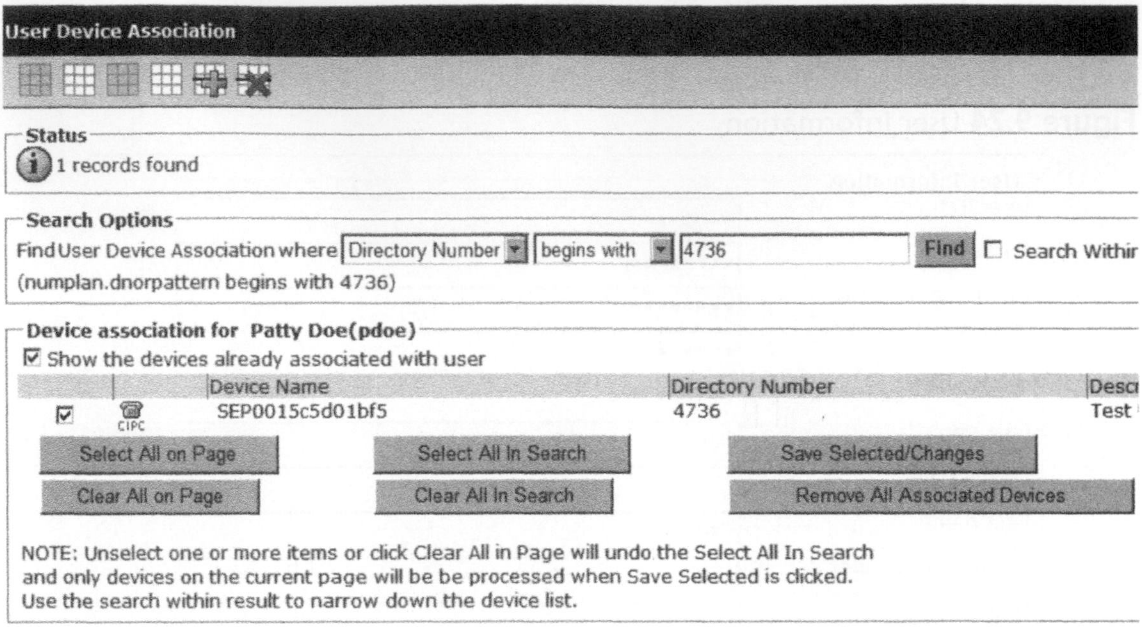

Click **Find**. When your phone is returned from the search, check the box next to the phone icon and then click **Save Selected/Changes**. This will associate your user with his or her IP phone.

Back in the user configuration page, click on the **Capability assignment** button. This gives your user access to CUPS and allows presence information to be gathered and published for every user who is enabled for CUPS. The CUPC client checkbox is needed only when you are using the Cisco CUPC client; because we are using the OCS client we don't need to check this box.

Check the **Enable CUPS (Cisco Unified Presence)** box, but do not check the **Enable CUPC (Cisco Unified Presence Client)** box. Click **Save**.

Configuring Application Dial Rules

When we configured CallManager for Enterprise Voice/SIP integration with OCS, I noted that CallManager cannot handle the + sign that OCS sends with all its outbound calls. The way we dealt with it then was by limiting the significant digits on the SIP trunk and thus stripping off the leading +.

Unfortunately, Remote Call Control does not work the same way because, once again, calls do not come through the SIP trunk in this type of integration. The OCS client sends the digits to dial to CUPS and CUPS passes these digits to CallManager. The only way for us to strip out the + is to configure an application dial rule.

Open the CallManager administrative Web site and click on **Call Routing | Dial Rules | Application Dial Rules**. Click **Add New**.

With this dial rule, I am going to strip out just the + and then add a 9 to the beginning (see Figure 9.26). This will change the number +13125551212 to 9 13125551212, which CallManager can then have my IP phone dial. If I don't add the 9 prefix, my IP phone will try to dial just 13125551212 and will fail because I need a 9 to dial an outside number.

Figure 9.26 Dial Rule Configuration

Application Dial Rule Configuration

Status
ⓘ Status: Ready

Application Dial Rule Information

Name*	CUPS-OCS rule to remove + sign
Description	Strip the + sign and leave the rest
Number Begins With	+
Number of Digits*	12
Total Digits to be Removed*	1
Prefix With Pattern	9

Save

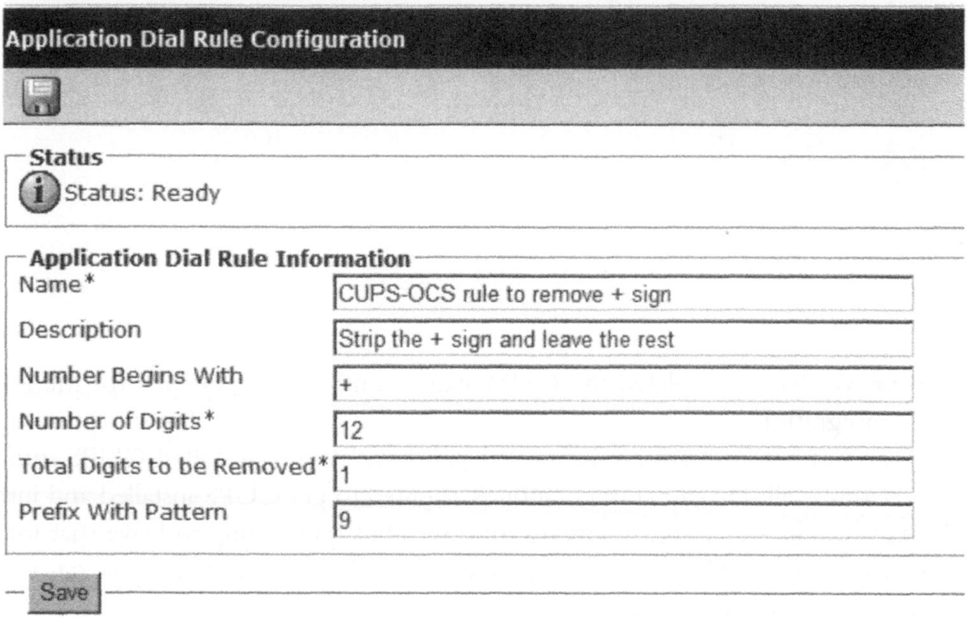

Notice that I have 12 as the number of digits: CallManager considers the leading + to be a digit. Click **Save**.

Create another rule that will handle incoming calls bound for users' extensions. This time, we will strip off everything except the last four digits (see Figure 9.27). And because these are internal calls, there will be no need to add a 9 prefix.

Figure 9.27 Dial Rule Configuration

Application Dial Rule Configuration

Status
(i) Status: Ready

Application Dial Rule Information

Name*	CUPS-OCS rule to remove all but the last 4 digits
Description	Strip the + sign and everything but the extension
Number Begins With	+
Number of Digits*	12
Total Digits to be Removed*	8
Prefix With Pattern	

Save

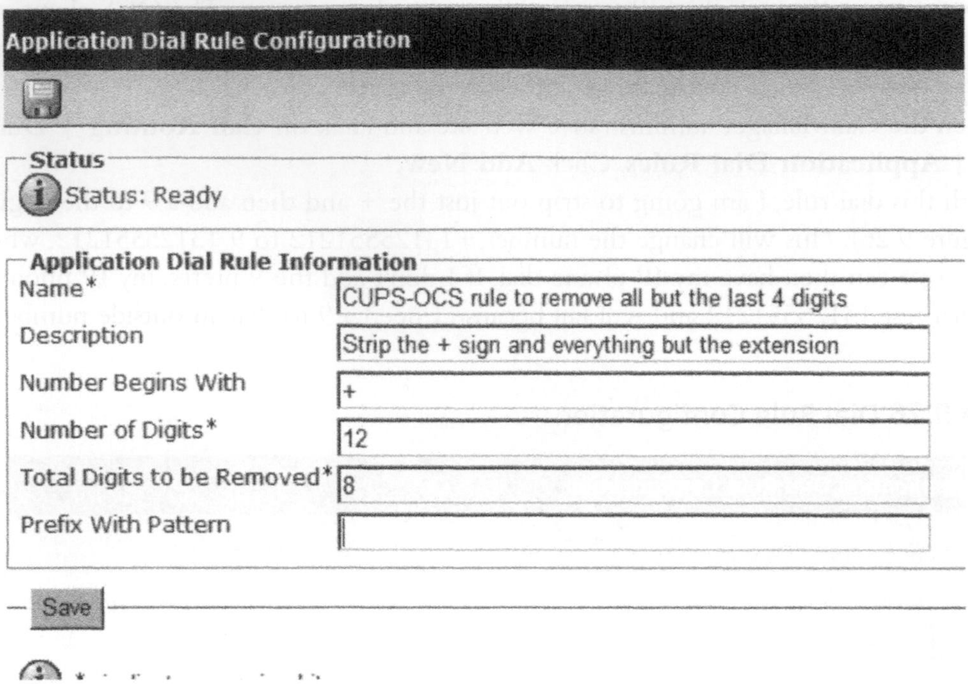

Click **Save**. We have completed the CallManager configuration needed for the Remote Call Control integration.

As I mentioned before, I am assuming that you have already installed CUPS into your environment. More CallManager configuration is required to get CUPS installed and integrated to CallManager (such as creating an application user), but I am going to leave that for you to do on your own or with a Cisco partner. I have covered all of the necessary changes to a basic CUPS install for an OCS integration.

Configuring CUPS for an OCS Integration

Along similar lines, I will not go into detail regarding how to configure CUPS to integrate with CallManager; again, check Cisco's documentation for this. I will, however, point out the two things that you must do to get basic functionality:

1. Configure ACLS

2. Configure users for use with Microsoft Office Communicator (MOC)

Configuring OCS for a CUPS Integration

The OCS Standard Edition Server (or the Enterprise Edition front-end server pool) requires some configuration to integrate with CUPS and CallManager. The main objectives of this section are to:

- Allow OCS to listen on port 5060
- Set CUPS as a trusted host
- Create an OCS static route to CUPS
- Configure users for RCC
- Enable your Communicator client for integration to the PBX

Configure OCS to Listen on Port 5060

By default, the OCS front-end server only listens for SIP connections on port 5061 because 5061 is the port used for secure SIP communications using a multiline telephone system (MTLS). CUPS will not support this secure SIP signaling, so we need to configure OCS to use SIP over port 5060.

Summary

OCS 2007 does not yet support any direct integration with CSTA-capable PBXes. However, Microsoft expects to officially support this in the near future. Currently, you can integrate with Cisco CUPS to allow your Office Communicator client to act as a remote control for your Cisco IP phone. To make this happen, you need to configure CallManager, CUPS, and the OCS Front End server all to communicate. You also need to enable the Remote Call Control feature for each OCS user and configure each client to be able to take advantage of the phone system integration.

Remote Call Control is a good option for customers who aren't yet ready or willing to make phone calls using a software-based phone. RCC provides an easy way for users to look up contacts' phone numbers and make calls all from one single interface.

Solutions Fast Track

Using a Gateway

- ☑ Integrating with a PBX allows you to extend the functionality of your phone system to OCS.

- ☑ PBXs that don't have IP capability can now support remote users who use the Communicator client.

- ☑ PSTN integration to OCS gives users the ability to call anyone, anywhere, anytime.

- ☑ Use a gateway to enable OCS clients to make calls to users on other phone systems.

- ☑ Gateways translate between OCS and a PBX/PSTN connection.

- ☑ Even if your PBX supports SIP, you need a gateway.

CSTA/SIP Gateways

- ☑ CSTA/SIP gateways allow you to enable Remote Call Control.

- ☑ CSTA/SIP gateways let OCS users see the status of your IP phone.

- ☑ There are no supported CSTA/SIP gateways just yet.

Frequently Asked Questions

Q: Do I need a gateway to enable PC-to-PC calls with OCS?

A: No. By default, OCS users can make PC-to-PC calls.

Q: Do I need a gateway to make calls to the PSTN?

A: Yes. OCS requires a gateway to translate between SIP and the PBX or PSTN.

Q: My PBX supports SIP. Do I still need a gateway?

A: Yes. Even if your PBX supports SIP, Microsoft doesn't support direct integration with SIP yet.

Q: I have CallManager 5.1. Can I integrate with OCS and use Remote Call Control?

A: No. Not only does Microsoft not support direct integrations with Cisco, but also you need to have the Cisco Unified Presence Server (CUPS) for RCC to work.

Q: Where can I find a list of supported gateways for OCS integrations?

A: Visit http://technet.microsoft.com/en-us/office/bb735838.aspx.

Q: Will my PBX support an OCS integration?

A: It's hard to say for sure, but almost any PBX that supports T1/PRI or FXO ports should work with one of the supported gateways.

Chapter 10

Integration with Exchange 2007 Unified Messaging

Solutions in this chapter:

- Exchange 2007 Unified Messaging
- Exchange 2007 Architecture
- Configuring Exchange 2007 Unified Messaging
- Mailbox Configuration: Combining OCS and Exchange 2007 Unified Messaging

☑ Summary

☑ Solutions Fast Track

☑ Frequently Asked Questions

Introduction

In this chapter, we will explore Unified Messaging (UM) and how to integrate Exchange 2007 UM with Office Communications Server (OCS) 2007. I will provide a high-level overview of Exchange 2007 UM and cover how to integrate OCS 2007 with an existing Exchange 2007 UM deployment.

Exchange 2007 Unified Messaging

UM is an exciting new feature in Microsoft Exchange Server 2007. UM provides the ability to *unify* your various mailboxes including e-mail, voice mail, and fax. Exchange 2007 UM brings many of the traditional voice mail features to e-mail in the same way OCS brings Private Branch Exchange (PBX) features to instant messaging (IM).

What Is It?

Exchange 2007 UM allows you to access your voice mail, e-mail, and faxes all from a single inbox via your Outlook 2007 client or even Outlook Web Access. Exchange 2007 UM also incorporates a feature known as Outlook Voice Access (OVA), allowing end-users to access their voice mail, e-mail, and even Outlook calendar via any telephone. OVA uses voice recoginizition technology to perform commands based on the spoken voice. For example, OVA allows you to call Exchange and enter your mailbox number and passcode just as you would typically access voice mail remotely. However, with OVA you can access new voice mail messages by simply speaking into the phone the words *voice mail*. OVA will then play any new voice mails waiting in your inbox. Alternatively, you can simply launch your Outlook client and listen to voice mails through your computer speakers.

How Does It Work?

UM works by integrating Exchange Server 2007 with your existing PBX phone system. Connectivity between the PBX and Exchange Server 2007 typically involves a Voice over IP (VoIP) gateway device linking the two systems. The VoIP gateway accepts unanswered incoming calls from the PBX and routes them to the appropriate Exchange mailbox to allow the caller to record a voice-mail message. The VoIP gateway also accepts incoming Outlook Voice Access calls from the PBX. To make this clearer let's walk through a couple of examples.

First, let's take a look at voice-mail. A caller picks up the phone and dials your phone number. The call comes inbound to your PBX and is routed to your phone and it rings. If you do not answer your phone in a predetermined amount of time, the PBX routes the call to the VoIP gateway. The VoIP gateway then hands the call over to the Exchange UM server. The UM server will then record the voicemail for the intended receipt. Next the Exchange UM server will send the voicemail to the hub-transport server which will in turn route the voicemail to the correct mailbox on the mailbox server.

Great, you now have a new voice mail. However, we'll pretend you're at a client location with no Internet access. So, how do you check your voice mail? Remember, that message no longer resides in a tradition voice-mail system; instead, it's waiting for your review in your Exchange mailbox. No problem. You pull out your cell phone and dial the OVA number. You then enter your mailbox number and pin code. OVA then presents you with a menu of options. You simply say *voice mail* and OVA begins to play the new voice-mail message. After hearing the voice-mail message, you decide you need to check your calendar. You speak into the phone, saying the words *calendar for today*. OVA opens your calendar and speaks your appointments for today over the phone.

The preceding were just a couple of examples of Exchange 2007 UM features and how you can use them in the real world. Next, we'll discuss in a little more in detail the requirements to implement Exchange 2007 UM.

What Does It Work With?

Exchange 2007 UM has a few requirements to work properly. Exchange UM, in most cases, will require a VoIP gateway installed. These can range from around a thousand dollars to several thousand dollars, depending on the capacity required. The VoIP gateway is needed to route traffic between a traditional PBX and Exchange 2007. By implementing a VoIP gateway, you can integrate most phone systems with Exchange 2007. Depending on your PBX vendor, you may not need to implement a gateway device. Some IP based PBXes provide integration with Exchange 2007 out of the box or with an add-on to their software. The main requirement is that they can route IP-based calls using the SIP protocol. These types of PBXes are then configured to route SIP-based calls bound for OCS users to the OCS mediation server.

NOTE

Exchange Server 2007 supports the standard SIP over TCP; however, some IP-PBXes use SIP over UDP. These PBXes will still require a gateway or a SIP router to convert SIP/UDP to SIP/TCP.

Exchange 2007 Architecture

Implementing UM requires a properly architected and implemented Exchange 2007 infrastructure. In most cases, you will need to be sure that not only Exchange but also Exchange connectivity to your PBX is highly available. With all of the great features provided by Exchange UM comes the risk of "putting all your eggs in one basket." Traditionally, if you lost your e-mail system, voice mail would still be available, or vice versa. However, after implementing Exchange UM, if your e-mail system goes down, so does your voice mail. This is why it's important to ensure that you properly design your Exchange environment before you deploy. If you require 99% uptime, you had better plan accordingly.

To properly implement Exchange 2007 UM, it is important to understand how Exchange is architected and deployed. Implementing Exchange 2007 is somewhat different than Exchange 2003. You will remember that implementing Exchange 2003 required installing all Exchange components, then disabling those that were not needed, and then properly configuring a server to provide a specific service. For example, after installation you must properly perform a series of configuration steps to designate that server as a front-end server. Exchange 2007 introduces a concept known as *server roles*. Server roles allow you define a server's purpose before installing Exchange. By doing so, only the components needed to perform that specific function are installed. Exchange 2007 incorporates five server roles, each performing a particular function (See Figure 10.1).

Figure 10.1 Exchange 2007 Server Roles

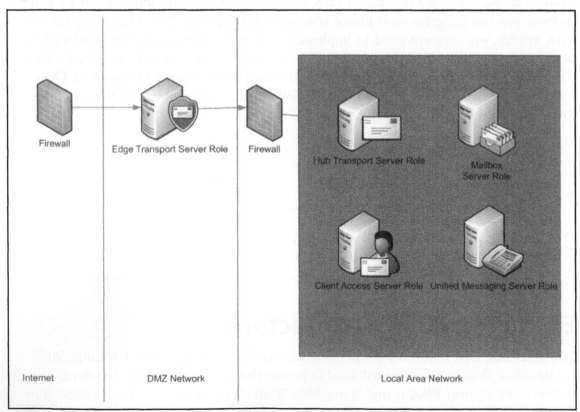

BEST PRACTICES ACCORDING TO MICROSOFT

Before deploying Exchange 2007, you should be sure to properly plan for capacity. No matter how many new features are implemented, end users still want quick, easy access to their e-mail messages. If you don't properly plan for capacity, you may see performance issues immediately after or during your deployment. Luckily, Microsoft provides tools and guidance on how to properly plan for Exchange capacity. Microsoft provides several deployment documents that are freely downloadable from TechNet. Microsoft also provides several tools for testing your deployment. These tools should be used to test your environment before considering its production. The tools include:

- **Exchange Server Jetstress** Provides ability to test performance of your disk drives by adding large workloads to them.
- **Exchange Server Stress and Performance** Provides the ability to simulate hundreds or thousands of simultaneous client sessions connecting to your Exchange servers.
- **Exchange Server Best Practices Analyzer (BPA).** The Exchange Server Best Practices Analyzer checks the configuration of your Exchange Server deployment to ensure best practice configurations are being followed. The BPA makes recommendations for correcting any known configuration problems.

Requirements

Before you jump in and deploy Exchange, it is important to understand the necessary requirements, both hardware and software. The biggest difference between Exchange 2007 and the previous version of the messaging system is that it requires 64-bit processors and a 64-bit version of Windows. You can install Exchange 2007 on Windows Server 2003 Standard or Enterprise. Service Pack 1 for Exchange 2007 provides the capability to install Exchange on a Windows Server 2008 system as well. If you plan to use UM, you will need to make sure you have a compatible IP-PBX or a VoIP gateway that will provide connectivity between Exchange and your PBX.

Server Roles

We previously discussed the new server role concept in Exchange Server 2007. You can install Exchange 2007 as five distinct roles, each designed to perform a specific function. Keep in mind that server roles do not necessarily mean that separate physical servers are required for each role. For example, you can deploy an Exchange server with both the Mailbox server role and the Client Access server role. Let's briefly cover each role and its purpose in an Exchange 2007 deployment.

Mailbox Server Role

The Mailbox server role in Exchange Server 2007 is where mailboxes for users are stored. The Mailbox server role in Exchange 2007 is synonymous with a back-end server in Exchange 2003. A mailbox server role must exist in an Exchange 2007-only server environment. The Mailbox server role can exist on the same physical server as other server roles.

Hub Transport Server Role

The Hub Transport server role performs the task of internal message routing and encryption. The Hub Transport server role also is in charge of applying internal policies on message routing. The Hub Transport server role can exist on the same physical server as other server roles.

Client Access Server Role

The Client Access server role in Exchange 2007 is similar to the front-end server in Exchange 2003. The Client Access server role provides Outlook Anywhere Access, formally known as Outlook Web Access and HTTP/RPC. The Client Access server role also supports connectivity for Windows Mobile devices. The Client Access server role can exist on the same physical server as other server roles.

Edge Transport Server Role

The Edge Transport server role resides in the DMZ of your network and is not a domain-joined server. The Edge Transport server role is in charge of external SMTP connectivity and provides antivirus, antispam, and encryption services for messages received from or destined to the Internet. You cannot install the Edge Transport server role on the same server as other roles, as it should reside in the DMZ of your network.

Unified Messaging Server Role

The Unified Messaging server role is necessary if you plan to provide UM services in your Exchange deployment. The Unified Messaging server role provides connectivity between the VoIP gateway and your Exchange 2007 infrastructure. Though not recommended in most production environments, you can install the Unified Messaging server role on the same physical server as other server roles.

Configuring Exchange 2007 Unified Messaging

Now that you are familiar with the Exchange 2007 architecture basics, it's time to set up and configure Exchange 2007 UM. Assuming that you have an existing Exchange 2007 infrastructure set up and configured properly, let's install and configure a new UM server to support UM.

Installation

First we need to install the Exchange 2007 Unified Messaging server role. In our example, we will use a server that already has Exchange 2007 installed and just add the Unified Messaging server role. In the example in this section, we install the UM role on the same server for simplicity. In a production environment, you will more than likely want to install the UM role on its own server. Perform the following steps to install the UM Server role:

1. Go to **Start | Control Panel | Add or Remove Programs**.
2. Locate Microsoft Exchange Server 2007 and click the change button (See Figure 10.2). The Exchange 2007 Setup Wizard will launch.

Figure 10.2 Windows Add or Remove Programs

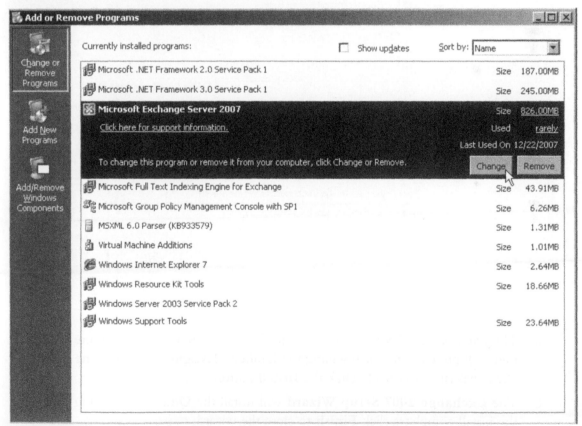

3. From the main page of the Exchange Setup Wizard, click **Next**.
4. From the **Server Role Selection** page select the checkbox next to the **Unified Messaging Role** (See Figure 10.3). Then click **Next**.

Figure 10.3 Exchange Server Role Selection

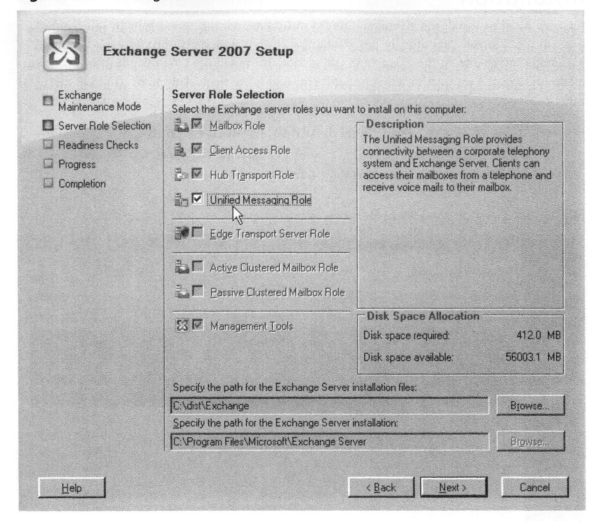

5. The Exchange 2007 Setup Wizard will perform a readiness check to ensure the system meets all prerequisites for installing the Unified Messaging role. After the readiness check has run successfully click the **Install** button.

6. The **Exchange 2007 Setup Wizard** will install the Unified Messaging role. After the install completes click **Finish** to close the wizard.

You have now completed the installation of the Exchange 2007 Unified Messaging Role. You can now proceed to creating a Dial Plan and Auto-Attendant.

Auto-Attendant and Dial Plan Configuration

After installing the Unified Messaging server role, we need to set up a dial plan and auto-attendant on the Exchange 2007 UM server. To create a dial plan and auto-attendant follow these steps:

1. Open the **Exchange Management Console**.
2. Locate and click on the **Unified Messaging** tree node in the left pane of the console.
3. In the **Action Pane**, click the **New UM Dial Plan** link. This will launch the New UM Dial Plan Wizard.
4. In the first step of the **New UM Dial Plan** wizard, type a name for the dial plan. In the **Number of digits in extension numbers** text box enter the number of digits to use for the dial plan.
5. Now click the **New** button.

Now that we've set up the dial plan, let's configure an auto-attendant:

1. In the **Exchange Management Console**, locate and click on the **Unified Messaging** node in the tree in the left pane of the console.
2. From within the work pane, click **UM Auto Attendants**. Then click **New UM Auto Attendant** in the Action pane. The **New UM Auto Attendant Wizard** will launch.
3. From the **New UM Auto Attendant Wizard** screen, enter a name for the new attendant into the **Name** text box.
4. Click the **Browse** button located next to **Select Associated Dial Plan**. Locate the dial plan you created earlier in this section, and then click **OK**.
5. Back in the **New UM Auto Attendant Wizard** enter an extension number to use for the auto-attendant in the **Extension Numbers** text box.
6. Select the options to **Create the auto-attendant enabled** and **Create the auto-attendant as speech enabled**. Then click the **New** button.
7. Now click the **Finish** button to complete the wizard.

You have now successfully created a dial plan and auto-attendant for use with Exchange 2007 UM.

> **NOTE**
>
> Microsoft provides a free software-based IP phone that is installed with Exchange Server 2007. This softphone allows you to test the unified messaging functionality in Exchange without a PBX and gateway device. The phone is located in the Exchange program directory and named ExchangeUMTestPhone.exe.

Mailbox Configuration: Combining OCS and Exchange 2007 Unified Messaging

In the preceding section, we set up and configured Exchange 2007 UM with a dial plan and auto-attendant. You now need to configure user mailboxes for UM and OCS 2007–Exchange 2007 connectivity.

Benefits

Before we jump into configuring OCS 2007 and Exchange 2007 connectivity, let's discuss the benefits of integrating Exchange 2007 UM and OCS 2007. So, what exactly does integration between the two products provide for your end-users?

- Missed call notification in both Outlook 2007 and Communicator 2007 clients
- Call and leave voice mail from the Communicator 2007 client
- Access Outlook Voice Access from the Communicator 2007 client
- Access to voice mail from the Communicator 2007 client

Configuration

Now let's finish configuring OCS to Exchange 2007 integration. First you need to enable users for UM. Perform the following steps:

1. Open the **Exchange Management Console**.
2. Locate the **Recipient Configuration section** in the tree and expand it.
3. In the middle pane, click to select the user you want to enable for UM.
4. In the **Action pane**, click **Enable Unified Messaging**. The **Enable Unified Messaging Wizard** will launch.
5. Click the **Browse** button to select a UM policy. Then click **OK**.

6. To configure a pin choose to **Automatically Generate Pin to Access Outlook Voice Access**. Then click the **Next** button.

7. In the **Extension configuration** section, select **Automatically generated SIP resource identifier**. Then click the **Next** button.

8. On the next page, click **Enable** and then click the **Finish** button.

You have now configured a user for unified communications. Now let's set up the connection between OCS 2007 and Exchange 2007. This process involves several different configurations, and it can get complicated. Luckily, Microsoft has provided us with a powershell script and OCSUMUTIL to configure and link the two systems. The OCSUMUTIL creates contacts for Exchange auto-attendants and the phone number for subscriber access to Exchange unified messaging. The OCSUMUTIL also ensures that Enterprise Voice location profiles in OCS match up to an Exchange UM dial plan.

To integrate Exchange 2007 and OCS 2007 do the following:

1. From your Exchange UM server open the **Exchange Management Shell**.

2. From the **Exchange Management Shell** run the script **exchucutil.ps1** which is located in the Exchange installation folder. This script performs several configuration steps, including providing OCS 2007 access to Exchange 2007 objects.

3. After running the Exchange configuration script, note the **UMIPGateway**.

4. From the **Exchange Management Shell** type **Set-umipgateway –identity** *name from step 3* **–port 5061** and press **Enter**.

5. Now let's link OCS to the Exchange environment. Log on to the Exchange UM server.

6. From a command prompt, run **ocsumutil /domain:***yourdomainname* and press **Enter**.

7. Finally, restart the **Unified Messaging** service on your Exchange 2007 UM server and restart the **Office Communications Server Front-End Service** on your OCS 2007 server(s).

You have now completed the process of setting up and configuring connectivity between Exchange 2007 UM and OCS 2007.

NOTE

Exchange 2007 and OCS 2007 UM integration requires the installation of Service Pack 1 for Exchange 2007 to be fully supported.

Summary

In this chapter, you learned how Exchange 2007 UM works and how it integrates with OCS 2007. We also discussed the advantages of integrating OCS 2007 with Exchange 2007 UM. In addition, we covered how to set up Exchange UM and connect it to an OCS 2007 deployment.

Solutions Fast Track

Exchange 2007 Architecture

- ☑ Exchange 2007 has several prerequisites that must be met before installing an Exchange server.

- ☑ Exchange 2007 uses 5 distinct server roles to support the Exchange infrastructure.

- ☑ Several freely downloadable tools are available from Microsoft for planning and testing an Exchange 2007 deployment.

Configuring Exchange 2007 Unified Messaging

- ☑ UM Requires installing and configuring the Exchange 2007 Unified Messaging server role.

- ☑ Exchange 2007 UM requires you to properly configure a dial plan.

- ☑ Exchange 2007 UM requires you to properly setup and configure an auto-attendant.

Mailbox Configuration: Combining OCS and Exchange 2007 Unified Messaging

- ☑ Exchange Server 2007 and OCS 2007 integration provides voicemail and missed called notifications in both Outlook 2007 and the Microsoft Office Communicator (MOC) client.

- ☑ Configuring Exchange Server 2007 and OCS 2007 integration requires running both a powershell script and the OCSUMUTIL utility.

- ☑ Exchange Server 2007 and OCS 2007 integration requires Exchange Server 2007 with Service Pack 1 installed.

Frequently Asked Questions

Q: What version of Exchange is required for UM and connectivity to OCS 2007?

A: Exchange 2007 RTM is required for UM. Exchange 2007 RTM is required to enable all integration features with OCS 2007.

Q: Is there any additional hardware required to support UM?

A: If your PBX does not natively support Exchange 2007 VoIP you will need to purchase a compatible VoIP gateway device.

Q: Do I have to deploy a new server to support Exchange 2007 UM?

A: No. If necessary resources are available, you can install the Unified Messaging server role on an existing Exchange 2007 server.

Frequently Asked Questions

Q:

A:

Q:

A:

Q:

A:

Chapter 11

Upgrading to Office Communications Server 2007

Solutions in this chapter:

- **Understanding the Migration from LCS 2005 to OCS 2007**

- **Planning Your Migration from LCS 2005 to OCS 2007**

- **Upgrading Perimeter Servers**

- **Upgrading Front-End Servers and Performing User Migration**

- **Removing LCS 2005 from the Network Environment**

- **What to Do Once You've Completed Your Migration to OCS 2007**

☑ Summary

☑ Solutions Fast Track

☑ Frequently Asked Questions

Introduction

Organizations that currently have Live Communications Server (LCS) 2005 and want to upgrade to Office Communications Server (OCS) 2007 have a defined upgrade path to follow. That path is simple, primarily because there is only one way to upgrade: Use the "side-by-side" method of migration. There is no in-place upgrade option of putting a CD into the old server and performing an upgrade. To perform a side-by-side upgrade, you must have a new OCS 2007 server set up and working; then you need to migrate user accounts and configure settings on the new OCS 2007 environment, and then decommission the old LCS 2005.

However, the migration process isn't as simple as replacing each LCS 2005 server one for one with a new OCS 2007 server. If it were that simple, I wouldn't have anything to write about in this chapter. Because the path for migration is well defined and has little flexibility, following the procedures outlined in this chapter will ensure a successful migration from LCS 2005 to OCS 2007.

Understanding the Migration from LCS 2005 to OCS 2007

To migrate from LCS 2005 to OCS 2007 you must follow a specific sequence of steps. Understanding this sequence is important. For example, if you upgrade an existing Microsoft Office Communicator (MOC) client to the new 2007 edition, the user will not be able to access LCS 2005 because MOC 2007 is incompatible with LCS 2005. Similarly, if you move a user to OCS 2007 and enable enhanced presence for that user, he won't be able to access his account with the old MOC 2005 client software because enhanced presence requires the MOC 2007 client.

As I've mentioned, planning and then executing a migration from LCS 2005 to OCS 2007 requires specific steps that you need to follow in a prescribed order. The first step is to plan for the migration and make sure you have the proper sequence for migration, that you've performed all prerequisites before migrating, and that you enable features at the right time so that you don't get ahead of yourself during the migration process.

Understanding the Coexistence of LCS 2005 and OCS 2007

When you are upgrading from LCS 2005 to OCS 2007, because there is no in-place upgrade that will allow you to simply insert a CD into a server and upgrade a system all at once, LCS 2005 servers and OCS 2007 servers will coexist in your environment at some point. The question is whether the two environments will coexist for a short period specifically to migrate users from one environment to the other, or whether the coexistence will last for a lengthy period. The choice is a matter of feasibility and comfort factor in terms of performing the cutover.

Feasibility of a Short Coexistence Time Frame

It is unlikely that an organization with dozens of LCS 2005 servers spread around the world will be able to migrate all of its servers and potentially hundreds or thousands of its users all at once. The reality that it "just takes time" to get around to a large number of users dictates that a long coexistence will likely occur for this organization's migration process. However, an organization with a single server and, say, 50 users could have a short coexistence time frame, and could migrate entirely from LCS 2005 to OCS 2007 in an evening or a weekend.

Comfort Factor of a Long Coexistence Time Frame

Even organizations with a limited number of servers that could migrate from LCS 2005 to OCS 2007 in a short period may choose to migrate over a long period, methodically putting in new OCS 2007 servers and testing all aspects of the new installation before migrating users to the new environment, and most certainly before decommissioning an older LCS 2005 server.

Choosing a Coexistence Time Frame That Works for You

Fortunately for you, nothing is forcing you to migrate slowly or quickly; that decision is entirely up to you. No doubt, there will be both LCS 2005 and OCS 2007 servers in your environment because the migration process is a side-by-side migration. However, you can keep the old LCS 2005 servers in place for a long time if you want.

Most administrators who have many servers to migrate tend to start conservatively in that they leave the old LCS 2005 environment running for a lengthy period after they have implemented OCS 2007. However, over time, these administrators become more comfortable with the migration process and tend to drop the LCS 2005 systems off the network soon after they have an OCS 2007 replacement server in place.

The only real decision to make is to not drop the old LCS 2005 server if users still depend on it to access their IM and communications services, or if it is being used to route messages or communications for the environment. You should decommission the server only when the organization truly is no longer using it. I will cover how to validate that your LCS 2005 server is no longer being used before you remove it in the "Removing LCS 2005 from the Network Environment" section later in this chapter.

Choosing the Migration Path from LCS 2005 to OCS 2007

If you decided on a short coexistence migration path from LCS 2005 to OCS 2007, you can take the "big bang" approach for migration. If you decided on the long coexistence migration path, you can follow a phased migration approach.

Performing a "Big Bang" Migration to OCS 2007

With a "big bang" migration, you migrate the entire organization from LCS 2005 to OCS 2007 all at once; as such, you don't have to worry that some people will be using LCS 2005 and others will be using OCS 2007. Also, you don't have to extensively test the cross-communication between the LCS 2005 servers and the OCS 2007 servers. Once you add the new OCS 2007 servers and migrate the user information to them, you can give the new servers the same IP address as the old servers and users can launch their client software and access the OCS 2007 environment without even knowing the environment was upgraded.

Performing a Phased Migration to OCS 2007

If your organization has dozens of LCS 2005 servers around the world, it likely won't be feasible to get to all of the servers and the hundreds, if not thousands, of client systems to upgrade all users simultaneously. In the phased migration, your organization would typically migrate server by server and site by site in an orderly and timely manner. Specific users will be migrated from LCS 2005 to OCS 2007 in groups. The groups will typically reside on specific servers. And servers within one site will be migrated before you move on to the next site.

A key to performing a phased migration is that you cannot easily enable certain features that are available in OCS 2007 (such as one-to-many video conferencing or Voice over IP [VoIP] telephony) until all users in the organization have been upgraded to OCS 2007. You can have some users have these new features and other users not have these features; however, users become confused when they can videoconference and have telephony conversations with some users and not with others. So, a best practice is to wait until all users have been moved to OCS 2007 and have had their client software upgraded from MOC 2005 to MOC 2007, before you turn on the new features of OCS 2007.

Choosing the Right Time to Migrate from MOC 2005 to MOC 2007

Besides migrating servers and user accounts from LCS 2005 to OCS 2007, you will also need to choose the right time to migrate from MOC 2005 to MOC 2007. The first thing you need to know is that MOC 2007 won't work in an LCS 2005 environment, so it is clear that the client software migration will not happen until after you migrate your servers to OCS 2007.

Because the MOC 2005 client will run against a new OCS 2007 server, you may think that keeping the MOC 2005 client and not migrating to the new MOC 2007 client will make the migration easy because you won't have to touch user desktops. However, if you don't plan to migrate to the MOC 2007 client, you shouldn't waste your time migrating the front-end servers to OCS 2007 in the first place. Most likely, you are migrating from LCS 2005 to OCS 2007 to get the new features in OCS 2007. And you cannot take advantage of those new features until you actually have the users running the MOC 2007 client. So, you will need to migrate the client systems from MOC 2005 to MOC 2007; the decision is really a matter of "when."

Migrating Immediately to MOC 2007

One approach for migrating the client is to migrate the user's system from MOC 2005 to MOC 2007 as soon as the user's account is migrated from LCS 2005 to OCS 2007. Effectively, the migration is performed in groups, whereby a group of 50 user accounts is migrated from LCS 2005 to OCS 2007, and then the client systems are migrated from MOC 2005 to MOC 2007. Once that grouping of 50 has been migrated, select the next group of 50 users to migrate from LCS 2005 to OCS 2007, and then migrate those users' client software.

This approach of migrating small groups of users to the MOC 2007 client is typically selected for organizations that expect the migration process to take awhile (i.e., there are hundreds, if not thousands, of users to migrate). Rather than waiting several weeks or months until the final user has been migrated, stage the migration such that groups of users can gain access to the new features of OCS 2007 relatively soon after their account has been migrated from LCS 2005 to OCS 2007.

Waiting to Migrate to MOC 2007

The other approach is to migrate all accounts from LCS 2005 to OCS 2007, and once all of the accounts have been migrated, then have a phase in the migration process during which all of the user systems are upgraded from MOC 2005 to MOC 2007. This method effectively has the entire organization wait until all LCS 2005 server data has been migrated to OCS 2007, and then all users are migrated at the same time. This is feasible for an organization with a limited number of users in which the time it takes to migrate accounts and install the new MOC 2007 software on client systems isn't necessarily lengthy. This may also be selected if the organization wants consistency, whereby everybody in the organization has the same client software and access to the same features.

SOME INDEPENDENT ADVICE

The real decision of whether to migrate groups of users to the new MOC 2007 client versus waiting until you can switch all users to the new MOC 2007 at the same time comes down to how your users communicate. If your IM traffic is purely group or department based migrating smaller groups of users to the new MOC 2007 client will work. However, if your entire organization intercommunicates, and users get antsy and want to try out features of the new MOC 2007 client, you should wait to switch over the client software until all users can have access to the same client software features. Because the MOC 2007 client does a lot more than its predecessor, users will become frustrated if they try to use a feature in their client software that someone else in the organization doesn't have access to.

Planning Your Migration from LCS 2005 to OCS 2007

As mentioned at the start of this chapter, the key to migrating from LCS 2005 to OCS 2007 is to follow a methodical process. The process begins by making sure you understand your existing LCS 2005 environment so that when you perform the migration, you are migrating all of the servers and server roles from LCS 2005 to OCS 2007. If you forgot you had an LCS 2005 server hosting users and you do not include that server in your migration plan, you may forget to migrate the users on that LCS 2005 system.

Identifying Existing LCS 2005 Servers

The first step in the planning process is to identify which servers in the organization are running LCS 2005, where the servers are located, and what server roles are currently installed on the systems. The server roles would identify whether the system is an access proxy server on the perimeter, a director server in the organizational network, or a front-end server hosting user accounts.

> **NOTE**
>
> Director Servers are noted throughout this chapter as optional server systems. If your organization has existing LCS 2005 Director Servers, they would be migrated to OCS 2007 Director Servers just as the replacement of other server roles being migrated from LCS 2005 to OCS 2007.

Identifying existing LCS 2005 servers is a relatively simple process. By accessing the LCS 2005 Administrative tool, you can see a list of servers associated with the organization's LCS 2005 environment. Specifically, the process to identify existing LCS 2005 servers is as follows:

1. Log on as an administrator to an LCS 2005 server in the environment.
2. Launch the LCS 2005 Administrative tool.

3. Expand the control tree so that you can see the Live Communications servers, archiving servers, and proxy servers, as shown in Figure 11.1.

Figure 11.1 Viewing the LCS 2005 Console to See the Servers in the Organization

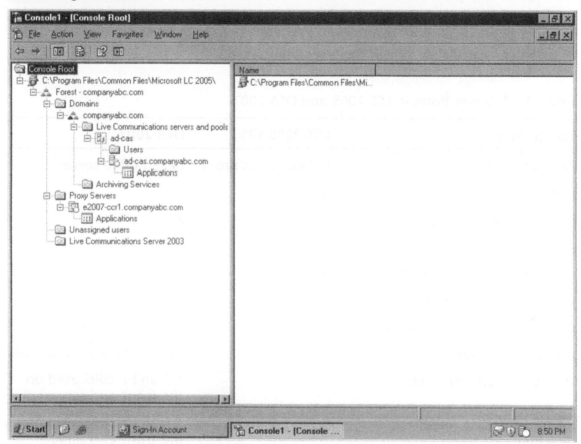

4. Note the names of all of the LCS 2005 servers that the Administrative tool has identified.

5. Identify the location of each server (which might require asking someone in the organization, checking what IP subnet the server is on, or physically looking for the server) as well as note which domain the server(s) resides in. This information will help you map out your plan to make sure you migrate all existing servers in the right order.

Identifying Existing LCS 2005 Server Roles

Once you have a list of the LCS 2005 servers, create a table listing their server roles. This will help you group the servers into logical blocks of systems so that you can migrate them from LCS 2005 to OCS 2007 in the proper sequence. OCS 2007 adds new server roles to account for its new functionality, such as Web conferencing and VoIP telephony. However, for IM or presence, or for Public IM Connectivity (PIC), those servers can be mapped one for one between LCS 2005 and OCS 2007, and will likely identify the migration grouping you will use to migrate servers from LCS 2005 to OCS 2007.

Table 11.1 lists the server roles in LCS 2005 and OCS 2007. A couple of the server roles have changed in name or function, and new servers have been added to OCS 2007 and will be referenced accordingly through the balance of this chapter.

Table 11.1 Server Roles in LCS 2005 and OCS 2007

Server Role	LCS 2005 SP1	OCS 2007
Perimeter server	Called access proxy	Called edge server
Director	X	X
Front-end server	X	X
Archiving server	X	X
Communicator Web access	X	X
Standard Edition front-end server	X	X
Enterprise pool front-end server	X	X
Address Book server	X	No longer a separate role
Web conferencing server		X (can be colocated on the front-end server)
IM conferencing server		X (can be colocated on the front-end server)
Audio-video conferencing server		X (can be colocated on the front-end server)
Mediation server		X
Quality of Experience Management server		X

Mapping the Path
of Communications between LCS 2005 Servers

With the physical LCS 2005 servers identified and their roles documented, the next step is to confirm the communications path for both incoming and outgoing communications between the LCS 2005 servers. As much as it might seem obvious that communications flow from the client, to the front-end server, to the director, to the access proxy, amazingly I've found that some organizations have director server roles that are completely bypassed in the flow of messages. Somebody put in a director server and never properly configured the front-end server to communicate with the director, so messages actually flow from the front-end server directly to the access proxy.

To check the flow of communications look at the configuration of each server to determine their settings. Do the following for each LCS 2005 server in your environment:

1. As an administrator, from the LCS 2005 Administrative tool right-click on each **LCS 2005 front-end server**, choose **Properties**, and click on the **Routing tab** to view the outbound connection routes of each server, as shown in Figure 11.2.

Figure 11.2 Viewing the Outbound Connections on a Front-End Server Configuration

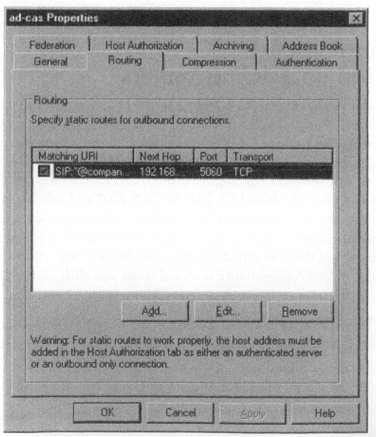

2. Write down the routing configuration information for each front-end server.

3. Right-click on each **LCS 2005 director server** (if you have them in your LCS 2005 environment) and choose **Properties**, and then click on the **Routing tab** to view the outbound connection routes of each director server.

4. Write down the routing configuration information for each director server.

5. Right-click on each **LCS 2005 access proxy server**, choose **Properties**, and click on the **Routing tab** to view the outbound connection routes of each server.

6. Write down the routing configuration information for each access proxy server.

NOTE

The changes between LCS 2005 and OCS 2007 made it easier to set up firewall rules for communications to OCS 2007 servers. Whereas LCS 2005 used a proprietary port 5061 for communications, OCS 2007 uses port 443. Those configuring OCS 2007 will find it much simpler to set it up for communications.

Understanding User Distribution on Existing Servers

Now, with a good understanding of the front-end, internal, and perimeter server infrastructure configuration of LCS 2005, the next step is to understand the client side of LCS 2005. First you need to determine which users are on which server in the LCS 2005 environment. When you pick your pilot users to migrate from LCS 2005 to OCS 2007, you want to know where to find the users so that you can easily migrate them to OCS 2007. Likewise, if you are going to be doing a phased migration from LCS 2005 to OCS 2007 and will be migrating users by departments, workgroups, sites, or roles, you'll need to know where the users reside in LCS 2005 so that you can choose those users and migrate them to OCS 2007 in a logical manner.

Identifying users and their associated servers is easy because you will see the users when you go into the LCS 2005 Administrative tool, and when you click on each server you will see the users associated with each front-end server. The specific process is as follows:

1. While logged in as an administrator and in the LCS 2005 Administrative tool, expand the console tree and expand the tree for each front-end server.

2. Select the **Users container** that is under each front-end server in the tree. You will see in the right-hand pane a list of users associated with the front-end server, as shown in Figure 11.3.

Figure 11.3 Viewing Users Associated with a Front-End Server

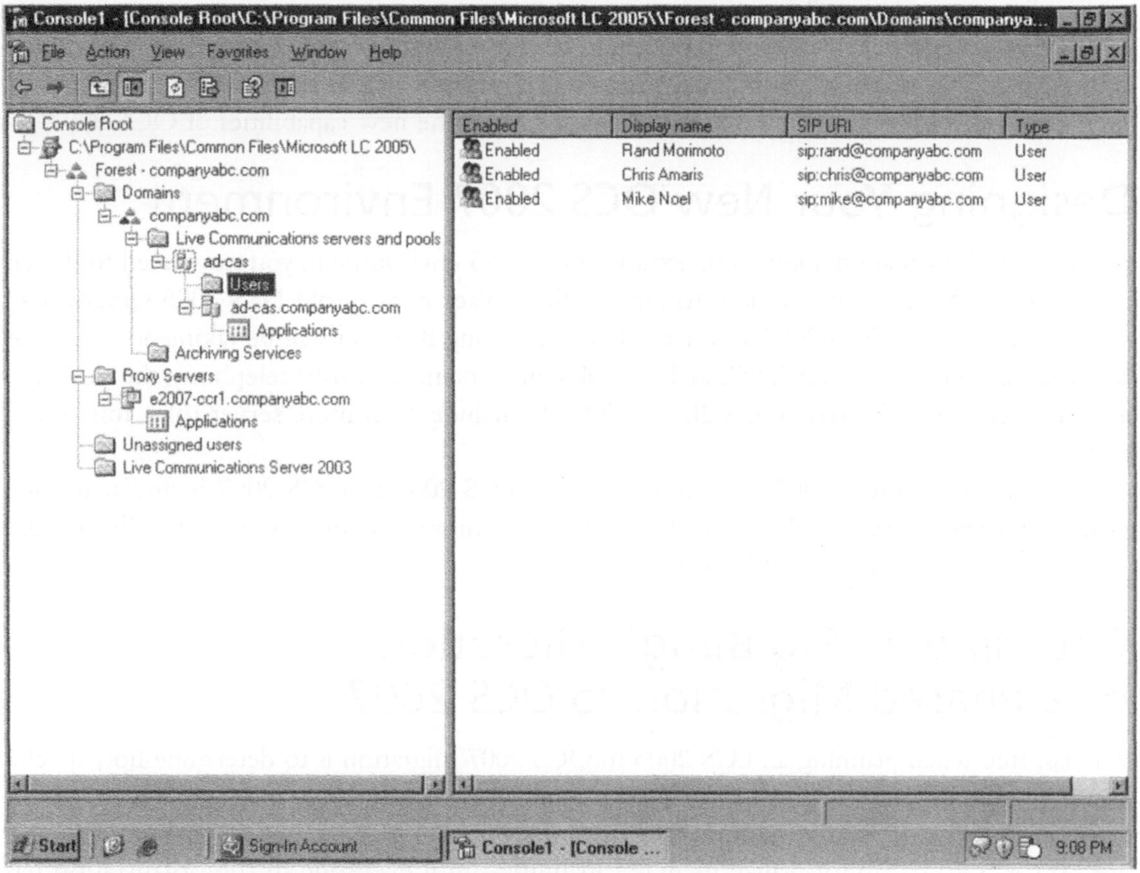

Determining Your Ability to Update Client Software Packages

Another best practice during the existing LCS 2005 assessment and planning phase is to understand how you will be able to push out the new MOC 2007 client to replace the existing MOC 2005 client software. If you have a product such as Systems Management Server (SMS) 2003 or System Center Configuration Manager (ConfigMgr) 2007, you can easily create a scripted process that will uninstall the existing MOC 2005 client and install the new MOC 2007 client in its place.

Some organizations that use Active Directory Group Policies for software distribution can create and push a package via a software distribution Group Policy during a user's logon process. Other third-party tools exist for updating the client as well. Or, if your organization does not have any automated tools and usually visits desktops and laptops manually to uninstall and install software, you need to take into account the time required to access all systems that will be migrated from LCS 2005 to OCS 2007 that will need their client software eventually migrated as well.

Having an automated software distribution system will enable you to more quickly migrate from MOC 2005 to MOC 2007 and ultimately will provide a more automated path to shift users from LCS 2005 to OCS 2007 to take advantage of the new capabilities of OCS 2007.

Designing Your New OCS 2007 Environment

Armed with information about your existing LCS 2005 environment, you now need to design your new OCS 2007 environment to include the replacement of old LCS 2005 server roles with corresponding OCS 2007 server roles. And assuming that you will be taking advantage of the new capabilities of OCS 2007, such as Web conferencing and VoIP telephony, the design and architecture of the new OCS 2007 will likely include even more server roles, functions, and features.

The design of OCS 2007 in a migration from LCS 2005 to OCS 2007 is similar to the design of a brand-new installation of OCS 2007. For more information, refer to Chapter 2, which covers the design of OCS 2007.

Choosing a "Big Bang" Migration or a Phased Migration to OCS 2007

The last step when planning an LCS 2005 to OCS 2007 migration is to determine how quickly you'll be migrating to OCS 2007. It is always preferable to keep the coexistence between LCS 2005 and OCS 2007 to a minimum. With some users on OCS 2007 and others not, those that are on OCS 2007 cannot utilize its new capabilities until everyone in the organization has been migrated to OCS 2007 and is using the MOC 2007 client. So, do what is necessary to make the migration timeline as quick as possible!

An organization with one LCS 2005 server and 50 users can do a "big bang" migration for the entire organization because the scope of the migration is limited to a single server and a handful of users. An organization with dozens of LCS 2005 servers and hundreds of users will likely perform a phased migration.

Upgrading Perimeter Servers

Migrating from LCS 2005 to OCS 2007 is an "outside-in" process, meaning that servers on the perimeter are migrated first, then intermediary servers are migrated, then front-end servers, and finally user client software. Servers are fully backward-compatible, so perimeter and intermediary servers can be migrated early and will allow existing LCS 2005 servers to interoperate and communicate with the new servers. This drastically minimizes the downtime for clients, as servers can be upgraded without impacting user communications.

With this in mind, first we are going to migrate the access proxy servers in LCS 2005 that will be replaced by OCS 2007 edge servers. Because migration from LCS 2005 to OCS 2007 is a side-by-side process, a new OCS 2007 edge server is added to the network first, properly configured to routing information in and out of the network environment. Once the system is working properly, the final switchover of communications is done to the edge server.

Preparing DNS

Because all OCS 2007 servers use the domain name system (DNS) to find and communicate with other servers, the first step in upgrading perimeter servers is to make sure DNS is set up and configured properly to support the new OCS 2007 edge server system. You need to configure three groupings of DNS settings:

- Set internal DNS so that LCS 2005 director and front-end servers can route outbound messages through the new OCS 2007 edge server.

- Set external DNS so that inbound messages can find the OCS 2007 edge server to route inbound messages through the new server.

- Change the fully qualified domain name (FQDN) external route for communications to formally route public IM information and federated IM communications through the new OCS 2007 edge server.

All of these configuration settings require a properly configured DNS name and IP address on a zone such that users or servers can find the servers they are to connect to. For example, if a user needs to access a server for IM, the FQDN of the server the user needs to access must be published externally for the user to access the server externally. However, if the user only needs to access the server from within the organization's firewall, the server only needs to be published in the organization's Active Directory for the user to find the server.

Likewise, if an internal server needs to route messages to an edge server in the perimeter, the edge server and its corresponding IP address and DNS name need to be published internal to the network. And if an edge server needs to communicate with an internal OCS 2007 server, although the organization likely won't publish the DNS name of the internal server to mask the server for security purposes, the IP address of the internal server needs to be accessible from the edge server.

Note that OCS 2007 uses Secure Sockets Layer (SSL; port 443) for encrypted communications between servers instead of the proprietary port 5061 that was used for LCS 2005. For all external access from clients either using Office Communicator or Live Meeting, the servers these users will access for communications to OCS 2007 need to now have port 443 opened on the firewall to provide the proper flow of communications.

Preparing Certificates

Because the key to any communications that are external to an organization is to ensure that the communications are secure, the use of certificates was standard with LCS 2005 for federated communications or with remote LCS 2005 clients. When replacing servers from LCS 2005 to OCS 2007, you need to transfer the certificates. Because certificates are keyed to server names, if you keep the same server name for the new OCS 2007 server as the old LCS 2005 server, you can simply export the key from LCS 2005 and import it into the OCS 2007 server with the same name. If you add a new OCS 2007 server with a completely different name, you will need to request a new certificate that matches the new server name.

SOME INDEPENDENT ADVICE

The decision to reuse an existing server name (and thus preserve the existing certificate) versus creating a brand-new server name for OCS 2007 is a matter of simplicity in issuing certificates. If your organization depends on an external certification authority (CA; such as Verisign, Thwart, or Chosen) and pays for certificates to be issued, you will likely want to use the same name for your new edge server as you used for your access proxy. Using the same server name will allow you to export your certificate from LCS 2005 and import it into OCS 2007.

However, if you have your own internal PKI setup where you can issue your own certificates relatively easily, you can choose a new server name and insert a new secured server to your OCS 2007 environment.

You can issue certificates to the new OCS 2007 server in one of two ways: have a new certificate issued to OCS 2007; or have an old LCS 2005 certificate exported so that it can be imported into OCS 2007. The two methods are detailed in the following sections.

Exporting a Certificate from LCS 2005

If you will be using the same server name for OCS 2007 as one of the LCS 2005 servers that currently exist, export the certificate from LCS 2005 and import it into OCS 2007. To do that, follow this procedure:

1. Log on as an administrator to the LCS 2005 access proxy system from which you plan to export the certificate.

2. Click **Start** | **Run**, type **mmc**, and click **OK**.

3. From the MMC program, click **File | Add/Remove Snap-in**.

4. On the **Add/Remove Snap-in dialog box**, click **Add**.

5. Scroll down and highlight **Certificates**, as shown in Figure 11.4, and then click **Add**.

Figure 11.4 Choosing the Certificates MMC Snap-in

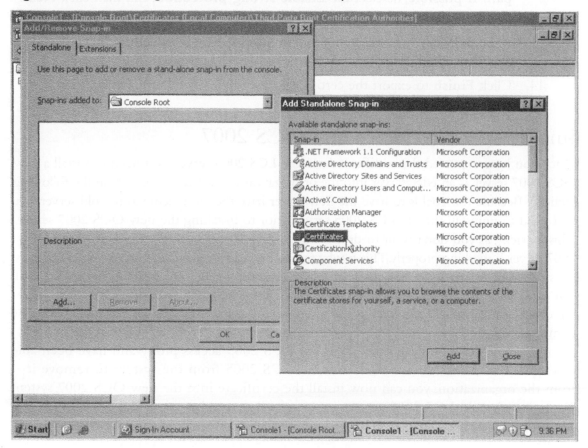

6. When prompted with "This snap-in will always manage certificates for:" select **Computer account**, and then click **Next**.

7. When prompted to select a computer to manage, choose **Local computer**, and then click **Finish**.

8. Click **Close** to close the snap-in page, and then click **OK** to get back to the MMC program view.

9. Expand the **Certificates (Local Computer)** branch of the tree, and then expand the **Personal branch**.

10. Right-click the certificate that you want to export from the LCS 2005 access proxy server, select **All Tasks**, and then select **Export**.

11. From the Certificate Export Wizard, click **Next** past the **Welcome page**.

12. On the **Export file format** page, click **Personal Information Exchange – PKCS #12 (.PFX)** and select **Include all certificates in the certification path if possible**, deselect the **Enable strong protection**, and then click **Next**.

13. Type in a path and filename where you want to export the certificate, such as **c:\LCS-Proxy1** (a .cer extension will automatically be added to the end), and then click **Next**.

14. Click **Finish** to export the certificate.

Importing a Certificate into OCS 2007

Once you have exported the certificate from the LCS 2005 server, you need to install a new OCS 2007 server as an edge server into the organization (we cover this process in the following section). Because the goal is to have the new server have the same name as the old server, you will need to uninstall the old LCS 2005 server prior to installing the new OCS 2007 server. This is tricky, as you don't want to drop an LCS 2005 server until you know the new OCS 2007 server is working properly. This is why this process of exporting and importing certificates is usually done when an organization has more than one LCS 2005 access proxy system and can easily afford to uninstall one LCS 2005 access proxy to build up a new OCS 2007 edge server when it has other LCS 2005 access proxy systems actively routing inbound and outbound communications.

Assuming that you have more than one LCS 2005 access proxy and have been able to export the certificate and then uninstall LCS 2005 from the system to remove it from the organization, you can now install the certificate into the new OCS 2007 system. To import the old LCS 2005 access proxy certificate to the new OCS 2007 edge server, do the following:

1. Log on as an administrator to the OCS 2007 edge server system that you plan to import the certificate.

2. Launch Microsoft Office Communications Server 2007 (select **Start | All Programs | Administrative Tools | Office Communications Server 2007**).

3. Expand the console page and highlight the **OCS 2007 edge server**, then right-click and choose **Certificates**.

4. When the Certificate Wizard begins, click **Next** past the **Welcome screen**.

5. For the **Available Certificate Tasks page**, choose **Import a certificate from a .pfx file**, as shown in Figure 11.5, and then click **Next**.

Figure 11.5 Choosing the Method of Certificate Importation

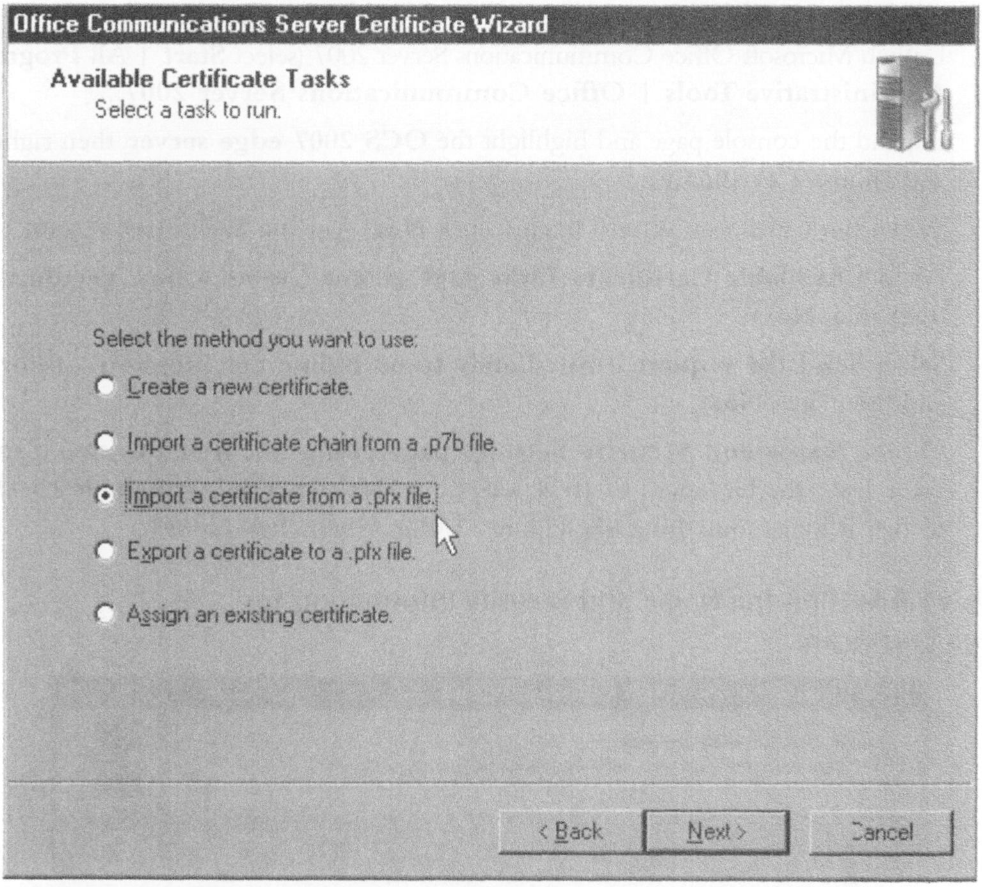

6. Enter the name of the certificate that you saved when you exported the LCS 2005 certificates in the "Exporting a Certificate from LCS 2005" section earlier, and then click **Next**.

7. When prompted for the password associated with the exported certificate, enter the password and click **Next**.

8. Verify that you have all the parameters set, and then click **Finish**.

Installing a New Certificate onto an OCS 2007 Edge Server

If you are creating and installing a new OCS 2007 edge server and will be using a new server name on the network, follow the installation and configuration directions in the next section of this chapter. Then perform the following steps to create and install a new certificate to this new OCS 2007 edge server:

1. Log on as an administrator to the OCS 2007 edge server system that you plan to import the certificate.

2. Launch Microsoft Office Communications Server 2007 (select **Start | All Programs | Administrative Tools | Office Communications Server 2007**).

3. Expand the console page and highlight the **OCS 2007 edge server**, then right-click and choose **Certificates**.

4. When the Certificate Wizard begins, click **Next** past the **Welcome screen**.

5. For the **Available Certificate Tasks page**, choose **Create a new certificate**, then click **Next**.

6. Select **Send the request immediately to an online certification authority**, and then click **Next**.

7. On the **Name and Security Settings page**, change the friendly name if you want, leave the bit length to 1024, select the **Mark cert as exportable** checkbox so that it looks something like Figure 11.6, and then click **Next**.

Figure 11.6 Setting the Name and Security Information for an Edge Certificate

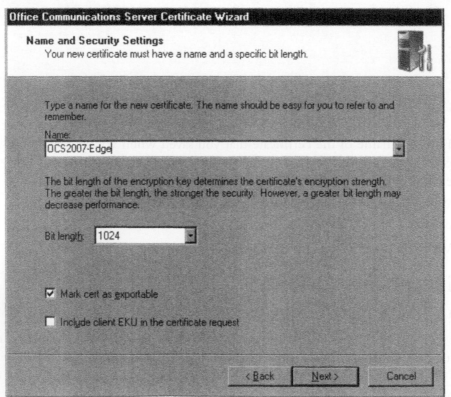

8. Enter the name for the organization and the organizational unit, and click **Next**.

9. For subject name and subject alternate name, make sure the subject name matches the FQDN of the OCS 2007 edge server that is published by the internal firewall, and then click **Next**.

10. Enter your country/region, state/province, and city/locality, and then click **Next**.

11. Review the Request Summary page and make sure everything is correct, and then click **Next** and then **Finish**.

Installing and Configuring the Edge Server

Once you have DNS configured and the certificates are ready for the new OCS 2007 edge server(s), you need to install the OCS 2007 edge server with the proper settings to provide inbound and outbound communications. Chapter 5 covers the installation of an OCS 2007 edge server, so we won't discuss it here.

Continue with the OCS 2007 edge server installation process until you reach the **Enable Features on Access Edge Server page**. Then proceed with the following:

1. On the **Enable Features on Access Edge Server page**, choose the components that you want to enable on the OCS 2007 server. To enable remote users to use this OCS 2007 edge server to view presence status and exchange IMs, you need to select the **Allow remote user to access your network checkbox**. To enable users to federate or communicate with a public IM provider (e.g., Yahoo! Messenger, AOL Messenger, or MSN Messenger), choose the **Enable federation checkbox**.

2. When you select the **Enable federation checkbox** to do public IM, select the **Federation with selected public IM providers** checkbox, and then select the IM providers (AOL, Yahoo!, MSN) that you want to federate with. Click **Next**.

3. If you are using an LCS 2005 director, on the FQDN of the Internal Next Hop Server page enter the full DNS name of the LCS 2005 director server. If you are not using an LCS 2005 director, just enter the LCS 2005 server name of the system that is the next hop.

4. For each Session Initiation Protocol (SIP) domain in your organization, on the **Authorized Internal SIP Domains page** enter the name of the SIP domain, click **Add**, and then click **Next**.

5. For **Authorized Internal Servers**, specify each internal server that you want to have connectivity to your OCS 2007 edge server, and then click **Next**.

6. If your settings are correctly summarized, click **Next** and then **Finish**.

Once you have the edge server installed, return here to continue the migration process from LCS 2005 to OCS 2007.

Redirecting Internal LCS 2005 Servers through the New Edge Server

Once the new OCS 2007 edge server has been installed, it is actually doing nothing on the network. Because no inbound or outbound servers acknowledge that this new server exists, the server is effectively installed, but not processing any communications. When choosing to switch over inbound or outbound communications to the edge server, the standard process is to switch over outbound communications to the new OCS 2007 edge server. You do this by directing the outbound communications from an LCS 2005 director server or an LCS 2005 front-end server.

When you make a relatively simple configuration change on either the LCS 2005 director or the LCS 2005 front-end server, all outbound communications will now go through this new OCS 2007 edge server. Configuring all outbound communications through an OCS 2007 edge server will effectively minimize half of the responsibility of the LCS 2005 proxy. The process of redirecting internal LCS 2005 server communications through a new OCS 2007 edge server is as follows:

1. While logged on to an internal LCS 2005 server, click **Start | All Programs | Administrative Tools | Live Communications Server 2005**.

2. Expand the LCS 2005 tree.

3. Right-click the forest node, and then click **Properties**.

4. On the **Access Proxy tab**, click **Add**.

5. Enter the FQDN of your new OCS 2007 edge server, and then click **OK**.

6. The **Live Communications Server Global Properties Access Proxy tab** should look something like Figure 11.7. Click **OK** to accept the configuration change.

Figure 11.7 Setting the Name and Security Information for an Edge Certificate

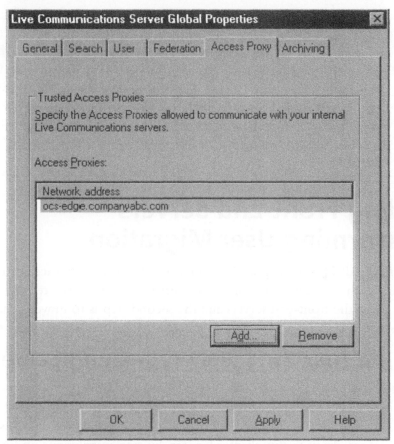

Redirecting Inbound Traffic to the New Edge Server

With an OCS 2007 edge server now handling outbound traffic successfully, the next step is to redirect inbound traffic through this new OCS 2007 edge server as well. Redirecting inbound traffic is a little trickier because the rerouting is done through a modification of public DNS records. Again, though, if the new OCS 2007 edge server has the same server name and IP address of the old LCS 2005 proxy server, the minute the new OCS 2007 edge server is back on the network, communications will go to this new edge server instead of to the old access proxy server.

As long as the external FQDN is set to route inbound traffic through the new OCS 2007 edge server, the new server should take the connections and route the communications to the internal servers for delivery.

> **NOTE**
>
> Traffic going to the edge server and going from the edge server to internal servers with go to and from the director server(s) or to and from the front-end server(s) depending on whether the organization is using director servers. If your organization has director servers, the traffic being redirected internally in your organization will go to and from the director server to the edge server. However, if you don't have director servers, the redirection of internal communications will be between the edge server and your existing LCS 2005 front-end servers.

Upgrading Front-End Servers and Performing User Migration

You're almost finished! The last step in the migration process is to replace the old LCS 2005 front-end servers with new OCS 2007 front-end servers. This is a two-step process, as the first step is to switch out the front-end servers and the second step is to move the users associated with the front-end servers. So, this section of the chapter covers both of these steps.

Installing a New OCS 2007 Front-End Server

The process of installing a new OCS 2007 front-end server during migration is identical to the process of installing a new OCS 2007 front-end server in a new production environment. For a recap, see the "Installing and Configuring OCS 2007 Standard Edition" section in Chapter 3. Then come back to this chapter for step-by-step instructions on how to install a new front-end server in the OCS 2007 environment.

Once you have the front-end server installed, return here to continue the migration process from LCS 2005 to OCS 2007. Unlike the installation of OCS 2007 edge servers and OCS 2007 director servers that requires the communications routing to be configured to acknowledge the new servers, when you add a front-end server to your environment the server automatically acknowledges the route of communications based on the configuration of the edge servers and director servers. So, all you need to do is add or move user accounts to the new OCS 2007 front-end server system to have that system integrated with the OCS 2007 environment.

Adding a User Account and Testing Front-End Server Operations

Before migrating users to the new OCS 2007 front-end server, the best thing to do is to add a new user to the new OCS 2007 front-end server and test that user account for successful inbound and outbound communications. This new account will validate that you have outbound communications from OCS 2007 out of the network and inbound communications back into the network working properly. If the test account works, you can begin the process of moving existing LCS 2005 user accounts to OCS 2007.

To create a new user account and to test a new user account with OCS 2007, see Chapter 4. This chapter will guide you through the process of creating and testing a user account in OCS 2007.

Moving Pilot User Accounts from LCS 2005 to OCS 2007

With the test user successfully able to send and receive IM communications, the next step is to move LCS 2005 users to OCS 2007. You do this by selecting a user, a group of users, or all users and moving them from LCS 2005 to OCS 2007 (what you choose depends on how many accounts you highlight in the migration tool). It is recommended that you start with just one account and make sure you can successfully move that account, and then move over a small pilot group of users that will be used to test OCS 2007 communications.

To move one user (or a small group of users) from LCS 2005 to OCS 2007, do the following:

1. Log on as an administrator to the new OCS 2007 front-end server system that you just added to the network.

2. Expand the console tree and expand the tree for the LCS 2005 branch to expose the LCS 2005 front-end servers still on the network.

3. Click on the **Users container** and select the user you want to migrate, as shown in Figure 11.8.

Figure 11.8 Choosing a User to Migrate from LCS 2005 to OCS 2007

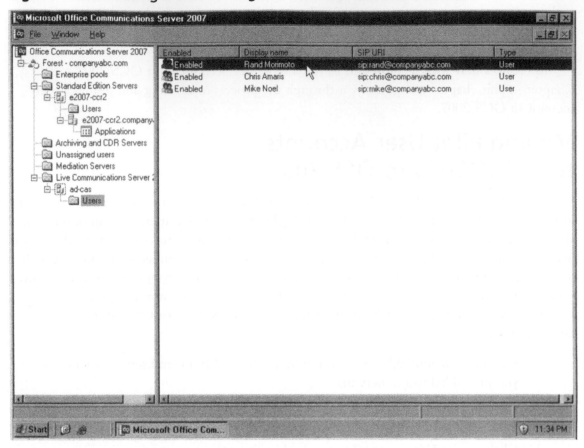

4. Right-click the user and select **Move users** to launch the **Move Office Communications Server Users Wizard**.

5. Click **Next** through the **Welcome page**.

6. Choose the server to which you want to migrate this user (this would be one of your new OCS 2007 front-end servers). Click **Next**.

7. Do not select **Force the user to move** if the server or pool is unavailable. Click **Next**.

8. Confirm that the move was successful, and click **Finish** when done.

Testing Pilot Users on OCS 2007

Have the user(s) you just migrated from LCS 2005 to OCS 2007 launch their MOC 2005 client software and IM each other. Also have this pilot group of users communicate externally (if you use public IM communications) and make sure that they continue to have full internal and external IM communications capability. In addition, have this group of users IM with users that haven't been migrated yet and are still on LCS 2005 to confirm that the new OCS 2007 users can communicate with LCS 2005 users within your organization.

To recap, the testing process should include:

- Pilot OCS 2007 users successfully sending and receiving IM communications to other pilot OCS 2007 users

- Pilot OCS 2007 users successfully sending and receiving IM communications to existing LCS 2005 users

- Pilot OCS 2007 users successfully sending and receiving IM communications to individuals outside the organization (if public IM is set up and used in the organization)

If communications continue to work for the pilot users, the process of migrating the balance of the organization's users from LCS 2005 to OCS 2007 should commence.

Moving and Testing the Balance of UserAccounts from LCS 2005 to OCS 2007

Migrating the rest of the organization's users from LCS 2005 to OCS 2007 involves nothing more than selecting more users or all users, as described in the step-by-step instructions outlined in the section "Moving Pilot User Accounts from LCS 2005 to OCS 2007." From the step-by-step process, either hold the **Space key** down and select all of the users to migrate, or hold the **Ctrl key** down and choose specific users you want to migrate. The procedure is identical and just takes into account the balance of the users.

Part of the migration process may include consolidating LCS 2005 users from multiple LCS 2005 front-end servers to one or a limited number of OCS 2007 front-end servers. Users can be migrated across servers as long as they have access to the domains where the new OCS 2007 front-end servers reside. A user in DomainA can be migrated to any OCS 2007 front-end server in DomainA. However, a user in DomainA cannot be migrated to an OCS 2007 front-end server in DomainB unless that user has rights or a trust has been established to allow the user to reside in a server in a different domain.

Removing LCS 2005 from the Network Environment

Because you've already removed access proxy servers and director servers from the environment, completely removing LCS 2005 from the organization requires just the removal of the remaining LCS 2005 front-end servers. The process is as follows:

1. Make sure all users have been moved from LCS 2005 to OCS 2007.

2. Remove LCS 2005 Standard Edition servers.

3. Remove LCS 2005 Enterprise Edition servers.

SOME INDEPENDENT ADVICE

If you properly inserted a new OCS 2007 front-end server and all communications are now flowing in and out of the new OCS 2007 environment, you can drop the old LCS 2005 front-end server(s) at any time because the old server(s) aren't doing anything on the network. However, to be extra safe and conservative, you can leave *one* of the old LCS 2005 front-end servers still running for a few days, and in case you have problems, you can reconfigure to communicate back to the old LCS 2005 system.

Although this is a nice fallback option, it is highly recommended that you pick a date to bite the bullet and drop LCS 2005 from the environment, typically within 10 days of installing OCS 2007. The longer you wait to remove LCS 2005 from your environment, the further it is in your mind to do so. I've seen organizations that have stray servers in their networks two or three years later and when asked why they have the old systems, they say no one in the IT department was around when the new configuration was put in, and no one wants to fiddle with removing the old system because they do not know what might happen. So, clean up your network and get rid of LCS 2005 within a week to 10 days of OCS 2007 taking over user communications.

Validating That All Users
Have Been Migrated Off of LCS 2005

To begin to completely remove LCS 2005 from the environment, you want to make sure all users have been migrated off of LCS 2005 and onto OCS 2007 front-end server systems. This task simply involves checking the Administrative tool to confirm that no users are still homed to an old LCS 2005 server. The process is as follows:

1. While logged in as an administrator and in the LCS 2005 Administrative tool, expand the console tree and expand the tree for each front-end server.

2. Select the **Users container** that is under each front-end server in the tree. If you have successfully migrated all users off of the LCS 2005 front-end servers, you should *not* see any users in the right-hand pane being associated with any of the LCS 2005 front-end servers, as shown in Figure 11.9.

Figure 11.9 Confirming That No Users Remain on LCS 2005

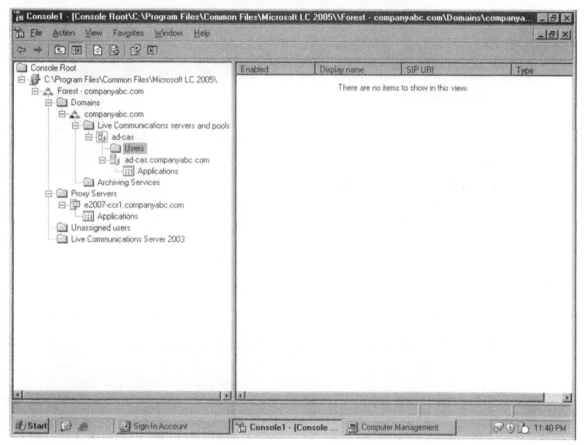

Once you confirm that no users exist on LCS 2005, remove the old LCS 2005 servers from the network. If it appears as though some users have remained on LCS 2005, select those users and move them to OCS 2007 until all of the users have been moved.

Removing LCS 2005 Standard Edition

When removing LCS 2005 from the environment, start by removing LCS 2005 Standard Edition systems first. These systems are the easiest to remove, as each server can be removed individually. The process to remove an LCS 2005 Standard Edition server is as follows:

1. While logged on as an administrator of the LCS 2005 environment, expand the console tree and select the **LCS 2005 Standard Edition server** you want to remove.

2. Right-click the server and select **Deactivate**.

3. Click **Next** through the **Deactivation Wizard Welcome page**.

4. Click **Next** through the **Deactivation Option page** shown in Figure 11.10.

Figure 11.10 Choosing to Deactivate LCS 2005

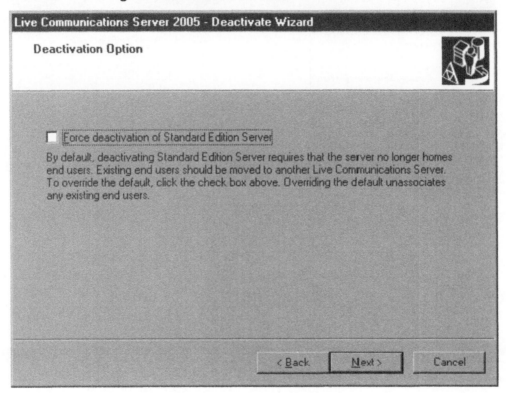

5. Click **Next** through the **Ready to Deactivate page**.

6. Click **Finish** once the deactivate process has been completed.

7. Uninstall the LCS 2005 code from the server by selecting **Start | Control Panel** and choosing **Add or Remove Programs**.

8. Highlight **Microsoft Office Live Communications Server 2005** and click **Change**.

9. Check the **Keep the user database checkbox** and then click **Remove**, as shown in Figure 11.11.

Figure 11.11 Removing LCS 2005 from the System

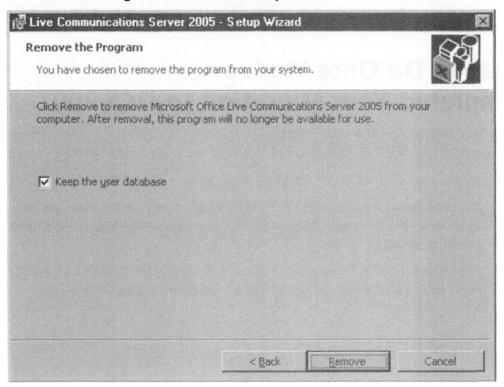

If you had only LCS 2005 Standard Edition servers in your environment (not LCS 2005 Enterprise Edition systems), you are done. You have successfully migrated from LCS 2005 to OCS 2007, and have successfully removed LCS 2005 from the environment with the removal of the last LCS 2005 Standard Edition system from the network.

Removing LCS 2005 Enterprise Edition

If you have LCS 2005 Enterprise Edition systems in the environment, the removal process is a little more involved, as you have to remove servers within an enterprise pool before you can delete the pool. However, the process is effectively the same, and it requires that you follow these steps:

1. Follow the steps outlined in the "Removing LCS 2005 Standard Edition" section to remove each server.

2. To remove the Enterprise Edition of LCS 2005, right-click the pool and then click **Remove pool**.

With the last LCS 2005 Enterprise Edition server removed from the system, and with the removal of the enterprise pool, you have finished the process of removing LCS 2005 from your environment.

What to Do Once You've Completed Your Migration to OCS 2007

Once you've migrated your servers from LCS 2005 to OCS 2007, you can take advantage of the new capabilities of OCS 2007. Some of the more common next steps are as follows:

- Migrate users off of MOC 2005 and onto the new MOC 2007 client software.

- Enable enhanced presence in OCS 2007, which now provides users not only with online or offline status information, but also with integration with Outlook calendaring data.

- Add new OCS 2007 capabilities, such as Web conferencing, VoIP telephony, and multipoint video conferencing, which are enhancements to OCS 2007.

Summary

Migrating from LCS 2005 to OCS 2007 requires that you follow certain steps in a certain order. These steps comprise installing new OCS 2007 servers into the environment, integrating the new servers into the new environment, and then removing old LCS 2005 servers once the new OCS 2007 servers have successfully taken the place of the LCS 2005 system.

When migrating, it is a best practice to start from the outermost servers and work your way in to the internal servers. In the side-by-side migration process, you install new OCS 2007 edge servers in place of old LCS 2005 access proxy servers; replace old LCS 2005 director servers with new OCS 2007 director servers; and add new OCS 2007 front-end servers and move users from old LCS 2005 front-end servers to the new OCS 2007 servers.

If a server or user fails to migrate to OCS 2007 you can still move the organization back to LCS 2005. With limited or no impact to users, you can perform a side-by-side migration to OCS 2007 without shutting down total services to the organization.

Once you have migrated the users from LCS 2005 to OCS 2007, you can add new features of OCS 2007 such as Web conferencing, VoIP telephony, and multipoint video conferencing. The migration from LCS 2005 to OCS 2007 is one of the easier migrations among the Microsoft Windows server system migrations.

Solutions Fast Track

Understanding the Migration from LCS 2005 to OCS 2007

☑ You cannot upgrade client software from MOC 2005 to MOC 2007 until after the user has been migrated from LCS 2005 to OCS 2007.

☑ You cannot activate enhanced presence until the client has been migrated to OCS 2007 and is using the MOC 2007 client software.

☑ Choose the "big bang" method of migration from LCS 2005 to OCS 2007 to minimize the need to run both an LCS 2005 and an OCS 2007 environment in parallel for an extensive period of time.

Planning Your Migration from LCS 2005 to OCS 2007

☑ Identify the locations of *all* existing LCS 2005 servers so that you can make sure you migrate all servers to OCS 2007 in your environment.

☑ Know the server roles of all LCS 2005 servers so that you can properly map a migration of those servers and roles to OCS 2007 in the right sequence.

☑ Map the routing of communications between servers so that server-to-server communications is set up properly between systems in the new OCS 2007 environment.

☑ Understand which users are associated with which LCS 2005 systems so that you can more easily move users to new OCS 2007 systems in the right sequence.

☑ Have a strategy regarding how you will upgrade client software from MOC 2005 to MOC 2007.

Upgrading Perimeter Servers

☑ Prepare DNS so that other LCS 2005 and OCS 2007 servers can properly see perimeter servers on the network.

☑ Plan for time in advance to order or request SSL certificates required for internal and external communications of the LCS 2005 and OCS 2007 systems.

☑ Continue to use the same external FQDN for IM communications.

☑ Redirect outbound communications through a new OCS 2007 edge server before directing inbound communications to the server system.

Upgrading Front-End Servers and Performing User Migration

☑ Add new OCS 2007 front-end servers capable of handling the demands of the organization, including performance capabilities that are able to handle the new features of OCS 2007.

☑ Take this opportunity to consolidate LCS 2005 servers to fewer OCS 2007 systems, because users can be migrated across servers at this time.

☑ Create a test user on the new OCS 2007 front-end server and make sure the test user can successfully communicate before moving LCS 2005 users to the new OCS 2007 system.

☑ Highlight and move users from LCS 2005 to OCS 2007 once you know the new OCS 2007 is working properly.

Removing LCS 2005 from the Network Environment

☑ Have a plan to remove LCS 2005 from the network within seven to 10 days of completing your migration to OCS 2007.

☑ Remove LCS 2005 Standard Edition servers first.

☑ For environments with LCS 2005 Enterprise Edition, remove all but one enterprise server from the network first, and then remove the enterprise pool to remove the last enterprise server from the network.

What to Do Once You've Completed Your Migration to OCS 2007

☑ Migrate users off of MOC 2005 and on to the new MOC 2007 client software.

☑ Enable enhanced presence in OCS 2007, which now provides users with not only online or offline status information but also integration with Outlook calendaring data.

☑ Add new OCS 2007 capabilities, such as Web conferencing, VoIP telephony, and multipoint video conferencing, which are enhancements to OCS 2007.

Frequently Asked Questions

Q: Can you perform an in-place upgrade from LCS 2005 to OCS 2007?

A: No, you can only perform a side-by-side upgrade to OCS 2007.

Q: Should you upgrade client software to MOC 2007 before migrating to OCS 2007?

A: No. MOC 2007 will not work against an account on LCS 2005, so you must migrate the organization from LCS 2005 to OCS 2007 before you migrate clients from MOC 2005 to MOC 2007.

Q: Can I have LCS 2005 and OCS 2007 coexist in the environment?

A: Yes, you can have LCS 2005 and OCS 2007 operate in the same environment for a long time. However, usually the coexistence occurs for only the time of the migration.

Q: If I extend my Active Directory schema to support OCS 2007, will LCS 2005 continue to run?

A: Absolutely. The extension of the Active Directory schema has no impact on the operation of LCS 2005.

Q: Can a user who has been migrated from LCS 2005 to OCS 2007 still communicate with someone running off of LCS 2005?

A: Yes, there is complete interoperability between LCS 2005 and OCS 2007 during the migration process.

Q: Can someone who has been migrated to OCS 2007 carry on a Web conference with someone still on LCS 2005?

A: Yes, a person still on LCS 2005 can participate as a member of an OCS 2007 Web conference as long as the LCS 2005 individual has the Live Meeting client installed on his or her system. However, the LCS 2005 person cannot initiate an OCS 2007 Web conference until that individual has been migrated to OCS 2007.

Q: Do I need to inform external PIC providers (e.g., Yahoo! Messenger, MSN Messenger, or AOL Messenger) that I've upgraded from LCS 2005 to OCS 2007?

A: No. As long as you maintain the same FQDN, you do not need to inform external PIC providers of your migration to OCS 2007, as your environment will remain operating as it has been in the past.

Q: During the migration of user accounts, can I consolidate users from multiple LCS 2005 front-end servers to fewer OCS 2007 front-end servers?

A: Yes. As long as the new OCS 2007 front-end servers are accessible to the LCS 2005 clients through security rights or trusts, the users can be consolidated during the migration process.

Q: Can I replace a Standard Edition LCS 2005 server with an Enterprise Edition OCS 2007 server?

A: Yes. Throughout the entire migration process, you can replace Standard Edition systems with Enterprise Edition systems, or Enterprise Edition systems with Standard Edition systems.

Q: Can I add new OCS 2007 features such as Web conferencing and VoIP telephony before the entire organization has been migrated off of LCS 2005?

A: Yes, but just remember that those still on LCS 2005 have limited or no ability to use the new OCS 2007 capabilities until they have been been migrated to OCS 2007 and MOC 2007. However, users who have been migrated to OCS 2007 and MOC 2007 can take full advantage of the new OCS 2007 capabilities.

Chapter 12

Managing and Monitoring OCS 2007

Solutions in this chapter:

- **Using Call Detail Records**
- **Using the Client Version Filter**
- **OCS Troubleshooting Tools**
- **Quality of Experience Server**
- **Validation Wizard**
- **System Center Operations Manager 2007**

☑ **Summary**

☑ **Solutions Fast Track**

☑ **Frequently Asked Questions**

Introduction

Most administrators are aware that all critical systems in their production infrastructures should be properly managed and monitored at all times. Office Communications Server (OCS) 2007 is no exception to this rule. Luckily, Microsoft provides several tools to help you to keep your OCS deployment happy and healthy. These tools also allow you to troubleshoot and diagnose problems when they arise, and they allow you to review archived Web conferences, instant message (IM) sessions, and Microsoft Office Communicator (MOC)-based phone usage. Most of the utilities introduced in this chapter are available for free via download or are included on the OCS installation media.

Using Call Detail Records

Call detail records (CDRs) are part of the archiving features in OCS 2007. CDRs are logs of usage statistics from conference, IM, and phone sessions that take place across OCS servers in your enterprise. CDRs are archived to a SQL database which allows you to easily create reports on OCS usage. It is important to understand that CDRs are not data from the actual conferencing, IM, or phone sessions, but simply usage statistics related to those sessions. You can create reports on CDR data using a variety of tools, including Microsoft SQL Server Reporting Services. Reports from the CDR database may prove to be useful when you need trending statistics for capacity planning. CDR capabilities are installed when you set up an OCS archiving server in Chapter 7.

Before we can look at CDRs, we need to configure OCS to begin logging CDR data. We do this through the OCS Server Microsoft Management Console (MMC):

1. Open the OCS Server MMC by going to **Start Menu | Administrative Tools | Office Communications Server 2007**.

2. Within the MMC, we need to locate the forest root node in the tree in the left pane of the console. This should be the first node just below the OCS 2007 root node, and it should be named *Forest – yourdomain.com* (see Figure 12.1). Right-click and select the **forest node | Properties | Global Properties**. This will open the **Global Properties window**.

Figure 12.1 OCS MMC: Global Properties Menu Option

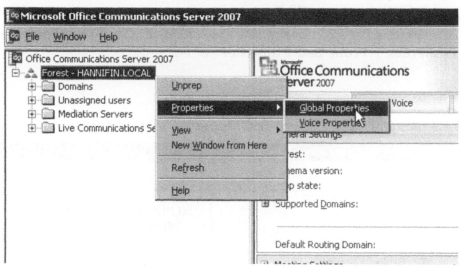

3. From the **Global Properties window** click the **Call Detail Records tab**.

4. To enable CDRs click the **checkbox** for each respective session type, as seen in Figure 12.2, and then click **OK**.

Figure 12.2 The OCS Global Properties Window

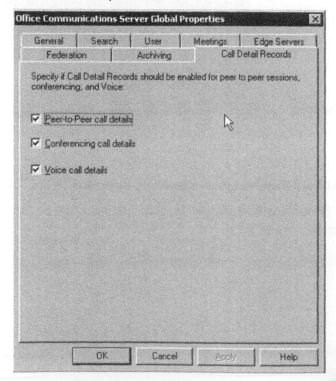

5. Now expand the tree in the MMC and locate the OCS server where you want to enable CDR (see Figure 12.3).

6. After locating the server in the MMC tree, right–click and select **YourServer | Properties | Front End Properties** (see Figure 12.4).

Figure 12.3 OCS 2007 MMC: Front-End Properties Menu Option

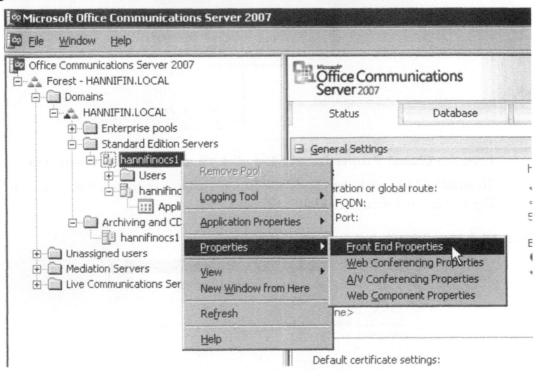

7. The **Front End Properties window** will open. Select the **Archiving tab**.

8. From the **Archiving tab** place a check in the box next to **Activate call details recording** (see Figure 12.4).

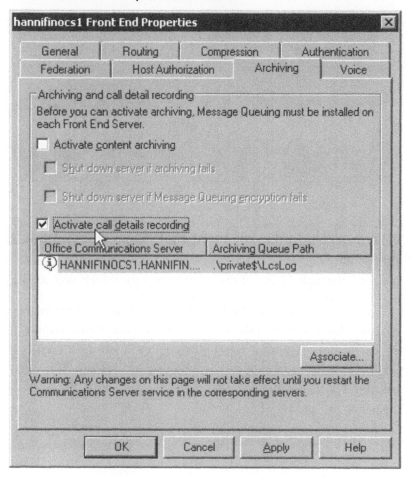

Figure 12.4 The Front End Properties Window

9. Click the **Associate button** to open the **Associate Queue Path window**, as shown in Figure 12.4.

10. Enter the name of the OCS archiving server and queue folder name in the **Associate Queue Path window** and click **OK**. If the archiving service is installed on the server you are currently configuring, you can just enter a period (.) instead of the full server name, as seen in Figure 12.5.

Figure 12.5 The Associate Queue Path Window

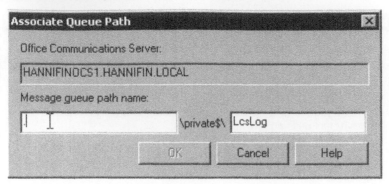

11. You will now be returned to the **Front End Properties window**. Click **OK** to close this window.

12. Repeat steps 5 through 11 for all the other servers for which you want to enable CDR.

OCS is now configured to log and store CDRs. Now that we have enabled CDRs, let's explore CDR stats in a little more depth. Microsoft includes the Archiving CDR Reporter application in the OCS 2007 Resource Kit. This tool allows you to view some of the most common usage statistics without having to write reports or perform SQL queries against the archiving database (see Figure 12.6).

NOTE

You can download the OCS 2007 Resource Kit from the Microsoft Download Center at http://download.microsoft.com.

Figure 12.6 The Archiving CDR Reporter

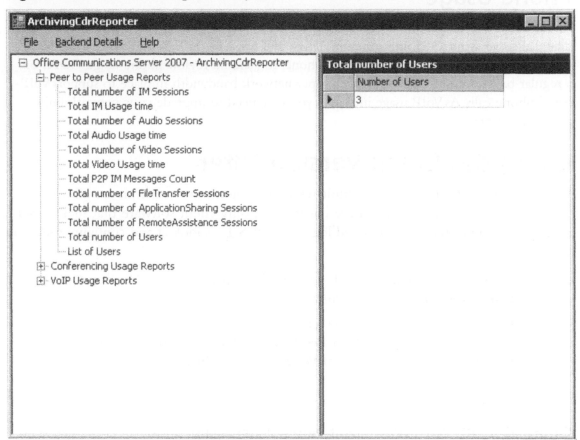

Conference Usage

Conference usage CDRs provide statistics regarding on-premises Live Meeting sessions in your organization. These statistics include counts such as n umber of conferences and conference minutes. You can use these statistics to trend Live Meeting usage to make more informed decisions about network capacity and the number of Web conferencing servers needed to support on-premises Live Meeting.

IM Usage

IM CDRs give you a view into MOC IM sessions in your organization. These stats provide information such as the number of IM sessions, number of IM users, and P2P audio/video sessions. As do the statistics provided by conference usage, these counters provide information that allows you to properly plan for network and server capacity.

Phone Usage

Phone-based CDRs provide usage statistics of Voice over IP (VoIP)-based phone calls that take place over your OCS infrastructure. These will typically be calls initiated by the MOC client or Communicator client-based IP phone. You should review phone usage CDRs on a regular basis to ensure that you have proper network bandwidth in place to support VoIP-based phone calls. As VoIP usage increases, you may need to upgrade your network links and connections.

Using the Client Version Filter

OCS 2007 includes the ability to limit which Communicator versions are allowed to connect to OCS servers. This feature ensures that only client software that meets your corporate IT policies can connect and log on to OCS. Let's look at and configure the client version filter:

1. Open the OCS MMC by going to **Start | Administrative Tools | Office Communications Server 2007**.

2. Expand the tree and locate the server you want to configure. Right-click the server name and select **Application Properties | Client Version Filter**, as seen in Figure 12.7. The **Office Client Version Filter window** will open.

Figure 12.7 OCS 2007 MMC: Client Version Filter Menu Option

3. Check the **Enable Version Control checkbox** to turn on version control.

4. We can now choose to allow or disallow different clients and versions. The allow/disallow list is already populated with most available clients, including various versions of MOC and Windows Messenger (see Figure 12.8).

Figure 12.8 The Client Version Filter Window

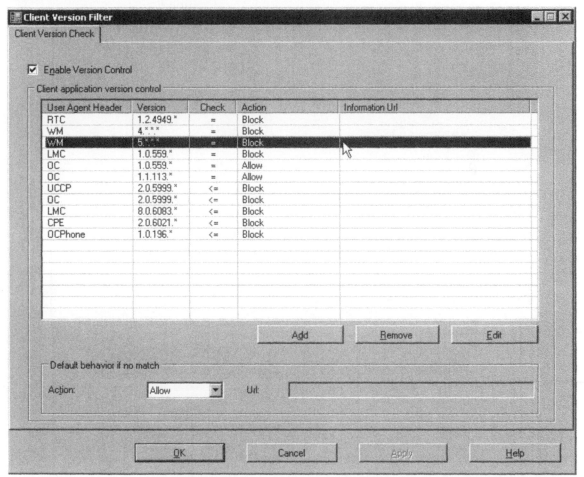

5. To disable or allow a particular client, click on that client name in the list to highlight it, and then click the **Edit button.** The **Edit Version Filter window** will open.

6. In the **Edit Version Filter window** locate the **Action to apply to this version** drop-down box and select the action you want to perform when the client of the selected version attempts to connect. The available options are **Allow**, **Block**, and

Block with URL. If you select **Block with URL** you will be allowed to enter a URL containing a message to present to the user when he or she attempts to connect to the OCS server with this client version (see Figure 12.9). Choose the appropriate action for the selected client version and click **OK**.

Figure 12.9 The Edit Version Filter Window

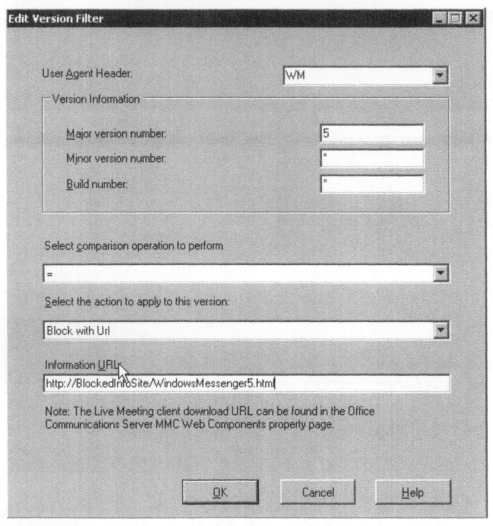

7. After choosing the appropriate action for all client versions, click **OK** in the **Client Version Filter window**.

OCS Troubleshooting Tools

OCS comes with several troubleshooting tools to help you diagnose problems when they occur in your deployment. It is important to understand the basics of these tools so that you'll be equipped to fix problems and, when necessary, work with Microsoft support services. The troubleshooting tools are simple to access and use, yet they provide in-depth and useful diagnostic information.

Diagnostics

OCS 2007 provides a ton of great features to enable end-users to be more efficient in their jobs. It is important for OCS to have good diagnostic information to help keep your OCS deployment happy and healthy. Good diagnostics allow you to proactively find issues and prevent downtime as well as restore services quickly when there is an outage. This section covers some of the great diagnostics features available in OCS 2007.

Diagnostics Headers

Microsoft has provided what is referred to as *MS-Diagnostics headers* in OCS 2007. MS-Diagnostics headers are used to allow servers to pass detailed diagnostics and suggested resolutions to client computers. MS-Diagnostics headers are included in most Session Initiation Protocol (SIP) Response errors. Diagnostics headers typically include the error source, components, reason, and any other details relevant to the error (see Figure 12.10). Because diagnostics headers are included in the SIP Response instead of the SIP Request, they are sent by the server to the client. The client then processes the headers to display the information in the client event log.

NOTE

For security reasons, MS-Diagnostics headers are not passed to federated partners. MS-Diagnostics headers often contain detailed information regarding your OCS infrastructure.

Figure 12.10 Sample Event with Diagnostics Header Information

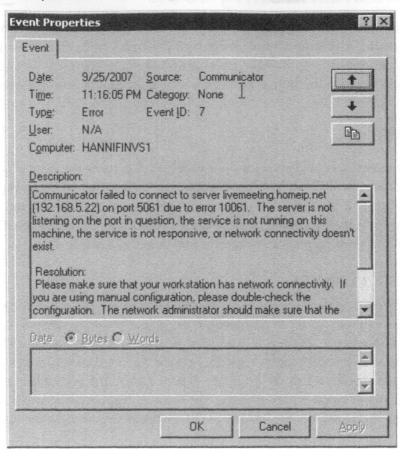

Runtime Server Diagnostics

Along with MS-Diagnostics headers, OCS provides runtime server diagnostics to assist with troubleshooting server problems. These include things such as connection issues, certificate validation failures, and client authentication problems. These diagnostics are similar to the MS-Diagnostics headers and you can view them in the OCS 2007 event log on the OCS server. Figure 12.11 shows an example of a runtime diagnostics event.

Figure 12.11 Example of a Runtime Server Diagnostics Event

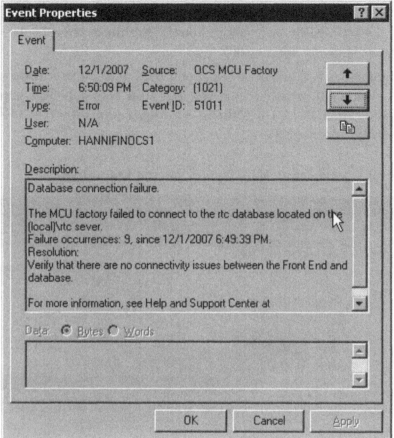

Logging Tool

OCS provides a detailed logging tool that is automatically installed with the installation of the core product. The logging tool allows you to start detailed logging sessions that create trace logs of various components of OCS. You can use these logs to review detailed diagnostic information when troubleshooting OCS issues. The logging tool even includes a command to prepare the logs to send to Microsoft Professional Support Services (PSS) in situations when you need to work with Microsoft to troubleshoot your OCS deployment. Let's take a more in-depth look at the logging tool.

The first thing we need to do is enable a new debug session. This will create the trace logs for storing diagnostic information. To enable a new debug session perform the following steps:

1. Open the OCS MMC by going to **Start | Administrative Tools | Office Communications Server 2007**.

2. Expand the tree and locate the server you want to begin to start the debug session. Right-click the server name and select **Logging Tool | New Debug Session**, as seen in Figure 12.12. The **Office Communications Server 2007 Logging Tool window** will open.

Figure 12.12 OCS 2007 MMC: New Debug Session Menu Option

3. Locate the **Components** section and select the components for which you want to enable logging (see Figure 12.13).

4. While selecting each **component**, you need to select the **level** of logging and any additional **flags** you want to capture in the debug session (see Figure 12.13).

5. Next, you need to select the **Log File Options**. First select a log type. The types of logging available are Circular, Sequential, and New File. Circular logs will replace log entries as needed when a log reaches its maximum size. Sequential logs will stop logging after the maximum log file size has been reached, and New File will create a new log file when the maximum size is reached. Select the logging type that is most appropriate for your situation (see Figure 12.13).

6. After selecting the logging type, select the **maximum size** to which you want your log files to grow. By default, this setting is 20 MB. This setting is important to ensure that logs do not fill up your disk drive.

7. Next, you need to decide whether you want to monitor the session in real time or just have it written to the log files. By enabling **Real-Time Monitoring** you can watch the debug session in the trace console. If you choose the **Display only** option, the debug logs will not be written to log files but just displayed in the trace console.

8. You can optionally enable filters to only capture data that is specific to a particular SIP Uniform Resource Identifier (URI) address or the fully qualified domain name (FQDN) of a specific computer. To filter data enter the appropriate **URI address** or **FQDN address** in the respective text box.

9. Now type the location where you want to save the log files in the **Log File Folder** text box (see Figure 12.13).

10. You should now be ready to begin the debug session. Click the **Start Logging button**.

11. You can close the **logging tool** by clicking **Exit**.

Figure 12.13 OCS 2007 Logging Tool Window

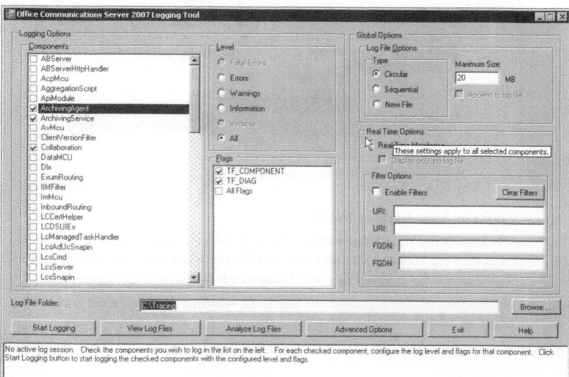

Now that you have turned on logging you need to know how to review the logs. We will now open the debugger and see what we've captured in the log files:

1. Open the OCS MMC by going to **Start | Administrative Tools | Office Communications Server 2007**.

2. Expand the tree and locate the server you want to begin to start the debug session. Right-click the server name and select **Logging Tool | Existing Debug Session**, as seen in Figure 12.14. The **Office Communications Server 2007 Logging Tool window** will open.

Figure 12.14 OCS 2007 MMC: Existing Debug Session Menu Option

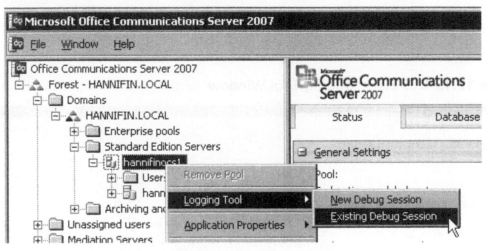

3. Click the **Stop Logging button**.

4. Click the **View Log Files button**. This will open the **View Log Files window**. Select the log files you want to view and click the **View button** (see Figure 12.15). The logs will be displayed in a new Notepad window, as seen in Figure 12.16.

5. After reviewing the logs, close the **Notepad window** and click **Exit** to close the **logging tool**.

Figure 12.15 The View Log Files Window

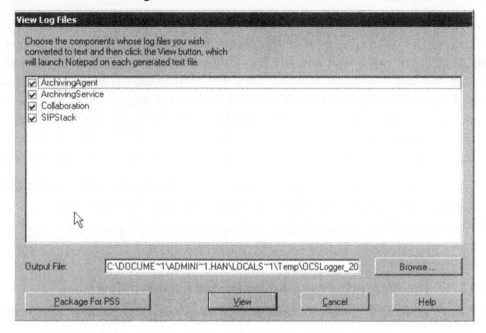

Figure 12.16 Sample Log Data in the Notepad Window

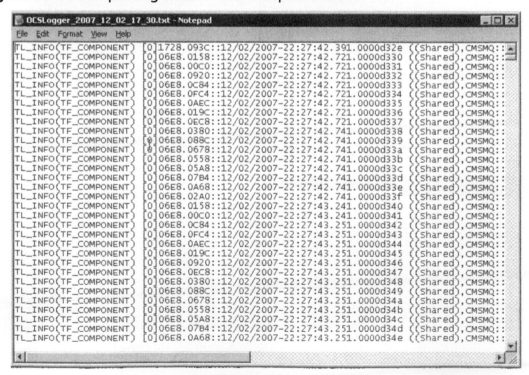

Route Helper

The Enterprise Voice Route Helper is a tool included in the OCS 2007 Resource Kit. The Route Helper allows you to perform tests that ensure that your phone number normalization and voice policies are configured properly. The Route Helper allows you to enter a phone number as an end-user would, and then tests the ability to route the call to the specified number. The Route Helper then returns information related to the route the call took through various servers and gateways and whether the call was routable at all. If the call is not routable, the utility will return the same error code that the client would see. The Route Helper tool can be helpful when trying to troubleshoot VoIP call issues. Let's look at the Enterprise Voice Route Helper tool:

1. To open the Router Helper go to **Start | Microsoft Office Communications Server 2007 | Resource Kit | Enterprise Voice Route Helper**.

2. The Route Helper main window will open, as seen in Figure 12.17.

Figure 12.17 The Enterprise Voice Route Helper Main Window

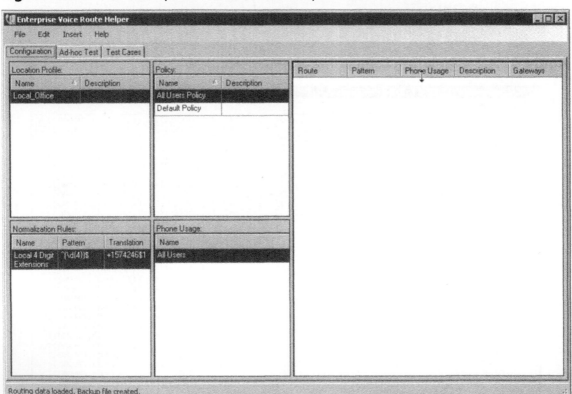

3. You will see three tabs in the main window. The Configuration tab will display any location profiles, policies, normalization rules, and assigned phone usage groups that you have configured. From this tab, you can edit, remove, or add any policies that you have configured.

4. Now let's look at the ad hoc test settings. Click the **Ad-hoc Test tab**.

5. From this tab, you can set up a test of your VoIP routing. Type a number you want to dial, choose a location profile and policy, and click **Test** (see Figure 12.18).

6. The results of your test will be displayed in the Results message box and any matching normalization rules will be highlighted under the normalization rules section, as seen in Figure 12.18. If the phone number you are testing would need to route through a gateway, this would be displayed in the Selected Routes section.

Figure 12.18 An Ad Hoc Route Test

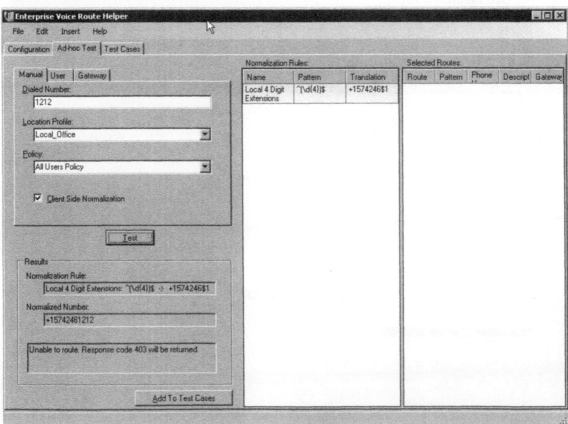

Snooper Tool

The Snooper tool is an advanced SIP and C3P troubleshooting tool for OCS. The Snooper tool is part of the OCS Resource Kit. The Snooper tool will parse logs and display messages related to SIP and C3P protocols. You can launch the Snooper tool from within the OCS logging tool or independently. Let's look at the Snooper tool in a little more detail.

1. First we need to start a new debug session to create new logs for us to analyze (for more details on using the logging tool see the "Logging Tool" section earlier in this chapter). To do this open the OCS 2007 MMC by going to **Start | Administrative Tools | Office Communications Server 2007**. Expand the tree and locate the server you want to begin to start the debug session. Right-click the server name and select **Logging Tool | New Debug Session**. The **Office Communications Server 2007 Logging Tool window** will open.

2. For our example, let's select **SIPStack** and then click the **Start Logging button** (see Figure 12.19).

Figure 12.19 The OCS 2007 Logging Tool

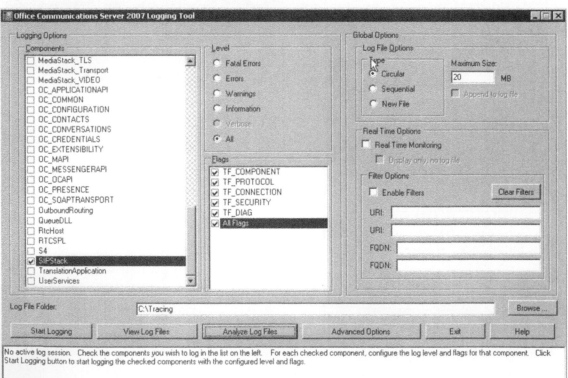

3. Now that you've turned on logging, launch the MOC client and log in.

4. After logging in, click the **Stop Logging button** in the **Logging Tool window**.

5. Click the **Analyze Log Files button** to launch the **Snooper tool**.

6. The Snooper tool will display detailed information captured from the collected logs. From this window, you can review and examine different SIP stack-based events that occurred. Notice in Figure 12.20 that there was an issue making an outbound connection to the edge server hannifinocs3.

Figure 12.20 The Snooper Tool Main Window

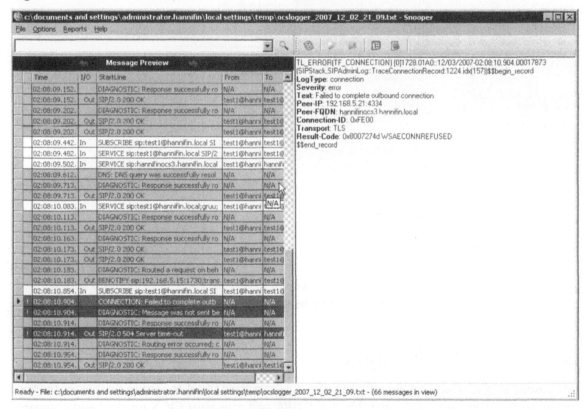

7. You can also search for specific data using the search text box. In the example in Figure 12.20, we find that there was some issue connecting to the server hannifinocs3. Let's search for that server name to see whether any other events are related to that server. As you can see in Figure 12.21, several other errors are pointing to problems with server hannifinocs3.

Figure 12.21 The Snooper Tool Search Results

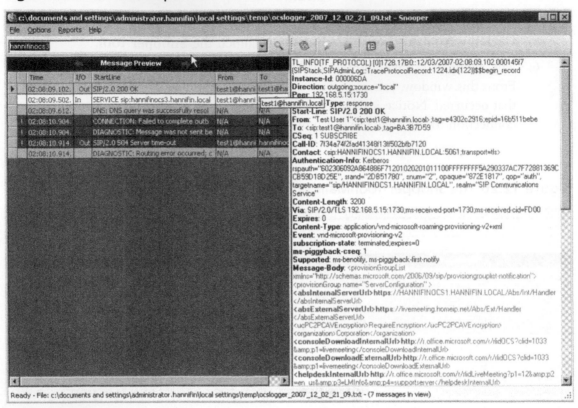

You can use the Snooper tool to troubleshoot and diagnose various SIP- and C3P-related errors in an easy-to-use, searchable interface. Keep in mind that you can launch the Snooper tool via a Logging Tool Debug session or independently by running Snooper.exe in the Resource Kit directory.

Best Practice Analyzer

Microsoft has started to provide a *Best Practices Analyzer* (BPA) tool to ensure that server products are properly set up and configured. The OCS BPA will scan your OCS server(s) and compare the configuration and settings to a predefined set of best-practice rules provided by Microsoft. The BPA will then generate a report showing discrepancies between your configuration and the best-practice configuration rules. This tool is a quick and easy way to ensure that your OCS environment is set up and configured properly. Any configuration errors revealed by the BPA could point to trouble spots in your deployment. The following will guide you through using the BPA in your deployment:

1. First you'll need to download and install the BPA. You can find it by doing a search at http://download.microsoft.com.

2. After installing the BPA, you can access it by going to **Start | All Programs | Microsoft Office Communications Server 2007 | Best Practices Analyzer | Best Practices Analyzer**. The BPA Wizard will launch.

3. The first step of the wizard is to check for new updates to the BPA. Click the **Check for updates now** link to have the BPA search for and download new updates from Microsoft. This step is important, as Microsoft regularly updates rules and features of the BPA (see Figure 12.22).

Figure 12.22 OCS 2007 Best Practices Analyzer Update Window

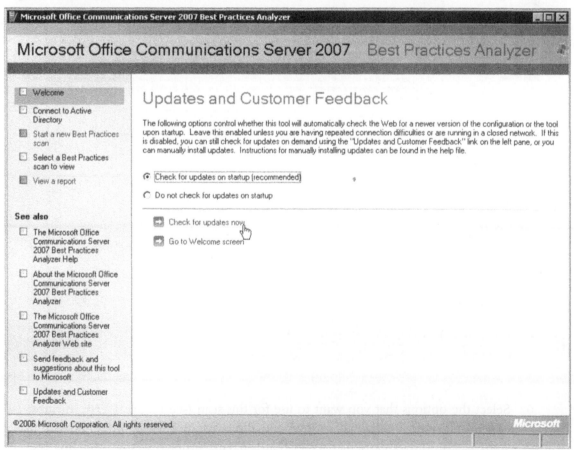

4. After checking for updates, you are ready to choose your options for a new scan. Click the **Select options for a new scan** link to continue. You will now see the **Connect to Active Directory page**.

5. Ensure that a domain controller is entered into the **Active Directory Server** text box and click the **Connect to Active Directory Server** link (see Figure 12.23). This will initiate a connection to the domain controller. The BPA will then move to the **Start a new Best Practices scan page**.

Figure 12.23 OCS Best Practices Analyzer: Connect to Active Directory Page

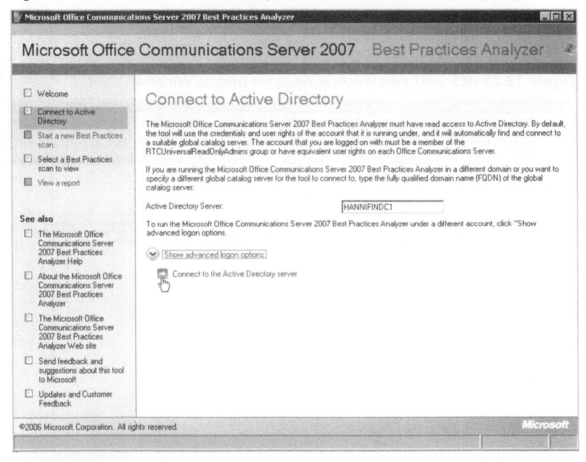

6. Select the options that you want to use for this scan (see Figure 12.24). In most cases, you'll want to select all settings and all servers; however, sometimes you may want to scan only a particular server that is having problems. After selecting the appropriate options, click the **Start scanning** link.

Figure 12.24 OCS 2007 Best Practices Analyzer: Start a New Scan

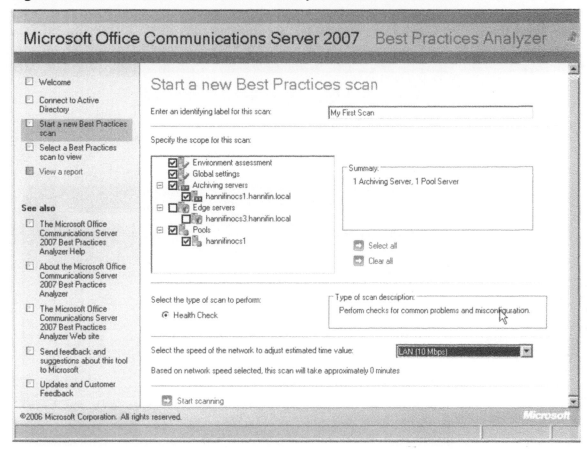

7. The BPA will begin to scan the selected server(s). This process may take a few minutes depending on your server and network speed. You can track the progress of the scan on the **Scanning Progress page**.

8. After the scan completes, the **View Best Practices Report page** will be displayed. Here you can look at the results of the scan in a variety of views. By default, the results will be grouped into three tabs based on how critical the issues are (see Figure 12.25).

Figure 12.25 OCS Best Practices Analyzer: Results Page

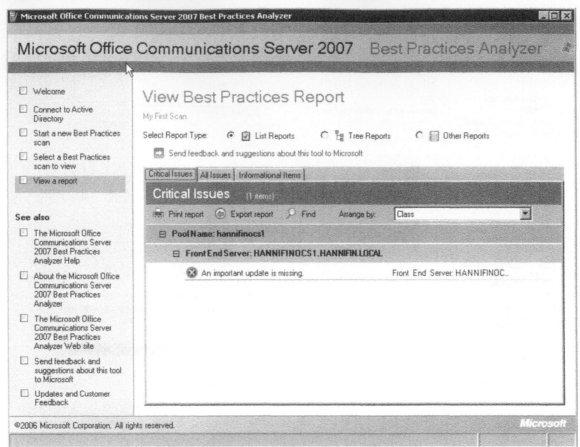

9. You can click on any of the issues listed to see more details and, in most cases, detailed instructions regarding how to resolve the problem. This can be beneficial when trying to track down misconfigurations in your environment. In the example in Figure 12.26, we notice that the OCS server is missing a critical update and we are even notified of the update number. We can now download this update which may fix problems we may be experiencing in our environment.

Figure 12.26 OCS 2007 Best Practices Analyzer: Best Practices Report Issue Details

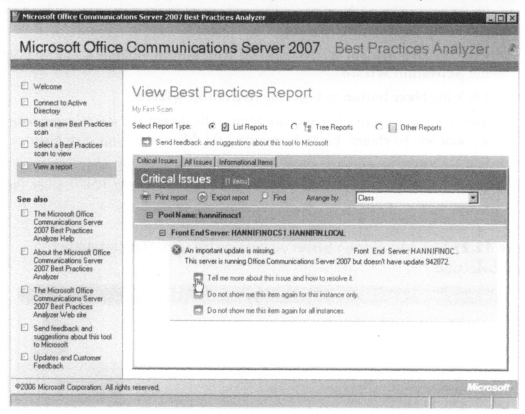

Microsoft has committed to providing BPAs for most server products. The OCS BPA is a great way to quickly identify configuration issues or missing updates. You should run the BPA on a regular basis to ensure that your OCS deployment remains properly configured.

Quality of Experience Server

Microsoft recently released a free downloadable product to allow more proactive monitoring of the various media services provided by OCS. The Quality of Experience (QoE) Monitoring Server allows you to monitor voice and videoconference session quality in real time. The QoE server is actually a new server role for OCS 2007 and you set it up and configure it as you would other server roles. The QoE server even includes sample reports that you can load into SQL Server Reporting Services. Let's set up a new QoE server:

1. First, launch the **Deployment Wizard** by double-clicking the **setup.exe** located in the installation directory.

2. From the **Deployment Wizard**, click the **Install button** from **Step 1**. This will launch the **Install Wizard**.

3. Click the **Next button** twice, and then choose the directory to which to install the QoE server and click **Next** again. This will complete the installation and return you to the **Deployment Wizard**.

4. From the **Deployment Wizard**, click the **Run button** for **Step 2**. This will launch the **Activation Wizard**.

5. Click the **Next button** to begin the **Activation Wizard**.

6. You will now need to select a service account. By default, the *RTCComponentService* account will be chosen. Enter the password for this account and click **Next**.

7. Choose a SQL instance to create a new database for the QoE server. This can be any instance of SQL, including SQL 2005 Express (see Figure 12.27). Click **Next** to continue.

Figure 12.27 QoE Monitoring Server Activation Wizard: SQL Database Server Selection

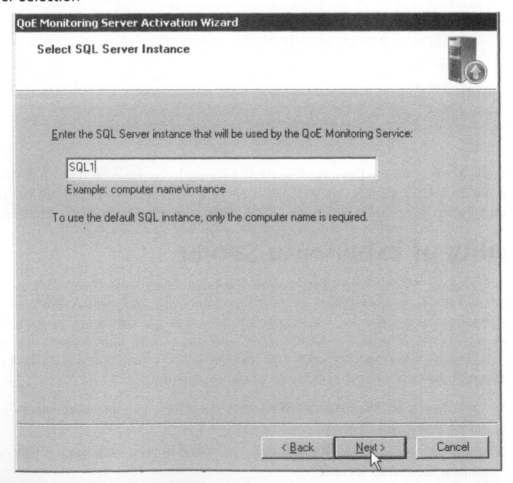

8. Choose the option to replace any existing QoE databases and click **Next**.

9. Choose the directory to install the database and log files (see Figure 12.28). Then click **Next**.

Figure 12.28 QoE Monitoring Server Activation Wizard Database Files Install Location

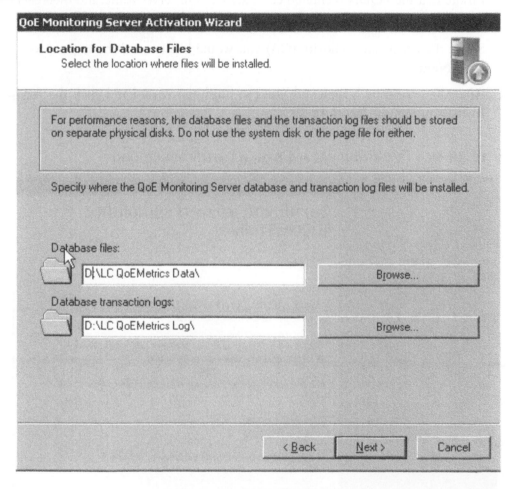

10. Verify the information on the summary screen, and then click **Next**. This will return you to the **Deployment Wizard** main screen.

11. Click the **Run button** next to **Step 3**. This will launch the **Certificate Configuration Wizard**.

12. Click **Next** to begin the wizard.

13. Choose a method to acquire a certificate. In this example, let's select the option to **Create a new certificate**. Then click **Next**.

14. Now let's choose to **Send the request immediately to an online certificate authority** and then click **Next**.

15. Enter a name for the new certificate and click **Next**.

16. Enter organizational information as seen and then click **Next**.

17. Ensure that the FQDN is entered correctly for your server name, and then click **Next**.

18. Enter **geographic information** and click **Next**.

19. Select the certificate authority (CA) you would like to send the request to and click **Next**.

20. After the certificate is approved, you can finish the wizard and click the **Assign button**, as seen in Figure 12.29.

Figure 12.29 OCS Certificate Wizard Assign Certificate Option

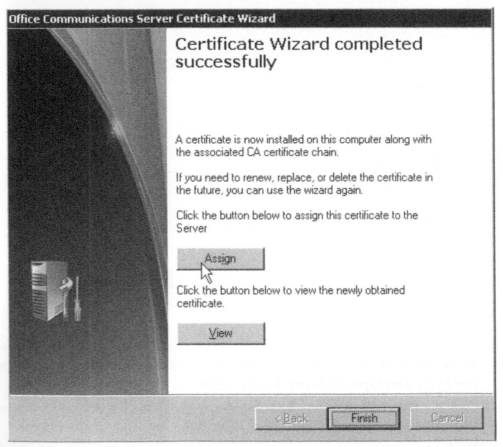

21. You will now be returned to the **Deployment Wizard**. Click the **Run button** next to **Step 4**. This will launch the **Start Services Wizard**.

22. From the **Start Services Wizard** click **Next** twice. The QoE services will now be started.

23. You will return to the **Deployment Wizard** main menu. Click the **Run button** next to **Step 5**. This will launch the **Configure Associates Wizard**. Click **Next**.

24. From the **Unassociated Pools** section, choose the standard edition servers or enterprise pools you want to monitor and click the **Associate button** to move them to the Associated Pools pane, as seen in Figure 12.30. Then click **Next**.

Figure 12.30 QoE Configure Associations Wizard Pool Selection

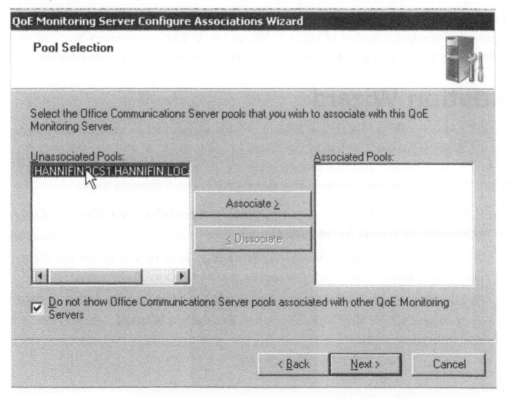

25. On the **Mediation Server Selection window**, choose any mediation servers you want to associate with the QoE server for monitoring, and click the **Associate button**. Then click **Next** and **Finish**.

26. You will be returned to the **Deployment Wizard** main window. You can now deploy the QoE Report Pack if you have SQL Server Reporting Services installed.

27. To deploy the Report Pack click the **Run button** in **Step 6**. This will launch the **Report Pack Deployment Wizard**.

28. Click **Next**. Then enter the URL of the reporting server and click **Next** again.

29. If you want to grant an Active Directory group access to the reports by default, enter the name of that group in the **Name of existing group** text box and then click **Next**.

30. Click **Next** again to complete the wizard.

You have now completed the deployment of the QoE server. It should immediately begin to monitor and track the quality of voice, video, and A/V Web conferences. You can view the example reports by browsing to your reporting services server in your Web browser.

Validation Wizard

OCS 2007 comes with the Validation Wizard, which allows you to validate the functionality of your OCS deployment. The Validation Wizard runs a series of tests to ensure that OCS core services are available and functioning properly. To use the Validation Wizard simply log on to an OCS server in your deployment and perform the following steps:

1. Open the OCS MMC by going to **Start | Administrative Tools | Office Communications Server 2007**.

2. From the MMC, expand the tree in the left pane until you locate the server you want to validate. Then click the **server name** to expand the node.

3. Right-click the FQDN of the server and choose **Validation | Front End Server** (see Figure 12.31). This will launch the **Validation Wizard**. Click **Next** to begin the validation process.

Figure 12.31 OCS 2007 MMC Validation Option

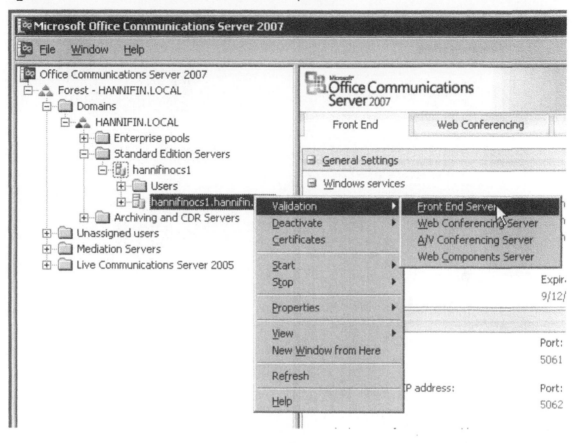

4. Choose the validation tests you would like to perform (see Figure 12.32), and then click **Next**.

Figure 12.32 OCS 2007 Validation Wizard Validation Steps Selection

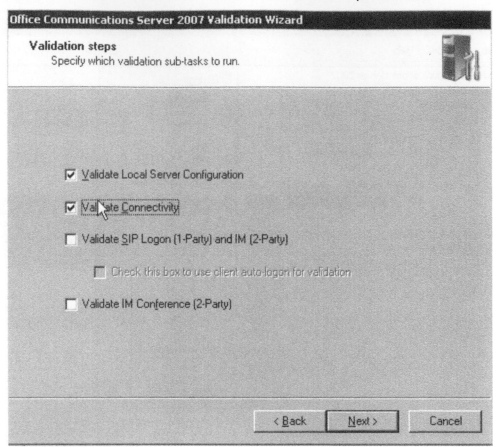

5. The Validation Wizard will perform the requested tests and return the results in an HTML report, as seen in Figure 12.33. You can use this report to locate any issues with your deployment and resolve them.

Figure 12.33 Validation Wizard Report

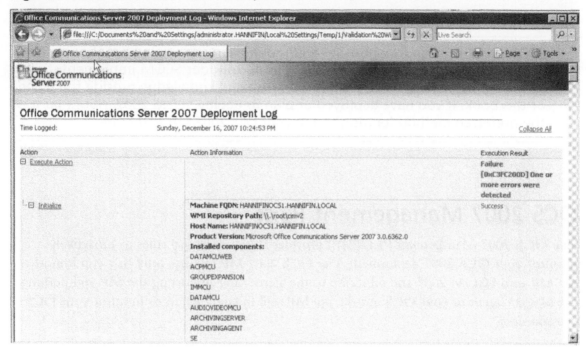

You now know how to run the Validation Wizard to verify the functionality of your OCS deployment. You can use this wizard to validate your Front-End Services, Web conferencing server, A/V conferencing server, and Web components.

System Center Operations Manager 2007

System Center Operations Manager (SCOM) 2007 is Microsoft's premier solution for monitoring your Microsoft infrastructure. SCOM 2007 provides detailed rules and alerts to properly monitor your systems and applications. One of the key advantages of using SCOM 2007 is the fact that you do not have to figure out *what* to monitor for most Microsoft applications. Microsoft provides predefined, best-practice rules for each of its server products. The collection of these rules is known as a *management pack*. Using a management pack is as easy as importing the pack into the SCOM server. For example, to properly monitor Microsoft SQL Server you simply need to import the SQL Server management pack into your SCOM deployment and complete a couple of tuning steps. This applies to most management packs, including OCS 2007.

SOME INDEPENDENT ADVICE

SCOM 2007 is not a free product and requires proper implementation to accurately monitor your OCS servers. You should consider SCOM implementation a project of its own, as it will require expertise and knowledge outside the scope of this book. If you have deployed or plan to deploy SCOM 2007, note that it is the preferred method for monitoring your OCS 2007 infrastructure.

OCS 2007 Management Pack

The OCS 2007 Management Pack (MP) provides all the necessary rules to proactively monitor your OCS 2007 deployment. The OCS 2007 MP requires only that you import the MP into SCOM 2007 and subscribe to the alerts. After importing the MP and pushing the SCOM agent to your OCS servers, the MP will instantly begin to monitor your OCS environment.

Summary

This chapter introduced several tools for monitoring and diagnosing problems with your OCS 2007 infrastructure. You also learned how you can use these tools to locate, diagnose, and resolve problems that can occur in OCS 2007. In addition, you were introduced to CDRs, which allow you to track usage trends. Tracking these trends allows you to properly plan for network and server capacity. Finally, you discovered how the OCS 2007 MP for SCOM 2007 will allow you to proactively monitor your OCS 2007 infrastructure.

Solutions Fast Track

Using Call Detail Records

☑ You can use CDRs to track and trend usage statistics.

☑ CDRs are maintained in a SQL database to maintain historical data.

☑ CDR reports can be easily generated by Microsoft Excel or SQL Server Reporting Services.

OCS Troubleshooting Tools

☑ OCS provides several tools for diagnosing and troubleshooting problems.

☑ You can install the OCS 2007 Resource Kit to provide additional diagnostic tools, including the Snooper tool.

☑ You can use the Best Practices Analyzer to search for configuration problems.

System Center Operations Manager 2007

☑ System Center Operations Manager (SCOM) is the preferred system for proactively monitoring an OCS 2007 infrastructure.

☑ You can configure SCOM to monitor OCS 2007 deployments with a minimal amount of effort setting up rules and alerts.

Frequently Asked Questions

Q: What is the proper process to troubleshoot problems with OCS 2007?

A: Review the event logs or SCOM alerts; run the post-install Validation Wizard; run the Best Practices Analyzer to ensure that your servers are configured properly; run the OCS 2007 logging tool; run the Snooper tool if you're diagnosing SIP issues; contact Microsoft PSS.

Q: Where can I get the OCS 2007 Resource Kit?

A: You can download the Resource Kit tools from Microsoft's Download Center, or you can purchase the full Resource Kit Book from most bookstores.

Q: Is it important that I learn how to use the diagnostic and troubleshooting tools?

A: Yes. Even if you will rely on Microsoft PSS to help resolve issues, you'll need a basic understanding of how to run and use the tools.

Appendix A

Customizing the MOC Client

Solutions in this chapter:

- Adding Custom Presence States
- Adding Tabs
- Adding Menu Commands

☑ Summary

☑ Solutions Fast Track

☑ Frequently Asked Questions

Introduction

In Chapter 4, we covered installation and configuration of the Microsoft Office Communicator (MOC) client. In this appendix, we'll discuss how to customize MOC to extract more features out of this product. Specifically, we'll discuss adding custom presence status messages, adding more tabs to MOC, and customizing menu commands.

Adding Custom Presence States

Once you sign in to MOC, you'll find various status options available to you. You can also set the status during sign-in. The following options are available to you (see Figure A.1):

- Available
- Busy
- Do Not Disturb
- Be Right Back
- Away

Figure A.1 MOC Default Status Messages

In addition to these, you can also add more specific presence messages by tweaking the client application. Let's work through this short exercise to configure custom presence states:

1. Open **Notepad** (you may also use XML Notepad 2007) and create an XML configuration file with the following code:

```
<?xml version="1.0"?>
<customStates xmlns="http://demo/newsite/customStates"
xmlns:xsi="http://www.w3.org/2001/XMLSchema-instance"

xsi:schemaLocation="http://demo/newsite/customStates
http://demo/newsite/CustomActivities.xsd">

<customState ID="1" availability="Online">
  <activity LCID="1033">Working from Home</activity>
  <activity LCID="1044">activity 2 for 1044</activity>
  <activity LCID="1055">activity 3 for 1055</activity>
</customState>
<customState ID="2" availability="busy">
  <activity LCID="1033">In a Meeting</activity>
  <activity LCID="1036">In Conference Room-1 </activity>
</customState>
<customState ID="3" availability="busy">
  <activity LCID="1033">Meeting with Customer</activity>
  <activity LCID="1055">Meeting with Client</activity>
  <activity LCID="1036">Meeting with Team</activity>
</customState>
<customState ID="4" availability="do-not-disturb">
  <activity LCID="1033">Interviewing</activity>
</customState>
</customStates>
```

NOTE

XML Notepad 2007 is available for download from www.microsoft.com/downloads. XML Notepad gives you an easy-to-use, intuitive interface to create and view XML files.

2. Save the file as customp.xml on a shared folder of your server (\\demo\share).

3. Click on **Start | Run |** and type **regedit**.

4. Locate the HKEY_LOCAL_MACHINE\SOFTWARE\Policies\Microsoft\ Communicator key.

5. Right-click on the **right pane**, select **New | String value**, and type the name **CustomStateURL**.

6. Type **file://\\\\demo\\share\\customp.xml** (on the local server, or the complete URL where you will upload the customp.xml file created earlier) in the **Value column**.

7. Close **regedit**.

8. Start MOC (**Start | All Programs | Microsoft Office Communicator 2007**).

9. Click on the **Down arrow** of the status buttons. You'll notice the newly added presence states (see Figure A.2).

NOTE

Incorrectly editing the Registry may damage your computer. Make sure you back up the Registry as well as your data before making any changes to the Registry. Perform all your customization tasks on a test machine before you roll out the modified MOC in your network.

Figure A.2 Custom Presence States

You can also save the Registry settings in a text file with a .reg extension (e.g., customp.reg), move it to a shared folder available to clients, and execute the Registry file at the client computer. To do so follow these steps:

1. Open **Notepad**.

2. Enter the following code:

```
[HKEY_LOCAL_MACHINE\SOFTWARE\Policies\Microsoft\Communicator]
@=""
"CustomStateURL"="file://\\\\demo\\share\\customp.xml"
```

3. Provide a name, such as customp.reg.

4. Save it in the shared folder (\\demo\share).

5. Double-click on the **customp.reg file** to execute.

6. Click on **Yes** to the Registry editor message **Are you sure you want to add the information in c:\share\customp.reg to the registry?**.

7. Click on **Yes** to the **Confirm Restore Key message window** (see Figure A.3).

Figure A.3 Importing the Registry Key

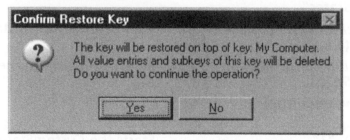

Consider the following points while configuring custom presence states:

- The length of the status message should not exceed 64 characters.

- Custom presence states are available only with Available, Busy, and Do Not Disturb status messages.

- You can add only four custom states.

- While mentioning the location of the XML file, only file:///, http://, and https:// addresses are supported.

> **NOTE**
>
> Knowledge of XML is essential to tweak the code. Administrators with prior HTML experience can learn XML very easily. XML files consist of three essential components: a Document Type Definition (DTD) file or schema, a style sheet, and the main XML program. You can learn more about XML through tutorials available at www.w3.org/XML.

Let's look at the XML file closely to understand the tags that are used (see Table A.1).

Table A.1 Custom Presence XML File

Code	Description
<?xml version="1.0"?>	Defines the XML version
<customStates xmlns="http://demo/newsite/customStates"	Points to the XML namespace
xmlns:xsi="http://www.w3.org/2001/XMLSchema-instance"	Points to the XML instance
xsi:schemaLocation="http://demo/newsite/customStates *http://demo/newsite/Custom-Activities.xsd">*	Points to the XML schema definition file
<customState ID="1" availability="online">	Starts the *CustomState* tag. *ID=1* refers to the first state of availability. *Online* is the state. *Busy* and *Do Not Disturb* are the other two states you can configure to use custom presence.
<activity LCID="1033">Working from Home</activity>	*Activity* refers to the custom presence state available under Online, Busy, and Do Not Disturb. *LCID* stands for local ID.
</customStates>	Closes the *CustomState* tag

Adding Tabs

Adding custom tabs is another way to customize MOC. Custom tabs give you the power of displaying Web content on the MOC screen directly (see Figure A.4). Displaying a corporate newsletter Web page when the user logs on to the Office Communications Server (OCS) server can be a great idea. You can add multiple tabs below the MOC client window. Users can navigate through these windows to access various Web pages. In this appendix, we'll use the SharePoint server that is used in Appendix B to demonstrate SharePoint and Project server integration.

Figure A.4 The MOC Window

Let's add a few custom tabs:

1. Exit the MOC client if it's already open.

2. Open **Notepad** and create a sample HTML page with the following code:

```
<HTML>
<HEAD>
<TITLE>Sample Page</TITLE>
</HEAD>
<BODY>
This is a sample Page
</BODY>
</HTML>
```

3. Save it as index.html to the shared folder (\\demo\share).

4. Once again open **Notepad** and enter the following code:

```
<?xml version="1.0"?>
<tabdata>
   <tab>
     <image>http://demo/_layouts/images/titlegraphic.png</image>
     <name>Share1</name>
     <tooltip>This is my SharePoint site</tooltip>
     <contenturl>http://demo/newsite/default.aspx</contenturl>
     <userid>false</userid>
     <contactid>false</contactid>
     <accessibility>inside</accessibility>
   </tab>
    <tab>
     <image>file://demo/share/titlegraphic.png</image>
     <name>Share2</name>
     <tooltip>This is my SharePoint site</tooltip>
     <contenturl>file://demo/share/index.html</contenturl>
     <userid>false</userid>
     <contactid>false</contactid>
     <accessibility>inside</accessibility>
    </tab>
</tabdata>
```

5. Save it as tabs.xml to the shared folder (\\demo\share) that is accessible to everyone.

6. Add a string value, *TabURL*, with the value *file://demo/share/tabs.xml* to the following locations:

```
HKEY_LOCAL_MACHINE\SOFTWARE\Policies\Microsoft\Communicator
HKEY_CURRENT_USER\Software\Policies\Microsoft\Communicator
```

7. Start MOC.

8. Notice the two tabs that appear at the bottom of the MOC client window. You may notice the SharePoint Web site displayed on the first tab. Observe the code you wrote in tabs.xml. The tool tip *This is my SharePoint site* appears when you move your mouse over the tab (see Figure A.5).

Figure A.5 A Custom Tab Displaying Web Content

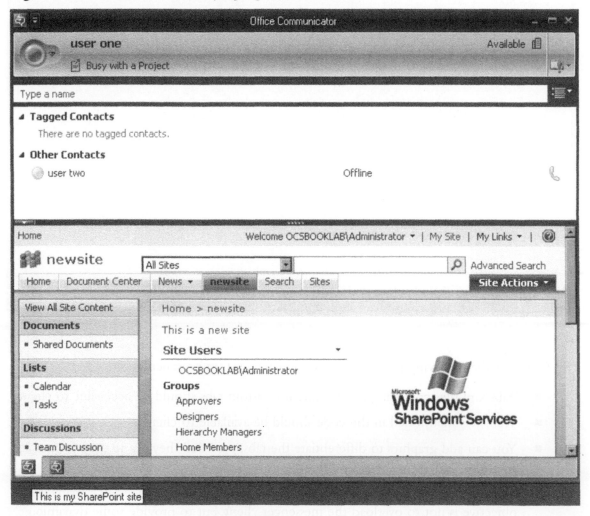

9. Click on the second tab. You will notice the sample HTML page we created earlier (see Figure A.6).

Figure A.6 HTML Page Displayed through a Custom Tab

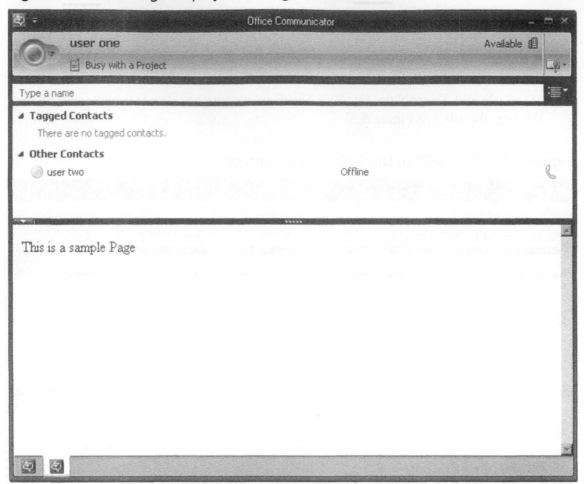

Consider the following points while configuring custom presence states:

- Tabs.xml files consisting of the code for custom tabs should be accessible to clients.

- Web sites mentioned in the code should be available to clients.

- You can add graphics to differentiate the tabs, provided they are in .png format and are either 16×16 or 32×32 pixels.

- You can have a maximum of 32 tabs (however, you may not need that many; the objective is not to overload the messenger client, but to provide some dynamic content).

Let's look at the XML file closely to understand the tags that are used (see Table A.2).

Table A.2 Custom Tabs XML File

Code	Description
<?xml version="1.0"?>	Identifies the XML file
<tabdata>, </tabdata>	Opening and closing tags for the tab data
<tab>, </tab>	Opening and closing tags to identify information for individual tabs
<image>, </image>	Location of the graphics for the Tab button
<name>,</name>	Name of the tab
<tooltip>,</tooltip>	Opening and closing tags for the small text balloon that appears when the user moves the mouse over a tab
<contenturl>,</contenturl>	Opening and closing tags that point to the Web site URL to be displayed inside the tab
<userid>, </userid>	Optional parameter that passes user information (currently logged in)
<contactid>, </contactid>	User's contact ID
<accessibility>, </accessibility>	Tag to inform whether the information should be available when the user is logged in to MOC from inside or outside the network. Organizations may not prefer that an internal newsletter be available when the user logs in from the outside.

NOTE

For more information, download the "Microsoft Office Communicator 2007 Deployment Guide," available from www.microsoft.com/downloads.

Adding Menu Commands

You can also add customized menu commands that will appear in the Tools menu (in the Conversation window), in the Actions menu, and while the user right-clicks anywhere in the Contacts list. Customized menus are utilized to launch an application that is installed in the client computer or any collaboration tool that is used by a group of users. Figure A.7 shows a typical Conversation window.

Figure A.7 MOC Conversation Window

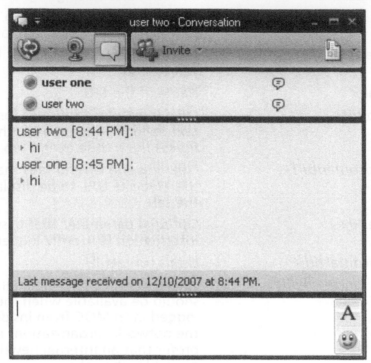

Follow this exercise to learn how to add a custom menu:

1. Start MOC and sign in.

2. Initiate a conversation with another user in your Contacts list.

3. Click on the **Down arrow** on the top left of the Conversation window.

4. Observe the menu items. These are the standard commands that are available to you (see Figure A.8).

Figure A.8 Menu Items from a Default MOC Installation

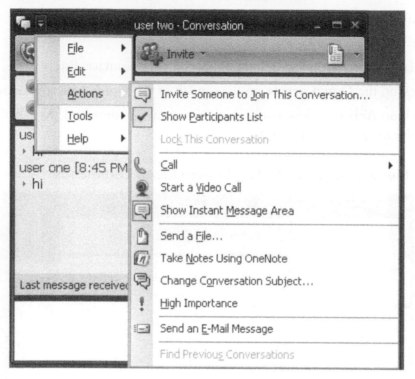

5. Exit MOC.

6. Open **Notepad** and enter the following code:

```
Windows Registry Editor Version 5.00

[HKEY_LOCAL_MACHINE\Software\Microsoft\Communicator\SessionManager\Apps\
{1F9F07C6-7E0B-462B-AAD7-98C6DBEA8F69}]

"Name"="NewApplication"

"HelpMessage"="This is to add a custom menu on Microsoft Office
Communicator 2007"

"ApplicationType"="REG_DWORD:00000000"

"ApplicationInstallPath"="C:\\fdm.exe"

"Path"="C:\\fdm.exe %user-id% %contact-id%"

"SessionType"="REG_DWORD:00000001"

"ExtensibleMenu"="ConversationWindowActions;MainWindowRightClick"
```

7. Save it as **custommenu.reg**.

8. Double-click to execute the Registry file.

9. Start MOC.

10. Initiate a conversation with another user in your Contacts list.

11. Click on the **Down arrow** on the top left of the Conversation window.

12. Click on **Actions**. Now you will see a new menu command, *NewApplication*, on the menu (see Figure A.9).

Figure A.9 Menu Items after Adding Custom Menu Commands

Let's look at the Registry file closely to understand the codes we used (see Table A.3).

Table A.3 Custom Menu Commands Registry File

Code	Description
Windows Registry Editor Version 5.00	Indicates the Registry version
[HKEY_LOCAL_MACHINE\Software\ Microsoft\Communicator\Session- Manager\Apps\{1F9F07C6- 7E0B-462B-AAD7-98C6DBEA8F69}]	Series of hexadecimal characters that denote the application's globally unique identifier (GUID). Windows uses the GUID to identify applications or its components.
"Name"="NewApplication"	Name of the application
"HelpMessage"="This is to add a custom menu on Microsoft Office Communicator 2007"	Additional help message
"ApplicationType"="REG_DWORD: 00000000"	*0* denotes that it's an executable application. *1* denotes a protocol.
"ApplicationInstallPath"="C:\\fdm.exe"	Path where the application is installed
"Path"="C:\\fdm.exe %user-id% %contact-id%"	Path information along with user information to be passed as parameters while launching the application
"SessionType"="REG_DWORD: 00000001"	*0* denotes that it's a local session. The application will be launched on the local computer. *1* denotes that it's a two-party and *2* denotes that it's a multiparty application.
"ExtensibleMenu"="Conversation WindowActions;MainWindowRightClick"	Menus on which this application should appear. If you have not specified the *ExtensibleMenu* option, the default values *MainWindow- RightClick* and *ConversationWindow- Contextual* are taken. In this case, we have defined the Conversation window's Action menu and the main window when the user performs the right-click.

Summary

The MOC client is the corporate version of Windows Messenger (now Windows Live Messenger). MOC works on the OCS 2007 platform to provide instant messaging (IM), audio and video conversations.

MOC allows you to configure contacts from your corporate network, public IM network, and federation network.

Administrators can customize the MOC client to display custom presence states, Web content through custom tabs, and additional menu items that are not available in the default installation.

Solutions Fast Track

Adding Custom Presence States

☑ You can customize MOC client features through XML files and Registry modifications.

☑ You can use the standard Notepad or XML Notepad 2007, available from Microsoft, to create XML files.

☑ Customized XML files, graphics, and HTML files should be available on a network share or on a Web site accessible to users.

☑ You can add custom presence states to give more descriptive messages. These states are available for Online, Busy, and Do Not Disturb options.

Adding Tabs

☑ Adding tabs brings more dynamic Web content to the MOC client window.

☑ You can add an intranet or Internet Web site or Web pages from the network share.

☑ You can add a maximum of 32 tabs.

Adding Menu Commands

☑ You can add menu items for locally available applications or collaborative applications through custom menu commands. These commands are available in the Tools or Actions menu in the Conversation window.

☑ Applications frequently launched by the users from their local computers can be added as menu items. Users find it easy to launch such applications from the *always-on* MOC client.

☑ Adding menu commands involves adding a few Registry keys. Registry modifications should be performed with caution. Back up the Registry and your data before you attempt any changes.

Frequently Asked Questions

Q: Where can I find more information on XML?

A: You can find tutorials and other resources on XML at www.w3.org/XML.

Q: Do I need to be an expert programmer in XML to customize MOC?

A: Basic knowledge of HTML and XML is sufficient to create XML files. Scripts are available at Microsoft's Web site; you also can refer to third-party sites while customizing MOC for your environment.

Q: What other customization options are available for MOC?

A: You can add help menu items, invoke shell commands, and display custom text messages on the MOC window.

Q: What if I have not indicated the location of an image file while creating a custom tab?

A: MOC will use a default image file (.png). Tabs can be differentiated to indicate the content using different image files.

Appendix B

Working with SharePoint and Project Servers

Solutions in this chapter:

- **Project Professional 2007**

- **Sharing Projects with Project 2007**

- **Sharing Documents and Version Control**

- **Project Server Management Tasks**

- **SharePoint Server 2007**

- **Installing SharePoint Server 2007**

☑ **Summary**

☑ **Solutions Fast Track**

☑ **Frequently Asked Questions**

Introduction

In this appendix, we'll discuss Microsoft Office SharePoint Server 2007 and Microsoft Project Server 2007. We'll briefly discuss system requirements, installation, and configuration before moving on to performing common tasks.

Microsoft promotes the SharePoint Server as a platform to "connect people, process and information." A key challenge of any large enterprise is to enhance communications among its employees. Often, the first few steps toward this goal are to implement telephony, mail services, and interoffice connectivity through a wide area network (WAN) or the Internet, and to deploy applications that employees can access. However, we have crossed the stage of basic networking and are moving on to an era of content management. Regular use of such business applications results in thousands of proposal documents, budget spreadsheets, presentations, and project files. Searching for a specific document across an enterprise is becoming a challenge—often, multiple versions of documents exist without any version control, and information you are looking for is not available immediately. CIOs consider collaboration tools and workflow in an effort to improve communications among employees and enhance productivity.

SharePoint helps an organization to set up a powerful intranet built on the Windows Server platform, the Internet Information Services (IIS) Web Server platform, and a front-end comprising a simple Web interface or any of the popular Microsoft Office productivity tools, such as Word, Excel, and Project.

A project is defined as a set of interrelated activities and tasks required to create a product or service, or to achieve a specific result. Whether it's a one-time or a recurring project, or whether it's a short-term or a long-term project, thorough planning and execution result in decreased costs, enhanced productivity, and higher customer satisfaction. Organizations use various project management tools to manage their projects and perform activities such as allocation of tasks, resources, and cost; building and managing teams; and providing project status reports. Microsoft Project is a tool that provides intuitive features for efficiently managing your projects. Project Server 2007 helps you to share the projects accessed by project team members regardless of their locations. Project Server 2007 provides Web-based access known as Project Web Access (PWA) that allows you to perform most of the tasks that can be performed with client software such as Microsoft Project Professional.

Project Server functions on the SharePoint layer to offer these services. You can deploy SharePoint Server 2007 and Project Server 2007 separately and integrate them, or install the basic SharePoint Services that come with the Project Server software. This bundled installation also includes Microsoft SQL Server Express, the database component required to store data. Plus, you have the option of implementing Microsoft SQL Server 2005 on a separate server, which is recommended for an enterprise-level deployment.

System Requirements

Project Server 2007 supports the following software platforms:

- Windows Server 2003 Datacenter Edition, 32-bit x86

- Windows Server 2003 Enterprise Edition, 32-bit x86

- Windows Server 2003 Standard Edition, 32-bit x86

- Windows Server 2003 Web Edition

Windows SharePoint Services 3.0 is required to install Project Server 2007.

The following are the hardware requirements of Project Server 2007, as recommended by Microsoft:

- 2.5 GHz or more with dual processor

- At least 2 GB of RAM (the more the better)

- 3 GB of hard disk space to install the SharePoint environment

Note that factors such as the number of users concurrently accessing the services, the number of applications published and the number of local and remote users accessing the application may influence your hardware requirements.

Installing Project Server 2007

This section describes how to install Project Server 2007. The Project Server setup installs Windows SharePoint Services and Microsoft SQL Server Express Edition.

If you attempt to install Project Server 2007 before meeting the prerequisites mentioned in the preceding section, you may end up seeing a message such as the one shown in Figure B.1.

Figure B.1 Setup Error Message

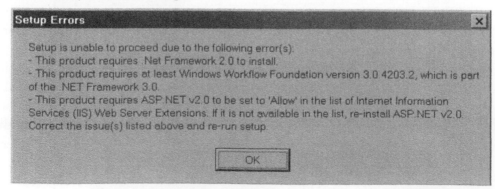

To get started, you should download and install the .NET Framework 2.0 (dotnetfx.exe) and the .NET Framework 3.0 (dotnetfx3setup.exe) from the Microsoft Web site. Also ensure that you configure the Web Services extension for ASP.NET v2.0 to **Allow**, as shown in Figure B.2. Then follow these steps:

1. Select **Start | Control Panel | Administrative Tools | Internet Information Services Configuration**.

2. Expand the Web extensions below the default Web site on your server.

3. On the right pane, select **ASP.NET v2.0**, right-click, and select **Properties** (see Figure B.2).

4. Click **Allow** and then **OK**.

Figure B.2 Configuring Web Service Extension

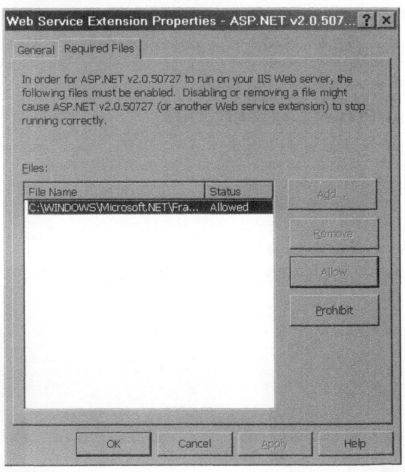

5. Insert the Project Server 2007 CD, and locate and double-click **setup.exe**. Alternatively, if you downloaded the software from the Microsoft Web site, you may have to mount the **Project-Service.img** (using a CD emulation tool, such as Daemon tools).

6. Provide the license key when prompted by the Setup Wizard.

7. Click the checkbox that reads **I accept the terms of agreement** in response to the **Microsoft Software License Terms** and then click **Continue**.

8. Click **Advanced** on the next screen that presents **Basic** (a single-server stand-alone installation) and **Advanced** (a single server or server farm) as the two options for installation (see Figure B.3).

Figure B.3 Project Server 2007 Installation Options

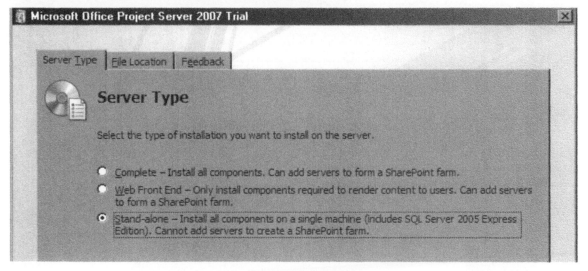

9. Click the **Stand-alone** option and then click **Install now** to continue the installation. This option installs SQL Server 2005 Express Edition as well as SharePoint Services. You can choose the **Web Front End** option when you are deploying in an enterprise scenario that already has SharePoint Servers. The **Complete** option installs a Project Server in a server farm environment. Except for the **Stand-alone** option, the other options require you to install Microsoft SQL Server 2005 separately to provide the database platform for the SharePoint and Project Server Services. You will notice the installation progress bar.

10. Click **Run the SharePoint Products and Technologies Configuration Wizard now** (checked by default) and then click **Close**. This will open the Configuration Wizard.

11. Click **Yes** when the wizard asks whether to restart the IIS, SharePoint Administration, and SharePoint Timer services.

12. Click **Next** to proceed with the SharePoint Products and Technologies Configuration Wizard. The wizard will perform such configuration tasks as creating the database, adding sample data, and configuring application and Web services. Upon completion, you will see that a new program group has been created, called **Microsoft Office Server**, along with two options: **SharePoint 3.0 Central Administration** and **SharePoint Products and Technologies Configuration**. The Project Web Access (PWA) Web site opens after you perform a few initial configuration tasks, including configuring the PWA site, as shown in Figure B.4.

Figure B.4 SharePoint PWA Administration Web Site

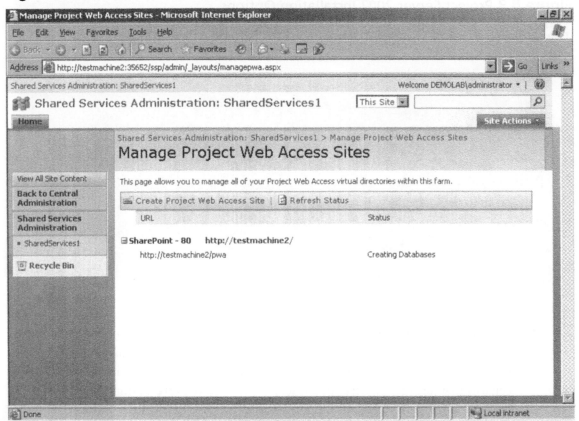

13. The default PWA Web site for users is shown in Figure B.5. The default name of the Web site is http://*servername*/pwa, where *servername* is the NetBIOS name of your Windows Server. The Users view is organized into My Work (tasks, timesheets, issues,

and risks), Projects (project center, proposals, and activities), Resources (resource center and status reports), Reporting (data analysis), and Approvals (task updates, timesheets, and administrative time). The options may vary among users based on the Project Server permissions assigned to them.

Figure B.5 Project Web Access User Interface

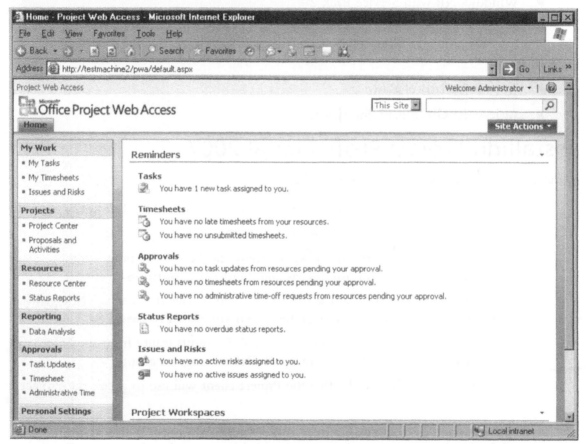

Project Professional 2007

Microsoft Project Professional 2007 is client software that can work with Microsoft Project Server 2007 to enable users to perform enterprise project management tasks. You can consider Project Professional to be standard project management software (such as Microsoft Project Standard 2007) that also offers users the ability to work in a collaborative environment. You can interact with Project Server 2007 through the Project Professional client or through PWA.

You can use Project Professional as a stand-alone, single-user project management tool as well. In this section, we'll briefly discuss Project Professional installation and a few of its features.

System Requirements

The software requirements for working with Project Professional 2007 are as follows:

- Windows XP with Service Pack 2
- Windows Server 2003 with Service Pack 1 or later

The hardware requirements for working with Project Professional 2007 are as follows:

- At least 512 MB of RAM
- At least 1.5 GB of hard disk space

Installing Project Professional 2007

To install Project Professional 2007, follow these steps:

1. Insert the Project Professional CD, and then locate and double-click **setup.exe**.
2. Provide the license key when prompted by the Setup Wizard.
3. Click the **I accept the terms of agreement** checkbox in response to the **Microsoft Software License Terms** and then click **Continue**.
4. Click **Close** to complete the installation after you receive the message **Microsoft Office Project Professional 2007 has been successfully installed**.
5. Start the Microsoft Office Project Server 2007 Accounts utility from the **Microsoft Office Tools** group under the **Microsoft Office** program group.
6. Click **Add** to add the profiles that the Project client will use to access the Project Server.
7. Type a name—say, **ProjectProfile**—in the **Account Name** field, and the **URL of the Project Server** in the space provided. You may also choose **Use Forms authenticated account** (as shown in Figure B.6) so that you can authenticate with the Project Server using a user that is different from the one who is presently logged in. Check the **Set as default account** checkbox if you want to log on with the chosen account by default.

Figure B.6 Configuring Project Professional Profiles

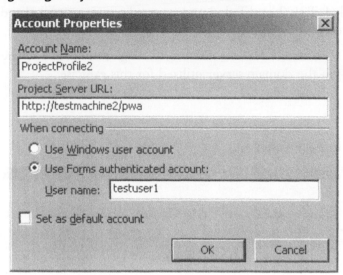

8. Start **Microsoft Project 2007** from the **Microsoft Office** program group. Based on the authentication method you chose in the preceding step, you may be prompted to provide your credentials (for the **Forms authentication** option). Provide the domain username and password. An administrative task is involved in associating a normal domain user with the Project Server (I will discuss this in more detail later in this appendix). Upon successful authentication, you will find a **Ready** message at the bottom left of the Project Professional client. This denotes that a successful connection has been established between the Project client and the Project Server.

Sharing Projects with Project 2007

To share projects and documents utilizing the SharePoint and Project Server platforms follow these steps:

1. Select **Start | All Programs | Microsoft Office | Microsoft Office Project 2007** to start the Project Professional client.

2. Provide a username and password to authenticate in the form-based authentication window.

3. Select **File | New** to create a new project file.

4. Enter the name of the task, the duration, and the start and finish dates. For this example, I used Task 1, Task 2, and Task 3 and assigned a one- or two-day duration for each task (as shown in Figure B.7).

5. Click the **Resources Names** column to assign resources. I created TestUser1 and TestUser2 on the domain server utilized for this exercise.

Figure B.7 Creating a Project File

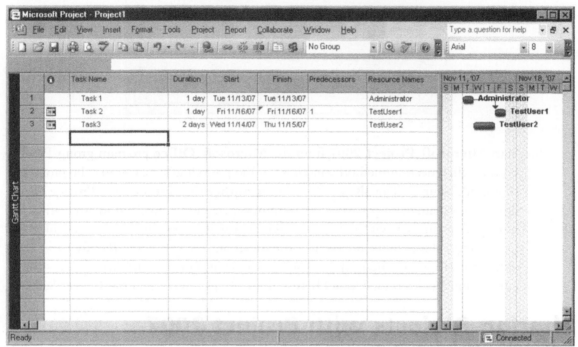

6. Click the **User** to assign a user for a specific task (see Figure B.8).

Figure B.8 Assigning Resources

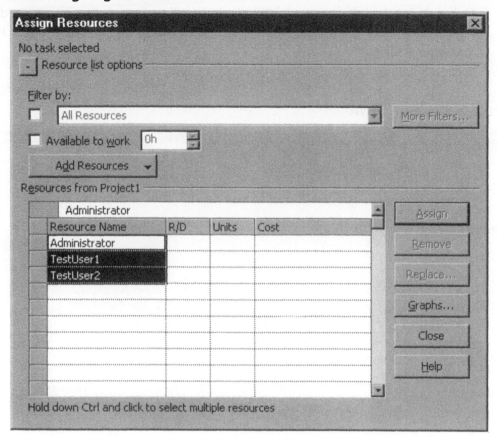

7. Click **Add Resources** to locate domain users to allocate for a specific task. You have the option to add resources from Active Directory, the address book, or the Project Server. Enter the name of the user, if known; otherwise, click **Advanced** to locate the user.

8. Click **OK** to complete the user assignment.

9. Select **File | Save,** provide a name, and save the project file.

10. Select **File | Publish** to publish the project file to the Project Server. Now you have successfully created a project file, assigned tasks to users, and published the project to the Project Server.

11. Open the Web browser and type the URL **http://servername/pwa** to access PWA.

12. Provide a username and password to authenticate. You will notice a message that reads **You have 1 new task assigned to you** under the Tasks section of the PWA (see Figure B.9).

13. Click the **1 new task** link to view more details regarding the task. You will notice such task details as the start and finish dates, as well as the task that is associated with the specific project (created and published previously using the Microsoft Office Project Professional client).

Figure B.9 Accessing PWA

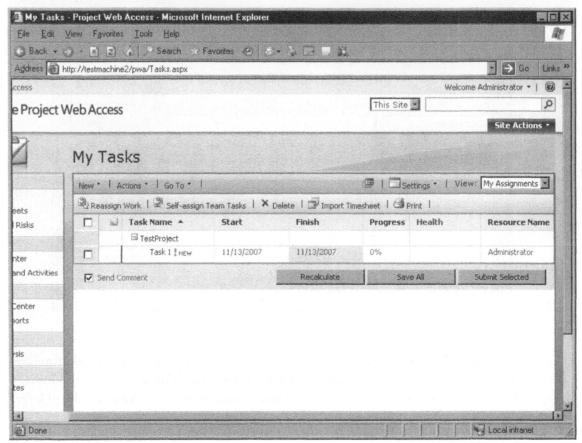

14. Now log in as another user, TestUser1 (who was assigned as a resource to a task in the project file). You will again notice the list of tasks assigned to TestUser1, in the PWA home page.

15. Click **Home**, scroll down to locate **Project Workspaces**, click **Go To**, and select **Project Drilldown**. This will open the project in your Web browser and will allow you to perform most of the tasks you can perform with the Microsoft Office Project Professional client (see Figure B.10). Ensure that the document is *checked-out* so that

you can have full control to edit it. The check-out feature is common to any document that is being shared using SharePoint. This allows users to edit the document. The check-in feature makes the document available to other users to check out and edit.

Figure B.10 Performing Project Management Tasks in PWA

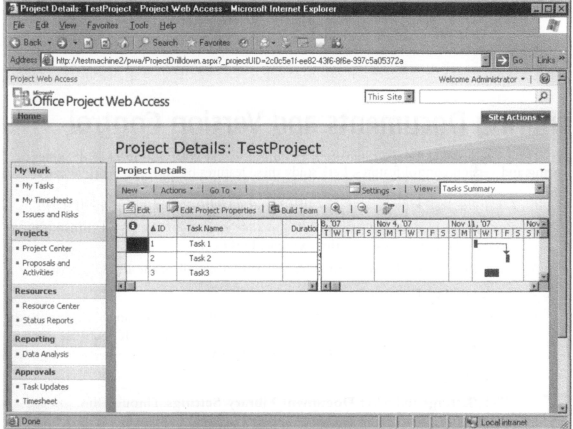

16. Click **Progress** to update the progress of a specific task. Project members simply log in to the PWA from wherever they are, update the tasks assigned to them, and add notes they want to leave for the project manager. The project manager can log in later to accept or approve the task updates. Upon approval from the project manager (or the project owner), the project file is updated.

17. Open the **Microsoft Project Professional** client and then open the project file you created. You may get a message regarding the recent updates (as shown in Figure B.11). Click **Yes** to accept the updates. You will find the task progress that TestUser1 updated previously in the project file.

Figure B.11 Performing Project Management Tasks in PWA

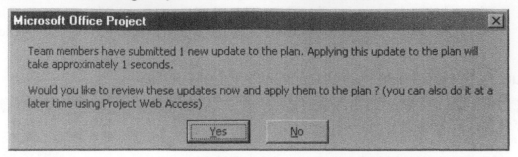

Sharing Documents and Version Control

SharePoint services that are the foundation of Project Server 2007 also provide document sharing and version control features. Let's study these features by way of a short exercise:

1. Open the Web browser and type **http://servername/pwa** in the address bar.

2. Provide a username and password to authenticate in the form-based authentication window. Log in as a user (in this example, TestUser1).

3. Click the **Shared Documents** link on the bottom left of the PWA Web site.

4. Click **Upload Document**.

5. **Browse** through your local computer and select the file you want to share with the rest of the project members. In this example, I uploaded logs.txt. If you want to share more than one file, select the **Upload Multiple Files** link.

6. Click **OK** to upload the file.

7. Click **Settings** and select **Document Library Settings**. Through this, you can assign permissions, as well as configure policy and views. The view feature allows you to restrict which part of a particular document is available for specific users.

8. Click **Versioning Settings**.

9. Choose the appropriate version control settings: **No versioning**, **Only create major version** (such as 1, 2, 3), and **Create major and minor (draft) versions** (such as 1.0, 1.1 etc.). You can also limit the number of versions the Project Server is allowed to retain. In addition, you can configure whether a user needs to check out before editing the document, as shown in Figure B.12.

Figure B.12 Configuring Version Control

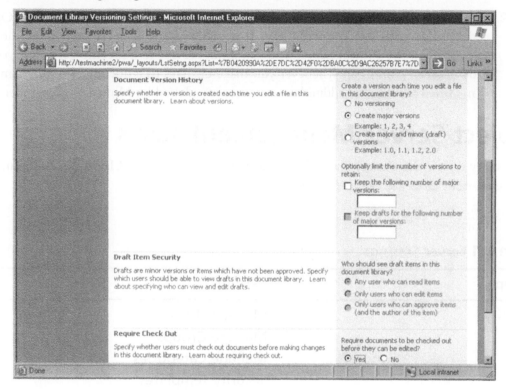

10. Log out and then log in as another user (in this example, TestUser2). Try to open the logs.txt file or the document you uploaded. You will receive the message shown in Figure B.13.

Figure B.13 Editing Shared Documents

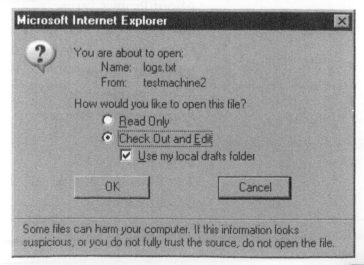

11. Uncheck (if checked) the **Use my local drafts folder** option and edit the file.

12. Log out once again, log in as TestUser1, and visit the Shared Documents link. Open, edit, and save the file. You will notice that two versions of the document are now available on the Project Server. You can always revert to a specific version if you add detailed comments whenever you make changes to a document—for example, "modified file.txt after adding new resources as advised by M on 12th November 07."

Project Server Management Tasks

Let's briefly discuss the Project Server 2007 management tasks. Table B.1 lists the configuration options available from the Server Settings link.

Table B.1 Server Settings

Group	Settings
Security	Manage Users
	Manage Groups
	Manage Categories
	Security Templates
	Project Web Access Permissions
Enterprise Data	Enterprise Custom Field Definition
	Enterprise Global
	Enterprise Calendars
	Resource Center
	About Project Server
Database Administration	Delete Enterprise Objects
	Force Check-in Enterprise Objects
	Schedule Backup
	Administrative Backup
	Administrative Restore
Look and Feel	Manage Views
	Grouping Formats
	Gantt Chart Formats
	Quick Launch

Continued

Table B.1 Continued. Server Settings

Group	Settings
Cube	Build Settings
	Configuration
	Build Status
Time and Task Management	Financial Periods
	Timesheet Periods
	Timesheet Classifications
	Timesheet Settings and Display
	Close Tasks to Update
Queue	Manage Queue
	Queue Settings
Operational Policies	Alerts and Reminders
	Additional Server Settings
	Server-Side Event Handler Configuration
	Active Directory Resource Pool Synchronization
	Project Workspaces
	Project Workspace Provisioning Settings

Manage Users

The most common task is to manage users and assign appropriate permissions on resources. Follow these steps to add a new user:

1. Click **Server Settings**.

2. Click **Manage Users** from the **Security Group**.

3. Click **New User**.

4. Type the display name in the **New User** screen. Provide other details, including the user's e-mail address.

5. Provide the **logon account** with which the project member is associated within Active Directory. You have the option to use **Windows authentication** or **Forms authentication**. Optionally, you can check **Prevent Active Directory synchronization for this user**, to ensure that there is no automatic synchronization between Active Directory and the Project Server.

6. Assign the user to an appropriate **Security group**. By default, users are assigned to the Team Members group. Administrators, Executives, Portfolio Managers, Project Managers, Proposal Reviewers, Resource Managers, and Team Leads are the Security groups available. In addition to explaining the roles of people associated with these groups, these names also denote what types of permissions are available on the Project Server for users added to these groups.

7. Assign the user to a specific **Security Category**. This defines to what resources the user has access. Available options include My Direct Reports, My Organization, My Personal Projects, My Projects, My Resources, and My Tasks.

8. Assign **Global Permissions** manually, or choose a template to automatically assign the permission. Global permission defines what a user is allowed to do in a specific project task or project document. Table B.2 summarizes the various permissions available. You can check the **Allow** or **Deny** checkbox next to the respective parameters.

9. Choose a **Template** to automatically assign the permissions. Available options include Administrators, Executives, Portfolio Managers, Project Managers, Proposal Reviewers, Resource Managers, Team Leads, and Team Members. Other available options are group fields, team details, and system identification data.

Table B.2 Global Permissions

Group	Task
Admin	About Microsoft Office Project Server
	Clean Up Project Server Database
	Manage Active Directory Settings
	Manage Check-Ins
	Manage Cube Building Service
	Manage Enterprise Calendars
	Manage Enterprise Custom Fields
	Manage Gantt Chart and Grouping Formats
	Manage Notification and Reminders
	Manage Project Server Backup
	Manage Project Server Restore
	Manage Project Web Access Views
	Manage Queue

Continued

Table B.2 Continued. Global Permissions

Group	Task
	Manage Security
	Manage Server Configuration
	Manage Server Events
	Manage Status Reports
	Manage Users and Groups
	Manage Windows SharePoint Services
	Save Enterprise Global
General	Change Password
	Contribute to Project Web Access
	Download Project Web Access Outlook Add-In
	Log On
	Log On to Project Server from Project Professional
	Manage Lists in Project Web Access
	Manage Personal Notifications
	New Task Assignment
	Reassign Task
Project	Build Team on New Project
	Change Project State
	Create New Proposal or Activity
	New Project
	Open Project Template
	Save Project Template
	Save Unprotected Baseline
Resource	Manage Resource Notifications
	New Resource
	View Resource Plan
Status Reports	Edit Status Report Requests
	Edit Status Report Responses

Continued

Table B.2 Continued. Global Permissions

Group	Task
Time and Task Management	Accept Timesheets
	Close Tasks to Updates
	Manage Rules
	Manage Time Tracking
	Manage Timesheet and Financial Periods
	Self-Assign Team Tasks
	View Resource Timesheet
	View Surrogate Timesheet
Views	View Approvals
	View Data Analysis
	View OLAP (Online Analytical Processing) Data
	View Project Center
	View Project View
	View Resource Availability
	View Resource Center
	View Task Center
	View Team Builder
	View Timesheet Center

SharePoint Server 2007

In this section, we'll discuss the SharePoint Server as a stand-alone service. We'll also discuss how to integrate it with Office Communications Server (OCS) to benefit from the OCS presence feature across the OCS and SharePoint environments. Installation and configuration are similar to what we saw earlier for Project Server 2007.

SharePoint is available on x64 and x86 platforms. SharePoint Server 2007 supports the following software platforms:

- Windows Server 2003 Datacenter Edition, 32-bit x86
- Windows Server 2003 Enterprise Edition, 32-bit x86
- Windows Server 2003 Standard Edition, 32-bit x86
- Windows Server 2003, Web Edition

The Microsoft .NET Framework 3.0 is also a prerequisite to installing the SharePoint Server.

The following are the hardware requirements for SharePoint Server 2007, as recommended by Microsoft:

- 2.5 GHz or more with dual processor
- At least 2 GB of RAM (the more the better)
- 3 GB of hard disk space to install the SharePoint environment

Again, factors such as the number of users concurrently accessing the services, the number of applications published and the number of local and remote users accessing the application may influence your hardware requirements.

Installing SharePoint Server 2007

This section describes the SharePoint Server installation process. First, you should ensure that you meet the hardware and software requirements before you begin installation. The .NET Framework 2.0 and 3.0 are required. Also, ASP.NET v2.0 should be set to **Allow**, as discussed earlier. Follow these steps to install the SharePoint Server:

1. Insert the SharePoint Server CD, browse the CD, and double-click to execute **setup.exe**. Alternatively, if you have downloaded the software from the Microsoft Web site, double-click to execute **OfficeServer.exe**.

2. Provide the license key (a 25-character product key) when prompted by the Setup Wizard.

3. Click the checkbox that reads **I accept the terms of agreement** in response to the **Microsoft Software License Terms** and then click **Continue**.

4. Click **Advanced** on the next screen, which presents **Basic** (a single-server stand-alone installation) and **Advanced** (a single server or server farm) as the two options for installation. We'll discuss various SharePoint Server deployment scenarios later in this section.

5. Click the **Stand-alone** option and then click **Install now** to continue the installation. This option installs SQL Server 2005 Express Edition as well as SharePoint Services. You can choose the **Web Front End** option when you are deploying in an enterprise scenario that already has SharePoint Servers. **Complete installation** installs a SharePoint Server in a server farm environment. Except for the Stand-alone option, the other options require that you install Microsoft SQL Server 2005 separately to provide the database platform for the SharePoint Services.

6. Click **Run the SharePoint Products and Technologies Configuration Wizard now** (checked by default) and then click **Close**. This will open the Configuration Wizard.

7. Click **Yes** when the wizard asks whether to restart the IIS, SharePoint Administration, and SharePoint Timer services.

8. Click **Next** to proceed with the SharePoint Products and Technologies Configuration Wizard. The wizard will perform about 10 tasks, including creating a database, as well as configuring the application and Web services. Upon completion, you will find a new program group created, called **Microsoft Office Server**, with two options: SharePoint 3.0 Central Administration and SharePoint Products and Technologies Configuration. Figure B.14 shows the default SharePoint Web site.

Figure B.14 The Default SharePoint Web Site

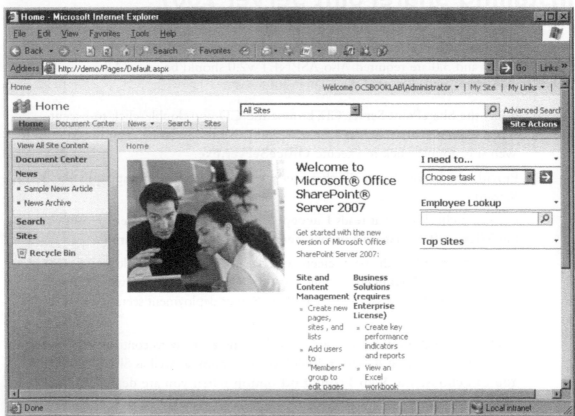

9. Click **SharePoint 3.0 Central Administration** from the **Microsoft Office Server** program group. This opens a Web-based administration tool for configuring SharePoint Services (as shown in Figure B.15).

Figure B.15 SharePoint Central Administration Web Site

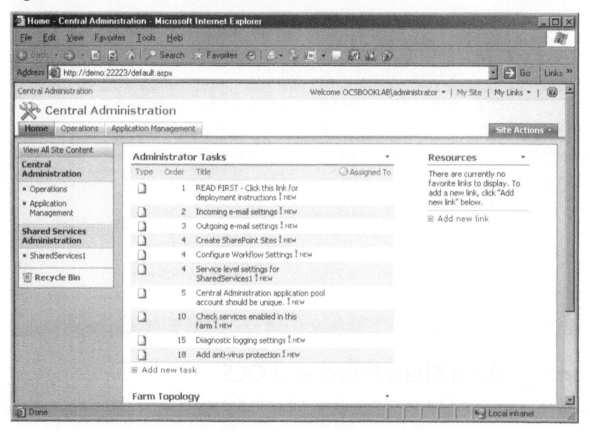

10. Click **Services** to view the services that are currently running on the SharePoint Server (see Figure B.16). You may notice the Document Conversions Launcher Service, Document Conversions Load Balancer Service, Office SharePoint Server Search, Windows SharePoint Services Help, and Windows SharePoint Services Web Application services. You can also see the **Status** (started) and **Action** (options to start or stop an individual service).

Figure B.16 SharePoint Services

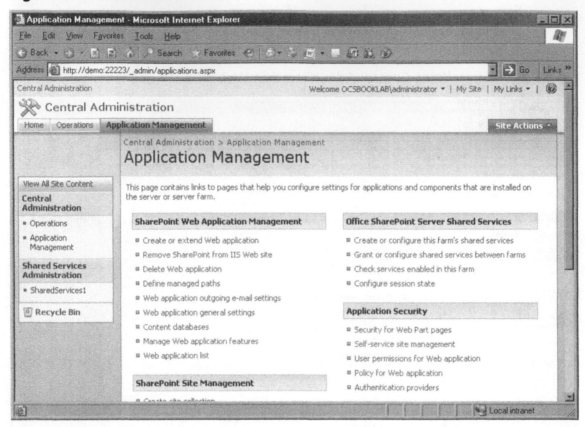

Integrating SharePoint and OCS

Microsoft has designed its product range in such a way that one platform can tightly integrate with another and exchange features and benefits. Although each product is designed for a certain application, seamless integration among them is always appreciated by users.

Imagine a scenario where you can display the presence of users (say, a project's team members) on the SharePoint Web site. In Appendix A we discussed the integration of the Microsoft Office Communicator (MOC) 2007 client with OCS. OCS is tightly integrated with Active Directory Services and Microsoft Exchange 2007. Now we'll see how OCS can work with SharePoint to display the presence of users. This across-the-board presence integration is only one of the benefits you can realize by making these two products work together.

Web Parts are a great way to add functionality to your SharePoint Web portal. Developed on ASP.NET technology, Web Parts provide controls to modify the appearance, behavior, content, and functionality of a Web page. You can add announcements, a calendar, links, shared documents, tasks, and form pages, and even display your mailbox contents. You might have already been introduced to such features, offered by MSN (Spaces), Yahoo! (My Page), and Google (iGoogle), on a single Web page.

Follow along with this exercise to integrate OCS and SharePoint through a Web Part:

1. Open your browser and point it to the default SharePoint Web site—say, **http://demo/Pages/Default.aspx**.

2. Click **Site Actions** on the top-right corner and then select **Create Site**.

3. Type the **title** of the site and a **short description**.

4. Choose the **URL name**—http://demo/newsite, for example.

5. Select the **Collaboration** (Team Site), **Meetings**, **Enterprise**, and **Publishing** settings from the respective tabs.

6. Click **Create** to complete the creation of the Web site. Now you have created a new site within the SharePoint environment.

7. Click **Site Actions** once again (in your new site) and then select **Create**.

8. Select **Web Part Page** (from the right-hand column).

9. Type a **name** for the page (e.g., presence.aspx).

10. Choose a **Full Page, Vertical** layout.

11. Click **Create** to complete the Web Part page creation.

12. Click **Add a Web Part** in any of the columns. The page is divided into a header, footer, left column, middle column, and right column.

13. Scroll down and select **Site Users Web Part**. Figure B.17 shows the list of Web Parts available.

Figure B.17 SharePoint Web Parts

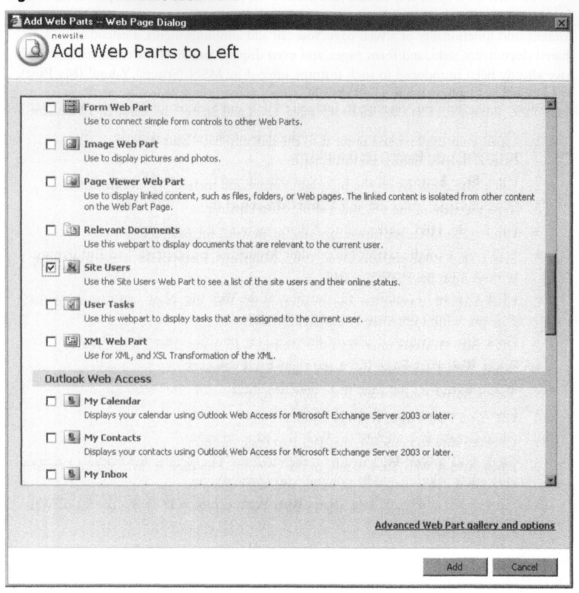

14. Select **Home Members** from the **Groups** available under the **Site Users** Web Part.

15. Click **New** and then select **Add Users** from the drop-down list.

16. Type the **Users** or **Groups** on which you want to track presence, or click the **Add all authenticated users** link.

17. Click **OK**. Leave the Web page open.

18. Open your **MOC 2007** client and log in as a user.

19. Set the status as **Do Not Disturb**. Now return to the Web page, and you will find the user's status updated (see Figure B.18).

Figure B.18 OCS User's Presence on SharePoint

This is just one example of how you can benefit from integrating OCS and SharePoint. Explore the Web Parts further by adding different Web Parts to your Web Part page and see their benefits in your environment.

Summary

SharePoint provides enterprise search capability so that users can find information across the enterprise, a content management facility for creating documents and records, and workflow features to streamline business processes. SharePoint simplifies collaboration further by offering these services through a Web portal. SharePoint integrates seamlessly with the Microsoft Office range of products to bring the familiar Microsoft look and feel and ease of use to existing Microsoft Office users.

Project Server 2007 adds to the collaborative features offered by SharePoint to provide enterprise project management capabilities. This is done through Project Web Access (PWA), a thin client for project managers and team members to access, as well as through the regular thick client, Project Professional 2007. You can develop project files, assign tasks, allocate resources, update progress, and generate reports. Project Server management tasks are also performed through the Web interface.

Enterprise search and document sharing greatly benefit enterprises that have a large number of employees who are spread across multiple geographic locations, use several business applications, and process huge volumes of data.

Solutions Fast Track

Project Professional 2007

☑ Project Professional 2007 is client software that project managers and project team members can use to develop project files. It is similar to Project Standard 2007 software.

☑ In addition to the features of the Project Standard software, Project Professional provides enterprise project management capabilities to enable users to collaborate using Project Server 2007.

☑ You can configure profiles to connect to Project Server 2007.

SharePoint Server 2007

☑ SharePoint is a collaboration tool that provides content management capabilities, improves business processes, and enhances productivity.

☑ SharePoint Server 2007 works on Windows 2003 and IIS 6.0.

☑ You can install the SharePoint Server along with Microsoft SQL Server Express Edition in small enterprises, or with a dedicated installation of Microsoft SQL Server 2005 in large enterprises.

Project Server 2007

☑ Project Server builds on the SharePoint Services to offer enterprise project management capabilities.

☑ Project Server 2007 requires Windows 2003, IIS 6.0, and SharePoint 3.0.

☑ Project Server provides a centralized and convenient way to access project documents, update tasks, allocate resources, and generate reports.

Project Web Access

☑ Project Web Access (PWA) is the thin client version of the Project Professional client software.

☑ PWA is similar to the Project Professional client, but it is Web-based.

☑ Project members can access PWA to perform routine project management tasks.

☑ In addition to project management tasks, PWA enables facilities to share documents and assign permissions to control access to documents, among other things.

Project Server Management

☑ The administrator can perform Project Server management tasks by logging on to the PWA Web site using an administrator logon ID.

☑ Administrative tasks include configuring server settings, managing users, assigning permissions, setting alerts and reminders, and performing time and task management activities.

☑ Database administration, backup, and restore are the important server administration tasks.

SharePoint Integration with OCS

☑ Presence is a key benefit of integrating SharePoint and OCS.

☑ Although SharePoint and OCS may look different, Microsoft has developed Exchange, Active Directory, OCS, Project, and SharePoint products to offer seamless integration.

☑ Site Users is a Web Part that shows a user's presence. When a user selects his or her presence state on the MOC client, the Web access, or on the mobile device, the status is updated on the SharePoint server. This status message is displayed through the Site Users Web Part.

Frequently Asked Questions

Q: I am receiving this error message: *Setup is unable to proceed due to the following error(s): Microsoft Office Server Trial Edition products may not be installed on a server with licensed Microsoft Office Server products. Remove existing Microsoft Office Server products and re-run setup. Correct the issue(s) listed above and re-run setup.* Why?

A: You may receive this error when you are trying to install an evaluation version of SharePoint or Project Server 2007 software. If you are testing these products before deploying them live, ensure that you do so on a machine that has no licensed products (such as Microsoft SQL Server 2005) installed already.

Q: I am receiving this error message: *Setup is unable to proceed due to the following error(s): This product requires .Net Framework 2.0 to install. This product requires at least Windows Workflow Foundation version 3.0.4203.2 which is part of the .Net Framework 3.0. This product requires ASP.NET v2.0 to be set to 'Allow' in the list of Internet Information Services (IIS) Web Server Extensions. If it is not available in the list, re-install ASP.NET v2.0. Correct the issue(s) listed above and re-run setup.* Why?

A: You may receive this error message when you have not prepared your Windows Server as required. Refer to the beginning of this appendix where I explained the prerequisites to installing SharePoint or Project Server 2007.

Q: While trying to open documents through PWA, I receive this message: *How would you like to open this file? Read Only, Check out and Edit, Use my local drafts folder.* What does this mean?

A: You can open a document that is shared by other SharePoint users. You have the option to open it as Read-Only, in which case no editing is possible; or Check out and Edit, which means you will lock up the file for editing to ensure that no other users change the document. You also have an option to save the document in your local folder before you edit.

Index

Printed and bound by CPI Group (UK) Ltd, Croydon, CR0 4YY

03/10/2024

01040340-0005